FROCKING LIFE

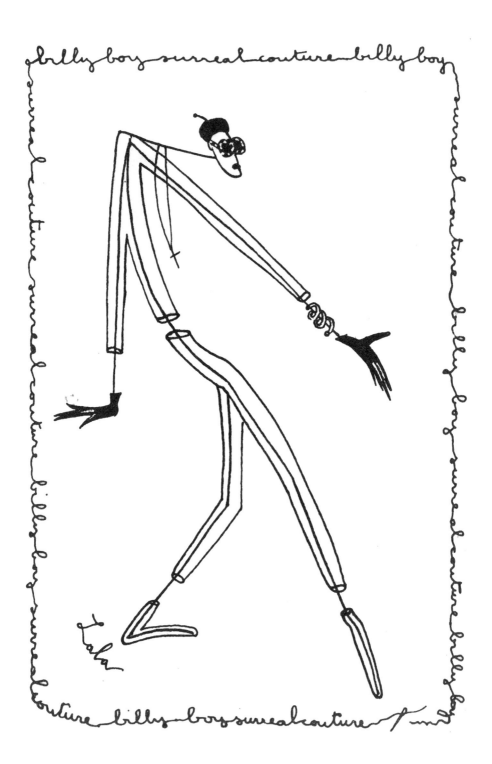

FROCKING LIFE

SEARCHING FOR
ELSA SCHIAPARELLI

BILLYBOY*

EDITED BY JEAN PIERRE LESTRADE
A.K.A. LALA

Rizzoli
ex libris

First published in the United States of America in 2016 by
Rizzoli Ex Libris, an imprint of
Rizzoli International Publications, Inc.
300 Park Avenue South
New York, NY 10010
www.rizzoliusa.com

Cover design by Gabriele Wilson

2016 2017 2018 2019 / 10 9 8 7 6 5 4 3 2 1

Distributed in the U.S. trade by Random House, New York

Printed in the United States of America

ISBN-13: 978-0-8478-4386-2

Library of Congress Catalog Control Number: 2016935324

FRONT COVER: BillyBoy* photographed in a Paris interior surrounded by
Schiaparelli ensembles for Edmund White's article "Billy Boy in Paris—
The Jewelry Designer's Crush on Schiaparelli—and Barbie," *Architectural
Digest*, summer 1989. Photograph © Marina Faust.
ENDPAPERS: A montage of illustrations by Lala, BillyBoy*'s husband, from
1982, the year they first met.
PAGE 2: BillyBoy*'s business card, designed and illustrated by Lala in 1982.
BillyBoy* wears the glasses he designed in the late 1970s and his signature
Byzantine cross and black Hermès suede gloves, which he was often seen
wearing at that time, too.
PAGE 5: One of a series of illustrations by Lala from the 1980s. Called
Glamorous Living with BillyBoy*, the series illustrates humorous scenes
from their life together.

(vintage shop in
le Marais)

CONTENTS

FOREWORD

n 1978, early in my curatorial career at the Costume Institute of the Metropolitan Museum of Art, BillyBoy* called for an appointment to see clothes designed by Elsa Schiaparelli. Not knowing who someone named BillyBoy* might be, I was delighted to find a young man (younger, in fact, than I realized) well informed and intensely interested in all things related to Schiaparelli. He was respectful as we looked through the collection and fascinated by the smallest details of Schiaparelli's work. He then showed me the pieces of his own Surreal Couture that had become part of the Costume Institute's collection. Over the years, when he came to New York, he would call for an appointment and with each one I would learn a bit more about him and his unfettered energy and enthusiasms. From our early meetings I admired his imaginative ability to express a very personal creativity by dressing up.

He believes that fashion is a means of self-creation and not an end in itself, and that clothing should remind you of the joy in life. Influenced by the work of Schiaparelli, by the work of the designers he chooses to patronize, and by a spontaneous combination of elements—for example, in vintage couture, with a 1930s Schiaparelli hat, 1950s Chanel costume jewelry, a 1970s Dior top and contemporary Galliano newsprint jeans—he individualizes his personal style and dresses according to his mood. The look is not premeditated fashion, but the creation of an artist approaching a specific moment in time—it is both ephemeral and unique. In Billy's view, self-expression trumps any issue of conventional appropriateness or the expectations of those he meets. Dressing imaginatively reveals his sense of humor, his aesthetic sensibility, and his mood. Encouraged from childhood to be spontaneous and creative, he believes in living his life and being himself.

Within the several collections that he has amassed, including his extensive collection of Schiaparelli, Billy's personal wardrobe is remarkable. Primarily English and French in origin, many pieces represent the most extreme of the gay underground club scene of the 1970s and 1980s, but equally the most traditional of bespoke English tailoring and classicism appropriate for the most conservative circumstances. There are Vivienne Westwood and Malcolm McLaren pieces from their first boutiques, along with a veritable who's who of designer clothes. Vinyl catsuits, printed mini kilts, "brothel creepers," and early punk attire also rounded out his style. He wore the most advanced conceptual designers: the colorful whimsies of Kansai Yamamoto, the stark designs of Issey Miyake, the deconstructions of Rei Kawakubo for Comme des Garçons, Yohji Yamamoto (for whom he'd model menswear), and even the earliest work of Kenzo. For one of our early appointments at the Costume Institute, Billy, who is over six feet tall, appeared in a huge Paco Rabanne maxi coat of black fake fur with bleached blonde marcel waved hair and a cigarette holder emulating what only could seem like Cruella de Ville or Jean Harlow. At the opening of the *Surrealism* exhibition at the Fashion Institute of Technology in New York, he wore a red wool hat, a tailored suit from Westwood's "Harris Tweed" collection, and shoes by Pierre

Cardin with toes molded in the leather of each foot. Although he has carefully maintained his wardrobe, Billy has a refreshing and pragmatic attitude toward it. He writes, "Clothes for me are amusing, silly, camp, and to be played with like fire or Tinker Toys. You dress up with them, you have a nice time, you take them off, you forget about them. I collect them to remind myself of this. I keep physical evidence of the absurdity of fashion. It's seriously superficial and creates any reality you'd like." Billy is a master at creating his immediate reality through clothes.

It was when I went to visit Billy in Paris in the early 1980s that I discovered that he was a collector: a serious collector with the passionate knowledge of his subjects that only a dedicated collector can have. In his apartment at Place Adolphe Max, I found myself surrounded by paintings and sculpture, Barbie, Bleuette, Alta Moda Tre Esse, and Kamkins dolls, cascades of couture costume jewelry, amazing Schiaparelli accessories. My particular memory is of a Schiaparelli powder compact from 1935 in the form of a telephone dial inspired by Salvador Dalí. All of these different groups of objects showed the same kind of all-consuming desire to acquire comprehensively— to have everything possible. The talent that makes a collector is an exceptional eye for ferreting out the objects of desire from unrelated contexts. In the case of Billy's Schiaparelli pieces, for example, it was finding treasured couture garments and accessories in flea markets and thrift stores, and later given to him by those who knew of his passion for Schiaparelli. The reward of this sleuthing is not only the objects themselves, but also the relationships with those who knew Schiaparelli, who were her clients, or who worked with the artisans who created the parts of the whole: the fabrics, the buttons, the jewelry, the hats and gloves, the perfume. Along the way he has acquired an encyclopedic knowledge of all things related to Schiaparelli and an extraordinary amount of original documentation from published sources and private letters, accounts, and oral histories.

I am especially pleased to have been asked to write the foreword for this book because I have watched the trajectory of Billy's career since he was a teenager, eager to see the Schiaparelli clothes in the Costume Institute. Billy works as an artist who creates in various media rather than as an entrepreneur. He has no hesitation in moving on to other media once his interest in a particular project or genre has waned, and his recent work includes both sculpture and painting. For more than thirty-three years he has worked side by side with his partner (and now husband), Jean Pierre Lala Lestrade. Together they have achieved success and seen their artistic lives flourish. One of Billy's prized works, begun in 1975, is a huge, heavy bandolier strung with dozens of Bakelite bangle bracelets. He has titled it *Self-portrait*: it is a collection, it is modern but old-fashioned, it is colorful, and it is a work in progress. He considers it a unique metaphor. Of course, Billy is still actively collecting: painting and sculpture, Schiaparelli, dolls and dolls' houses—I don't think he could ever stop.

Jean L. Druesedow
Kent, Ohio
June 2016

PREFACE

All my life, I've followed an invisible thread from one Elsa Schiaparelli dress to another, from a Schlumberger button shaped like a snake to a Schiap hat garnished with carrots, and from one serendipitous and surprising meeting to another amazing story. Everything, every tiny element of her life and her work that I encountered—whether through the garments and creations themselves, or through stories people would tell me about her—seemed to spell out an incredible tale about this woman's personal vision of beauty. I earnestly tried to tape record everything and write down all I learned because the entire Schiaparelli experience I was having was metaphysical, as though I was under a charmed magic spell, compelled to capture everything lest it be lost. It felt at times not only like a moral duty, but moreso like a soulful duty. I felt I may have been born and put in this life to be a sort of Mercury, a messenger delivering from one generation to another an important message about life through the arts and that I'd do this through my collecting and studying, my writing, and my artwork.

Since the beginning of my career at a rather young age I often had my name linked to Schiaparelli's. I was immediately associated with her because of my passion for her work. The more press coverage I received, the more doors opened for me and for my Schiap research. All those couturiers, artisans, photographers, stars, artists, and socialites revealed incredible meanings to her work. Those meanings—sometimes obvious and sometimes hidden—in Schiaparelli's designs still fire my imagination. In every epoch, her sense of timing was perfect. She is most often remembered for her avant-garde designs, but I believe she had an astute understanding of glamour and precisely how to highlight a woman's beauty, and how to release her sexuality and charms. She gave women (and not just the wealthy) the opportunity to express themselves in ways that conventional haute couture clothes did not. Her invention of franchising and licensing her ideas, with ready-to-wear, patterns, all sorts of accessories from buttons, jewelry and menswear allowed millions more women (and men) everywhere to afford a Schiaparelli experience. She forged the world of fashion we know today and her influence can still be seen clearly in both women's and men's fashion. If she has an equal it was Paul Poiret, who often inspired her work, and in his own time changed the way women were dressed, giving them the same sexual awareness and freedom as Schiap. She changed the way women were perceived, but also the way that the act of seduction was perceived. Eroticism was a strong topnote to her vision of fashionable dressing. She knew, perhaps instinctively, that down to the tiniest detail, clothes can speak endlessly about so many other things.

I can only put a fraction of what I have learned over the past forty-two years in this book. I have endeavored to put all these friendships and acquaintances, experiences I had and documents I collected to good use, and have processed this accumulated information in a creative way to document Schiaparelli's extraordinary career. I want to do so to honor all the many who have helped me. I am sure the future holds many occasions to continue to share the fruits of my research. I tend to be very academic and by writing this book, I hope to broaden Schiap's appeal to people who can be interested in her but who don't necessarily want a three-page description of a button. Ideally, I hope to bring the results of collecting Schiaparelli not only to an academic audience, but also to introduce everyone and anyone interested in her work and era to my own work and era, as well. They are cosmically linked in any case. Schiaparelli, one of the first designers to bring fine art and outright sexiness to fashion, called her autobiography *Shocking Life*. How could I resist paying homage, and calling this elaborate story by one title only: *Frocking Life?*

BillyBoy*
February 2016

BILLYBOY*
A QUEER GENTLEMAN OF FASHION

At an early age, BillyBoy* chose two mentors. From his childhood in the United States, he found a TV star as his ultimate role model: Bugs Bunny. As a teenager in France, he chose one of the greatest masters of fashion history: the Italian-born Elsa Schiaparelli, known as "Schiap" to her closest companions.

From Bugs Bunny, he learned the basics of how to behave in society and how to manage life's wicked turns; to be coy, smart, witty, and to always dress appropriately with the assurance of Beau Brummell. He also learned how to eat an ice cream cone in a hundred different ways, from alluring to annoying (depending on who you're dealing with), how to strike a pose and blink your long eyelashes with perfect timing, and a few other tricks of seduction. He learned sartorial skills such as how to pull off a dainty hat, a wig or two, or even a ruffled Byronian-era gown that fits like a glove for a torrid *pas de deux* on the battlefield. But most of all, his cartoon mentor taught him a lighthearted approach to life, and an entertaining charm that is to personality what humor is to good conversation.

From Schiaparelli, who he discovered at age fourteen through a very strange hat in a Paris flea market, he learned the meanings of Love and Art. His human mentor opened doors that he "never even dreamed existed," as the title character says to her nephew in *Auntie Mame*. As Schiap turned into a genuine passion, she became a golden thread that led to all sorts of discoveries, encounters, and inspirations. He naturally became a collector of her creations, and in vast numbers. What else was there for a young man to do in a world filled with treasures that nobody paid attention to? He loved anything quirky, groovy, or glamorous, so hunting for them became second nature. With rapidly acquired taste and extraordinary flair, he found amazing things—often for a pittance—almost every day. Such was his gift. He traveled all over the world and beautiful things seemed to find him, adding to his collection and his life. He has never ceased to be enthralled by beauty and art, beginning from his earliest years, when he crawled among the jeweled Roger Vivier-shod feet of his great aunts at cocktail parties.

In true Montessori student style, he managed to express his Surrealist-imbued visions and eclectic tastes in his own fashion, art, and performances. Ideas sprung forth from his peculiar and fertile imagination. He revived, for the fun of it, the words "surreal" and "groovy" long before anyone even remembered them. His life as a young queer in Manhattan, led to a role as a protégé of Diana Vreeland and later as one of Andy Warhol's last Superstars. And then he left this life in New York to settle down in Europe without a single hesitation. We met in Paris when he was twenty-two and I was twenty-eight. Not long after, I helped him bring back what he casually called his "stuff": about 100 steamer trunks, filled with his odd-ball collection of 1960s and 1970s Marimekko, Cardin, Courrèges, and Jacques Esterel, bespoke suits and accessories from Savile Row, and a long list of American, European and even South American and Russian fashion of the last three decades of high fashion by designers from the most conservative to the most eccentric. His own personal history of 20th century fashion was all neatly stored in a mountain of 1930s Louis Vuitton trunks. Each trunk was doused in the heady scent of Shocking de Schiaparelli perfume, which I will forever associate with these early years of our relationship.

BillyBoy* has always been a strange fruit and it must be said, not everyone could have a bite of it. The press adored him since he was, as author Edmund White wrote, "good copy."[1] One day he looked like a dazzling rock star in a skintight silver lamé studded outfit by Nudie Cohen (the designer of Elvis Presley's elaborate ensembles) originally made for David Cassidy. For a tea with the Begum Aga Khan at the Ritz, he would be a dandy in a conservative suit with impeccable tie, topped by a Vivienne Westwood/Malcolm McClaren Buffalo hat adorned with a silk lettuce leaf. For an interview at home with German *Vogue*, he became a sex kitten in hot pants and an Yves Saint Laurent sheer blouse. Waiting in line for a taxi on Place de Clichy in Paris around the corner, he might wear a Kabuki wig with a marbleized silk pajama suit by Stéphane Plassier, much to the bewilderment of Brazilian drag queens going to work in the Bois de Boulogne who just could not *read* him. Somehow, unlike Anna Piaggi, Leigh Bowery, or Quentin Crisp, he never really seemed eccentric, a term he says he doesn't like. But the attention was not just about his looks. The press frequently featured his collections and cited his accomplishments in the first Elsa Schiaparelli exhibition, the *Nouveau Théâtre de la Mode* Barbie, Surreal Bijoux, and Mdvanii, the first fashion doll ever created for adults. BillyBoy* seemed to have a jet-set lifestyle, but few understood or even realized how hard he (and we) worked. As Andy Warhol wrote of BillyBoy* in the *Andy Warhol Diaries*, "How does he have time to do this—collect his antique couture clothes and design his jewelry?"[2]

Therefore, since the 1970s BillyBoy* was an enigma for most of his contemporaries, even in the most sophisticated *mondaine* circles in New York, Paris, London, and countries all over Europe. Lying naked in bed at the Chelsea Hotel in New York with William Burroughs he would wear a Cartier diamond necklace and a few real squash blossoms and cornflowers behind his ear, with a pair of striped blue and silver Fiorucci disco socks. At Jean-Charles de Castelbajac's party given in Paris in honor of his friend Jean-Michel Basquiat, who came only for five minutes (this was a few weeks before his tragic death), Mr. Boy* wore a provocative see-through crochet jumpsuit Rudi Gernreich gave him, a cod-piece of leather and steel he designed, a necklace made of multi-colored resin penises with tear-drop pearls, also of his own design, Westwood rocking horse shoes, and a big Biba fedora hat. The look was all *too much*, even for the smug young editors of *Marie Claire* and *Elle*.

I have been endlessly amused watching the reactions of others to him, and fascinated by how oblivious he is to these responses. Of course, as a collector by nature, he has kept everything, *all* of it, down to the last Play-Doh button on a John Galliano ensemble from his earliest days as a designer. During the era of Schiaparelli, many society women gave their frocks to the maid after having worn them just a few times. Well, that was not the *genre de la maison* chez BillyBoy*! One day, while looking through a Christie's catalogue announcing "The Collection of a Lady with a Title" I joked about seeing his own personal clothes gathered as the *Wardrobe of a Queer Gentleman of Fashion*. We laughed, but seriously liked it. We kept it in mind as a name for an upcoming exhibition on the subject by his longtime friend Jean Druesedow at Kent State University Museum in Ohio.

BillyBoy* is probably one of the most knowledgeable individuals in the field of fashion history today. While most people think Schiaparelli is all about the 1930s—and sum up her contributions to fashion in the shoe hat, the color "shocking pink," and a few iconic garments—BillyBoy* has gathered information, documentation, and all kinds of other material that covers her entire career, from the early 1920s until she retired in 1973. For him, Schiaparelli's creations are equal to those of any great artist. BillyBoy* has always said that if you love a subject, be sure to not turn it into a business in any way. From his perspective as a historian and a collector, Schiap's work in the 1960s, undervalued and misunderstood today, is as valid as that of her golden age in the 1930s. Her merchandizing in the early 1930s and her hundreds of licenses are tremendously interesting. She was incredibly prolific in this sense, and also a pioneer in the field long before Pierre Cardin. Her association with artists and artisans of her times has also been a constant inspiration for BillyBoy*. The Surreal Bijoux, entirely hand-made in our rue de la Paix atelier next door to Schiap's first house of fashion, were created in the same spirit as a Giacometti button or a Comte Etienne de Beaumont necklace. Let's talk about "possible conversations"!

One door opening on another, this book features a fascinating cast of stars, celebrities, oddball characters, and personalities. Several exhibitions and books have appeared since the first exhibition in 1984 (initiated by BillyBoy*) dedicated to the genius of Schiaparelli, but none of them equal the scope of what BillyBoy* has done with the experience he has. Knowledge and discovery walked hand in hand through his constant expeditions to grungy flea markets, snobbish antique shows, and luxurious auction houses. It never ends! "This is the only thing that truly relaxes me. It's meditation," he said to me. As a result, his collection, in the field of fashion history only, covers two centuries.

Frocking Life: In Search of Schiaparelli, is about this unique passion that BillyBoy* has made part of his life and his relationships with some of the world's most fascinating, and often legendary, people he knew and befriended. It reads like a thrilling voyage in time through fashion history, art, and culture, most of it researched with the faith of a believer and gathered with the perseverance of an archaeologist.

It is a wonderful dose of glamour and the quirky chic of both the oh-so-contemporary decades BillyBoy* has humorously and charmingly lived so far, mixed with the truly brilliant story of Schiaparelli's fascinating life and career as a singular artist.

Jean Pierre Lestrade
a.k.a. Lala
June 2016

PART ONE

CHAPTER I

"OH, IT'S A HAT"

When I was fourteen years old, I found a strange hat at a Paris flea market for a few francs. The hat, which looked like a crushed clown's headpiece with an insect quietly munching on it, utterly entranced me. Even before I held it, I distinctly recall feeling bubbly and terribly amused at seeing it. Imagine, a gold fly. How hilarious, I thought. Then I picked it up. The label read, "Schiaparelli, Paris." I brought it back home to my glamorous great-aunt Sylvia in New York who explained that it had been made by "that nice old lady" I'd met years ago when I was a child.

I couldn't explain why this hat intrigued me so. I wore it to my Montessori school, much to the amusement of the class. I was teased and tormented mercilessly because of that hat. I hadn't realized that it was supposed to be a lady's hat. It really did not look like any sort of hat one could recognize like a beanie, a trilby or a Stetson cowboy hat. When I put it on I felt at the time the way a little boy would feel wearing his team's baseball cap (I never had such a cap so it was all childish conjecture): I felt totally normal. I could not for the life of me understand what all the fuss was about.

Like most Surrealist artwork, however, this hat was not just a hat, it was an object of desire, a symbolic artifact that was nothing and everything at the same time. A bit like my peculiar, unexplainable, and powerful attraction to my Crayola shocking pink and gold crayons that were hidden in my childhood box of secret things of superb sacredness. Without question, I did not know at the time that this odd fashion accessory would turn out to be the beginning of a lifelong adventure, the earthly commencement of a soul contract.

My spiritual love affair with Schiap started simply enough with a small flea market find when I was a young teenager. Immediately after arriving in Paris in June of 1974, after a prolonged world tour that concluded in the Middle East and having absconded (played hooky if you will) from my Montessori tutor, I had decided to go directly to the flea market, almost practically from the Orly airport. In my ever growing excitement and happiness to see antiques and ephemera of all sorts I arrived at the mythical place I loved most in the world, the Marché au Puces de Clignancourt right on the outskirts of the city, which is a whole world in itself. It was still dark when I arrived, the sun just coming up as I wound around hazy silhouettes of junk and curiosities of all kinds. My adopted father had introduced me to flea markets at age four, but it wasn't until around age ten that I was allowed to seek them out on my own, so this was all still new and especially thrilling to me. To this day I am grateful to my father for guiding and encouraging my varied interests in history. He always told me that in order to be successful at something you had to be driven by passion and desire for the purest version of the truth. He also said it will be very hard, sometimes discouraging work but to persist and overcome all obstacles. Hunting down anything, be it cerebral information or material objects is like a big game safari and the hunt will be a true test of endurance. He was right.

I was prepared with my version of a hunting kit, comprised of a flashlight, an apple for a snack, Band-aids, cotton gloves, check-books in nearly all European currencies, cash (of course), a Larousse French-English dictionary, aspirin, blank cards, a tape measure, a darning kit, a notepad, my diary, pencils, and a small Minolta camera and film, which was the only way to record something at that time. I wore my favorite bespoke black cotton velvet Christian Dior redingote that I had aquired after seeing a photo of Paul Morrissey in such a coat. I still have this coat and whenever I even just glimpse it I am reminded of this fateful day. I wore blue suede and denim square toe cowboy boots that my dad had bought for me a few years earlier. Unlike almost everyone else, who dressed in blue jeans and dirty workshirts, I wore a pair of slinky black heavy jersey Halston pants and an oversized black cable knit Balenciaga turtleneck sweater, and topped it all with a black beret. So French, I thought, convinced I was blending in.

It was unusually brisk that morning, though with the promise of sunshine. The famous Parisian light dazzled even the darkest colors on every surface of every object into swimming pools of intenseness. Wandering a flea market for me has always been a peaceful activity that allows my thoughts to flow easily and languidly, fluttering from thing to thing, spurred by all the objects and their histories. To this day, roaming around an antique store or thrift shop or flea market relaxes me tremendously.

It was that day that I found, lying on the floor on a dusty cargo blanket, *the* hat. The hat by Elsa Schiaparelli. The sun had come up and I noticed the sparkling insect first. A gilt fly that was sewn to this *thing*, not yet acknowledged as being anything else than a mass of something attached to this insect. Looking back on it, I had an out-of-body, somehow supernatural experience. The moment I focused my eyes on the gold insect, my vision enlarged; as if on a movie screen my view opened up and I understood this teeny detail, this gold insect, was attached to some sort of peculiar headgear. My spiritual vision opened up, too, and I had what can only be called an out-of-body experience. For a few moments, I understand the entire meaning of the multiverses and especially my own universe. It was intense! Yet all I said to myself when that strange trip faded back into a three-dimensional reality was "Oh, it's a hat." I think I said it to myself, but I may have said it aloud because the seller, a disheveled dealer, crossed his arms, sized me up, and spoke a few banalities that I did not really listen to. A hat? An insect on a hat? It was a bluish-black dull satin, top-stitched into an accordion shape. I bent down and looked closer. I picked it up and I then felt a jolt of energy many times more intense than the first trip I'd just had and that, to this day, I don't think I have ever felt again. At that exact moment, I knew I was in love. But with whom? With what? I only knew that I was thunderstruck, truly so, and with a thunder made of unearthly divine positivity. The moment I touched this creation—and I recall this as vividly as if it had happened one minute ago—I said to myself, something along the lines of, "The soul contract I have starts right now." I actually felt something like a huge metaphysical blast when I touched that hat.[1]

It had clearly started in some other dimension in some expansive nonlinear place. I was aware there was a soul contract and that here on earth, my consciousness of its existence instantly appeared in my mind. Up until this point whatever thoughts about souls and other dimensions were something I thought about often, but this soul contract was in a complete somnambulistic state in me. I had no expectation in my life thus far to ever have such a personal experience of such concepts and beliefs. Although it was present in me since birth it only commenced when I touched this oddity. Immediately my consciousness became aware of its existence. The contact with the hat, in a split second, was a catalyst that instilled in me an immense sense of lucidity and awareness of this wild and clearly life-changing journey. I experienced this supracosmic blast of inner sight, a portal that unveiled a deep connection to the person who was responsible for crafting this refined combination of earthly materials into a *chapeau*.

The hat had opened my eyes to what love was, a kind of deeply satisfying, metaphysical love. It is no exaggeration to say the discovery of this seemingly banal object was, for me, the equivalent of discovering the Holy Grail. At that special moment I felt time was no longer linear, but something only Quantum theory could explain and that time was expansive, fluid, and biomorphic, a lucid crystalline ectoplasm that had no boundaries, no end, and forever and eternally moving. I understood multiverses and had a vision of my many other selves in many other realities. My experience with that first Schiaparelli creation transformed my life into a brilliant, gleaming rollercoaster ride. I have her to thank for making me see the sublime and amazing thing that is life on earth.

My adult life is in many ways a homage to the hat's maker, Elsa Schiaparelli. It has been an esoteric bouquet of personal manifestations and verbal flowers laid at her feet. One of my most beloved mentors, Diana Vreeland said in the opening to her autobiography, *D.V.*, "I loathe nostalgia."[1] Even though I feel the same, it is still essential to record and document one's own voyage through this earthly life. The Schiaparelli hat, designed for a lady in a time when I had not lived, made me nostaglic for something I had not experienced in my current incarnation. I used this longing to make my present. It contributed to my daily level of happiness and made my future not only interesting, but also offered a positive and inspirational influence on others in fashion and the arts. Finding the hat became the catylst for something very important for me, but also for those I would know and those who may know me.

It has been over forty years since that moment at the flea market, and still I am fascinated and astounded by Elsa Schiaparelli and her work. In every piece I discover something deeply revealing, beyond the already pleasing aesthetics. Her work brings an always-fresh sense of peace but also awe. Initially, it was the unusual juxtaposition of shapes, colors, and textures that engaged me: a blue satin bias cut gown matched to an orange tweed bolero; a rough knit jacket that appears to be Middle Eastern berber cloth but is surprisingly made on the Isle of Skye at the seat of Clan Macleod, dyed electric blue with a rough hewn, yet highly modernistic closure made by the artist Jean Clément; an oatmeal-colored, three-quarter length day coat made from a sturdy homespun lyric tweed, cut like a coachman's coat of the eighteenth-century, closing with hand-shaped buttons made of resin. Each of these items speaks to me deeply and ignites a sense of joy mixed with the odd feeling of calm that occurs when studying beautiful objects. They are a glimpse of my guardian angel. Peculiar as it may sound, Schiap put me on rails, like a train, and pushed me forward with the excitement of being alive, of being in the world.

Goethe wrote in *Der Gross-Cophta* (1791) that "you must be the hammer or the anvil." Schiaparelli was always the hammer. In her creations, she was a force who imposed her own eye, her own inimitable vision and sense of chic and savoir-vivre, on her era. For me, though, she was also a spiritual guardian hammer, sometimes banging me on the head to get moving, whether I wanted to or not. The feelings she evoked in me were stronger than my own consciousness, firing with explosive force my curiousity and imagination and driving me forever forward to learn about the most precious aspects of life—all through her work. From the moment our connection was set in motion it has been my dream to tell her story. And over time, her story intertwined with my own in such a way that I cannot seem to tell one without the other.

CHAPTER 2

CHILDHOOD

P rior to that Saturday in June 1974 at the Clignancourt flea market, I am not entirely sure I existed. I may have existed as a mass of organic matter floating in space and time, with the assigned age of fourteen, but something in that young person was not entirely turned on, not entirely alive. I always felt that even in my very first memories, I was merely observing humanity on a foreign planet, not really a part of it. It came as a sort of shock to me that I was supposed to be human, an earthling. There was nothing that made me feel this way at all. I felt only as if I was an observer and my human (-esque) form was a disguise. This was a deep and profound sentiment that contributed to my sense of alienation, sadness, and also, rather strangely, a strong sense of empathy. Though I still feel this separateness, I have come much closer to understanding my unusual journey and destiny. I realize now that the crucial puzzle piece missing from my childhood was the feeling and real knowledge of love.

I was born in Austria to two unmarried, underage, yet wealthy parents from different religions. I was put up for adoption practically as I was coming out of my mother. There was a mysterious story about my birth that involved a twin brother, a death, an inheritance, and a number of other things that have been completely impossible to know the truth about or get the facts straight, which would haunt me my entire life. So, the first excruciating years of my existence were spent in an orphanage and with a variety of foster families in Austria and then the USA. Before the process of adoption was finalized I had a beautiful Egyptian lady who was my caretaker and supervised which foster homes I'd be briefly staying at. When a couple finally expressed a serious desire to adopt me, I was allowed to live with them in the United States in a trial period not unlike one a car dealer offers a potential customer wishing to buy a car. This short trial period allowed them to make sure, I suppose, that they really wanted to adopt me. In 1964, at age four, the long legal wait to be adopted was over. I was now part of a big family of first generation Russian immigrants living in America.

All I can say about that time, which I sadly can still remember, is that it was spirit breaking, mostly terrifying, and left me with a memory of extreme hopelessness. I still have nightmares about it. The people who'd become my eventual adoptive parents were extremely careful and loving to me though, and as chance would have it, accepted me as their son. My mother always told me they were the only couple who had shown serious interest in me and that I seemed very dejected and melancholic even at that young age. I believe I was a difficult child to adopt due to a host of ailments that ranged from flat feet to a number of unpleasant congenital illnesses. My mental state was considered fragile and I suffered from panic attacks and eating disorders. My real family's refined pedigree and perception of my underage parents as children who committed a mortal sin would surely have thought these issues to be perfect justifications and alibis to get rid of me *illico presto* in any case. Besides, what "normal" couple would want a child with such a background and such troubles? It was always diffciult for me to understand why my adopted family actually chose me. I was, even by age four, a mess.

The same year I was adopted, my birth parents commited suicide. I discovered this information long after leaving home, as my adopted mother remained tight-lipped about my origins until the day she died. "It's better if you don't know anything about it" was the standard response. Over the course of many years and via private detectives I'd hired, I would learn a bit more about the situation. But even after going the route of a mild sort of espionage and bribing a few people, it's still very confusing to me. This horrible tragedy, this bottomless black hole of fate would prevent me from knowing more, no matter how I tried. In any case, I was severely traumatized by my circumstances, despite the considerable effort by my adoptive parents to make me feel loved and well adjusted. I was so deeply hurt that I slowly grew into a frightened and insecure child who continued to grow into a confused and angry teen. My first lesson in life was to take my trauma, my flaws, and my shortcomings, and learn how to make them work in my favor.

Early on I learned to use my imagination and creativity to withstand the constant struggles in my young, sheltered life. Even the smallest things seemed difficult and I found everyday life very confusing. Leaving the protective shell of my bedroom required considerable effort and so I regularly found ways to convince myself that everything would be fine and I would have some sort of happy ending. This was exhausting. It's not that I lived in a fantasy world—I never had an imaginary friend, for example—I just felt best alone and even better when I was left to enjoy thinking about beautiful things and imagining creating them. This was the way I coped. It distracted me from my situation and saved me from the harshness of the everyday world.

Through this deeply rooted sense of creation that I was born with, I developed an intense focus on all things beautiful. At first this manifested in making silly little things with my hands. I was contained in my own secret universe of glamour, beauty, and aesthetics, like a character in a Conrad Aiken story. Psychiatrists and child behavior counselors called me "emotionally disturbed," though one should bear in mind that back in the 1960s being autistic, left-handed, gay, or having difficulties that are now identified as bipolar, obsessive compulsive, post-traumatic stress, anorexia, bulimia, and hyperactivity would earn that label. Even just being mopey could doom you to that appellation. In reality I was just gay, depressed, and traumatized.

I was constantly afraid my adoptive parents would "give me back," even if I realize now this as an irrational fear. Later in life my mother swore up and down that nothing of the sort had ever been said, but I do have vivid recollections of hearing things in moments when my mother lost her patience. Usually though, this threat of being returned was doled out as a reminder when I'd disobey small demands. A demand usually entailed a request for me to participate in activites that involved contact with other people, which I was determined not to do. However, my mother swore that I was the nicest child in the world, quiet and good-natured. She said I was often melancholic, but my mood improved when I was left alone to my own devices to create art. So I was forehead deep in every type of art supply and medium, from cameras to paints and clays, and all their related apparatuses. When I was spoilt with these things I felt adored, as being smothered with gifts would make anyone feel, but the fear of being sent away was always lurking in my thoughts. I was very confused.

My parents were not to blame for my own psychogoical complexity; it was part and parcel of me from birth. One of the unfortunate consquences of adoption is that it can create an emotional impression of total abandonment. I belive this is a common issue, even for those children with less dramatic backgrounds. I think these oppressive feelings were problematic for my parents, but they coped as best as they could. My mother allowed me to be a "totally free butterfly," while at the same time seeking out ways to help me fit in. It was unrealistic to wish I would be normal. Asking for world peace and a cure for cancer would have been a lot more reasonable. However, during those first years after my adoption they did try to present a good front to outsiders, which must have been a burdensome and difficult task. It often felt as if I were participating in some sort of Pavlovian experiment. The results from this brief experiment with them were very hit-or-miss (though mostly miss) and questionably successful or even useful.

I had a total ignorance of what normalcy was supposed to be and I made mistake after mistake with my attempts to perform in life in general. Because as much as I hated it, I also hated to see them so disappointed in me and so seemingly sorrowful when I was alone for such long periods of time. So, I tried to please them. Yet, no matter what I did, I stuck out. Quite soon I abandoned the idea, deciding it was a massive waste of time to strive for something I could not achieve and that, frankly, as my awareness grew stronger, I did not want to do. I had a natural defiance for most of the things related to being my age in the 1960s and looking back to that time all the things that were considered "normal" made no sense to me. Along the road I would make detours, mistakes, and errors of judgement, but was lucky to be instilled with awareness of what I wanted from life from a very young age.

I knew I was different by age three. I was socially handicapped, excruciatingly timid, and actively disliked most things children my age were doing. I simply did not get it. My peers seemed like aliens from another planet and for the first few years of my life I had no friends at all. I hated to be around children of any age and I believe my parents had no idea how truly upset I was at the mere suggestion of being in any sort of contact with noisy, messy, and sticky children.

My peers must have found me more than just a bit bizarre as well, so I spent nearly all of my early childhood alone.

When I became a little older, from around age eight to twelve, my solitary tendencies mellowed into a stoically artificial politeness. I feigned a bare minimum of smiling. I turned my very melancholic indifference for most things not related to art or beauty into a *faux-semblant* of a nice young man. Going through the motions of the practical things in life bored me, but I had found a way to withstand them. By the time I was a teen I was able to successfully disguise my anti-social behavior. I managed to teach myself how to smile and how to fake a more pleasant demeanor. It was a learned behavior based mostly on movies and book characters. I also concocted a unique personality mix based on the characters I saw: a Lolita-like gay boy-cum-abnormally precocious lad who could be a rather naive angel or a spellbinding demon. I even became somewhat daring and very extroverted, which was a wonderful disguise and a workable self-preservation mechanism. It was also a response to the fear of being rejected. I learned later that this purposeful extroversion was a test I was imposing on people around me. I was so afraid people would leave me that I pushed the envelope to the extremes until most would run away screaming into the night. In the end, it was the ones who stayed through thick and thin and through my escalating eccentricities who mattered to me the most. I wanted proof of everyone's love for me and this was the crazy way I obtained it. If I wore a strange old hat, would my parents still love me? I think the whole early part of my career was this self-imposed extroversion. I must underline that this behavior was not calculated or intentional at the time. I was very much a work in progress. I was very much like a strange cosmic experiment in its early stages and a type of guinea pig in this human incarnation that I am. I learned how to articulate this only through many decades of experiences and harsh self-criticism, as the man I am now, to a great extent, is no longer that very insecure, naive young person. Through maturity, it's only now I can see clearly how I evolved with linear time and experience and have the means to express it through writing.

With my anti-social angst under control to an extent after a few years of adjustment to planet earth and humans, I made every effort to learn about this world and how it functions and I did this best when I was alone. My desire for knowledge and my determined avoidance of people my age afforded me a lot of time to do whatever I wanted, guided by my more positive creative instincts. These were complemented by and compensated for with an abundance of playthings. I was smothered with toys and dolls from the first day I was adopted. This gave me an endless range of entertainments: educational toys, Sasha dolls, Antonio Vitali wooden animals and farm sets, all sorts of European intellectual designer toys alongside the most commercial American versions. There was nothing too marvelous for me and my parents just gave and gave and gave. They distracted me with therapeutic outings to parks, aquariums, zoos, concerts, plays, dance recitals, and other cultural experiences. I had horses, slot cars, and a piano and lessons in everything from dance to tennis. Anything fun, educational, or unusual was made available to me. My parents believed this method of child rearing would inspire me to become whatever it was I wanted, and hopefully grow into a healthy individual in the process. They thought that their odd way of paying attention to me with constant approval, tokens of affection, and material abundance would be the magical combination for my happiness.

My dad liked to overdo things. He brought home a present for me every single day. Literally. Every. Single. Day. It could be a bag of lollipops with candy faces on them, a teeny doll, a board game, or even a big-boxed toy. I think he was particularly fond of the astronaut toys, especially one by Mattel called Major Matt Mason, so I had several of those. We played G.I Joes, Action Man, and astronaut dolls together, though when he was around they abstained from kissing each other, as they did when I played with them alone. He built me a rudimentary pup tent and furniture, but my biggest concern was if the table and chairs matched and if they would be formal enough. I wanted a stylish modern dining room, not a wartime bench and table. He tried very hard to mold me into someone who'd be considered normal, at least from the outside, though he knew it was a losing battle. Looking back I feel genuine sorrow for him.

My parents felt I had to define my personality by choosing the things that interested me. This was all part of my mother's determined conviction that I should be allowed complete and utter freedom to become whatever it was I'd become. I was given dolls only because I asked for them. In my mind, they offered me an opportunity to care for my own babies. I had marvelous Sasha dolls by artist Frau Sasha Morgenthaler. Having met her and known her back then endeared her dolls to me for life. She gave me a number of Sasha dolls painted and dressed by her for me. I had Italian dolls with lovely high fashion wardrobes by Furga called Alta Moda Tre Esse, which I had discovered on a trip to Rome as a child. By now, many people know about my relationship with the Barbie doll and are surprised when they learn that I had an equally as intense relationship to Britain's famous Sindy doll and I also had everything in between from the Gégé Mily series of dolls and the Ideal Toy Corporation's Tammy and Crissy doll. The company owner gave the latter to me because my father had a big business contract with that firm. To be truly clear about this, I must say I "collected" them to the point of hoarding which, along with all the other things that worried them, preoccupied my parents a great deal. My mother just wrote it down to me being "free" to express myself. I particularly favored the doll clothes—the little coats and suits and dresses, small accessories like sunglasses and hats. I liked the male doll's gear just as much, and tried often to interchange it with that of other dolls. Sterotypes about correct sexual identity through clothes were the furthest thing from my young mind. Mostly, I was drawn to the smallness and sensuality of the materials. Miniature objects put me in a rapturous spell. In the end, though, my favorite toys were the ones I made myself. Living in my imagination, creating things from anything on hand—scraps of fabric, old costume jewelry, paper, straw, colored glass found on beaches, even rolls of colored electrical tape I found in my adopted dad's workshop. I was endlessly drawing and trying to write down my feelings.

My mother is responsible for a particularly special toy. It was one of the first I had received when I was four. It was a girl's dress-up set from Marx Toys that contained a plastic hat-like wig (in a silver bouffant style), a pair of Lucite Spring-O-Lator style heels filled with glitter, and a matching vinyl clutch. The package stated it was for a princess, but it looked like it was better suited for a hooker. When I think about it now, I feel bad for my father but also cannot help but to laugh. My mother said the clicking across the parquet floors drove him up the wall. The poor man, what that must have done to his mind back then. His baby boy was in cha cha heels and a Pop Art-like plastic "do" with a coordinating clutch. In spite of this early experience, I was not fated to become a drag queen. I know that even from that early age I had no desire to look quite like a girl, but felt such joy being dressed in exotic ways. I did swoon for those heels though. Although I rarely wear them as an adult (there are a few exceptions), high heels have played a large role in my artwork over the years and it all stems from that Marx Toys Dress-Up kit. I was unknowingly cultivating my sexual orientation and my future as an artist and collector. From the first day I was adopted, my mother always made allegories of flowers blooming and spirits set free to develop into a butterfly. She was like Marlo Thomas reenacting her "Free to Be . . . You and Me" ideology. I was one very odd, rather floral, butterfly!

As a result of my mother's encouragement I pored over an old set of leather bound encyclopedias from the 1920s. I found a great deal of comfort and very much needed peace of mind in these books, with their fabulous glossy color illustrations. I recall the precision and detail of the pages on botany, especially the cactuses and flowers. The animal pictures were mesmerizing. The mysterious diagrams and drawings of shells, stones, minerals, insects, and fish enchanted me thoroughly. I was innately drawn to all beautiful objects. I found everything intriguing and lovely, whether it be an orange and black 1960s (what is now called "Fat Lava") pottery vase, the watercolor movements of a real goldfish, a Verner Panton chair, lavish embroidery of Roger Vivier shoes which my dozens of great aunts and aunts wore with an almost fetishistic need, or the scents of Diorissimo, Le Dix de Balenciaga, and Shocking that they all wore. I discovered that old films and music from earlier eras enraptured me, too, and they played a big role in my mental and sexual development. I was also enticed by human-sized clothing and the many ways one can play with it. I stimulated my mind to the outer reaches of my imagination.

By age ten I started to re-work old clothes I found in closets or the attic into my own dress-up outfits. I fashioned psychedelic Pucci and arty-looking Dior scarves into makeshift turbans, Balenciaga foulards turned into sarongs, and found that two Chanel scarves could conveniently be fashioned into a fetching mini tunic. I put flowers in my hair just like the song "San Francisco (Be Sure to Wear Flowers in Your Hair)" that I heard on my mother's hi-fi stereo. I made shell bracelets and bead necklaces. I draped myself in my grandmother's real and costume jewelry and anything else colorful or exotic looking that I could find. I'd take a pair of old 1950s men's pants and, using my rudimentary ability to work with a scissor and fabric, cut and pin them into new shapes. Often I would paint them to make a new texture for the old textile. Once the paint dried, I'd draw, glue, or sew designs on the newly shaped garment using everything and anything available. I was particularly fond of the blue and red fake fur that my mother had used to wallpaper my bedroom and I used remnants of it to make all sorts of things. I invented my own toys, my own games, and a sundry of *divertissements* and got my freak on rather early thanks to these two unsuited-for-each-other people who gave me the world on a golden platter.

During the earliest years of my life with these new parents, as one can see, they were overly generous to me and paid special attention to my behavior, responding to almost everything I did and giving me anything I needed. Evidently, though, it was difficult for them to be consistent with attention and as time passed, and the zeitgeist of the times changed, this became more and more sporadic. One day I was the center of attention, but the next I might not see them, or if I did, I felt invisible. At the same time, they held very high ideals, especially my mother, but it was impossible to live up to the standards they set for themselves and even for myself, I could not really keep up with trying to please them. As much as I may have tried to adapt to this adopted family, I found my new parents very foreign to me and I truly did not know why I was with them. I did not feel that thing I believed (and still believe) blood-related families have, that sense of being part of the same whole. My new parents loved me as if I were a child they'd conceived and tried everything to make me feel that I belonged. Despite their best efforts, I felt more like an exotic pet.

Needless to say, despite anything else confusing or negative I may have felt during the years that I lived with my adopted parents, I am eternally grateful to them for the freedom and sense of liberty they gave me right from the start. My mother was particularly adamant that I be given the best of the best education and I should be allowed to assert myself freely, because in her mind, it might help to "express the pain away." Alhough they encouraged my expression, I am quite sure they worried about what would come of all this freedom. They were particularly concerned for my safety when I was, on the occasional situation, with other children. My gayness was never an issue with them, though. My mother said she knew immediately and my father, who was always in denial, finally understood prior to my leaving home at age fifteen. It was obvious in my mind and very quickly became apparent in my manner of dress and in the overtly strange way I looked, behaved, and thought about life in general. The day before my mother passed away she told me that she was always proud of me, but when I was a child her biggest fear was that I'd be hurt by someone who didn't "get me." She said, "Only intelligent people can get you, people on your level. The rest you either frightened or made feel very uncomfortable or worse, jealous. I was worried about how you'd manage when you left home." Although it was obvious that I was not well-adjusted even before they adopted me, it much later became apparent that this was why they chose me in the first place. My mother confided eventually that she had decided she would give her attention to a child since she never loved my father, who was sterile from taking anti-malaria drugs during the Korean war. For her, the only resource was adoption, and it took quite a while to convince him and his family. No matter what anyone says, adopting children was a stigma back then and it made people question the sex life of a couple and the health of their marriage. For this emotive Russian family, adoption was cardinal to admission of incompatibility and sexual failure. My mother told me that adopting me was an endless battle, with guilt trip after guilt trip thrown at her and my father by the ensemble of both families. In the end, as usual, she got what she wanted. I guess I could say it was my mother who called the shots in our house and she told me as an adult that she wanted to have an "emotionally needy child" because it fulfilled her need to love and smother someone with her affection. She'd given up on trying to change my father early in their marriage, long before I was even born. She admitted to me it was a fundamental mistake to marry him, and she did so only so she could get away from her old-world parents. It was an error to think she could make my father into an exciting, party-loving husband, something he was not. As bizarre an admission as it is from a mother to a son, she chose me because of my flaws.

Though their marriage was a bit of a sham, at least concerning my mother's feelings for my father, they doted upon me in the early years of my childhood. To outsiders, it seemed we were an ideal family. When I think back to that time, it was clear my parents became more and more distraught with the constant challenge I presented as I learned to talk and express what was on my mind. After many psychological tests and a whole bunch of child psychoanalysis, I was deemed a genius with an IQ well above the 140 mark. In fact many specialists said that my emotional state was linked to my intelligence and recommended sending me away to a special school for children with very high IQs. This my mother adamantly refused. The suggestion terrified both my parents, but my mother took it on as a confirmation that her instincts were right and that her way of raising me was not only justified but necessary. My mother told me I was a "heavy trip" to worry about all the time. My incessant, often incomprehensible opinions about the world and life usually puzzled, occasionally alarmed, and always creeped her out. She repeatedly said I was an alien life form and that when I spoke to her about life she would actually become frightened, as my ideas seemed much too sophisticated and adult for such a young child to feel. I never got into trouble, or caused any typical childhood ruckus, but I was constantly the subject of conversations between my parents, something that had to be explained to their friends and family who may have been a little bit in the know. I was always dolled up in my ersatz turbans glittering with costume jewelry at parties and other family gatherings and I could hear the *sotto voce* of my relatives saying things like "Oh, he's turned out to be a little fairy," "I'd beat the crap out of my kid if he looked like that," and the worst for her (and even more terrible for my father) was "I heard he's emotionally disturbed, I can see now what they mean." My mother would become very defensive and even aggressive when she'd hear these offensive statements mumbled by people she loved. She defended me in many ways, explaining that it was because I was adopted, I was sensitive, and would probably be a creative person one day. I think my father was just humiliated. I would hear my parents say things such as "What will we do with him?" each time one of these unpleasant showdowns occurred or after one of my emotional meltdowns, which were as regular as the sunrise. The poor dears, they were not really prepared for such a basket case of a son.

My mother told me years later that she and my father wanted to make up for the terror of being in an orphanage and foster care during the first years of my life, but she also had her own life to live. She had an intense Russian beauty, with charismatic bright violet-blue eyes set against jet-black hair, and a great sense of humor. Always the life of the party, she had a passion for high-stakes gambling and other thrilling activities. She believed in living life with intensity! When I was young she had an illegal gambling salon in a brownstone for years. She simply adored having casino parties with her mafia friends. It was a scene right out of *The Godfather*. What I remember the most (sometimes fondly, sometimes not so fondly) about her in the 1960s and '70s was that she seemed to live in a never-ending Tiparillo cigarillo commercial with music, clinking glasses, gambling, and all sorts of men and women with great hair in cocktail clothing smoking, drinking, laughing, and dancing. I used to dance the latest go-go dance steps with her on the billards table! She was truly a glamorous woman of the times, and looked the part with her mod clothes, sports cars, limousines, and equally flashy friends.

I think my mother started to become emotionally unstable and frustrated with her marriage as my childhood progressed. Her instability worsened after her mother violently committed suicide when I was 13. My darling grandmother Leah (who everyone called Lee) was as glamorous as a movie star even in death and changed all of our lives forever. Just before she died, she gave me a miniature platinum, enamel, marcasite, and ruby enameled Fabergé egg that she claimed had been given to her mother by the Tsarina. I had no way to know she planned to kill herself and although I loved the gift, it seemed odd for her to give it to me out of the blue like that. I wore it to her funeral with a tartan suit in the fashionable pastel ice cream tones of strawberry, pistachio, and vanilla. I was very much criticized and scolded for my choice, but my grandmother had said I looked "dapper" in it and that is why I wore it. I wore it for her. Her death traumatized the family and things seemed to fall apart for everyone. I think it was one of the main reasons why I so suddenly decided to leave home in 1975.

The year after my grandmother's death, my mother was so severely crippled and emotionally damaged that she became unrecognizable to me. She was so deeply shocked, frustrated, and angry which turned into an "I don't give a fuck" attitude. It was truly horrible and scary to be around her, especially when she was high on amphetamines or barbiturates, which she popped randomly depending on her mood. Trying to predict her moods was pretty much impossible and thus, she was very hard to live with. I spent most of my time trying to avoid her and literally moved as far across the globe as possible to get away from her thanks to the world tours she arranged for me in order to learn about life and all the varied ways people live it.

She was, at best, a likeable bully with a need for control. My clothing and general outward appearance were the first and pretty much only problems between us when I turned into a teenager, though they started at age ten when I demanded bellbottom pants by Pierre Cardin and Biba. They were labeled unisex, but were overtly feminine. She was not a fan. After that debacle she developed an increasing fixation on my appearance. She wanted me to be totally myself but in the image *she* wanted for that self. After the suicide this focus became worse, and it seemed like she was backtracking on the idea of allowing me to be myself. I had been raised to express anything and everything I felt, but after my grandmother died, my mother no longer approved of anything. If even the slightest thing did not wholly please her, she would not hesistate to inform me so frankly, sometimes cruelly. She even called me a "queer" as an insult after that tragedy, something she'd never done before. It was as if she gave up on me. As I continued to grow up, the concept of being Queer seemed more and more a good thing to me (which is a long story destined for another time). Being Queer was a celebration. My great uncle, who was a handsome gay man, seemed not only to celebrate it, but went to Rio de Janeiro each year to get his party on. He even had the chic to drop dead there from a heart attack whilst mating with one of the exotic ephebe locals; *hélas*, being a Queer was not something to celebrate. This despite the fact she came to terms with her lesbianism and was living it fully by this time. In her defense she did repeatedly tell me, "It was never the gayness that worried me, that was fine, it was the clothing, the way you stood out so completely from anything normal and usual. I was so afraid you'd get killed one day for it." I want to underscore that it was not the homosexuality, but the bizarreness of how I looked and behaved that concerned her. She finally accepted me fully by the end of the 1970s, when she left my father to live her rather outrageous and very flamboyant lesbian life. She became a militant lesbian in Greenwich Village after having become lovers literally with nearly every woman in the vicinity of our house. I have been able to forgive her for some of the things I had resented for years but the most important thing is that I will be forever grateful for that amazing education, and the immense freedom rarely given to a child that she insisted I have. I owe her that.

Even during those difficult years we did have our moments of true bonding. She delighted in telling me about her belief in Paganism, Wicca, and Summum. We spoke about Goddesses and white magic non-stop. When we spoke of these things I felt very close to her and as if I understood why the universe entrusted me to her care. My mother had a very intense philosophy of life and unusual beliefs. She also possessed a great sense of dry humor and made pithy wisecracks that she used to charm everyone. We used laughter to avoid the anger and pain. We have a very similar sense of humor—ironic, campy, and devilishly dark. We were like the Addams family in that regard. She was a glamour puss party girl and I learned from her that I could become one, too.

When she died, my immediate reaction was to thank the universe for allowing me to speak candidly with her before she left this earth. I never had this opportunity with my father, who died long before she did. I could not have survived another missed opportunity to make final amends and say good-bye. She was genuinely the most supportive person in my life, dedicated to helping me become what she always called "the real me." Though our relationship was complex, I would not have lasted long in this world nor would I have achieved much without her firm belief in letting me be that "free butterfly."

When my father passed away nearly twenty-three years had gone by without any contact between us. I heard that he cried and could not understand why I'd abandoned him at the end of his life. This created a permanent crack in my emotions that will never heal. I confess that I was afraid of him, and am embarassed by my vanity and stupidity regarding him. I have never cried as much as I did the day I learned he was gone forever, at least for this lifetime.

I may have been closer to my mother but looking back, I think in a bizarre way I understood my dad better, which may not always be the case with a gay man. I came to understand the essential being of my dad only after his death. The opposite of my mother, he was also an extreme personality: dark and brooding, often called a "young Marlon Brando" by people who met him. I later realized that he was a very earnest man, typical of a certain generation of men born in the 1930s. He took huge risks that provided him with enormous success, but he lost everything in the end—his wife, his son, and his wealth. He was swarthy and saturnine in his nature, but could be very introspective and thoughtful. He was a loner, like myself. Apart from a young so-called cowboy who followed him about at rodeos (supposedly to help with all the gear, his junk and horses, though as an adult I understand it was mostly to help him with his junk), he never had a single friend to my knowledge except Al Pacino, who visited him often before he became a famous actor. Even though he could be as brutish as a Zane Grey character, he didn't possess any of the mean, cutting manipulation that my mother had. He didn't try to mold me at all, in fact. He believed in only a few things: his family, fidelity to his wife, and the best for his child. His only vices were buying horses and dogs, which he loved and on which he spared no expense. I understood rather early on that he was hiding deep insecurities about his sexuality and his manhood. My mother told me after he passed away that being sterile was a great shame for him.

My father gave me wonderful gifts that I am exceedingly appreciative of as an adult. I have a great respect for animals and nature that I learned from him. He taught me how to take risks and enjoy being alone. He gave me the love of knowledge and introduced me to flea markets and antiques stores, which spurred a deep love of history and objects from the past. In spite of his generosity, somehow I was always afraid of him. I thought he was somewhat barbaric and a brute, that I had to tiptoe around. In reality, my father was an exceptionally kind and simple man, very much like the cocky and uncouth Fred Flintstone and Ralph Kramden I imagined he was when I was young. I understood as an adult that like those two characters, he was also very likeable despite those characteristics. Sadly, my mother's family despised him, a fact they blatantly and relentlessly paraded in his face. They thought my mother had married beneath her even though his family was from a higher aristocratic class in Russia than hers. On the rare times that they extended a kind word they called him "Gentle Ben." Under the gruff exterior he truly was like the fabled bear of the late 1960s television show. To this day I regret not knowing him better and I miss him.

The roots of my complex personality may have been present from the beginning, in my genes, but observing my parents' behaviors only reinforced these traits. I think my experiences with them created a void that I filled with an obsession in the form of collecting everything I could about Elsa Schiaparelli.

CHAPTER 3

LEAVING HOME
"GOOD-BYE, AND
THANKS FOR ALL THE FISH"

n 1974, just prior to the trip to Paris during which I found the hat, my parents allowed me to open my first gallery. I opened another gallery a few years later, at age seventeen. I named both "Pizzazz" after Diana Vreeland's great use of the word, and both were equally short-lived projects. A motley crew of painters and somewhat unsavory people frequented them. I thought they were the chicest places possible, so I never seriously considered selling any of the contents because I loved the decor too much to disrupt it by removing anything. It was a typical, yet exceptional privilege that my parents allowed me to open this alternative art gallery at that age. I imagine they wanted to encourage my interests. I showed my own paintings, collages, and antiques alongside works by the mostly unknown artists who circled around the scene. A few of them were legitimate abstract expressionists and action painters from the 1950s who lived in the area. Many of them were also desperate alcoholics and drug addicts who were clearly taking advantage of my special situation. I didn't care. They were fascinating and told me interesting stories about artists like Jackson Pollock and Hans Hartung. These lavishly decadent misfits added color to my life, and my experience with the first gallery pushed me to further myself.

I recall stealing money from my father out of a huge 1940s kosher pickle jar he kept in his closet. I used this dough to paint the floors with designs in the manner of Kazimir Malevich, added Lucite shelves and installed Art Deco and mid-century Modern furniture. There I was, set up in my own gallery. Although still a young teen-ager, I appeared grown-up and put on many airs and pretentions about sophistication. My father came to see it once and brought a hamper of food for me to share with my starving artist friends. This act of generosity made me feel guilty for taking money from his pickle jar. He had a strong sense of camaraderie, which I attribute to his days in the military and the few friends he made in his unit during the Korean War. When he saw my own group bonding, I think he approved and paid a little bit more attention to me. However, when he told me it was foolish and a waste of time to support these "drunk losers" I immediately snapped back to feeling resentment and fear. His thoughtful gesture was destroyed, evaporated into the air, by his clear disapproval for my project. Though he apologized after all hell broke lose at home later that day my only thought, which I confronted him with, was, Why did he have to hurt me that way? I asked myself, When am I going to blow this popsicle stand? Thirteen years old and already I was somewhat jaded and dissatisfied with life.

In the mid-1970s my teenage life was a blast! I had a wonderful time pretending to be a grown-up. By then I had discovered that sex was a release for me. Starting at age fourteen, I literally slept my way up one street and down the other side in all the artsy neighbor-hoods of Manhattan. I found it all rather fun and glamorous. I must have been a wee bit insane, not to mention utterly clueless that this was not standard behavior for people my age. However, ever since I encountered that hat (and before I met the love of my life) I've felt like sex was just a rest stop between Schiaparellis for me. It has led me to some incredible people and places: the men's room of the Russian Tea Room with an American senator I dated secretly for a while; a Cardinal in Vatican City to whom I swore (with my fingers crossed) my devotion; endless train trips to visit a West Point Cadet on holiday in London; the back seat of a 1960s Austin-Healey. In between gasps for air from often-energetic sex, I longed to be in Paris looking for the mysterious details of the life of the woman who represented my most intense fascination.

My parents knew this somehow, or at least they knew how much more I related to Paris and London, so I was secretly sent back and forth to Europe in an attempt to prevent me from getting into trouble. Up until the year I played hooky from my chaperone, I traveled a great deal without any family members. My mother thought that Europe was a safer place for such a young teen and that the people I knew there were more refined with a certain *savoir-vivre* that Americans lacked. Unfortunately, she was not aware that the Old World was full of equally, if not more so, depraved men than any American boys I might have known.

When my parents eventually found out I was in Paris, alone and un-chaperoned, they were livid. I threatened never to come home, to live in the dangerous Latin Quarter and to become some sort of *Boul'Miche* style Existentialist (with divine clothes, of course). I forced them to wire money to a bank on the Champs-Elysées. Relieved, the first thing I did was buy sandwiches and walked to Place de la Concorde where I met a backpacking tourist from Norway who I would have sex with later that day. My next task was to purchase more "appropriate" clothes for Paris, as if I knew what that entailed. The clothes in Paris of 1974 were out of this world fabulous and I decked myself out in them like nobody's business. I also scoured the flea markets for vintage menswear that I re-worked and tailored to my figure. When a friend recently asked me which designers I wore back then, I drew myself up like Norma Desmond in *Sunset Boulevard* and said, "I wore them all!"

After traveling and being educated in Europe, I finally left my childhood home for good in late 1975. Not long after I returned from my travels, I met a new boyfriend at the terribly fashionable Razor Gallery in the trendy SoHo neighborhood of New York. His name was Christopher and he was the bastard son of a Kuwaiti prince and a Swedish prostitute. I had been arguing with my parents since the summer and sometime in December of 1975, right in the middle of the school year, I announced to my family that I was leaving. I had no resistance from anyone whatsoever.

In the midst of a snowstorm, Christopher and I put my Vuitton trunks into a brand new mini-van my dad gave me as a sort of "going away" gift. It was chaotic bringing everything to my new home in a funkier part of Manhattan, a huge suite at the Chelsea Hotel, and we moved in with snow and rain raging all around my rather cumbersome amount of basic necessities. You'd think that when a teen leaves home, he'd bring a toothbrush and a change of clothes, a few books and a television set, some practical and useful things. This was not my case at all. I took a miniature museum's worth of important art and design with me when I flew the coop. On the day I left my family, I recall my mother, a cocktail in one hand and a cigarette in the other, all aglow, practically shooing me out the door. Earnestly, and I am sure without intentional bad will, she said, "Oh, Billy, you know, my mother never let me live life the way I wanted and I just want you to do what you want, to go out there and do your stuff and have your own experiences." At the time I thought it also contained the coded sentiment, "I hope he doesn't get into trouble out there." I think she was also a little relieved to just get rid of the endless trail of worries I caused her. My dad was not there that day, though. My mother claimed in her somewhat bitterly joking manner that it was because "he hadn't the balls" to see me off. He did help me with all the details of the move and gave me an impressive wad of cash. I don't think it was lack of balls at all. I think he was sad and very quietly disappointed in me. Seeing my mother there that dreary day when I left home, standing at the door in all her 1970s glory, I can still feel the dreadful realization that I'd come to a junction in my young life. Whatever may have happened in the past it was now over, and as hard as I may have tried to think things would get better one day in regard to my parents, I knew deep inside that was not exactly true.

My mother's marriage was loveless, and so was my relationship with Christopher. My mother married my father to escape her family's house. Christopher was my ticket out. I found it sad and unsettling that I seemed to be following her path. It is a strange coincidence that Schiaparelli also left home very early and married hastily, perhaps without real love, as I learned from reading her memoir *Shocking Life*. If she could do it, so could I. But on that day, my sixth sense felt something, and it did not feel good at all. Oh dear, out of the frying pan and into the fire!

CHAPTER 4

A YOUNG QUEER
IN MANHATTAN

Armed with a ton of old Vuitton steamer trunks filled with groovy clothes, Art Deco bibelots by Demétre Haralamb Chiparus and Franz Hagenauer, paintings by Sonia Delaunay and Russian constructivists, 1920s and 1930s Bauhaus creations, Weiner Werkstätte ceramics, Andy Warhol artworks, toys, all kinds of vintage fashion dolls, and of course, my new stash of Schiaparelli hats, dresses, and jewelry, I moved away from home. I did not run away, but rather sashayed away all the while havering like a gay magpie. I headed for a hipper part of Manhattan and found my ideal home in the Chelsea Hotel. It was a very rock-'n'-roll, bohemian, and downright funky place to live. The wonderful "Old Skool" apartment suite was supposed to be temporary, but I ended up keeping it for years even though I had several other places all over Manhattan and in Europe. It was perfect for my 1970s arty teenage sensibilities. I instantly morphed from an oversexed ingénue into a hipster artist without being aware of it.

My eclectic group of neighbors at the Chelsea included Arthur Miller, Christopher Isherwood, Sid Vicious, and the temperamental genius fashion designer Charles James. Photographer Horst P. Horst dropped in regularly, as did William S. Burroughs, who was a frequent guest of mine. He shared his psychedelic writing ideas with me and listened to my wild Schiaparelli anecdotes while lying naked on the bed eating Stella D'Oro cookies and zapping through television stations. Burroughs said that Schiaparelli was an early anarchist who would have embroidered vomit and mud if she were still around today, beaded and jeweled to such perfection that from a distance, you would think it was the real thing. Up close, however, you'd know it was an elitist statement, a sign of power and wealth. He was not the only psychedelic thinker to say things to me about Schiap. A decade later Timothy Leary told me that he thought Schiaparelli was on the same wavelength with everything that is a little way out but instead of on LSD, she was spaced out naturally. He thought some people were like that, hooked into the vibes. Schiaparelli seemed to have been really in there and I was right alongside her.

My move to the Chelsea marked the beginning of my nights out in New York, when I'd occasionally wear Schiaparelli suits to the fashionable nightclubs—everywhere from Studio 54, Underground, and Area, to raunchy places like CBGB and Max's Kansas City. I was never faithful to one place and, as a dilettante I went where the ebb and flow of life led me. I saw amazing people, heard amazing music, and saw exciting performances at underground venues like the Mudd Club in New York, Le Palace and Les Bains Douches in Paris, and Kinky Glinky and Taboo in London. I could converse for hours with artists and musicians in New York such as Klaus Nomi, Joey Arias, Robert Mapplethorpe, Nico, Mimi Gross, Kenny Scharf, Keith Haring, Arthur Tress, and Diane Brill. In Paris and London I had a whole other set of people. Back on Park Avenue, where I could shed momentarily my ersatz underground skin, I would frequent the gatherings of the New York fashion elite, including Koos van den Akker, Halston, Perry Ellis, and later, Stephen Sprouse.

Perhaps I met such fascinating and diverse people because I had learned to be a rather beguiling young man. I was often called "chameleon-like" and was invited to all sorts of social outings. People seemed to appreciate the various looks I was cultivating. Although I was nothing like today's outrageous and talented drag queens, pansexual vloggers on YouTube, or the endless, very exclusive tribes all over the world—from bearded hipsters to pierced and tattooed bodybuilt bears and futuristic androgynes—I had the same sort of effect. But this was a different era, when standing out in a crowd was genuinely unusual. My look was not a costume or a disguise; it was usually French, Italian, Japanese, or Scandinavian high fashion and pure vintage from 1880 to 1960 that was pretty much a new idea in the 70s, all mixed with my own special style. That style, if I have to articulate it in words, I guess would be called essentially a television sitcom set in a psychedelic Art Deco musical of the 1930s. All singing, all dancing, all colorful. For me, everything had to attempt to be a balance between art and fashion, and was highly influenced by the past. All of these clothes and concepts were mixed like a strange type of dry martini with my various moods: Eastern Buddhism meets Art Deco, Cowboy Campitude, Pop Cartoonism, antagonist Crystal Allen from George Cukor's *The Women*, pin-up gone wild, or myriad other feelings that I would focus on from day to day and month to month. I was not entirely alone in my alternative fashions. There were people like the painters McDermott and McDough who wore period pieces and looked like they stepped out of an early twentieth-century photogravure. Others, like the lovely Katy K. Kattelman, looked totally rockabilly and country western. John Sex looked like Elvis and James Dean. Even RuPaul, when she started a decade or so after my youth, looked like something out of a fabulous 1960s underground film. Since I very frequently wore ultra modern designer's clothes mixed with genuine vintage haute couture (for either sex), you could be assured that with this kind of hocus-pocus love-potion-number-nine mixture, you never could really predict the final effect. Plus, the odd ball thrown into all of this is that I loved to be naked, as much as possible!

There were so many people I remember fondly from that time. One was Tina L'Hotsky, who was called by talented social observer Michael Musto "a good-time gal who was sort of the downtown Paris Hilton of that time."[1] She was a charming big blonde, and a bit of a rival to Diane Brill. I gave her my favorite Raymond Loewy designed hand-held hairdryer. I often photographed her in Schiaparelli clothes and hats from the 1950s and 1960s. Many of these photos ended up in underground newspapers and magazines like the *East Village Eye* and *Soho Weekly News*. Whenever she was happy with something she squealed with delight and was truly a vision to behold, in her posing and prissing about her appearance. I also knew a delightful girl named Ursula Rashoff. She lived in Chicago with a large, arty family of handsome brothers and sisters and a wonderful set of parents. Ursula was like a delicate bird, with refined features, chestnut brown hair and a perfect head for hats as some women have. She looked great in any hat you'd put on her head and introduced me to the work of Chicago hat-making legend Bes-Ben. Her taste was wonderful and she could spot couture amazingly well, so we'd spend hours, if not days, looking for it around the Chicago area. We'd go on Schiap hunts together and found quite a few pieces. With her I also found Callot Sœurs, Worth, Dior, Chanel, and many other important pieces by major designers. Chicago was a particularly good place for finding these types of treasures in the 1980s.

I was drawn into modeling, fashion, music, and the arts through chance meetings with many highly acclaimed talents, all of whom helped me in some way or another to understand both fashion and art. I was lucky to learn about fashion from such designers as Rudi Gernreich. He made me a few pieces of clothing over the years, including a mesh jumpsuit that was rather revealing. I wore his dresses because they never struck me as being just for ladies and he gave me a shocking pink shift with colored fringe as decoration that I adored. He said I looked good in Schiaparelli's pink.

Inspired by the artists around me, I became further fascinated by Schiap, and the post-war years especially, which I found mysterious. Her clothes were sometimes truly bizarre: buttons which don't close, pockets on the shoulders, highly graphic-looking shapes, scarves which were meant to look like a bottle of ink spilled on them, hats that looked like they were for invading aliens with cut-outs for a lady to beguilingly look through. I had never seen anything like them. It was thrilling to discover these fashions through the old pages of my vintage magazine collection lining the shelves of every place I lived in. I preferred Schiaparelli's post-war years to her Surrealist years, believe it not. My interest in fashion didn't stop with Schiap, though—I loved everything from the space-age designers like Pierre Cardin, Paco Rabanne, André Courrèges, Jacques Esterel, Emanuel Ungaro, to more contemporary designers like Louis Féraud and Ted Lapidus. I often wore their clothes as my everyday wardrobe and I felt wonderful in doing so.

Soon after leaving home, I started to further develop a project I called Surreal Couture that consisted of collages, paintings, sculptures, accessories such as hats and jewels, even clothes. My earliest Surreal Couture jewelry was shown on an eighteenth century Meissen statuette of a man whose head I broke off and replaced with a real lobster claw. I then added a leashed plastic lizard to the piece. My good friend at the time, the photographer Arthur Tress, staged an homage to Schiaparelli with me. In his photos you can see my assorted pet lizards, chameleons, and iguanas zipping around all the various Schiaparelli artifacts I was obsessed with at the time: a Schiaparelli 1940s stocking, some pairs of 1950s Schiaparelli shoes, pieces of her jewelry, her perfume bottles. We included a Schiaparelli hat, clearly inspired by Dalí, looking like a dresser drawer pull on a Lucite bust of Napoleon with my hand reaching into the photo. I thought it was very Dadaist. Arthur always has been such a unique and gifted photographer.

During this phase I identified with a new thing called "wearable art," which was clothing made with the intention of being art, either wearble or not. I made it my own by putting on live performances in the windows of prestigious department stores or art galleries. Nearly every other wearable art artist stopped at the creation. Apart from a wonderful artist named Colette Justine (later named Justine of the Colette is Dead Co), and the "Kipper Kids" (Martin Rochus Sebastian von Haselberg and Brian Routh) I knew of only a very few others, like the artist and performer Joey Arias and the opera singer Klaus Nomi who were adding performance to their *art plastique* back then, though others did exist allover the world. It was a small burgeoning zeitgeist of that era. Colette and I both had done performance art installations at a high-end vintage clothing shop called Victoria Falls on Spring Street in SoHo. One may recall recently the artist Colette, when Lady Gaga started her career. She claimed Gaga copied her work and protested her in Manhattan one rainy night in front of a store Gaga was doing a promotion in. This era of Colette and Klaus was when Calvin Churchman came into the picture and became the center of the landscape of my life. He was a brilliant man and a breath of fresh air.

Calvin was the art director of Fiorucci, an interactive art and fashion space originally created in Italy at that time by an acquaintance of mine, the vivacious and extravagant Elio Fiorucci. Even though most people could not afford the sexy jeans, plastic and vinyl outfits and accessories, and brightly colored knits designed by future friends Natalie du Pasquier and George Sowden, people came in the store to hang out, listen to the disco music, drink the free espresso coffee, and simply be seen peacocking around. Artist and performer

Joey Arias was like a futuristic Elsa Maxwell, floating around with brightly-colored hair, severe and beautiful make-up and the latest Fiorucci clothes. He worked the astonished crowds of shoppers like a glamorous circus barker. I think it was a solid commercial concept to blend art and fashion and it gave many underground artists an opportunity to express themselves uptown, something quite rare at the time. Calvin gave not only Joey Arias, but his best friend Klaus Nomi, and painter Kenny Scharf, and a number of other "underground" artists their first big breaks in New York.

My first show at Fiorucci was an exhibition of my Caran d'Ache and Crayola crayon drawings of speeding 1960s cars vrooming along horizonless vistas in Schiaparelli Sleeping Blue and Shocking Pink. The drawings were inspired by page sixteen of *Destination Moon,* which was one of the adventures of the Belgian cartoon hero Tintin. They also related to my dad's passion for antique cars. The hundreds of advertisements I had seen from the 1930 and 1940s where models in haute couture gowns posed with cars also did much to connect the automobile with glamour. This association was an important leitmotif for me. Many of my earliest artworks are drawings and collages of Schiaparelli clothes with vintage cars.

Calvin and I had a fantastic relationship. He was drop-dead handsome, with a vast knowledge of art and design, and gifted in both areas. We became friends and were inseparable for quite some time. We were clearly attracted to each other, so I decided to move to his building on Park Avenue where we'd see each other in the elevator nearly every day. He was sophisticated and we seemed to have endless common references in the field of the arts. Calvin and I went into rapturous ecstasy over pitched roofs, suburban barbeques, Formica kitchens, and the ultimate chic of Paul McCobb. He also knew who Balenciaga and Schiaparelli were, which made me feel less of an outcast.

Even though Christopher was still my boyfriend, I spent more time with Calvin. It was the closest I had ever come to being in love. He was also in love with me, but we sublimated this thing that we felt. Instead of just having sex with Cal, as I once would have done, I focused on our mutual artistic interests and common creative ideas. We had a truly cerebral relationship, with amazing discussions and exchanges of ideas. Gay men can do this despite popular beliefs. Even in the 1970s this was possible. Imagine that! We went to many exciting venues, like the budding drag ballroom scene where extraordinary queens were part of Houses (named for Parisian haute couture houses). We also went to another new phenomenon, the Mudd Club. It was named after the physician Samuel Alexander Mudd, who became a pariah by honoring his Hippocratic oath and treating the wounds of John Wilkes Booth, Lincoln's gay assassin (at least according to Larry Kramer, gay activist and writer). Anya Phillips, a party girl and previous art director at Fiorucci founded it with visionaries Steve Mass and Diego Cortez. The Mudd Club opened in October 1978 and immediately was the ultimate place to be. Everyone in the New York underground scene and even "aboveground" scene had something to do with it.

The performance artists that they were, Klaus Nomi and Joey Arias developed a series of New Wave Vaudeville acts with Tristan Tzara and Bauhaus graphics and Marlene Dietrich innuendos. Klaus had a definite charisma, and he fancied himself the Maria Callas of another galaxy, which, in a way, he absolutely was. He spent most of his life struggling to make ends meet by selling delicious pastries on the side, even though he arrived at his venues in limousines. This odd German man with a cubistic hairstyle and deadly white powdered skin was able to evoke high camp and classic opera in an entirely contemporary and briskly new manner. I think this was the reason his work was admired by a broad range of people, from fellow opera buffs to fashion people to sundry East Village *habitués*. He was a unique talent with an amazing knowledge of art history and opera music culture. Joey had the camp kind of humor that defined the era. He was prolific, a true chameleon, without a mean bone in his corseted body. He seemed always to be laughing a raucous, dirty laugh. He did a variety of musical and dramatic performances and seemed to be everywhere that was cutting edge. He'd often try on my Schiaparelli hats and strike great poses. I always thought I was witnessing living theater when he'd "play Schiaparelli" with me.

I had the good fortune to introduce Klaus and his act at the Mudd Club in New York a couple of times around 1979. I was dressed as the faun Pan, while Janus, the female band member, wore a Mermaid Gown I had designed. The dress was essentially a sheath of Schiaparelli's purple Frolic fabric that was a matte nylon satin, which I acquired at the defunct house of Schiaparelli. I shredded pieces of the same fabric to create a mermaid effect with a small train and I hand-beaded it with Swarovski crystals, seashells, gilded seahorses, seaweed, coral, and snails. The cape was a fishnet dyed a bright goldenrod yellow and covered with the same ornaments. The crowning glory was the necklace made from a huge, flat mother-of-pearl scallop shell, layered with dozens of other shells, beads, and spirals of gilded wire with garnets on the ends. Bill Cunningham photographed it for the *New York Times* and it was shown in *Women's Wear Daily*. With Janus's signature alien look and her pastiche hair made from colored electrical wire, the effect was, for myself and I think others, delightful and startling.

CHAPTER 5

SUPERSTARS

There was never a dull moment living in the East Village. I had to truck my tired tail back up to Park Avenue when I needed to sleep or just get away from all the drama downtown, and drama there was. I lived at 4 St. Mark's Place, right above Trash and Vaudeville, with my boyfriend Christopher and my roommate Peter Groby. Peter was a handsome Ivy League boy who wanted, like a lot of art school or trust fund kids, to be part of the scene (I guess you can say I was a teensy bit in this category, too). Jackie Curtis, an ex-Warhol superstar and local *ambigüe*, was dating Peter and madly in love with him. Jackie would pop by, impromptu, and perform a three-hour hyper version of his mega-drama plays *Glamour, Glory, and Gold* or *Vain Victory: Vicissitudes of the Damned*, whose titles changed with the mood and sexual incarnation of the playwright. He once asked me to make him a space helmet that fit his hairdo. I crafted one from materials that I purchased at Canal Street Plastics, a mythic place and, sadly, now gone. As Andy Warhol said, "Everything's plastic, but I love plastic. I want to be plastic."[1] And in knowing this, plastic defined all the things I liked, such as Schiaparelli's flagrant use of plastic to make fashion accessories and even clothes. Diana Vreeland told me a story of how, one of those gowns made of Colcombet's early synthetics that used some primitive form of plastic dissolved completely at the dry-cleaners, to the point it was unrecognizable. She asked to see it and saw, literally, the entire dress had melted into a puddle of gook! The 1930s Jean Clément-designed belts that I have found with huge, wildly eccentric, and crudely rendered plastic hooks, are exquisite in their barbaric-ness and are placed in unlikely places on clothes. My early finds of these pieces had me spiraling about in delight and to this day just looking at them makes me feel great. I love the texture, the colors, and the almost Art Brut aspect to them.

Naturally I loved using plastic in my work and I also associated it with the plastics from the 1920s and 1930s. At the 1975 Art Deco Exposition at Radio City Music Hall, I saw jewelry made from Bakelite and diamonds for sale. My aunts had worn similar pieces and those items had always fascinated me. I was surprised that it was so easy to buy them now at these specialized fairs and I longed to have as many as I could afford. Sadly, this was just a few. I placated myself by doing my own interpretions of such jewels and ordered all the components for my own creations from Canal Plastics and formed a wonderful friendship with the man in charge there. He helped me cut, miter, and assemble my plastic, and generally aided me with all technical aspects of my creations. I made space helmets inspired by Jackie's request, nuclear Judy Jetson-ish Lucite cuffs, Jupiter orbit belts, and a massive Lucite collar. I combined all of these pieces together for what I called my "Conquering the American Home after the Blast" outfit. I used them in a performance that received some very positive acclaim internationally. It was performed at a club called Hurrah's on West 86th street for the opening party of *Fetish: The Magazine of the Material World* that Terence Main co-published with two of his Cranbrook classmates. I even made the same bracelets for my friend

Jobriath, a singer who lived in the penthouse of the Chelsea Hotel. He had a marvelous outer space look and for a moment it seemed he was going to be the next David Bowie. Jobriath had wanted my entire cartoonish ensemble, but the Costume Institute at the Metropolitan Museum of Art had acquired it in 1980 along with a few other Surreal Couture pieces I produced.

I spent a great deal of time with Jackie, fiddling about with bits and bobs of plastic, making jewelry that I thought was very Buck Rogers and was inspired by 1920s modernism. I designed huge necklaces, à la Schiap after I discovered (and subsequently purchased) Hoyningen-Huene photos of European socialites wearing her clothes with African-inspired large-scale necklaces. Adorned in those out-of-scale earrings and bracelets, we would go out on the town to test how the jewels "worked." Sometimes we'd doll ourselves up as a svelte 1940s couple and visit the Carlyle. I was infatuated with the murals by Schiaparelli's preferred illustrator, Marcel Vertès, in the highly camp venue of Café Carlyle. I also adored the ones in Bemelmans Bar by Ludwig Bemelmans, the illustrator of the classic *Madeline* children's book series. Sitting at a table under these whimsical drawings, I would read Jackie passages from Warner Fabian's 1923 cult book *Flaming Youth*, melodramatically reciting the sexual adventures of its heroine, Patricia, a flapper who tried everything and ended up disillusioned. I did my best impersonations of the character as I sipped my Sidecar or Fallen Angel cocktail, but Jackie would snatch the book away and continue reading with more dramatic flair and earnest intensity than I could muster. So I'd just sit back and sip a drink, studying his animated face, caked in face powder. Caught up in the character of Patricia, Jackie would become loud and we'd sometimes be asked to leave or at least simmer down.

Jackie was a very tiring person, but I knew somehow I was in the presence of a real twentieth-century talent. He was no Sarah Bernhardt, but he was a genius of sorts. Even though he was older than me, I felt like an older brother to Jackie, as if our little moments were a good thing for him instead of the more reckless adventures he had with others.

I remember fondly many very amusing and slightly incoherent afternoons at the Chelsea Hotel and on St. Mark's Place, doing our usual routine of trying on Schiaparelli hats in a most "blonde-on-a-bum-trip" way. We were very close at that time. We'd drink cocktails in fancy Desny sterling silver Art Deco glasses from my collection and giggle about the old Hollywood we never knew. Sometimes Jackie was very demure and really played the role of a high society matron of the 1940s, and quite well. He had great affectations and with his high camp remarks went straight into outer space with the incarnation of the day. "Sugar, doesn't this look fabulous on me? Although I do look like those ladies at B. Altman's . . ." he'd say. A few times we actually did go to Charleston Gardens at 34th Street, the flagship store of B. Altman's, to the restaurant where, even in the 1970s, little old ladies lunched wearing bibbity-bobity hats. We dined in my Schiaparelli hats, nibbling on cold salads, the daintiest tea sandwiches, and strawberry shortcake. The place itself was wonderfully camp as you took your lunch in front of a life-sized facade of the Tara mansion from *Gone With the Wind*. We also had hilarious dinners at the Oak Room at the Plaza where we pretended to be old society matrons, ridiculous patrons of the arts and we maintained our characters thoughout the entire dinner. It was like some crazy, gay, Schiaparelli-soaked version of Method Acting.

We'd pass days and days at places like Bonwit Teller, Saks Fifth Avenue, Henri Bendel, and Bloomingdale's. Sometimes we spent an entire day in one of those stores, looking at everything: the clothes, the perfumes, the make-up, the jewelry. It was a heady experience and to this day when I smell certain perfumes I recall Jackie and his overly made up face asking me, as he held up a dress to his Raggedy Ann silhouette, "What do you think of this?" He really could be a great lady when he wanted, but he was also the most hysterical, neurotic woman I knew. Once in a while I'd lend him a beaded Mainbocher sweater or a Schiap hat for his underground "one-woman" shows in such Lower East Side theaters as La Mama and others, now mostly all gone. I collected a wig of Jackie's from Joe Franklin, TV host extraordinaire who had Jackie and other Warhol Superstars on his show more than once. My friend Craig B. Highberger did a marvelous documentary and wrote the definitive book about Jackie, both called *Superstar in a Housedress: The Life and Legend of Jackie Curtis*.

I have known Holly Woodlawn since I was a kid, when I visited Andy Warhol's Factory with one of my young, groovy aunts. Holly was a totally freaky, alcoholic transvestite who could pass as a real woman thanks to her androgynous features. She understood camp and Hollywood glamour. Lou Reed immortalized her in his song "Walk on the Wild Side," too: "Holly came from Miami, Fla. / hitch-hiked her way across the USA / plucked her eyebrows on the way / shaved her legs and then he was a she," but she is best known for three films: *Women In Revolt* and *Trash*, both directed by Paul Morrissey and produced by Andy Warhol and *Broken Goddess*, a Peter Dallas film. The latter is a truly gorgeous film despite the fact that Holly was completely drunk during the filming. The director must have been quite the genius, since it really doesn't show that much in the end. Holly was unique in all ways and I adored her then, despite the fact that she was highly unpredictable, slovenly, sometimes violent, and a drunk. I always felt Holly was a victim not of Warhol or Morrissey, as she'd like to have you believe, but of her crazy times coupled with an incredible lack of restraint and a non-existent academic education. She appreciated the basics of life and if you give her a nice bed, a good meal, and some Chardonnay, she would be perfectly happy. I lost contact with her for a number of years until 1989, when Greg Gorman photographed her for an article I did for *Harper's Bazaar* Italia called "BillyBoy* Goes to Hollywood." When I saw her again she was just as before, alternating between charming camp and mean-spirited bitterness.

Holly came to Switzerland for the L.U.F.F. film festival in 2007 and she lived at our house for a couple of weeks. It was pure madness. First, the bottles of Dom Pérignon champagne started to mysteriously disappear only to be found later, *sans* champagne, under her bed. We gave a huge party at the Château de Rosey with the theme of Schiaparelli and Warhol's *Ciao! Manhattan*. Dom Pérignon sponsored it and everyone was dressed up to the nines. The party was held at the bottom of an immense indoor swimming pool covered with gold Murano tiles and lit by candelabras.

On that same trip, we did a photo shoot of Holly wearing Schiaparelli clothes at the Hotel Le Palace in Lausanne, a five-star hotel that reeked of Hollywood glamour and oldy-worldy European charm before the decor was made over to be modern. She wore a reproduction Skeleton gown I'd made. Holly was a snarling heap of nerves during the shoot, but the resultant images are truly stunning. She looks like the iconic Warhol Superstar she is. When Holly left, she lovingly gave me her half-empty bottle of Chanel No. 5, her dark red lipstick, and her sequin gown by our mutual friend the late Giorgio Sant'Angelo for my collection. We kept her bedsheets, cigarette butts, empty Dom Pérignon champagne bottles from under her bed, and lipstick-stained pillowcases in a Lucite tube as an ex-voto reliquaire artwork we called *Trash*. When she passed away on December 6, 2015, my husband, Lala, and son, Alec Jiri, and I genuinely went into introspective silent grieving, as she touched us to tenderly when she lived with us just a few years ago. Recently a friend pointed out her Wikipedia page has a photo of her wearing my jewelry as she had heaps of it over the years. That actually made me break down and cry. And worn out, battered high heel pumps and sticky old wigs all over the world sighed and shed a crystalline tear in sorrow for the passing of one of the last rainbowed *précieuses ridicules* Warhol Superstars.

Ondine was another Warhol Superstar I knew in the late 1970s. He was extremely clever, knowledgeable about theater and art, but abnormally cruel and very mean. He once said to me, "I've *had* your boyfriend," referring to Christopher. Ondine was almost a cliché of the 1960s underground personage. He was loud, lavish with metaphors, and camp. He used to yell at me from across a room, "Come here, you little vixen!" or ask, "When are you going to pull out those Schiaps (pronounced She-apps) and go full drag?" Vixen? Me? Preposterous! It irritated me to no end. He did like it, though, when I dressed in full 1930s style with my Schiap jackets and Dietrich-inspired look. Taylor Mead also loved my Schiaparelli obsession. He remarked about my hats, "And who are you today, BillyBoy*? Lady Astor? Buck Rodgers? Millicent Rodgers?" His apartment was unlike anything I'd ever seen. It was literally a pile of rubbish halfway up the walls, utterly filthy and in a permanent state of chaotic disarray almost identical to Francis Bacon's London studio that I'd been in. They were like identical bookends made of a miasma of vermin-infested garbage, a bit like the talking trash heap Marjory on the puppet tv show *Fraggle Rock*. Despite his Oscar-the-Grouch living space, Taylor was one of the more amazing Warhol Superstars, like Jackie, for whom every single minute was a creation.

CHAPTER 6

ALL STYLES BIG AND SMALL

S tyle can be very quirky and is unique to each individual. It has nothing to do with fashion or designer clothes. Even as a teenager, I firmly believed that it was completely nuts to stick to a particular look just because someone in a magazine said you should. I collect historic haute couture and contemporary avant-garde fashion because they prove to me that there are many ways to understand life through different styles. To me, objects that support that idea seem well worth preserving and maintaining. At the same time, clothes are for covering the naked body, and something amusing to be played with. You dress up, you have a nice time, you take them off, you forget about them. I also collect them to remind myself of this. I keep physical evidence of the absurdity of fashion. People should devote the time to analyze fashion, but it's futile to take it too seriously. On a symbolic and even metaphysical level, things that are in contact with human beings vibrate people's stories and retain the essence of human life on earth during a concise and specific linear time period. Clothes have a way of speaking to me that I am unable to put words to. They resonate stories almost as if I were watching the individual person's life on a screen. I have a profound psychic link to things and when I touch them an entire picture is shown to me in my mind that tells me all about the individual it had been in close contact with. At times the picture can be frightening but usually it is very engaging. The experience is like watching a whole film in my head about the previous owner. To this day, I find it rather difficult to express what really happens because I do not possess the words to tell the depth and force of these experiences. All I can really say is that humanity, like art, is not black or white. It is an extremely deep and vast palette of infinite subtle nuances of feelings, thoughts, and senses, and when I touch a garment, I get all of this and in a strange way it's very moving. People are so diverse and so individual that they range from the truly evil to the truly saintly and everything in between (which is the case most often). In a word, I think I am seeing their souls. Though I feel detached from these feelings and dare I say, from the souls revealed, I have a very great sense of empathy for these people. Sometimes they seem so lost and often rather sad. And if not sad, reckless. I can know all about the person, sometimes in minute details. The more attached to the object an individual was or the more they loved it—and in the case of collecting clothes as much as the garment was worn—the more powerful the communication of that person is to me. Unfortunately as much as I have tried to explain this phenomenon, it's simply something I am unable to truly express completely. This book is an attempt at doing so.

When I was young, life seemed like a wonderful bag of contradictions, absurdities, and peculiar associations. I wanted to be accepted, but I also longed to wear clothing that reflected my moods and fantasies. I created a wonderful shell to protect myself, inspired by Schiaparelli. Her clothes were like armor for me. I could become another character, safe from judgments about my choices. At my Montessori school, my peers acted as if I was from outer space. However, when I wore the same clothes to an art opening or a party with older people I received positive attention. At these events I met people who also dressed in unusual ways and made a few like-minded friends. The success of these initial experiments encouraged me to continue to explore the ways that I could use clothing to express myself.

I dressed to suit my varied moods and a wide range of designers on both sides of the Atlantic (and even Japan and South America) helped me fulfill some of my most extreme expressions. Ironically, the clothes were never that important to me and once they were no longer on my radar, they were assigned an eternal resting place in my collection, sometimes never to be seen again. They merely allowed me to communicate fleeting sentiments. Frankly, I find almost all of the so-called fashionable designer clothes I wore then somewhat ugly when you compare them to those of other eras. As Oscar Wilde famously wrote, "Fashion is a form of ugliness so intolerable that we have to alter it every six months."[1] I could not agree more. Yes, they were stylish and glamorous in a moment in time, but the only clothes I find truly chic and elegant, that can be worn every decade since their invention, are those from 1920s and 1930s.

At that time I appeared mostly as an ambiguous, androgynous creature. I genuinely did not identify with either sex and truly felt I was something else I could not (and still cannot) completely express. I felt then (as I still do now) as if I am not quite in the right body. I feel as if I am from somewhere else, disguised as a human. Laugh as one might at such a preposterous confession, I genuinely felt like an observer wearing a skin which I was just borrowing temporarily on earth. I could easily look like a young girl if I wanted to, and sometimes did, though it had less to do with clothes and more to do with behavior. I remember going to a cricket match in Brighton with the British poet David Robilliard in the early 1980s, dressed so androgynously that he pretended I was his girlfriend. I fluctuated back and forth in my sexual and physical identity. This was instinctive rather than having anything to do with style, art or artiness. Clothes and accessories, especially vintage ones gave me an additional field for expression and let my mind feel the true joy of creation. Bear in mind though, this was the era of gender rebellion and the credo of "Do you really want to hurt me?" sung by Boy George when he was in the band Culture Club. Androgyny was increasingly seen as acceptable. Elements of it appeared not only in music but in fashion and art. I may have only been a reflection of my generation's zeitgeist at times, but I do know that during those years my "eccentric," alien-life form looks, as others called them, were appreciated. Somehow, I felt like my androgyny offered me a way to understand human feelings of all sorts. Clothes were my entry into exploring empathy. I owe this understanding of human nature directly to Schiaparelli of course.

I was regularly wearing vintage couture from my collection, very selected pieces that were not immediately identifiable as female attire—suit jackets from Dior, Chanel, and Schiaparelli suits from the 1940s to the 1960s. I chose them for their squared shoulders and small waists, which evoked the David Bowie/Marlene Dietrich silhouette I wanted. I'd combine them with leather boxing boots and silk, acrylic, Lycra and even mylar dance tights (by Larry Legaspi, whom I adored) in stupidly wonderful colors. I scrunched the sleeves up and tied my hair in a black gauze turban. I'd wear the whitest Christian Dior powder and reek of Shocking de Schiaparelli. I'd put a few brooches here, a few beads there, and among the Schiap jewels and the real jewels by Cartier and some of Maripol's now-iconic black rubber "Madonna" bracelets it made for quite a peculiar and at times maybe even provocative look. When I wasn't dressed up in bespoke clothes, making me look much older and wiser than I was, I often wore very revealing clothes that showed off my body. More than once this got me into some naughty trouble, but it was delightful for a brief while. I wore the more period-piece menswear (mixed with women's clothes) and the more body-hiding garb (which could almost make me look prudish compared to my nearly naked ensembles) for everything: grocery shopping in the East Village, an art opening in London, a *grand bal* in Paris. I was a rather conspicuous curiosity. At a very early age I had the great pleasure to meet and become friends with Alexandre de Paris, who is probably one of the most famous hairdressers in the world. Since then, Alexandre has styled, cut, and colored my hair. On rare occasions Vidal Sassoon in London did it, but for the most part it was the charming Alexandre. Though it is common as dirt now to dye hair bright colors and have extreme cuts, in the early 1970s, it was considered outrageous. He also made me elaborate and fun wigs and gave me many now iconic ones, notably those of Courrèges. He made me all the shades of silver and gold, blonde, and white (when I was seeing Rainer Werner Fassbinder and during my Veronika Voss period in the early 1980s). He invented styles for me that included ephebe Greco-Roman, pompous Louis XIV complete with jeweled hair combs, a fairy, a pixie, a sinister Dracula-like creature, my "Get Groovy" 1960s Mod, a 1930s starlet, a punk rocker, and even 1950s Rockabilly. He made my hair cherry red, citrus orange, bubblegum pink, baby and sky blue, and even the BillyBoy* Blue that Andy Warhol invented for his painting of me as a Barbie doll. He'd use flowers, vegetables, candy, and all sorts of antique lace and hair ornaments on me. For galas he would put my eighteenth-century diamond pins beautifully in my curls. Through his artistry, he allowed me to walk a very fine line between masculine and feminine. Incredible as it may sound now, I was the embodiment of androgyny and this was before it could be seen on every YouTube user under twenty-five. Paradoxically, even though I loved women's clothing and the feminine aspects of myself, I did not want or have even the slightest desire to be a drag queen. Though I had many drag friends I did not understand from where it came, this desire to dress entirely as a women. Transgender I believe

I understood. I had had a few very exciting and very meaningful relationships with transgender people, both male-to-female and female-to-male, however outright drag was something I respected but did not fully relate to. That was just not in me. I was merely naturally and instinctively performing and channeling the alternate universe character of a society woman of the 1930s, dressed by Schiaparelli. Simple as that. Later in my life, once haute couture collecting was established, people would ask me how I could desecrate valuable iconic pieces by wearing them. I really couldn't have cared less about such nonsense at the time because I did not associate monetary value to the clothes I'd collected. I loved them and took care of them. I was vividly aware of their historic importance and my responsibility to be their guardian for a spell but I also liked to wear them. They *are* clothes, after all.

There were a couple of men in particular who taught me how to break gender roles. One of them was the delightful Quentin Crisp. He was an English eccentric and a very determined Gay Rights activist, a "stately homo" as he referred to himself in his book *The Naked Civil Servant*. He would tell me about being on the furthest fringes of the grand high society world of his contemporaries such as Stephan Tennant and Cecil Beaton. He shared my affection for Schiaparelli and recounted owning a sad little tube of her lipstick and in the 1950s spraying himself head-to-toe in her perfume at some department store counter. Quentin admired my nerve to wear Schiap hats and would occasionally try them on himself, preening in front of an old Art Deco-style mirror. Memorably, he told me once that their elegance transcended the fact that they were designed for members of the opposite sex.

The other influential man in my gender education was Romain de Tirtoff, better know by his pseudonym, Erté. He was one of my heroes as a young man and I never imagined that we'd become good friends. Erté's career started around 1912, when he moved to Paris.

He briefly worked with Paul Poiret, the king of Paris couture at that time (and another of my obsessions). He then spent the next decade or so at *Harper's Bazaar*, illustrating fantastic covers of ladies dripping in pearls and furs, looking as if it took a great deal of strength to hold up their arms laden with pearl ropes and glittery swags of lamé. He designed for the Folies Bergères and the L'Opéra de Paris, the Ziegfeld Follies, Irving Berlin's *Music Box Revue* in America, and created a number of iconic sets and costumes for MGM Studios. He touched on all that was fashion: gowns, suits, dresses, shoes, jewelry, and interior design. His own place in Paris had what looked like a genuine Baroque grotto on the ceiling, with gilded shells on every inch of surface, aligned in a geometric order exactly like one of his drawings. I learned so much from him. I posed for some of his photos on the beach in Palma de Majorca as one of his alphabet letters. He was a noble queen in the grand French manner and I adored the fact that he was effeminate without the slightest of inhibitions, much like Quentin.

Sometime around 1975, I was introduced to Horst P. Horst, the German-born fashion photographer who created some of the most memorable images of the mid-twentieth-century. He was adorable. He had an eye for detail that was remarkable. When I was a teen, Horst did a series of nude photos of me in my Art Deco-filled Park Avenue apartment. They are typical of his sensibilities and conjure the 1930s. I still have the copies of the negatives that he gave to me. Before he died in 1999, he told me quite a few stories about Schiaparelli, and his long-term boyfriend, Valentine Lawford, gave me a formal introduction into gossip over regular lunch dates. He would tell me stories about all the people I'd met related to Schiaparelli. He was never mean and it seemed like everything he told me was the flat out truth. Most importantly, he gave me his slant on style. They taught me what was and what was not "chic," a word I think I heard the most from them.

CHAPTER 7

ART DECO—CHROME— MY INNER ANTI- BOURGEOISE WOMAN

I vividly recall the pleasure of attending the Art Deco exposition in Manhattan in 1975, at the glorious Donald Deskey-designed Radio City Music Hall. It was a full-blown Schiaparelli explosion for me. My obsession was in full bloom by this point and I made quite a few new friends thanks to it. I eagerly babbled on about my Schiaparelli fantasies to anyone who'd listen. And people did listen. At this scintillating show held in the foyer of that stunning Art Deco palace, I bought a multitude of chrome objects: a pair of ice buckets with stylized penguins all over them, skyscraper-like cocktail shakers by Norman Bel Geddes, sets of spun aluminum tableware by Russell Wright, prancing Frankart statuettes in that peculiar shade of faux bronze patina green, and anything that evoked Borzois and Josephine Baker. It was here that my plastic fetishism was indulged, and I bought as much Bakelite and Galalithe as I could carry. I understood that I was very close to becoming a glutton for beauty. I had to reel it in at times, reminding myself that Poiret died a pauper and that I was extremely lucky as it was, that I shouldn't push the limits too far. But honestly, everything, every surface, every texture, every color, struck me as exquisite. It was orgasmic just to see so much beauty in one place.

My personality was entirely based on a fictitious, capricious 1930s Schiaparelli woman modeled after Bettina Bergery, a friend of Schiap's whom I had known since childhood who became a very close and dear friend of mine. She is amongst the most important women in my life. Thanks to her endless stories about life in Paris in the 1930s and how seductive it all was, I decided my inner anti-bourgeoise would devour and seduce men, notably bourgeoise men with artistic pretentions and naked sexuality. Anti-bourgeoise is a term that I thought up as a teen to describe the type of person I wanted to become. I saw it as being slightly wanton like Anaïs Nin or the Marchesa Luisa Casati, and completely unlike those boring conventional women who loathed sexually deviance.

It was around this time that I created a piece of art that I thought was quite clever. I still get a great kick out of it as I usually have it (and others which followed) in my bedroom. Hung on a wall always just in front of me, it's there to allow me to contemplate its textural beauty and to remind myself of so many things in life which interest or fascinate me. Each element had a story, written down in my diaries. It's quite a simple idea. I took all of my newly acquired Bakelite bracelets, strung them together, and wore them as a necklace. That was its first incarnation. I considered it a work in progress and added a bangle or two periodically. In fact, I added to it rather regularly so it grew and grew over the decades. This first one is no longer wearable at this point and has become pure sculpture. It is over five meters long. I called it *Self-Portrait*. I had to start others as time went on and it's a great pleasure to anticipate adding to the most recently started one.

When I started to feel that strange tingly feeling of conscious sexual attraction, my artwork started to make more and more sense to me, especially on a symbolic level. Until then I think I applied many of these sexual themes to myself, using sex as artwork and not entirely for my own pleasure. The drawings and samples for my earliest wearable art clothes were of pants for men with attached penises on the zippered fly front or built-in bulges, or cut away fronts so the real penises could be shown, based on chaps my father's cowboy friends wore. I did dresses with areas cut out for breasts to be exposed and vagina-shaped hats. I instilled erotica into all sorts of details. I made penis buttons out of wood and painted them with oil paint, and I took delight in pornographic collages, inspired by Bill Burroughs, Allen Ginsberg, and Jacques Prévert, among others, to be made into fabrics.

The German play *Pandora's Box* (1904) and the 1929 film of the same name, starring Louise Brooks, had a profound effect on me. I thought I was in love with her. I felt something no real person had ever made me feel. It was intoxicating, and gave me a feeling of great freedom to admire and emulate her. For quite a long time I became Brooks's libertine Lulu in my attitude towards sex at that very crucial point in my early adolescence. I adopted a white 1920s hair style, powdered make up from Shu Uemura, and started smoking shocking pink Balkan Sobranie cigarettes tipped with gold, using a coral, diamond, and jet Cartier cigarette holder from the 1920s that Erté had given me. I loved the sense of aesthetic liberty it gave me. I started to shed the very last remnants of my cloak of innocence and childishness. I became Art Deco.

My attraction to chrome-plated objects, which are so integral to Art Deco, could be perhaps linked to the notion of reflection. Looking in a shiny object held the same appeal as imagining myself in those old movies, but I did not have the same feelings as Narcissus. I thought I was simply an awkward and gawky person. I was terribly skinny, long-waisted and plain. So, I learned how to use what heaven gave me and make it as nice looking as possible—same for my personality. I studied my flaws and tried to round them out as best as I could. I knew I was not handsome or really special, but I thought of myself as a male version of Schiap's *jolie-laide* and I made the most of my admittedly strange looks.

My role models, besides Schiap, were the stars of black and white films. *Broadway Melody of 1936* with Eleanor Powell in silver sequined tails and top hat was the height of aesthetic aspiration for me. Or the scene from *Sensations of 1945*, where she dances in a gigantic pinball machine to fabulous jazz by Woody Herman and his Orchestra—I was that pinball! *Blonde Venus*, where Marlene Dietrich emerges from a gorilla suit and sings "Hot Voodoo," a style that was later parodied by Madeline Kahn in *At Long Last Love*, Peter Bogdanovich's homage to 1930s musicals, made me understand that's what life should be about. However, when I met and befriended Marlene Dietrich later in my life, the reality of the Blonde Venus was a stark contrast to my childish dreams. My relationship with her sparked a serious session of self-reflection regarding my idolization and romanticizing of the arts and artists. The origins of the word glamour concern enchantment and magic, spellbinding someone with an illusion. Surely this is what had happened to me when she emerged from a gorilla suit into spangles. The magic only ended when I met the sad, unkempt, and lonely woman she was in her later years. Keeping a dream alive, or aspiring to a dream, became a major element in my work as an artist and in the artworks I collected.

Mesmerized by the sets, the scenes, and the language of movies from the past, I spent hours imagining my dolls in movie situations. Once I had the idea of photographing my dolls in the Chrysler Building, a monolith of fabulousness that I adored. In the early 1970s, I had discovered the Cloud Club on the building's sixty-sixth floor. It was a strange place. The waiters wore Chrysler Building-inspired uniforms in a bizarre mix of Hollywood-style kitsch rooms mixed with the glamorous William van Alen steel and glass. By the time I was seventeen, I was going there on my own, getting plastered on cocktails, and feeling very Art Deco despite the plank floors, the Tudor-style lounge, and the Magritte-esque paintings of clouds and stars. More often than not I struck up a conversation with someone and would end up in bed with him a few hours later, my doll and camera in my big bag. My doll photos usually ended up looking blurry, but through trial and error I eventually learned how to take better pictures. Sadly, the place became a bit seedy and rundown, and eventually closed sometime in 1979. Good-bye, Cloud Club and *adieu*, innocence.

CHAPTER 8

MONEY AND SOUL CONTRACTS

M oney and soul contracts are always linked. One of my soul contracts surely gave me the knack to cope with this potentially evil thing, money, and to render it beautiful and useful. Even though I do not hold wealth in high esteem, I've always been able to earn money when necessary. Money is just a tool that allows me to be myself and to do what I do: make art and collect.

Almost immediately after leaving home, I started to sell my drawings and paintings to all sorts of people I'd meet. Sometimes I could earn a few hundred dollars for a single piece, which was quite a sum at that time. By 1976, I had sold my Surrealistic clothing designs to some of the most fashionable and famous stores in New York, such as Henri Bendel, Bonwit Teller, and Bloomingdale's. I tried to maintain a balance between working and selling my art, and buying and occasionally selling objects. In the course of pursuing my obsession with Schiaparelli, I was able to obtain other amazing objects, some rather valuable. When I ran out of cash or wanted to purchase an expensive item, I could be resourceful.

I never parted with things from my "personal" collection, but I enjoyed finding things that were relatively important but that I did not want to keep. Back then one could find incredible things for nothing, things that now are completely unaffordable. For example, I once found a diamond bracelet comprised of flawless whites in a bag of costume jewelry at a flea market in Connecticut. When I was in New York, I sold it to the jeweler known as Fred Leighton (his real name is Murray Mondschien), whom I became friendly with and saw in both New York and Paris. Another time I found a series of Hans Arp silkscreens in a portfolio for ten dollars in a bookshop on the Lower East Side. I traded these for a pair of adorable Cartier brooches shaped like ladybugs, which were later traded for something else. The Costume Institute purchased an early Chanel black satin coat that I bought from the surviving sister of a pair of twins who had two of everything. I kept one of each and sold the second examples, notably to museums. I also sold things through auction houses such as Christie's, Phillips, and Bonhams, not so much for the money, but for the thrill of it all. It brought me great pleasure to identify paintings, sculptures, objects, books, and bibelots. I liked everything, so it was always a struggle to decide what I wanted to keep. In retrospect, I think I hoarded objects instead of cultivating intimate relationships with people my own age because I thought objects were more reliable than people. Beautiful material objects would not ever disappoint you whereas people, even beautiful ones, could.

My habit of wanting to research, collect, and have discussions with like-minded people has brought me into contact with a variety of interesting individuals and places. The older dealers I knew had a great sense of all things historic, and their mission often was all about historical accuracy. Though their goal was to sell these objects and artifacts, they took great pride in uncovering their backgrounds, too. It took a huge amount of work to discover the dates, the names, and the histories of objects in order to place them in the firmament of culture and art. When a piece was sold to a museum or a major collector it was akin to receiving a medal of honor. It's essential to bear in mind that at that time many people did not collect art (or haute couture) as an investment—that was decades away. In fact, collecting fashion had not yet come into full existence and was far from being really established, aside from a handful of people—including myself—who were passionate about textiles, fashion, and related subjects. Most of the people in these new territories collected for the thrill of being able to hold these beautiful things in their hands or see them up close and to boast about the new knowledge they acquired in regard to them. The "wow" factor amongst collectors was the big high, the Nirvana promised and delivered by these esoteric things. It felt like it was almost a symbiotic relationship between the collector and the object of desire. As a teen, I looked at this manner of seeing art and collecting as a true expression of joie de vivre, something I admired and aspired to. This way of thinking made sense to me and these specialists' attention to my little person made me feel appreciated and admired back. At times I even felt a strange form of love, which, as I pointed out previously, was particularly important to me. The fact that I was a mere teen selling rare objects to established dealers and museums directly or through serious auction houses gave me confidence in my taste. Clearly, this was what I needed at that time.

On one of my visits to the Brooklyn thrift shops, I chanced to meet the vintage clothing dealer and fellow lone wolf collector Beverley Birks, who became a life-long friend. Bev, born a Canadian but a true Manhattanite, was a former Dr. Pepper poster girl and a really brilliant young woman. She was one of the first people I knew in New York who collected fashion with a special interest in the prewar era. She claims that I was the one who made her see the light about post-war fashion, as I was equally as passionate for both. I soon realized that Bev was one of the chicest people in that newly emerging field. She was one of the very first people to buy and wear my Surreal Couture jewelry, which was quite daring and eccentric of her. She has a huge barbaric necklace made of shell, brass wire, and amethysts that I'd made that she wore wonderfully.

We had so much fun trading clothes, swapping endless stories, "tales of old frocks" I used to say. Our friendship transcended collecting. Once in a while, we'd argue about trading. I felt, for example, that my Yves Saint Laurent trapeze dress was historically as important as a 1930s Schiaparelli suit, but to her dealer's mind they were not equivalent in monetary value. This aggravated me to no end. We often discussed the draping genius of Schiap and her technical innovations. We bonded over special pieces. For example, Bev owned a dazzling Schiaparelli Leaf Cape that I would have coveted if I were the jealous type. The cape was elbow-length and simply cut, with hundreds of expertly assembled organza leaves in shades of green that ran the gamut from pale to dark, each tacked in place with a small bead. It was captivating to see in real life and it was the inspiration for my own version, which is in the collection of the Union Française des Arts du Costume in the Louvre.

In Margaret Towner's book *The Vivien Greene Dolls' House Collection*, about the extraordinary collection of doll's houses assembled by my friend Vivien Greene, the author writes that the passionate collector makes a contribution that is not always appreciated for its value. Towner further observes that collectors start acquiring things that are not at all in demand, selecting items that stand out to them on their own. Within time the lack of previous scholarship on the subject yields a collective renaissance in the larger community. This seems to completely summarize my own experiences as a collector, especially the early times of my life as a teenager and young adult, prior to the Internet and Google, when obtaining information was a wildly different process. As Vivien Greene once said, there is a "strange way in which certain objects . . . gravitate towards anyone who will love them."

When I traveled between Paris, London, and New York during the mid-1970s and late 1980s, it seemed, to my naive eyes, that haute couture was just about everywhere. This changed by the early 1990s, when collecting fashion started to become an acknowledged field, but until then it was practically effortless to find great pieces all over the place. In the flea markets the sellers of *fripes* (inexpensive used clothing) and just about any woman you met seemed to have amazing clothes tucked away in the back of a closet or an attic, and they were usually happy to get rid of them. Unwanted designer dresses were once casually given to maids, family members of lesser means, or to schools for productions of amateur plays. My friend Bettina Graziani gave me an amazing Balenciaga haute couture gown and evening coat. The ensemble was to be included in her trousseau for her marriage to the Prince Aly Salman Aga Khan. Tragically, he died in car accident before they were wed, which forever changed the fate of Bettina. It also changed the fate of her wedding trousseau wardrobe. The gown is beautifully embroidered with minute stitches that create intricate arabesques of floral patterns intermingled with birds. The full-length Watteau-style coat is made of shocking pink taffeta and is an excellent example of Balenciaga's masterful tailoring. Bettina's sister had however not noticed the mastery of the garment and proceeded to patiently undo all the seams of the gown and coat in order to make, of all things, cushions from the silk linings. Thankfully, she never got around to it and it sat disassembled for about twenty-five years, neatly packed away in tissue paper in a box in a closet in her house in Normandy.

In New York, one had to simply make an effort to search for real treasures, as they were there for the taking if you knew where to look. In America, clothes were more likely to be donated to charity shops or simply thrown away. It is important to remember at the time that these garments, which may have had a glorious old past, were just out-of-fashion used clothes for most people. Absolutely no one was interested in them, and the ones who could have been—curators of a handful of museums—certainly would never imagine finding something in a thrift shop. Going to thrift shops was for freaks and oddballs like myself. More conservative folks would not deem it of any interest for themselves to even breach the front door of a thrift shop for any reason. As for myself, just like any hardworking miner from the Gold Rush, I instinctively knew that you sometimes have to get your hands dirty to find a gem.

In Manhattan for example, I spent whole days wandering from Upper West Side junk shops to Lower East Side thrift shops, searching for (and regularly finding) amazing vintage clothes. I could walk for miles if I smelled something in the air, following the telltale tingling feeling that comes from knowing that I am about to find something amazing. Inevitably, the discoveries that excited me most were the Schiaparellis. In a florist's window, of all places, I found a miraculous cache of Sleeping de Schiaparelli perfume bottles with the original shipping cartons. They were using the bottles for bud vases and hideous sand art. In my feverish enthusiasm I even tracked down unclaimed Schiaparelli garments in a dry-cleaning shop on Madison Avenue. The mid-1970s saw the very first telltale beginnings of what would become a boom in vintage clothing, with shops springing up in the funky neighborhoods of big cities in the U.S. and throughout Europe. The dealers were unusual, often with a great sense of style and panache, and all the shops I frequented those last few years of the 1970s were mostly a pure delight for my spirit.

Around the same time, Christie's in London started selling twentieth-century textiles, and I would buy literally every single piece of haute couture that came up for auction that interested me. The catalogues of that era were hilarious: very plain lists dotted with a lot of typos and dreadful black-and-white photos of drab assistants in sensible and scuffed flat shoes modeling the clothes. They had the most minimal descriptions: "Dress, black silk with embroidery: label 'Schiaparelli, 21 place Vendôme, Paris' estimate £40-£50." I was in heaven! It was so easy and so inexpensive that I found myself in a tricky position. In Paris, I kept maps which traced the line I'd walked from the moment I stepped out the door in the morning to my return at night. Each line was numbered in my diary and annotated with what shops I found and what I bought. I was gleefully amassing a collection of haute couture along with innumerable related documents at an alarming rate. What's a boy living in Manhattan to do? In fact what is a boy to do who lived in several cities at a time to do? It was a question of transportation—how to get the clothes from the famous old auction houses and into storage somewhere in one of the cities I lived in. I already had a trail of Schiaparelli garments in apartments scattered about New York City: apartments on Saint Mark's Place, Hell's Kitchen, and Park Avenue; a brownstone in Park Slope; a loft in Flushing Meadows, Queens. They were all crammed with stuff—gorgeous stuff, but stuff nonetheless. I'd plunged into this obsession with indescribable relish, all in the earnest desire to record and document each and every one of Schiaparelli's fashion collections.

CHAPTER 9

MISTER MODERN

invented the character of Mister Modern as a type of performance art during my teens. He was a post-modern dandy and artist who lived amongst 1950s artifacts. Similar to the Anti-Bourgeoise woman in origins, Mister Modern sprung forth from the depths of my sub-conscious, conceived during long waits at airports, bored evenings in luxurious hotels, and lonely walks in forests or parks where I'd find a nice spot and write for hours. Mister Modern was a product of fifteen years worth of television sitcoms, Tupperware, I.B.M., and highway billboards, slick and completely emotionless. Fascinating and androgynous, cruel and obsessive, he was a peculiar blend of refined yet irrational traits. I realized later that Mister Modern was a paragon of the qualities and flaws that I valued and despised most. He was as extreme as I was.

Mister Modern was a necessary and important part of my transition into adulthood. In his world, there were time travel, alternate universes, and gender switching. All of these elements are directly linked to my love of Virginia Woolf's *Orlando* and Aldous Huxley's

Brave New World, and the writings of Philip K. Dick and William S. Burroughs. Mister Modern was an outlet for explorations in hallucinogenic drugs, mind control, sex therapy, super powers, social decay, and elitism. He often recited film quotes from *Sunset Boulevard* and *Valley of the Dolls*. In my imagination, Mister Modern was a spokesman for Schiaparelli and atomic energy, the focus of my artistic pursuits at the time.

I started to write very amateurish stories for my avatar called *Tales of Mister Modern*. They read like comic books, novellas, TV scripts, and recipes. Each one began with the same line: "Nobody really remembers when he came about. Just one day he was there, right on our television screens, all sparkly and cellophane-like. Sharp as ice, crystalline, yet you felt as if he were one of the family." Every story mentioned Schiaparelli or related to her in some way. Mister Modern had a daily TV show sponsored by a futuristic monopoly I dreamed up called Seers and Röbot. In one episode he reveals Schiap Atomic, a small orb that will end all household drudgery. A rare lipstick by Schiaparelli with the same name inspired this moment. I found the tube in its original packaging and the teeny domed object opened like a miniature star observatory. It inspired me for years. A lipstick name did this! One tiny object, a detail of life, a lipstick, sent me into outer space with pleasure and sparked my imagination forever. Many of these original scripts and artifacts are in a museum of science fiction in Switzerland called La Maison d'Ailleurs.

I complemented these B-movie style scripts with highly affected photographs of my friends and I as characters in his futuristic domain. Mister Modern even hosted a World's Fair set in the far off future of 1987 whose theme was "Fashion through Understanding" in homage to the 1964 World's Fair's theme of "Peace through Understanding." I staged the "March of Modernity" pavilion in the windows of Fiorucci in New York City, using designer furniture and accessories from the 1950s, 1960s, and 1970s. The store had a field day with my imagery and we were able to summon forth those interested in the new images of hard stylishness and severe camp. I was able to supply clients with peculiar-looking Miro-esque painted boomerang desks, spiky Eames chairs, Russel Wright dishes, sputnik torch lamps, and plastic flowers galore. It caused quite a stir in the art and fashion world at the time, since that type of furniture had not been considered a legitimate design interest before then. These items are now considered classics and have immense value. In those days, it was immensely difficult to sell a rare 1940s Eames plywood chair for five hundred dollars; today, you'd have people killing each other to get one for such a low price.

Mister Modern was the subject of various storyboards, photographs, Super 8 short movies, video (which was brand new at the time), and happenings. Leonard Abrams, the founder of the *East Village Eye* newspaper, ran several Mister Modern photos and stories that I wrote, which was very exciting artistically. Sometimes he and I would have borderline stormy debates about the bourgeoning scene around us, especially its aesthetics. Leonard was purely downtown and I don't think he ever really understood me. The *SoHo Weekly News*, *Details*, and *The Manhattan Catalogue*, along with other trendy punk and new wave publications, also did several features on me, associating my artwork with Schiaparelli, and devoting articles to my Surreal Couture designs and Mister Modern character. Everyone aspired to be in these magazines back then since they were the highest form of avant-garde culture in the United States.

"The cloning of humans is on most of the lists of things to worry about from science, along with behavior control, genetic engineering, transplanted heads, computer poetry, and the unrestrained growth of plastic flowers."[1] I've often thought about this Lewis Thomas quote from *The Medusa and the Snail: More Notes of a Biology Watcher*. Transplanted heads? I've always assumed half the people I saw back then each day had transplanted heads. My "Science Fair of Art," held at St. Mark's Place in 1980, was my homage to behavior control clones, plastic flowers, Schiaparelli-ian chic, and irony for all things fake and puerile. I would turn on an old radio or television to play static noise because I thought it was a type of futurist music on "Mister Modern Magnavox TV." I called it "Cosmic Static" after Schiaparelli's "Cosmic Net," a 1930s synthetic tulle that had a strange texture and is another example of her use of modern technology in fabrics. Mister Modern was the ultimate mind-control television host and pre-dated Max Headroom by twelve years. His seductive smile, nuclear recipes for getting rid of stains, and traditional values conjured up a larger than life aura that swept a nation (or at least he did so in my imagination). The "Science Fair of Art" participants contributed artistic inventions like a time travel machine for pets and lima beans that sprouted Gertrude Stein clones (called "Les Beans"). We dissected frogs and featured space travelling Hermit crabs who were orchestrated by Scarlatina Lust and Alex Torrid Zone Igloo. These two artists were the founders of *Smegma the Magazine*, which was a genuine concept zine that featured art for art's sake. It was Dadaist in feeling, utilizing collage and a wonderful new thing, the color Xerox. Sometimes my friend Jean-Michel Basquiat or Keith Haring and I would do these color photocopies together; it was a ritual unto itself. While the *East Village Eye* was all about new wave and punk music and things actually happening in the East Village, *Smegma the Magazine* was a work of art in and of itself.

A series of performances I wrote, called *Conquering the American Home After the Blast*, were about post-war glamour in a dystopic world. As Mister Modern, I performed a piece entitled *A Synthetic Nuclear Blast*. I also performed a nude ballet called *La Mort de Cupidon* at Habille L'Art, an avant-garde gallery for wearable art in Montreal. The dance was set to Igor Stravinsky's "Après-midi d'un Faun" and was my interpretation of Marcel Vertès' illustrations for Schiaparelli and the pre-war paintings of androgynous women with armor and wings the Surrealist painter Leonor Fini painted. All of Schiap's ads by Marcel Vertès had fauns, cupids, angels, and pixies prancing about naked. Leonor's work also had naked fauns in erotic poses. I wanted it to be a homage to these perfume ads and Leonor, whom I'd been friends with since an early age.

I danced around the windows of the SoHo wearable-art gallery Victoria Falls as *Harlequin Hold Onto Your Hat* in another one of my mini-ballets. I adored Rena Gill, who owned the gallery, which sold vintage clothes. She was deeply into these clothes and I truly admired her. I think I even had a crush on her (she later married Stefan Brecht, who authored an iconic reference work called *Queer Theatre* at that time). I vividly recall trying to trade couture with her and she, being savvy, always made it a challenge to seal any deal. Fittingly, I showed my *Les Choses de BillyBoy** (in homage to *Les Choses de Paul Poiret*) there, where my boudoir doll from the 1920s—a Paris flea market find from my childhood—was displayed dressed in Poiret-inspired clothes that I had made as a kid.

Around 1979 I performed in two variations of something I called *Muʒak Madness* at Fiorucci where I related Schiaparelli clothes to the French music of the same era, such as Henri Sauget. I later staged *A Christmas Ball with BillyBoy** in the windows that starred all my friends, my assistant Beth, and the marvelous model Dovanna. Everyone swirled around a Schiaparelli-inspired ballroom dressed in vintage Schiaparelli gowns and ensembles from my Surreal Couture collections. It looked rather demented, totally baroque and very glamorous. We all literally danced our way into 1980, a year that changed the world forever with a new, mysterious plague. This hopeless disease was a theme regularly explored by Mister Modern. Huge social change and a new form of gay activism emerged from this crisis, but unfortunately I was oblivious for the first year or two as I was in Europe, living out my fantasies and blissful Schiaparelli obsession. I was still dancing.

CHAPTER 10

SURREAL COUTURE

must have thought up the term Surreal Couture around age twelve. I know for a fact I was pretty much the first person to start using this word again concerning fashion. For the most part, cognoscenti excluded, people my age hadn't a clue what I was talking about and older people said things such as, "You mean, like the melting clock?" In the 1970s, Surrealism was no longer a trendy subject and you never saw it anywhere, really. Maybe in isolated instances, but I was spreading it around like wildfire and often people were surprised by my use of the word. It made me feel very grown up to invent terms and phrases for the things I was doing, so the title Surreal Couture clearly linked my two loves. The name was a tribute to Schiaparelli's Surrealist designs and to the art movement in general and it expressed my ideas about art and fashion as an ensemble. My first collections started when I still lived with my adoptive parents, created and executed during my seemingly endless airplane trips. I once beaded an entire hat in the shape of a lamb chop on the way home from Australia on a Pan American World Airways flight. I started to build up my stride with the Surreal Couture "collections" after I moved to the Chelsea Hotel, but my apartment on Park Avenue is where it really became a steady and regular output. Apart from a handful of close friends, most people I showed my designs to probably considered these concoctions eccentric, though I do not like this term. It may have seemed outright weird at the time, but I was totally dedicated and invested in the work, so for me it was totally "centric." All my worries and fears seemed to fall away when I worked on these collections. They left me with a profound sense of happiness.

My Surreal Couture could be called a form of Schiaparelli fan art (though this term did not exist at the time) because they were created out of a true love for Schiap. I am convinced that the term "fan" is really just a pop culture way to say "love." Every piece made some form of reference to something Schiaparelli, whether it be obvious, like the lobster and lips motifs, or symbolically referential, as with the use of contrasts of materials such as blending very rough hand-made wool with elegant French silk satins. All of these things I depicted in my paintings, though the telephones looked like floating noodles and the lips vaguely like female genitals. I called all of these creations my "manifestos." I was dead serious about it all, too, which made it all the more hilarious.

John Ogle, a well-known American art dealer of that era wore several of my ensembles. Among the most memorable were a crocodile motorcycle jacket and a hooded, floor-length opera cape, both reversible in bright colors. The biker jacket had two zigzagged accessories that snapped onto the shoulder to create a reptilian effect. Tucked away inside a sausage-like collar was a rolled up hidden hood, also fashioned out of brightly dyed real alligator and snake skins and lined in thick silk velvet. Homer Layne, Charles James's last assistant, exquisitely tailored the cape. It featured pockets with vintage Schiaparelli Eclair zippers designed to hide all the things a gentleman might need, from condoms (a new, somewhat frightening, necessity) to a small flask of booze (also a necessity to get through those years of panic and havoc). The cape was perfect for a gay nineteenth-century vampire.

Inspired by the Dadaists and Surrealism, I approached design as an experiment in deconstruction. I used clothing that was damaged beyond repair and whatever accessories I could find. I cut up my Louis Vuitton, Dior, Gucci, and Hermès handbags and used the materials to spell out words and phrases like "Fuck Me, I Am a Queer" and "Cocksucker" on tight fitting, ribbed cotton jersey shirts and skirts for men. I used the hardware from these luxury handbags to give garments a belted look. I used gorilla and monkey fur from 1920s coats to create epaulettes. I chopped up old designer labels and sewed them on sleeves and waistlines in a chaotic manner. I used shredded Pucci prints, pieces of Poiret capes, and blowtorched scraps of Dior gowns. Melted Lesage embroidery took on a whole other mood this way. I'd splatter everything with paint: Klein blue, shocking pink, gold, and silver. Antique and vintage accessories would be added to the finished product, the more ridiculous the better. I also made my own, using gilded doll heads, silvered baby bottles, bronzed toy cars, and real baby alligator heads paired with pearls, gemstones, or coral. Anything and everything could be gilded and turned into something of value for the piece. I might even throw on a live lobster entangled in Chanel pearls as I'd go out the front door in one of my creations. Once I filled 1950s Chanel quilted handbags with bags of red paint and shot them with a rifle on a firing range. The resultant splatters made the bags look as though they had bled in some violent manner. I used the bags myself, and people still recall those handbags in detail. It was pure punk attitude, mixed with classic French haute couture and the chaos of Dadism. An artist "friend" in Switzerland later usurped this concept for a famous fashion brand for one of their "pop-up museums" in the mid-2000s.

A menswear shop near Greenwich Village bought one of my

Lobster tuxedos. I saw the owner a year or two later and he told me without a shred of kindness that he had thrown it out because no one in their right mind would have bought it. I only made two: the one I sold to them and another that was acquired by the Metropolitan Museum's Costume Institute. I found it fitting since several important Dadaist and Surrealist artworks suffered the same fate because they shattered conventional ideas of their era. I was honored to be in the league of artists whose work was deliberately destroyed by those who did not appreciate it.

I started to receive more attention from the press around this time, beginning with the European magazines. Their American counterparts quickly following. My collections were highlighted in *Women's Wear Daily*, *Vogue*, *Harper's Bazaar*, *L'Officiel*, *Elle*, and *Jardin des Modes*. In those years, prior to all the intensive Stepford-Wife branding that began in the 1990s, magazine and newspaper editors could show un-wearable, and even unavailable, clothes alongside the work of the most commercialized designers. This was a great era for the fashion press creatively speaking. I was very lucky, but it did not strike me as particularly important at that stage, since I did not consider this project a business. I think my blasé attitude may have factored into the added coverage, too.

In the 1970s and early 1980s, the concept of "Art Wear" was mostly unknown. It was new and exciting, but also a synonym for unsellable. I recall one *Women's Wear Daily* journalist whom I was particularly fond of named Lorna who, along with another writer named Ruth, wrote some daring articles about what I was doing and praised the Art Wear ideology. Art to wear was an exciting, up-and-coming movement, and I felt I was contributing in my own way. There were many others artists, designers, and even galleries popping up all over the world, making statements about things one could wear besides conventional fashion, but I was lucky enough to participate in a seminal show of the subject in SoHo at the Henry

Street Settlement, called "Regalia." Before the Art Wear movement, I worked in an isolated bubble on these creations. However, I still felt that Schiaparelli was always with me. Each time I invented something for Surreal Couture she was next to me, whispering wisdom and approval in my ear. Once I found my community, it was as if I had stepped in from the cold, protected by a world of artists, both alive and in spirit.

I used a studio apartment below the one I lived in as my Surreal Couture atelier. This alternative haute couture house was filled to the brink with Art Deco artifacts displayed in endlessly shifting arrangements interspersed with dolls. Since I thought of my designs as works of art that happened to be based on fashion, I didn't consider seriously selling them at first. Sometimes people would call to place an order after reading an article about me, but I was very reluctant to set appointments. I had not created an operation that could handle proper business transactions and I certainly had no interest in becoming a traditional designer like Bill Blass or Perry Ellis, as much as I liked and admired them at the time. I viewed my work as an artistic tribute to Schiaparelli, Surrealism, and haute couture. However, I eventually realized that I needed to earn (and should earn) a living, so I started reluctantly and selectively selling pieces. I allowed them to find homes with clients who were genuinely excited about my creations. I was both flattered and impressed that they understood my artistic objectives. I also worked with stores that held significance to Schiap's history, like Bendel's and Bloomingdale's, who carried her clothing in the 1930s and 1940s.

I staged Surreal Couture fashion shows as early as 1976. They were exercises in utter absurdity with no rules or rigid standard procedures. I did what I thought Schiaparelli would have done, given my era's means and zeitgeists. I became Schiaparellian! I held one in the amphitheater of the Fashion Institute of Technology that recalled Montmartre, Surrealistic collages, and Jean Paul Sartre's theatre. I had the immense privilege to have Daphne Hellman, one of the most famous harp players in Manhattan, as the musical accompaniment. She played in a classical style with a rakish atonal touch. I positioned her magical spirit smack dab in the middle of the stage, which was crawling with dozens of live soft shell crabs. The show was a real success and John Duka, *the* most influential fashion journalist of the time, gave it a rave review in the *New York Times*.[1] In 1982 I hosted a presentation at Art et Industrie gallery, in the former Razor gallery space. It was an ode to France and the invitation was a Mister Modern collage in electric blue, of the Mona Lisa ripped in half, her face scratched to resemble Duchamp's *L.H.O.O.Q.*, with an image of myself in front of the Eiffel Tower peeking out from between the ripped image. At the show, confetti fell and French flags waved as the models slithered down the runway to the strains of "Da, Da, Da," a now-obscure German hit pop song by a group called Trio. I showed sack back chemise dresses and sheaths, heavily embroidered at the neck in crystal beads in brilliant and bright Schiaparelli hues; colorfully feathered and veiled toques; and a number of oddly silhouetted suits, appliqued with telephone pockets, enormous bronze buttons à la Chirico. I was an oddball and an outsider in the fashion world, but my shows were attended by the established fashion elite, high society socialites, and fashion students in addition to a ragtag group of eccentrics and interlopers. I found these supporters rather encouraging, all of them.

A charming fashion buyer named Joanne Smith, who had a shop in Beverly Hills, approached me after one of my shows. She liked my Schiaparelli attitude and purchased tons of my cape coats, which caused a sensation after Bill Cunningham captured me wearing one in one of his photographs for the *New York Times*. Just before I sent them to her, I had them photographed on fifteen male and female models on the steps of the Metropolitan Museum of Art. In Paris, Orson Welles bought one from me that was shown in popular newspapers of the day in a lovely drawing by a very talented Fiorucci illustrator named Syd. Joanne also purchased a series of my colorful felt hats in classic 1920s shapes that I had made in the New York garment district by the old hat makers who did the hats for Adolfo, Mr. John, Halston, and for Schiaparelli (which was the real reason why I did so). They were adorned with bright feathers and bands of antique French textiles and scraps of Ducharne and Bianchini-Fèrier fabric that Paul Poiret's daughter Perrin had given to me. Around the same time I created a collection in collaboration with the artist Mimi Gross, daughter of W.P.A. artist Chaim Gross. The most unlikely Surreal Couture client was Mimi's mother, the archetype of the Jewish Mama. I loved her and she was truly a character. She drew wonderful cubistic 1920s-esque flowers on a background of large checks and printed it using her woodblock technique on crash linen from the 1930s that I used for coats and jackets. It was completely inspired by the Schiaparelli textiles I owned. This collection of Surreal Couture was a particularly successful one, and Madame Yvonne Deslandres, former costume curator at the Louvre, and my "spiritual mother," wore one of the jackets adorned with a jewel studded Surreal Bijoux starfish in all her official museum photos.

I felt what I was doing was purely absurd and a paradox within a paradox. I made no attempt to be avant-garde because I found it silly to think one can consciously do so. I wanted the individual pieces to carry a Dadaist message, though I did not know what exactly that would entail. I felt as if the pieces were almost alive and I was so curious as to how people would perceive them. Were they appealing or bizarre? Did they allow people to feel any sort of symbolic message, or did they just put people off? Not surprisingly I found the reactions very mixed. However, I received the greatest compliment of all when most of the clothes ended up in the Louvre's Union Française des Arts du Costume, thanks to the support of its founder and curator, Yvonne Deslandres. Before the clothes went into the Louvre's collection, I showed them one last time in the USA at the spectacular Manhattan club Danceteria. I treated it as a retrospective of a half-decade's worth of work and the event utilized the entire building.

I also had the incredible honor to be encouraged by wonderful people like Diana Vreeland, Jean Druesedow, and Paul Ettesvold, who incorporated a selection of my fashions and jewels into the permanent collection of the Metropolitan Museum of Art.

Diana was a miracle on two feet and another of my early Anti-Bourgeoise mentors. She was just as grand as her myth, which, even at that time, preceded her. I first encountered her as a child. I recall sitting on the floor at my mother's cocktail parties admiring all of my great aunt's embroidered and sparkling Roger Vivier shoes in their silk stocking-ed feet, with Diana's hearty laugh and elegant poses creating the backdrop. I was too young to interact with her then, but I was able to develop a real relationship with her as a teenager, when she was the empress of fashion at the Costume Institute at the Metropolitan Museum of Art. When we met again she shrieked from her fire engine red lips that I looked "just like Schiap." I was wearing a late 1940s Schiaparelli haute couture suit jacket with her signature quirky buttons with a pair of 1930's cuffed pants and a severely belted matching coat. The ensemble was topped with a Schiaparelli hat, perched at a jaunty angle, and a set of Schiaparelli jewels called "Champagne Morning" that consisted of two acid green bracelets and a massive brooch made from an assortment of glass stones. This look was an early incarnation of my Anti-Bourgeoise, but my resemblance to Schiaparelli was an unintentional result. Perhaps this is why Diana let me try on the famous Shoe hat in the Costume Institute's collection.

I spent many evenings sitting on a pouf cushion at Vreeland's feet in her New York apartment, decorated in shades of red and filled with all sorts of fascinating art, including portraits of her by Christian Bérard. I felt so small in the presence of her knowledge and wisdom. It was a wonderful feeling. I was always mesmerized and bewitched by her charm and her elegance. We drank freezing cold gin in tiny glasses and got a bit tipsy once in a while. Diana once told me that there was nothing more amusing and chic than a slightly tipsy cultivated young man. I must have fit that description because I often found myself a bit tipsy in her company. I also recall thinking she must have spent a great deal of time around gay men.

I enjoyed my correspondences with her greatly. I loved the way she wrote and how she signed her name the way it should be pronounced, Diane. She had such a bold penmanship. She regaled me with stories about Paris before the war, her love for Chanel clothes, and of course Schiap. We'd discuss everything: art, politics, theater, music, God, sex, money, greed, friendship, what to wear on a lapel, and how to select a tie. Sometimes we'd gossip about people we knew. Once she told me she disliked Karl Lagerfeld. It was the very beginning of his career at Chanel and she simply did not like the direction he was taking the house. For her, Chanel without Chanel was unthinkable. I often wonder what Diana would have to say about the now established practice of reviving Parisian haute couture houses after the deaths of their namesakes.

Diana was someone who valued the human experience, and her genuine appreciation of fantasy and humor made fashion an adventure. Every moment with her was wonderful and deeply meaningful. I learned so much through her eyes and knowledge. I adored her.

Through Diana I met a gentleman now practically forgotten by history. Paul Ettesvold worked at the Costume Institute and he was an inspired man, full of visionary thoughts. He was a mix between a dandy poet and an obsessive schoolteacher in many ways. Paul came to Paris in 1984 when I did my *Hommage à Schiaparelli* show. He was a very handsome and very dapper young man, a real beauty—tall, slim, and blond, with a great air of elegance that made him look like a 1920s ad for gentleman's shirts or cigarettes. I really wanted to please him and be his friend when I first met him. I always felt a boost of confidence when he acknowledged things I said or pointed out about Schiaparelli. I was devastated when he passed away from AIDS-related illnesses. He is barely remembered or acknowledged anymore, an example of the short-term memory for people who existed before the Internet could preserve their stories. I find it rather sad and always try to speak of him and the other unsung heroes of the 1970s and 1980s who established the field of conserving and preserving the history of twentieth-century decorative arts and haute couture.

I also have Diana to thank for the great friendship that I have developed with Jean Druesedow, now the director of the Kent State University Museum in Ohio. She has always been a tremendous help in my research on Schiaparelli. We still speak often about the responsibilities of collectors and what it reveals about ourselves. She recently told me it is important to collect fashion as an individual because clothes are an extraordinary indication of an individual's response to the aesthetic milieu of a certain time and place.

To this day I don't know why I garnered so much attention with my Surreal Couture, but it opened even more doors for me to meet interesting people all over the world. I met amazing people in the fashion and art worlds, and everywhere in between. Their support gave me a wonderful sense of connection to the universe.

CHAPTER 11

PARIS—LONDON—PARIS

t seemed as if a huge fork had appeared in the road in front of me when Schiaparelli entered my life. Choosing a direction and embarking on that first step changed my entire life's meaning. Before I settled down in one place permanently, I wanted to travel the world. In mid-1978, no longer sequestered by chaperones or tutors, I ventured to the Middle East, Asia, and Europe. I wound up in East and West Berlin, England, Scotland, Ireland, and Switzerland. I made a pilgrimage to Rome specifically to see where Schiaparelli had been born and to visit the monuments dedicated to her famous relatives. It was then on to Finland, Sweden, and Norway, with stops in Budapest and Hungary along the way. I felt most at home in Vienna, and returned there often. I rode on fabulous train lines, like the Orient-Express and Trans-Siberian Express. Sometimes I had chauffeured luxury cars driving me and sometimes I was knee-deep in screaming children on public transit, which was the only option available in some places. In Israel, I hitchhiked. Every single experience I had seemed to tell me that this was part of a big plan, a special life lesson taught through the lens of art and style. I didn't think I was special, but I did feel as though I was protected by the cosmos. My philosophies about life were forming; I was growing up and maturing. It became very clear to me what I had to do and also what I had to stop doing. In some unexplainable way, Schiaparelli was the matrix and star center of this.

England was a wonderful place for me. In a familiar pattern, I oscillated between underground funk and the highest echelons of society. I was always chattering away about Schiap, regardless of whom I was with. Oddly, though, it wasn't the society women who had worn her clothes that gave me the most insight into Schiaparelli. Rather it was newly established artists who were contemporary equivalents to the type of person Schiap might have been during her time in London. The English artists and designers I met were creating clothing that thrilled me with their newness. People like Judy Blame, Slim Barrett, David Holah, and Stevie Stewart (the creators of the now iconic BodyMap club clothes), John Galliano, and Alexander McQueen, who were all rapidly becoming famous for their highly original fashions and accessories. The drollery, the chic, and the camp of the London scene in the 1970s and 1980s made me to feel the way I imagined people felt when they saw Schiap clothing for the first time in the 1930s.

In London, I stayed at the Savoy and Ritz Hotels. Not only did I enjoy the luxury they offered, but because I can hardly cook or do anything practical, hotels seemed a better place to live than my overcrowded flat which always seemed to me to be just a mass of packing crates, clothes racks, dresses and dust. In the picturesque surroundings of these grand old hotels, I still ended up filling my rooms with Portobello finds that included Schiaparelli garments from her London house of fashion.

From the late 1970s to the mid-1980s, Kensington Market was to the club kids and the underground style mavens what the Ritz was to conventional doyennes of chic. The market was a cavernous old building on Kensington High Street in London that was filled with funky boutiques and small shops catering to the alternative crowd. I absolutely loved it there. Every boy seemed sexy. Every girl seemed so glamorous. Kensington Market, and for that matter, all of the flea markets and junkshops in and around London, were very comforting to me. In England, the young artists all seemed to have a "make do and mend" attitude, and seemed to be able to create something from nothing in the rough economic climate of the era.

I met David Robilliard when he was in his late twenties and we were friends until his death in 1988. He was simply too scrumptious to explain. I loved to knock about with him. We wandered around together cracking jokes and he was often my wingman while shopping for vintage clothing. He dazzled the storeowners with his wit and charm while I rifled through racks of clothes of all types. Fred Hughes, Andy Warhol's gifted business manager, was another shopping friend. He always introduced me as the "world's foremost collector" of Schiaparelli, which flattered me to no end. Fred was extremely cultivated, very ambitious, and a real bon vivant. He was often like a big brother that I could talk to when I had doubts about life. He knew all the things a gentleman needed to know: details about food, manners, table talk, everything. This made him appear as a modern Beau Brummell, though he did tend to have a problem with alcohol that could quickly deflate the illusion of grand refinement by the end of an evening. He looked like a young English Lord, a studied look he wanted and handled to perfection. We patronized a variety of English tailors and often purchased the same suits. He gave me his cast off clothing, which included bespoke suits and a particularly wild pair of psychedelic lamé pants that he had custom made in the 1960s at Renoma in Paris. He loved the idea that I could tell people that I had gotten into his pants.

By now I had traveled widely and thought it was time to decide where in the world I wanted to settle down. Where could I make a home and not just squander money on more traveling, collecting, and loneliness? Paris seemed to be the most sacred and breath-taking city on earth, a place where art and fashion merged seamlessly. Its attraction was like the pull of an invisible magnet, a fate I could not avoid. The City of Light was where Schiap had lived at my age. And it was where I'd found the hat after all! I installed myself there in the autumn of 1978 to locate Elsa's various incarnations and stories, and finally find someone who would love me forever. Both were of supreme importance to me. I was barely eighteen.

When I disembarked from the Concorde in Paris, I was surprised to find myself greeted by newspaper and TV crews and the newspaper *Libération* wrote an article on my obsession with Schiaparelli.[1] In 1980 the magazine *Actuel* featured a full-length story called "At Last A Normal Young Man," which presented me as the inventor of the "new Baroque," later considering the title, I suppose one could say I had come a long way from the days of being ridiculed at school for wearing a woman's hat. I arrived at a crucial moment in time and history. I was extremely lucky because I was able to see the very last vestiges of old Paris. In the late 1970s, Paris still looked like it had in the 1940s. You could find shops on every corner that appeared untouched by time. The *merceries* were the most thrilling of all. They still sold hand-made buttons from the nineteenth century as well as Schiaparelli-style buttons from the 1930s. Montmartre was a dreamscape: old bistros and cafés, cinema girls who showed you to your seat, and old men in berets. I could say the name Schiaparelli to anyone, even someone not involved with fashion, and they knew who she was, even if they'd never seen a Schiap dress in their life. Everyone seemed to have a cousin, an aunt, a mother, or grandmother who had some connection to haute couture, whether it be as a seamstress or a client, and had something to say about it, too. The old Paris disappeared within ten years of my arrival, but I feel lucky to have seen it dressed in all of its shambled glory when I landed there.

I spent time in museums, cafés, bookshops, antique stores, and gay bars, which were very different from those in the USA and England. The gay bars in France were more like a cabaret than just a joint to cruise, with singing and merry making in a style straight out of Paris in the 1920s. I drank mezcal, Pernods, Suzes, and took way too much Valium while fantasizing I was a modern day Max Ernst. Taking lovers was a great way to learn about a culture, I discovered, but if they didn't like flea markets and antiques fairs, there was no hope for them, no matter how divine and pleasing they may have been in other aspects.

I could not write about these years without mentioning Jacques Chazot. He was a delightful man, a sort of French Noël Coward. He was known for being Gabrielle Chanel's confidant and "walker." It was obvious that they adored each other from her interviews in the 1960s and he was possibly the only person Chanel was completely kind towards. He was also one of the gayest men in Paris, out and proud long before that expression came into use. He would only gossip about the most positive aspects of people and he taught me the best qualities. He was graceful and very dapper, right out of the 1940s, like the slang he liked to teach me when we ogled boys together. He was very close to Françoise Sagan, the French writer. He claimed she was the only woman he had fallen in love with.

When I first met Françoise she shared with me a famous quote of hers from 1982: "A dress makes no sense unless it inspires men to want to take it off you."[2] I thought it brilliant and echoed Schiaparelli's point of view. How could I not like her? I had come to France to immerse myself in French culture, and meeting someone like Françoise Sagan was a high point of that goal. She led a glamorous life, and wore clothing from Paris's greatest designers (which she received as gifts), though she tried to be discreet in her dress. She was a truly fascinating woman with a trail of mythic literary successes, scandals, and various racing car accidents. I also became friends with her lover, Peggy Roche, a brunette who always seemed very sure of herself. She loved fashion and was a noted designer in her own right. Both she and Françoise said they had been amused by Schiaparelli's clothes when they were growing up.

I met Prince Amyn Muhammad Aga Khan, a man of superior taste and knowledge, in the 1980s. I was invited to dinner at his sumptuous Parisian house with the composer Andrew Lloyd Weber. That evening we were shown a pair of small ormolu wall sconces from the Baroque period, from the Palace of Versailles that Amin had just acquired. He'd paid over two million pounds for them. I think this was one of the first times I realized not all collectors are the same. The idea of spending that much for such exquisite objects impressed me. For one of the first times in my life I understood that money, no matter how much one may have, is relative. Though I admire this level of collecting, I doubt that I would enjoy it as much as the serious hunting that I engage in, much like sniffing out truffles or chasing a fox. It's adventurous and exhilarating when you go out in the morning and have no idea what you may fall upon.

CHAPTER 12

LOVE, AND I MEAN
L. U. V.

I walked into *Vogue*'s offices on the Place de Palais Bourbon in Paris to meet Dorothée Lalanne on my birthday in 1980, a year after our first meeting in New York. She was celebrating the launch of *Vogue Beauté*, a short-lived magazine for Condé Nast, and we had worked together on a feature article about the life and work of Elsa Schiaparelli. Beyond a mutual interest in Schiap, Dorothée and I agreed on everything from spiritual matters to fashion, and, most importantly, the best type of strawberry jam. At her insistence, I moved into her family's 1950s modernist house in Suresnes, a bourgeois suburb of Paris. We instantly fell into something that closely resembled love and shared an immensely rich and creative life together for a while.

In Suresnes, Dorothée and I took long walks in the surrounding forest, talking and laughing, both of us looking like North African Zouaves or Spanish gypsies in the flowing tunics I made from antique fabrics topped with large chunky jewels. We imagined ourselves to be Nazimova and Valentino, or Isadora Duncan and Nijinsky. I sketched her portrait. She took funny polaroids. I would drape fabric on her to create Surreal Couture dresses. In between fittings, we drank verveine, Earl Grey, and thyme herbal teas. She drank gallons of that verveine infusion and teapots full of warm water from a chartreuse green Russel Wright teapot I gave her. I nicknamed her "Dorothépot" because she was always so particular about how to make and serve these teas in her quasi-oriental ceremonies. I eventually made a dark blue felt hat for her that resembled a teapot lid. I included this moniker in one of the little booklets filled with drawings, poems, or stories that accompanied the dresses I made for her. I called it "Dorothépot Couture—a dress to wear only after midnight and the rest of the day's dresses."

When I was not working on strange arty clothes, I channeled Edith Sitwell. I performed these imitations with a towel wrapped around my head, wearing a huge topaz ring on my index finger that Andy Warhol had given me and another that had belonged to Edith, given to me by her cousin, Joan Sitwell. My goofing around made Dorothée crack up in hysterics, a relief from her morose moods and contagious stress. She had a great, highly infectious laugh and I suppose this drove me to create these characters for her. It was laughter that held our strange relationship together.

We spent idyllic days and lovely weekends in Ury, a small village near Fontainebleau, with her father, François-Xavier Lalanne, and her stepmother, Claude Lalanne. He was a warm and welcoming man who created beautiful stylized sculptures of animals, some quite famous now. He is responsible for the sheep in Yves Saint Laurent's garden and the ivy-covered elephant fountains at Châtelet in front of Paris's City Hall in the first arrondissement. His wife, Claude, is also a gifted sculptor, whose stunning bronze jewels of flowers and animals recalled my childhood interest in the drawings in the dictionaries. They welcomed me into their home, where I spent a great deal of time painting. I met all kinds of people there, like the Mitterand brothers, Guy and Marie-Hélène de Rothschild, Emile and Charlotte

Aillaud, the Baron Alexis de Rédé, Betty Catroux, and many amazing others. Meeting these people gave me a wonderful opportunity to understand French culture. I felt as if I had entered a Jurassic zoo of fashion, mingling in a million-year-old jungle with jeweled old toads of art and society. I feel very lucky to have had the chance to know the Lalannes and witness their dedicated creation of art firsthand. I have a deep respect for them and they were genuinely wonderful people.

Dorothée spent a great deal of time trying to convince me I was not gay. Oh, what a bore that was. She would wake me early in the morning, interrogation style, to explain that I was just going through a phase. Aside from this huge error in reasoning, she was intellectually gifted, contemplative, and cultured. And yet she was a *Vogue* girl who wrote articles about fashion even though she hated it. Always at odds with her very plain looks, Dorothée wore sober chic clothing, almost in a compulsively draconian way, and never wore any make-up other than bright red Chanel lipstick. Her hair was severely cut and styled by one of the most elitist hairdressers of the time, Line Bertin. She wore impeccable flat shoes from Chanel and Walter Steiger. She was what Schiaparelli called a *jolie laide*. She was also an amazing klutz, always burning holes in her clothes from the fallout of the Indian beedi cigarettes she smoked, and clumsily tripping over herself. Keith Haring once gifted me a superb set of Japanese-inspired bowls with his drawings glazed into them from his Pop Shop. Dorothée, ever the snob, begged to drink tea from one and within minutes had dropped it, breaking it into pieces.

Dorothée was best friends with a curious fellow named Lala. She told me about him often, and I finally met him in early 1982. One day she was busy working and she conspired for us to go out to have a drink or something. She told me we'd love each other, probably meaning we would have plenty in common, but I don't think she realized how right she was. We did love each other. I never went back to that gloomy French suburban lair where Dorothée isolated herself after that. Lala became my partner almost immediately, and eventually would become my husband.

Jean-Pierre "Lala" Lestrade was the first and only person in my life who I fell deeply in love with, and still am to this day. The inexplicable sublime feeling of falling in love was a brand new, spellbinding sensation. It was not at all what I had experienced with anyone before, even unlike the love at first sight I had felt with Dorothée. I had made every attempt to learn about love and know what it felt like. I knew that I had used sex to see if I could feel that magical thing they call love, but each and every time, I was left with selfish sexual desire, but I never felt loved. In addition to these new feelings, Lala was the first and only man I ever met who did not depend on me financially. He was selfless in his love for me. We started working together right away and have never stopped.

On that first meeting, we drank vodka cocktails for hours at a café near the Jardin du Luxembourg. Actually, I was the only one drinking the cocktails. Lala drank a beer while I drank fast and steady, like a flapper, thinking it was glamorous. I disappeared into the restroom for about an hour, where I fell asleep from the Valium I had also taken (with an illegal absinthe chaser). At that time I was severely addicted to Valium. When I woke up, refreshed from my catnap, I was surprised to see Lala, baffled and more concerned than annoyed, still waiting for me. Then he took me to dinner at an Arabic restaurant called Le Troupeau, after the eponymous acclaimed Turkish film of the time. At the restaurant, over a couscous meal, Lala made a drawing of me that he still has. I was wearing a Serge Kruger jacket with a beret and a ton of Chanel accessories, which he pointed out in a humorous way with arrows on his sketch. Lala has done many drawings of me ever since, most notably a series he called *Billy Boy*'s *Art of Glamorous Living*. They have been published in *Tatler*, *Vanity Fair*, *Elle*, and elsewhere.

We spent the night together and I was in heaven. Soon after I made a brief trip to Geneva, to visit my demi-boyfriend, a Swiss artist named Patrick Imhof. My intention was to back away from the relationship, but the day I arrived his father died and I spent three weeks alone in his barren white apartment filled only with his intriguing paintings, listening to the B-52s and dying of total boredom. I knew many people in Switzerland but I had no desire to socialize because I felt my mind was filled like an egg. I could not bear to be out and about despite the boredom because I wanted to really figure out my feelings. Lala was truly my soul mate. I knew it immediately and with those weeks of thinking I was able to calmly confirm that was truly the case. So, I called Lala, got on the TGV train and he met me at the Gare de Lyon in Paris and took me to his brother Didier's apartment, where we lived for a month. By sheer coincidence, I had met Didier a couple years before meeting Lala. He was a party animal and I saw him all the time in the coolest places and nightclubs. At the time he was producing a now-cult magazine called *Magazine,* an early version of the acknowledged and popular *Têtu* magazine, while modestly earning his living as a clerk in a hotel. *Magazine* was about chic gay culture and filled with art and interviews, a cross between *After Dark* and Andy Warhol's *Interview.* The non-porn aspect of Didier's magazine was a true precedent for gay culture. (Lala released a flexi-record with his cult song "Jolie Fille d'Alger" in issue N°o). This was all before Didier became famous for his gay activism, as a journalist for *Libération,* for his many books, his founding of Act-Up Paris in France, and *Têtu* (a French gay magazine that he co-founded and which was financed by Pierre Bergé). He had never seen someone so obsessed with shopping and drinking cocktails. For a gay man at the time, I was a freak. While he wanted to cover the obelisk on place de la Concorde with a huge condom (this was eventually done in the 1990s by an activist gay group) and organize the lying down in the streets with other impoverished militant gays wearing bombers jackets, jeans, and Timberlands, I was having fittings and trying on outfits at Courrèges, Yves Saint Laurent, and Balenciaga Homme on Avenue George V.

Early on I invited Lala's brother to take a trip with me to London so I could shop and so he could see it wasn't such a bad thing after all. He accepted, but the trip turned strange when Didier realized he couldn't cope with my lifestyle. In his novel *Kinsey 6*, Didier mentions our Ritz experience along with his slant on our long relationship as being brothers-in-law, so to speak. He recently wrote, "Billy Boy absolutely had to go to London for some shopping and needed company because Lala was either away or busy. So Billy proposed to me that I come along, to spend two days at the Ritz and to keep him company during his shopping. The trip started in a typical Billy Boy comical way, but needless to say, with a true fashion flair: Billy was wearing a huge black fur coat (the Yeti type by Paco Rabanne), which was so enormous that it wouldn't fit in any luggage compartments of the plane. I spent quite a lot of time carrying that thing, it was like hanging around with twenty-five black sheep pelts in the airport. In the Ritz lobby, I was that close to making fun of all the luxury surrounding us. The next morning, I found the abundance of rare and unseasonal fruit that was adorning Billy's bed totally obscene. The worst moment came when, the day before leaving, Billy suggested, in all good faith, since I was hungry, to simply call for room service. When I saw the price of the simplest sandwich, I burst into such a rage that I slammed the door and rushed out furious into a full blizzard and headed to McDonald's on Piccadilly Circus.

He further explains that at the time, he was dressing like a gay skinhead and that "all this stuff" was exactly what he was deliberately trying to eradicate from his lifestyle. He admits in this regard that he was very much under the influence of the frugal way of dealing with success. But for him, our adventure was revealing and pretty clear: Billy wanted me to understand that futility and luxury can be amazing tools for change, especially when considered in a historical perspective, which he knows how to do like nobody else in the world. I was trying to make him see my point that political conviction must sometimes sound very primary in order to be understood. After all, I was eager to throw myself into the fight against AIDS. Billy always wanted to remind me that my origins, as middle class as I claim they were, never prevented me to develop a sincere interest and love for a culture that he was defending. In these quarrels, Lala was always the one we would call as a moderator. But we also both knew that Lala hates to be assigned to that role and that his love for Billy would always have the last word.

Lala was actively looking for a new place for me to move into, which he recalls as a depressing task because nothing seemed to be suitable. He finally found a place, on the right bank of the Seine in the eighteenth arrondissement. I liked the apartment a lot, but felt very nervous at the same time. Just before signing the lease, Lala and I shared a snack in an Arabic tearoom on avenue de Clichy and he made a funny cartoon of me, dressed in my all black Kruger out-fit, under a vintage 1960s lamp, saying, "God! I REALLY want this flat!" I signed, got the keys, and there we were, in an empty flat in the bright November sun. I presumed he'd move in with me and when I asked he looked at me, kind of surprised. Lala said to me years later that it was the second most important decision of his life and it only took five seconds to make. It was without question the most intel-ligent decision I'd ever made.

The apartment was in a 1960s building, very clean and com-fortable with a charming young concierge. There was a large, old-fashioned brasserie at the corner, a gay sauna on the opposite side, and an old family-owned toyshop with dead stock from the 1950s and 1960s on the other. There were fantastic antique stores, old fabric and button shops, and junk shops all along the back streets. It was dreamy. It was romantic. I was in love and settled in a quaint Parisian apartment with the man I knew I would spend my life with. We painted the salon in an exquisite shade of Schiaparelli violet and put down almond green wool carpet, the exact same shade of the color of Schiaparelli's leaf cape. The windows of the apartment, filled with Parisian sunshine, looked out upon a charming, rundown courtyard at the back of an old hotel. The hotel was very much frequented by South American transsexual prostitutes who worked the Bois de Boulogne at night, whom we'd befriend by waving to them.

We furnished our new apartment with flea market finds, incorporating Lala's nineteent-century steel and iron garden chairs painted Paris park green with things we made out of blocks of broken plaster found in the street. We had one bed à la Poiret covered in a zillion Indian cushions. In the kitchen we had a 1940s Le Rêve oven from Switzerland, the first thing we bought together. We hung an Adnet cubist chandelier in the foyer, a Jean-Michel Frank mirror designed by Bérard and executed by Alberto Giacometti, threw in a number of Art Deco designer master pieces, a bunch of Atelier Martine pieces, some Jean-Michel Frank tables, chairs, a dramatic plaster column, a few modern master paintings, and voilà! We were good to go.

My new mate encouraged my passion for collecting. Can you imagine, not only did he love me, but also he accepted my weird doll collecting! Even more importantly, he pushed me to collect more Schiap. He has even gifted me some of her pieces over the years. A man who accepted my Schiaparelli addiction, well, that is truly heaven sent. It was intensely obvious that we had a soul contract, as clear and crisp a connection as when I'd touched that first Schiap hat.

CHAPTER 13

SCHIAP SCHIAP SCHIAP

n 1983, I went to the appropriate people I knew in politics for the city of Paris and the Musée Galliéra to propose that I organize the first official retrospective on the work and career of my muse, Elsa Schiaparelli. They immediately agreed because they'd seen so much of the press about me and Schiaparelli. I traveled back to New York with Lala to prepare some of my collection for shipment to Paris. First, we went on a mission to hunt down every steamer trunk in Manhattan. We needed to pack everything into them because my collection of old Vuittons could not carry it all despite the large number of them that followed me throughout the world for years. It was without question an absurd, sitcom-like situation and a Surrealist experience in and of itself. We also made a trip to my art storage unit, a long, light-deprived room packed with all kinds of stuff, some of which I had totally forgotten. I opened boxes and trunks that reeked of Shocking perfume and old things. My letters, dolls, and other sentimental objects (some utterly useless and esoteric) were included here, too. We had to itemize every single object for Customs before transport. Lala wrote down everything on a list that read like a Surrealistic poem of eclectic memorabilia while I dictated in a slightly annoyed tone: "One pink felt hat with an insect shaped like a fly pinned on it, labeled Schiaparelli; one blue cloche hat with beadwork in the shape of an 'S' labeled Schiaparelli; a beat-up talking Bugs Bunny that says 'What's up, Doc?' and a thing, I don't know what it is; a green rubber Gumby circa 1964; one bronze and ivory statuette signed D. Chiparus; a complete set of Jensen silverware for 24; fifty copies of *Teen Beat* magazine 1969 to 1971, 'Oh, look, there are several with Eve Plumb on the cover, oh my god, she was so adorable!'" Lala later admitted that he had seriously considered running away from the warehouse and going back to the hotel, but felt so sorry for me that he decided to stay and help. With a literal ton of objects packed into steamer trunks, the entire portion of my collection that was stored in New York was finally on its way to be with me in Europe with the rest of my things. All the furniture, including an Art Deco piano, was sent, as well. We did the same thing in London for the Schiaps and a lot of other stuff I'd collected there. It was all converging together for my new mature, adult lifestyle complete with my charming and very much adored soul mate.

Since then, those trunks have followed Lala and me everywhere. The ones that became battered and beaten to death have been declared as *Mdvaniiism* artworks and were given to friends. (Selling them would have taken away the Wiccan positivity that they have been imbued with.) The remaining "survivors" are still covered in epitaphs marked "Schiaparelli one" and "Schiaparelli two," a tribute to their first incarnation as vessels that carried my collection to France. The exteriors also are covered in airline decals, Mattel Toys stickers from my Barbie projects, museum addresses, rusted corners and broken locks. Jean-Baptiste Faure, a Swiss friend, wrote in 2011 that they are the story of our life together, which continues to this day.

With my collection finally in one place, I began photographing my Schiaparelli clothes on women I knew socially, as opposed to just fashion models. This was an idea I continued to develop further over the next decades. The central concept is related to one of the main tenets of haute couture, that each garment is made to custom fit a specific woman's body. I wanted to show pieces from my collection, which come from a variety of women, on an equally diverse group of socialites, artists, celebrities, and others. The models were given period hair, make-up, and postures, but there would still be an unmistakable lens of the modern day with each. The results were quite thrilling and evocative of the photos Robert Doisneau and I did a few years later at the Musée d'Art Moderne in Paris. In those photos, taken in the spring of 1987 for an article I wrote for *Femme*, Doisneau photographed my friend Dauphine de Jerphanion wearing a 1933 Schiaparelli gown from my collection in a now iconic image.[1] I cannot think of a way to improve upon it. This was also only the second time that Doisneau used color photography—the first was a portrait of me at La Coupole wearing Issey Miyake and eating a banana split. In contrast to museums, where historic garments are infinitely precious and always handled with the greatest care, I am able to breathe life back to the garments in a way that mannequins cannot. For the most part, they look so forlorn and somewhat dreary when hung lifelessly on a mannequin, and a vintage Stockman or Siegel dress form is only a smidgen better. Lala aided me immensely in this effort and we soon co-signed the images we made because it'd be impossible for me to do them without him.

Just a few years prior to that photo shoot in 1987, I met Lala's friend Jane Xanthopoulos, an American girl with Greek origins. She was in flux, separated from her husband (Lala's best friend), living in a squat, and working as a waitress. It was love at first sight. She had a New Yorker's sense of humor and irresistible, shiny black eyes. She had the greatest screaming laugh in the world. I asked her to be my assistant and she proved to be amazing, professional and hard working, but also a true friend. Of course, I could not help but engage in a Pygmalion makeover, cutting her hair short and dying it Jean Harlow platinum, finishing the look with tailored 1940s Schiap suits and stiletto pumps. She looked sensational. She modeled my Schiaparelli clothing in the Musée Galliéra exhibition catalogue.

Jane was the first in my series, but many actresses and performers joined in this project immediately and it continued regularly over the years. Gabrielle Lazure and Philippine Leroy-Beaulieu, two of the young ingénues in French cinema, were photographed for *Vogue* feature stories wearing my haute couture Schiaparelli clothes and hats. They did a splendid job. Rock singer Catherine Ringer from the group Les Rita Mitsuoko posed for me just for fun. Djemila, the French punk rock singer and *Facade* magazine regular, had such an amazing flair. She looks divine in every photograph, even snapshots. Djemila truly knew how to move in the clothes. I have a photo of her in our Place Adolphe Max apartment, posed in front of floor-to-ceiling Shocking Pink silk taffeta curtains as a backdrop (made out of dead stock given to me by the Place Vendôme House of Schiaparelli). It was as if the black velvet 1949 Schiaparelli gown with Lesage embroidery and novelty built-in pockets was made especially for her. Once, at a dinner party in our home, Myriam Schaefer (the assistant designer to Jean Paul Gaultier at the time), Djemila, and Diane Brill got into a heavy competition as to who wore what best and it almost ended in a catfight. It was rather hilarious. Djemila was the clear winner, even though Diane was stunning and at the height of her modeling beauty. Myriam was hissing insults under her breath and the whole thing was right out of the film *The Women*.

My friend Dauphine was in the opening pages of a 1987 *Femme* article shot by Robert Doisneau. She was muse to Thierry Mugler and always dressed in the absolute height of fashion in his clothing. Dauphine came from a noble French family dating back to the 1460s.

She had an aristocratic face and the gift of making everyone and anyone feel at ease, a genuine noblesse oblige. Like Marisa Berenson and Joey Arias, she was one of those people who never said a bad word about anyone. Once, when we were in New York together, Andy Warhol invited me to a party and I asked if she could come. He was intrigued because it was rare for me to have any feelings beyond friendship for women, and he teased me about my crush on her. She wore a beige Mugler outfit, a turban, and my Surreal Bijoux jewelry. Let me tell you, she was the star of that party! People were so blown away by her that Andy at some point seemed almost jealous. Dauphine passed away, quite sadly on October 15, 2013 after a long illness. I was heartbroken. She was truly one of the greats of fashion of our times.

Another friend and our Surreal Bijoux house model of the time, Christine "Cricket" Vial modeled Schiaparelli for me from our first meeting onwards, including the shoot with Doisneau. She was a young model, perky and refreshing. She had stark white short hair and a great knack for posing. She loved to have fun. She wore my Schiaparelli trompe-l'œil sweater, the Circus print dressing gown, and many other outstanding pieces from my collection. We made a wonderful video, when the format was still new and used big bulky cassettes. She modeled several looks and we were able to show each from various angles to see the garment at its best. We used the Juliette Greco song "Si" by Henri Sauguet as the sound track, interspersed with clips from an interview with Bettina Bergery. I hope someday to be able to show this video to a larger audience.

On June 20, 1984, the Musée Galliéra presented the *Hommage à Schiaparelli* exhibition at the Pavillion des Arts in Paris. This show, which used many pieces from my collection, attracted considerable attention and had an immediate impact on the world of fashion. Suddenly, Shocking Pink was *the* color, not only in Paris but also on Seventh Avenue in New York and on London High Streets. The show was also the impetus for the 1987 *Fashion and Surrealism* exhibition at the Museum at FIT in New York City. It included a number of my important Schiaparelli items in addition to examples of my own work. Pieces from my collection have been loaned to museums all over the world, including London's Victoria & Albert Museum, Les Cours Mont-Royal, and Japan's Kyoto Museum. My entire collection is now housed in Switzerland with us and shown sometimes by Fondation Tanagra, the non-profit cultural organization I founded with Lala in 1997.

Schiaparelli was never far from my mind. On many auspicious occasions, I received signs from her. I always seemed to find a particularly fine Schiaparelli ensemble on my birthday. The day before I moved to Paris, my heart filled with mixed feelings, I found a labeled Schiaparelli compact lying on the street. Was it a reminder from her not to worry? It certainly was like a wink from outer space!

As early as 1979, the then-inactive House of Schiaparelli on the Place Vendôme contacted me repeatedly to discuss bringing me on to design new collections for them. I always declined the offer, much to the surprise of Schiaparelli's daughter, Gogo (whose full name is Marisa Luisa Yvonne Rahda). While I loved Schiap, I never wanted to *be* Schiap. However, I did accept, with pleasure, the challenge of putting the Schiaparelli documents in order. I happily browsed through the dusty old press releases, photos, and remaining archives for months on end, which supplied some of the foundation of information for this book.

I cannot emphasize enough the importance of Yvonne Deslandres in my life and my research, and also in the perception of Schiaparelli that we have today. Yvonne founded the Louvre's Union Française des Arts du Costume and gave me precious access to their collection of Schiaparelli's design albums. These books contained sketches by Drian, fabric swatches, trimming samples, and, of course, the clothes themselves.

She was my spiritual mother and a great inspiration to me as I studied Schiaparelli. Yvonne was always incredibly enthusiastic about Schiap's work and felt that it was necessary to collect and preserve contemporary and historical fashion for posterity. She had a strong sense of what was important to observe in a fashion and saw the great historical importance of Schiaparelli long before I was even born! She was responsible for the museum's acquisition of the most important Schiaparelli creations ever made. Yvonne approached Schiaparelli about the acquisition of her incredible design albums. She told me it had been difficult to convince Schiap to hand them over, but was entirely worth the effort. She should be thanked for her persistence, as these albums will continue to be of supreme importance for future generations. They were essential to my understanding of the richness and scope of Schiaparelli's work. Yvonne often told me that I should study them over and over, because in doing so, "you'll see slowly all the details, they will pop out at you, one after another, it's too much to take in a few sessions of looking at them. Each year she created is a masterpiece, you can see the history of Europe in them, the subtleties are many . . . and only hard work and a lot of patience and with your curiosity, with time, you'll understand her work."

She was right, looking at these startling Schiaparelli fashion albums over, and over I realized it would take a very long time to fully understand the unique art of Elsa Schiaparelli. I was enthralled by it; it spoke to me on so many levels, which I hope I've been able to express in this very personal book. After more than forty years of research and interest in her, I feel I still can continue to do research on Schiaparelli.

CHAPTER 14

THE TWO BETTINAS

Bettina Bergery, dubbed "my other Bettina" to differentiate her from Bettina Graziani, is my favorite Anti-Bourgeoise and possibly the prototype for this character. I felt this from the beginning, as I had known her nearly all my life. She was closer to me than absolutely anyone else, and probably the greatest influence on my personality. The rather intense fascination I felt for her meant she had a larger and more important role in my development as a person than my adopted parents did. We had a profound relationship, a bit like *Harold and Maude*, but less morbid and because of her *mondaine* view on life more glamorous. Apart from Lala, very few people could understand my devotion to her and hers to me. Bettina was quintessential to my understanding of life, chic, glamour, and being an artist. Lala and I always said she was an artwork unto herself. She transcended the here-and-now, linear time frame and was an astral creature of light, beauty and in-depth spiritual knowledge. She also was hilariously superficial, vague, and camp. She was the epitome of reckless intellectual beauty and the confirmation that life is utterly absurd and full of surprises. She was a friend to some of the most notable luminaries of the past six decades, a diverse group that included Pope John XXIII, Max Ernst, Francis Picabia, Salvador Dalí, and Schiaparelli. Her startling bedroom was a crazy mix of eighteenth-century antiques and Jean-Michel Frank furniture. Among the framed photos of her luminary friends were dozen and dozens of framed photos of me. Ever since I was a youngster, I have also had many framed photos of her in my bedroom. We seemed to inspire one another and our vibes were in total synchronization. She was also a fabulous writer, truly gifted with words. Bettina's constant affirmation of life was nothing less than amazing, to; she always took a positive perspective on things even though she was known for being rather sarcastic. She adored my Surreal Bijoux designs and wore them with unrivaled panache. She was my unofficial walking advertisement and was responsible for my introduction to many of the amazing artists, writers, and intellects in my life.

Bettina was born in 1900, a Shaw-Jones related to George Bernard Shaw. Throughout my life she spoke to me in the most poetic terms, but she made little sense to most people. Lala has always said that it took him a year to finally understand what she said. As Schiap's muse, high society model, window dresser, and public relations genius, she knew everything that happened behind the scenes. The information she entrusted to me before her death is filled with priceless anecdotes. It was Bettina who brought artists like Salvador Dalí and Jean Cocteau into the world of Schiaparelli. She had the cunning idea to dress her pet wistiti monkeys, named Pouchka, Riki, and Big Mama, in miniature versions of her Schiaparelli haute couture. This absurd foolery was considered at the time particularly Surrealistic and chicly amusing. Hollywood fashion designer Adrian and filmmaker George Cukor were directly inspired by this anecdote and included wistitis dressed in Adrian clothes in the 1939 film *The Women*. She was one of Schiap's greatest collaborators, her Gal Friday, and her public relations ambassador. Bettina was one of the most Surreal persons to be encountered, a perfect match for the somewhat mad and highly *mondaine* genius of Elsa.

In *Shocking Life*, Schiaparelli recalls her first encounter with Bettina, who she described as a very beautiful girl with a thunderous personality. The book recounts that Schiaparelli refused to hire Bettina for months, because although the girl was an ideal fit stylistically, she had no skills. She asked her "What can you do?" to which Bettina replied, "Nothing." Schiap, probably taken aback, replied to her, "Unfortunately, I cannot pay for 'nothing.'"[1] Bettina persisted and eventually Schiap gave way and never regretted it. Bettina, however, remembered it entirely differently. In a *Women's Wear Daily* interview in 1956 she remarked that she read memoirs because of her love of fiction and "there is nothing more fictitious than a memoir." She goes on to explain that Elsa had seen a George Hoyningen-Huene photograph of her from the 1920s in which she was wearing an early Schiaparelli ensemble. Bettina was very established in the highest of high society both in Paris and the United States and she literally "knew everyone" worth knowing. Schiap considered her a type of American royalty. She was associated with the best of all worlds: the aristocrats, the artists, and the writers, many of whom were inspired by her colorful and somewhat eccentric ways. Plus, Bettina looked superb in Schiaparelli clothes; she was an ideal Schiaparelli type. So, Schiap immediately asked to meet Bettina soon after seeing that first shot of her and hired her promptly thereafter.

Gifted with an incredible sense of élan and a fast, sharp tongue, she breezed through her work at Schiaparelli. One minute she would be amusing Madame Schiaparelli with rubber noses and penny arcade tricks to ease her out of a foul mood, and the next minute she'd be making color suggestions to famous customers. She was a provocative *attachée de presse* and a skilled diplomat like her famous husband, Gaston Bergery, France's ambassador to Moscow and to Ankara during the Second World War. Bettina would also ask her friends to mention Schiaparelli in their novels, articles, and poems, and she was the inspiration for a main character named Veronica Stevens in Dalí's novel *Hidden Faces*. Since Schiap was an anarchist in the fashion world and Bettina was the absolutely perfect example of Schiaparelli's ideal of beauty, it wasn't strange when this dynamic duo ended up in the works of such compatriots as Salvador Dalí, Nancy Mitford, Elizabeth de Gramont, Anaïs Nin and Aldous Huxley. Cole Porter even sang about them. Thanks to Bettina's enthusiasm, Schiap became even more famous. Dalí vividly described the House of Schiaparelli in his memoir, *The Secret Life of Salvador Dalí* (1941), and stated, "the soul and the biology of the Schiaparelli establishment was Bettina Bergery, one of the women of Paris most highly endowed with fantasy."[2] In *La Femme et la Robe* (1952), Elisabeth de Gramont called Bettina an "extraordinary person" and described her as "an elf who runs around to all the fashion salons and is welcomed everywhere and is treated with joy and celebrated."[3] Bettina always told me that she had one useful gift: the ability to persuade people to do her bidding.

I met my other Bettina, Bettina Graziani, at the Lalannes' home in the late 1970s. She was a socialite and former fashion model who was an early champion of my work and offered me enormous support throughout our decades long relationship. We enjoyed an extremely close friendship. Bettina Graziani, unlike Bettina Bergery, was a bourgeoise of the very highest kind.

Bettina, born Simone Micheline Bodin in Normandy, rose to fame through her modeling career, which began in 1944. She was on nearly every cover of *Elle* magazine for a decade, favored for her freckles and red, boyishly cut hair. She was fresh, with a provincial air about her. My other Bettina (Bergery) referred to her condescendingly. She'd say, "Oh, how is that lovely friend of yours, you know . . .

what's her name . . . that country girl?" which infuriated Bettina (Graziani) to no end. She was a couture model for the great post war designers, most notably Jacques Fath and Hubert de Givenchy. Even Chanel asked her to be a star model for her but she was soon fired because the press spoke more of Bettina making a "comeback" than the collection Chanel was showing. Bettina was also part of the Beatnik and Existentialist St. Germain des Prés crowd, friends with Juliette Gréco, Jacques Prévert, Albert Camus, Jean-Paul Sartre, Simone de Beauvoir, and Françoise Sagan. Somewhere within the first months of our very intense relationship, Bettina offered me a 1951 example of the famous fashion magazine *Album du Figaro* with her on the cover. This was no ordinary example of the magazine, because the Surrealist poet Jacques Prévert transformed nearly every page with his own original, very Surrealistic collages. The pages on which Bettina was featured in dresses by Dior and Schiaparelli were altered with (by using a second copy of the same issue and clipping apart other pages) photos of meat, vegetables, picture frames, floating heads, and diverse objects. He then made these images of Bettina into these crazy collages, some of which have the same image of her overlapping onto herself and interacting with the totally peculiar unrelated pictures. Knowing my passionate interest in Surrealism and fashion she thought this was a perfect birthday gift for me, and it was. Having known so little about Prévert at the time, and Bettina having been such good friends with him, her stories added considerable knowledge to my repertoire of classic French personages she felt were important I know about. I was an eager student and loved learning so much about this way of thinking in France after the war, a milieu Bettina was right in the middle of. Existentialism posits the idea that individuals create the meaning and essence of their lives, and Bettina cultivated those aspects in her luxurious life.

Bettina was a very beautiful young woman and had many conquests among the rich and famous men in her circle. But her true love was Prince Ali Salman Aga Khan. They met in 1955, around the time that she retired from modeling. I always loved the way she'd tell me, after downing several very chilled vodkas, that it was not a hard choice between Pablo Picasso and Aly Kahn when they both wanted her as a lover, because Aly was so much more charming and had great taste in choosing clothes for her. In a famous photo of her in Picasso's studio where she is dressed in a bright orange ensemble the old bull looks like he's going to explode out of his shorts. However, her relationship with Aly ended in tragedy. In 1960, the two were involved in an automobile accident on the way home from Deauville. Aly, who was driving, was killed instantly. Bettina and the other passenger, the chauffeur, survived with minor injuries. She was pregnant with his child at the time but, besieged with grief, she miscarried. When she told me the details of that tragedy, I felt her heartbreak almost viscerally. The accident happened the year I was born and I was struck with the realization that I am the same age that her son or daughter would have been.

Bettina lived the way I imagine an ambitious aristocrat under Louis XV lived at Versailles. As far as she was concerned, the world revolved around her and even the smallest detail had to be irreproachably flawless. Considering her simple Normandy country upbringing, she managed to reinvent herself rather amazingly and I loved that about her. Aly Kahn's aunt, Suzanne Magliano, who was one of the meanest, snobbiest, and nastiest bitches I ever met, decorated Bettina's apartment. It was a masterpiece filled with antiquities of the highest caliber. Wood paneling, pillaged by unscrupulous antique dealers in the 1950s from forgotten French castles, was re-installed in the living room salon. When Suzanne arranged a bibelot in Bettina's flat, like a seventeenth-century miniature, or an eighteenth-century silver incense burner, it stayed that way forever. She'd fly into hissing rages, spitting venom if Bettina so much as moved a trinket box from the left side of a small priceless antique table to the right side. Whenever Bettina had to have a shade custom-made for a new antique lamp or the lining of her curtains replaced, it was a big affair. It always started with an elusive "Je dois en parler à Suzanne," which would send Lala and me running as quickly as we could. However, having an apartment superbly decorated by that old crab was considered the height of old-fashioned chic. It was, for Bettina, the best you could have, so she didn't touch a thing until Suzanne died. Suzanne was a dragon to the very end. I think it was the slight displacement of a chair in Bettina's study or the hanging of one of my paintings in her smoking room that finally made the old girl pass to the other side. Or maybe what killed her was the Schiaparelli perfume bottle named "Sleeping," a crystal bottle in the shape of a candle that I gave to Bettina, who placed it without previous approval from Suzanne on a table among other expensive and refined bibelots. I really don't think it was the bottle that made her pass away. The old thing just had to go.

We went out every night, Bettina and I, possibly too much, as attested by Lala's mild annoyance. I was Bettina's escort for every relevant social event, all the formal balls, various art openings, haute couture fashion shows, cocktail parties, and amusing dinners in Paris. We never seemed to grow tired of each other. We dined at the Ritz with the Begum Aga Khan, who wore amazing jewels and loved photographing flowers and insects, or with Serge Goredefsky, the astronomer who had a great sense of humor. We'd often use the Restaurant Lipp to plan the following day's events. I recall one luncheon at Sao Schlumberger's sumptuous Parisian home, with a bevy of distinguished guests in attendance. Sao started describe a new diamond trinket she'd picked up at a Sotheby's sale or some such place. Prince Mubarak-El-Sabat, who is always so much fun and a classically camp person, happened to be wearing a diamond encrusted Chaumet watch, and started to talk about some bauble he'd just acquired. Sao retorted with another diamond description, and Mubarak, again, replied with a description of a bigger, more radiant, and more expensive stone. Before you could say caviar canapé, it turned into a full on sparring event over who possessed the biggest and best rocks. It was like a tennis match with diamond anecdotes. I turned to Lala and whispered, in a breath-y Marilyn voice "I just adore conversation, don't you?" and he nearly choked on his *tarte aux fraises*.

Bettina was still very beautiful when we met, but when she came to our house in a skintight lime green Azzedine Alaïa minidress and more makeup than a Knie clown, she was not at her best. I recall one dress by Loris Azzaro that looked like someone attempted to eat all the silver sequins from Lesage's atelier and then threw up on her. I was always honest when she looked too tarted up and refused to go out with her unless she changed her clothes or makeup. However, after nearly three decades of a hilarious and whirlwind friendship filled with endless adventures and a real love, I realized I had out-grown the relationship. Bettina had become too enamored of her own myth.

In 1972, more than twenty-two years after she retired, Françoise Sagan wrote an article about her for *Vogue* Paris called "L'Éminence Rousse." She was lauded as a fascinating fashion model with a great charisma, which caused Bettina to see herself as the eternal goddess of French fashion. Her ego became so enormous and heavy-handed that she started to bore me. Even as we drifted apart, I was eternally grateful to the universe to have hooked me up with such a wonderful friend, but also thankful that I was able to bow out of the relationship slowly and discreetly. Moving to Switzerland helped. Bettina contin-ued forward into the florid praise of all of the flatterers who paved the way for her later years. Bettina never stopped shaking things up and I believe she eventually reached some sort of self-satisfied nirvana for old fashion models, whatever that may be, without me at her side. In 2010 she was made Commandeur des Arts et des Lettres by our illustrious mutual friend and openly-gay man, Frédéric Mitterand, who was the French minister of culture and communication by then. Bettina was a marvelous model, a great person in many ways, and I always was the first to point out the great chic she contributed to French high fashion. We are all acting out an absurd, ridiculous play with our lives, no one is exempt from this fact. From a distance I was better able to observe, be amused and admiring of the genuine though often self-proclaimed fashion myth she continued to act out *par excellence* until she was reclaimed by the universe in death in 2015.

CHAPTER 15

SURREAL BIJOUX— MDVANII

I settled into my new life in Paris, emboldened by a new sense of confidence from my relationship with Lala. I started to work on my paintings, sculptures, and jewelry and clothing designs again with a thrilling fervor that topped all past feelings. I worked with my usual disregard for making both relatable and marketable products, since this was a very clear intention of mine. I found that I was pleased to continue my research process for this hybrid between my clothing and my paintings that I called artwork. Without even trying, my work became extremely famous in a short time and sought after by many. My creations were like ritualistic objects; each and every one meant something to me personally. I called them gris-gris and associated them with my belief in Wicca and Kabbalah. They could be carried on one's body, imbued with Wiccan magic spells for those who came into contact with them, even though they were disguised as necklaces and brooches, dresses and tunics. I also saw them as brightly colored Pop-Art versions of Wicca, Kabbalah, and Summum (a religious philosophy that began in 1975 that I followed very closely at the time). I made a bracelet for Lala that spelled his name out in very old rhinestones and Belle-Époque gilded and beveled crescent-shaped mirrors, which had a magic spell cast upon it for good luck and as a love talisman. When he wore it, I was amazed at how many people remarked on it and asked if I could make another. I didn't know whether to be flattered or a bit vexed, as I was concerned when too many people seemed to want something. However, I came to understand and accept it as the compliment that it was and not a sign that my work was appealing to the masses, which I equated with vulgar commercialism. Looking back, I think my feelings seemed often extreme and very black and white but I was aware of this and did not think it could be as easy as that. I did not want to be blind to so many things in the grey areas of life. I earnestly tried to see all these in-between grey areas of my feelings. It was a fascinating daily discovery to think about, the subtle aspects of all things one thought and did. I asked Lala to help me and together I was able to understand so much more about life on earth.

At that time, I felt to the very essence of my being that people had forgotten how to use gris-gris, talismans, and amulets that protect the wearer from evil and encouraged one to aspire to the heights of light and love. I complained to Lala that the era was becoming dulled by that false idea of modernism. Hadn't anyone been told that it died decades ago? Put more bluntly, costume jewelry was in a rut and what was being made seemed to be getting more and more conventional, small, and cheaply gold-electroplated. So, I made more of my manifestoes and tried to make the concept of Wiccan ornament and talismans known and better understood. This was wonderful for me because with the appreciation of people who came into contact with my stuff, it felt as if the world was really changing a teeny bit, step by step, for the better. In our large old-fashioned kitchen, we were experimenting with a brand new way to make the jewelry, too, a method much more related to ornament, objects, and gris-gris. At first we used plaster, which we tried to bake in our Swiss Le Rêve oven. It did not work very well for our intended result, but the burnt plaster brought about some pretty interesting textures. Baking the jewels in an oven turned into a sort of myth about the jewels that the press and our admirers found charming. We used strass and rhinestones, wood, *objets trouvés*, glass, metal, semi-precious and precious stones to make these odd, one-of-a-kind indescribable items that fluctuated between jewels, objects, statues, and ornaments. It was truly thrilling to make them with Lala.

A plethora of influences informed the work. There were a lot of 1960s Pop culture references, like the Funny Face drink characters Goofy Grape and Choo-Choo Cherry, Troll dolls, Gumby and Pokey's entire universe, Dr. Seuss and his world. Divinely cute Hasbro toys like "Peteena" (a Bettina Graziani-inspired poodle fashion doll who wore a YSL Mondrian dress) and My Little Pony figurines. The hilarious camp-itude of the Flintstone House, a cardboard dollhouse in the style of the beloved Hanna-Barbera cartoon show, and the Rube Goldberg style Mouse Trap game took form in our creations in strange new ways. The colorful and ironic flotsam and jetsam from various places, from all eras and epochs, from anywhere to everywhere inspired us equally. When Alec Head, the horse breeder of world-acclaim, gave a lunch in my honor at his famous stables in Normandy, my work took on quirky equestrienne references unlike anything Hermès could have dreamed up. All of these beautiful things were pondered upon and joked about and then rolled into one big concoction of tangible thoughts, as they were fashioned in a loving and lingering way into all sorts of things. Chic themes also came into play and were warped into an acid trip of mutational imagery. Nothing was too large, too baroque, or too weird for us to create. It seemed that after the initial shock wore off, people seemed to understand the work. Whatever the truth may have been, it made me happy. I think this was perhaps the last period when such crazy

stuff was made by artists and artisans all over the world and appreciated. Today, dark thoughts prevail in all domains, but our work then
(and still does now) sent out a very big, positive vibe because it was
made with happiness and love.

Lala and I opened an atelier, offices, and showroom called Billy-
Boy* Surreal Bijoux on the rue de la Paix, number six, literally next
door to where Schiap had started her own Paris career at number four.
Our new address was an amazing location considering that the street
hosts all the greatest names in *haute joaillerie*: Cartier, Boucheron,
Mellerio dits Meller, Van Cleef et Arpels. It was pretty nervy for a
costume jewelry designer to dare settle down in this exclusive area.
The workrooms were on the second floor and one had to walk up an
old Parisian-style staircase in a glass tower to get there. It was nothing fancy, just four rooms, but getting it was incredible luck and it
looked to me one more time like a cosmic wink from Schiaparelli.
We decorated it with black and white linoleum tiles, wobbly Art
Deco tables and chairs; antique bits and bobs; and early Ikea furniture, because their black desks were reminiscent of the versions that
Schiap's staff had used.

The original team at Surreal Bijoux was comprised of only four
people aside from Lala and me: my assistant Jane (who wore the jewelry exceptionally well and followed me everywhere); Bill Anderson,
a tall American friend of Lala, who also happened to be a talented
painter and the nicest person in the world; Chantal, whose father was
a Communist, was Lala's assistant and multi-tasking secretary; and a
girl named Nathalie who was a clone of Madonna in her *Desperately
Seeking Susan* period and who did not know how to do anything at all.
I have no clue why Lala hired her, but she was glamorous and quite
humorous, always dropping funny comments about everything with
her typical Parisian slang, using all the expressions of the time like
ça craint (it sucks). Lala eventually had to fire Nathalie after a couple
of months because all she did was make long distance calls to her

boyfriend in Los Angeles and we suspected her of taking drugs in the restroom, which she denied vehemently. One day, when I came back from a trip to America or London, she wasn't there anymore. Soon after, Lala hired three new employees who came from the school of jewelry in Paris. In spite of the skills and techniques they had acquired in their training, they all had to adapt it to make the Surreal Bijoux, which was not something that could be taught in schools. Everything was hand-made, even the metal pieces from prototypes made by Lala. Lala also found Youssef, who was from Kabile and worked for us in the atelier and also at home to take care of the house. He worked for us for many, many years. I had many assistants, and they were all vivacious. One rather playful and slightly naughty one was named Steve, an American boy who was very tall with very long blond hair. He did my correspondence and did many jobs including secretary and when necessary answered the phone, pretending to be me! There were many marvelous and quite adorable, always fashionable look-ing French boys, each one had a special something, a quality. Jacky was a brunette boy who worked very hard and was very faithful to the crew. He was always calm and very sweet, Jean Marc was sim-ply amazing and very knowledgeable about Pop and French art cul-ture. He was the essence of camp and part of the House of Aviance (of the Ballroom scene) in New York. He worked for us for a long time and his boyfriend, a sweet boy with thick glasses, helped when I did shows and exhibitions. They traveled with me often. There was Edward Hemingway, grandson of the author and an aspiring artist at the time who brought a good feeling to our team. Ricky was like a walking dictionary of English and film culture. He loved lunchtime because he was an epicurean in his way. In Normandy he loved the flans and the various cheese dishes Lala would make for lunch. He was my secretary and friend. There were many others over the years and I remained friends with nearly all of these people even after I left France. They all brought something really marvelous to our team.

The Surreal Bijoux used glass beads and hand-made glass elements. Some were made in *pâte de verre*, then practically a lost craft, which involved firing a layer of glass to the surface of a mold. The 1980s were the very last decade in which artisans were actually still doing this in France. The pâte de verre beads we used were made one at a time by an elderly woman in the Marais. They were very expensive, but I did not care because they were so beautiful: little blobs of opaque white glass with eyes and a smile on one side, and a pout on the other, which I called Happy Germs From Space. For the Ali Baba collection, I designed asymmetric shapes in gilt or silvered metal with molded glass stones inserted into them. It seemed too much even for the flashy 1980s. Andy Warhol regularly wore pieces from the first metal collection, named Joan of Arc, and he even immortalized some of them. We had special metal molds created, intending to use them for regular production, but it turned out to be a limited run as was the case for many of our designs. Almost no one else in the profession of making haute couture jewels could claim they used the traditional methods and materials that we did at the time. Even our boxes were made by the same box makers for Dior, Chanel, and Balenciaga. We worked with the most famous, the most Old Skool artisans still existing in Paris such as Maison Gripoix (I had known the family, notably the reigning queen of haute couture jewels, Mme Gripoix, since the mid-1970s), Maison Janvier, Mr. Desrues of Maison Desrues, Maison Lukes, Maison Michel for all types of trim and hat related pieces, Swarovski for the amazing stones (this was long before their name became more known, at this time only those in the métier knew of them), and even Mr. Lemarié of Maison Lemarié, who did the sumptuous feathers for us, and many, many others. I am so glad I had this chance as by the 1990s many of them slowly closed apart from those bought by Chanel Enterprises, like Desrues and Gripoix, who have become sort of commercialized. Paris no longer is the home of such Old Skool artisans. They are nearly all gone, though a few, much

reduced, survived. Thanks to such classic French haute couture artisans the Surreal Bijoux were very influential and vastly copied by
the most popular and commercial manufacturers of fashion jewelry
and even by quite a few haute couture houses. Nearly every aspect
of the jewels influenced the costume jewelry industry: the shapes,
the themes, the various styles, the use of resin (which had not been
used in ages), the Surrealistic references, and many other aspects of
it became big business for those who did commercial business of any
sort in the field of fashion.

In many ways the Surreal Bijoux were conversation pieces with
Schiaparelli. Some were directly inspired by her jewelry, like the
Gambettes necklace made of knit cotton. This was is a direct homage to her 1941 Ex-Voto necklace made of rough wool knit with
legs, which I have in my collection. Though my motifs, shapes, and
themes may have been different, the texture and sensual feel to them
was identical. They expressed lusciousness always with a touch of
humor; not gimmicks but statements of chic. You could not call these
pieces shallow. The jewelry was in line with the overall Surreal trend
I seemed to have inspired in 1980s accessories, from Karl Lagerfeld's
chair hat to Pierre Cardin's Magritte-inspired foot shoes (he and
Bettina offered me the first pair). It seemed as if I'd reinterpreted
Schiaparelli's artistic sensibility and put it back on the fashion map.
In creating art and fashion myself, I began to understand what might
have motivated her to create her startling work.

The official launch was held in the extraordinary galleries of
Jansen, the legendary interior decoration firm. No less than 1,000
pieces of Surreal Bijoux were displayed, announcing a new era in
costume jewelry: cartoonish and humorous, pop and new baroque,
luxurious and hand-made. We put on a show in the windows with
two go-go dancers. One was a beautiful girl from Africa with a massive hair-do, platform boots, and a Huckleberry Hound blue sequin
micro mini dress from my collection who did the Frug on an acid

green cube. The other was Mathieu Geoffroy Dechaume, the sexy
drummer in Lala's band, Lala et les Emotions, in mellow-yellow
polyester Jacques Esterel bell-bottom overalls, my authentic vinyl
Courrèges men's boots, and a Barbarella blond wig Alexandre de
Paris had personally made for me, who did his thing on his own
cube. We had done a film in the *Vogue* studios, which was shown at
the event and was essentially Mister Modern cut-up art work collage
of Mathieu dancing in a the same outfit and a ton of pearls and my
jewelry interspersed with 1960s cartoons like *Mr. Magoo* and *Magilla
Gorilla*, old monster movies, and old TV commercials. I had hand-
painted the film with brightly colored markers to give it that Velvet
Underground and Beat Generation feeling. This display caused three
minor auto crashes outside the windows of Jansen's rue Royale establishment. Inside, there were enormous polaroids of jewels strewn
about in front of a huge portrait of me wearing another version of the
custom-made blonde 1960s-style Alexandre de Paris wig, an ersatz
cowboy hat I'd made at Surreal Couture, a green glove on one hand
and an orange on the other, also from Surreal Couture, and dark Ray-
Ban glasses while making a 1960s-style gesture in front of my face. It
was plastered with my new motto and signature: "Get Groovy!" The
hand-made resin pieces casually arranged in the vitrines revealed
flower power necklaces, baroque crosses, hieroglyphic-like sym-
bols, goons, and monsters with rhinestone teeth. I thought it looked
like jewelry created by Daisy Duck. Surrealistically-inspired shapes
and motifs, eyes, lips, noses, the Hand of Fatima, and 1940-ish jewels were among the central themes. I came to the exhibition in a
chauffeured 1950 Mercedes in violet tights, yellow hot pants, and an
electric blue Biba fake fur jacket from the 1960s. I simply reeked of
Shocking perfume. My hair was dyed green by Mr. Alexandre and I
wore real tiger lilies in my hair and black Ray-Bans. The Ray-Bans
were something I wore, I think, throughout the entire 1980s, not for
the cool-dom of them, but for the darkness my eyes needed. Alice

Springs wrote in her book of photos that she managed to get them off me for one shot, as if it were a big deal. The exhibition was called *Get Groovy* and an obscure poem I had written was the invitation:

So, you're wondering . . .'What is it this time?' Well, let me tell you. Paris, très chaud . . . Jean Patou on an acid trip. Platform shoes and dropped-waist flapper dresses. Wigs, wigs, wigs by Alexandre de Paris. Leon Bakst has a deep rap session with Janis Joplin and he really digs it. DO YOU KNOW WHAT I MEAN? It's 1925 and 1975 in 1985. Irony and Time warp. You've heard of Balmain's "Jolie Madame," well this is "Jolie Time warp." Thé dansant. Motown. James Brown, high impact plastic Italian Deco. I am not Modesty Blaise, nor am I Gabrielle Chanel. I am not Diaghilev, or Nijinsky, or Rod Stewart, or Polnareff. Biba Nova is the coolest, most grooved-out place. Color and sketchy, dreamy, filmy, moving jewels to highlight an electric Kool-Aid acid test on Man-in-the-Moon Marigolds. Rainbows and butterflies, Daisies and Dragons, Birds and Fish and Peru and Goonheads? Fred Flintstone falls head over heels in love with Bonchacrova and finds her radish earrings charming and Yabba Dabba Dooberry. Nancy Mitford marries Josie and the Pussycats in Outer Space and they open a platform boot salon and wig emporium at the Algonquin Club: GO FOR IT. GET GROOVY!

At the Jansen venue, the avant-garde jewels looked perfectly at home and the show was a tremendous success.

Buyers, collectors, friends, and the curious came directly to our workrooms. Lauren Bacall would drop in, choose ten pieces, and then ask, in her inimitable voice: "So, what's the damage?" She always paid right away, too. When Elizabeth Taylor came we shared loads of laughs, although we could not escape the feeling that it was like hosting royalty. Prince Mubarak El Sabat brought a truckload of his entourage and literally bought every single piece in the place. I made very wacky eyeglasses for Ray Charles and his French lady friend, Arlette Kotchounian. He sung "Happy Birthday" to Lala over the telephone once. Fred Hughes would come with Andy Warhol, who would suggest pieces to Bianca Jagger, Paloma Picasso, and a ton of other celebrities. It was a real party when everyone was trying on jewelry and drinking cocktails right in the middle of the workday. Princess Gloria Thurn und Taxis would come dressed to the nines, wearing fantastic *haute joaillerie* (and sometimes famous pieces worn by ancient royalty). We'd have a hell of a good time, but it was always a toss up if she'd pay her bill or not. But in the end I did not care. The fun we had was worth much more to Lala and me than money.

Both Bettinas helped promote my jewelry, but I owe my success in New York to Bettina Graziani. One day, decked out in my jewels, she went to lunch with Geraldine Stutz, president of Henri Bendel. She was thrilled with Bettina's accessories and ordered 100 pieces for her store. That first collection sold out in one day. The pieces were made from plaster, hand-painted in delicate shades of turquoise, fuchsia, heliotrope, and saffron, with faceted crystal stones and cabochons (in equally luscious colors), silver and gilt chain and foil, all so fragile it seemed as if they would be smashed to smithereens if you just looked at them incorrectly. Lala and I also created jewelry for different couturiers and designers such as Emanuel Ungaro, Thierry Mugler, Bernard Perris, Hanae Mori, Francesco Smalto, Charles Jourdan, and many others. Surreal Bijoux was sold in the most fashionable shops in France, the United States, Japan, England, Italy, Germany, and Scandinavia. It was more expensive than most costume jewelry of the times. It was also sold throughout South America and Russia as well. In 1988 the *Observer* fashion editor voted me Man of the Year. In the accompanying article, Sarajane Hoare called my jewelry "uninhibited and irresistibly funny" and "larger than life, naive, eccentric, rebellious."[1] I was bowled over and honored, partly because I had briefly thought I had the honor of both man *and* woman of the year due to the article's wording. Earning this praise placed me in the company of Lady Diana Cooper, one of the great British women of style and grace, who was similarly honored. She was a *Vogue* contributor and was dressed by Schiaparelli. My jewelry was further heralded in the *New York Times* by John Duka, who was the make-or-break fashion journalist of the time. Although he was always supportive of my work, I was genuinely amazed at his flattering piece on the jewelry, which he called very innovative. The last time he'd seen me I had headed off into the sunrise in the direction of Paris with my Schiaparelli memorabilia. I was really surprised to read in the *New York Times* from December 18, 1984 that he called my collection "a free-form chic." I felt I owed my success to the intense inspiration and spiritual guidance of Schiap and I was always rather surprised by positive reactions to my work. It was if Schiaparelli had imbued them with some of her wit, frivolity, and gaiety.

Not long after this, Lala and I were invited to Moscow during the first days of Perestroika by my friend Fiona Cartledge's parents; her father was the British ambassador in Moscow. I was asked to develop an exhibition and lecture about my work, the history of *avant-garde* and innovative costume jewelry, and most dear to me, a series about Schiaparelli. Nearly all the ambassadors' wives of the world attended these events and afterwards it (unintentionally) became a Surreal Bijoux Tupperware party. We had an amazing adventure, went to museums which we closed just for us to visit, and were driven around in Mrs. Thatcher's Rolls Royce (the only one existing in Russia at the time). I wore a Schiaparelli 1960s minidress on Red Square and most of the trip modeled myself on the Duchess of Windsor with an Alexandre de Paris hairdo imitating the hairstyle he created for her in the 1960s, which emulated the one she wore in a Beaton photo of her wearing Schiaparelli in the 1930s. I wore my 1930s Schiap linen safari ensemble, which was one of the few men's ensembles by Schiaparelli I owned at that time. We were introduced to Moscow's only "haute couturier," Zeitsev, who I gave a bottle of Shocking de Schiaparelli to. I even collected some of his dresses for my collection. This included some given to me by the delightful Lady Cartledge, one of the most colorful and delicious personalities I'd meet in England.

We also held a memorable, but rather absurd show at Barneys in New York. I was reluctant to create anything for that store because I thought it represented what I disliked about selling fashion. The only way I could bear to do it was to make something I really wanted to do, so I came up with a sex-related collection. I called it Safe Sex and it consisted of totems comprised of various genitalia in 1970s motifs: smiley faces, soda pop bottles, colorful nipples, and penis necklaces with drops of pearls dripping like sperm and strung on hemp cord. They were entirely hand-lacquered in a secret resin formula exclusive to Surreal Bijoux made from my blood mixed with Lala's, some of my sweat, and even a few tears in the genuine Chinese lacquer. I even used melted Caran d'Ache crayons and rose tree sap in the mixture. "Alien beings celebrate life and rescue the world" was a recurrent theme for this collection. The pieces were exhibited on soil, wax, grain, and incense. The funny thing was that the soil created condensation on the glass cases, so all the pieces looked as if they were trapped in some heavy English fog. This was an unintended, yet perfectly Surreal thing to have happen. I hadn't allowed anyone from Barneys to see the collection or the display until ten minutes before the opening. When they finally saw it, someone exclaimed that they would lose their job. At the last minute, Lala and I decided that we loved the collection too much to allow anything to be sold, which totally outraged the store's owners. We kept the pieces until just recently, and have sold only a few at auctions in Paris. Barbara Berger, a sensational collector and now friend, has a few of those pieces.

Andy Warhol at this time did an amazing new advertising campaign called "Absolut Warhol" for the Swedish Vodka company. The head of the company, Michel Roux, an affable and very enthusiastic man who loved the arts and wanted to associate with artists, initiated it. Thanks to Andy, Keith Haring, myself, Kenny Scharf and David Cameron followed in this campaign. Absolut BillyBoy* was born out of this at a lunch Paige Powell and Andy gave me at the Factory of that era. We were the first five artists to do this campaign, which is now legendary with hundreds of people being "Absolut So and So." My participation was a silk scarf with my cartoon drawings on it depicting a man falling head over heels in love with a lady after having an Absolut Vodka martini. The scarves were made identically to how a Hermès scarf was made. They were top quality and made entirely in France, something rare these days. The jewel was a stylized cocktail tray, which when placed on the "table" drawn on the scarf made a Dadaist kind of association. On the gilt metal tray was a bottle of Absolut and a cocktail glass. The bottle was gilded metal, too, enhanced by *pâte de verre* with the name Absolut on it. There was a diamond and a ruby rhinestone accent and a cartoonish arrow pointing from the lip of the bottle into the glass that was made entirely of gilded metal, and even had a cartoon-y olive and toothpick. A thousand of these were made and along with the scarves were given to the top thousand women in business and arts in New York. Mr. Roux ordered solid gold versions made with rock crystal, ruby, and diamond that were executed in the truest fine jewelry tradition, French *poinçon* and all. It was a huge success for us. We all ended up in Sweden and received a dubious "Absolut Vodka Award." The whole experience was rather Surrealistic. Mr. Roux also bought a great many pieces of my artwork, Mdvanii, and tons of costume jewelry when he came to Paris. All his executives who came with their wives to the showroom referred to me as "Monsieur Rose Schiaparelli."

At the time in Paris, if you were a fashion designer you knew that you were successful if the Sentier garment district copied your designs. This was the place where one could find commercially-manufactured bits and bobs, large-scale production offices for ready-to-wear, and the place where many of Schiap's artisans worked back in the day. The Sentier was well known for its capacity to rapidly produce anything with a potential sales success. There were numerous workshops there and nothing was made in China. The Surreal Bijoux designs that were copied there mercilessly, however, always looked just like what they were: watered-down, cheap, mass-produced parodies of the originals. Flattering though it may have been (as copying, according to the old bat Gabrielle Chanel, is the highest form of compliment), I was often grossed out.

Not everything was creative and fun all the time, though. Gone were the days when I sat around filling my idle time with sketches. I had set up a bona fide business; there really was no other way to do these things than to be organized. I took the new task seriously, and tried to do everything the right way, but it was a huge learning curve. I had conflicted feelings about making a business but now with a partner, no longer a single agent, I had to think of ways to be part of the world and connected. Earning a living like "normal" people seemed to lose some of its taboo because I saw it was an important aspect of being adult. There was of course, as in any business, always a lot of work, some often very tedious tasks and problems of all sorts to solve. My father's words came back to me often those early years of this new way of working and creating. The Surreal Bijoux were extremely successful in Japan, which meant more and more orders, all of them made and shipped from our ateliers. The desire in the press to cover our designs was quite impressive and the girls who worked at *Vogue*, *Elle*, and *Marie Claire* would come to the atelier without any advance warning to choose pieces for a shoot. Others would just call and say silly things like "Hi, we're doing a sea theme. We need blue jewels. We'll take whites also. Can you deliver this afternoon?" One of the most frustrating aspects of creating jewelry was that I found that I could not control how it would be shown all the time. There was a brief moment when the trend was to photograph models in movement so you could not see the dress or the outfit. The jewels were a blurry streak of color at best or simply invisible under hairdos and hats. Sometimes the jewels would be given back just tossed in a shopping bag, the original silk paper we wrapped them in carelessly discarded. This infuriated Lala to no end.

Aside from the Surreal Bijoux activities, I had also reached a sort of turning point in my work. In 1988 my Barbie book was a best seller and had been published in many languages. The BillyBoy* Nouveau Théâtre de la Mode and Barbie Retrospective had toured France and the USA to great success and the most amazing international press (and some minor incidents such as a crazy Barbie collector arsonist setting a truck filled with a crate of my vintage 1970s dolls on fire). I had designed two very successful new styles of Barbie doll, which, for the first time in the doll's history, had the name of the designer on their boxes. Andy Warhol created a portrait of me as a version of the Pop culture doll. However, the charm and excitement of Barbie was wearing off for me. Though I had a worldwide success with all things related to my doll obsessions, I wanted to create something new, my *own* fashion doll, something that encapsulated my own vision of the world and all the things I loved about it. I envisioned a totally new and somewhat daring (perhaps even risky) concept which would allow me to do anything that I wanted, far from the endless restrictions linked to children's toys. I wanted a totally luxurious and artistic fashion doll exclusively made for adults.

With the complete support of Lala, I put Surreal Bijoux on standby, much to the annoyance of our Japanese and European representatives. I passionately dove into the new project. I had a vision in my head that had come to me in a dream. She was based on my mother's youthful good looks, but with the mondaine personality of both Bettinas. She was dressed in haute couture, a true Parisienne. We named her Mdvanii (pronounced Mid-vah-nee) after the 1920s Russian "princess" Roussia Mdivani, best friend of Bettina Bergery. The original Mdivani wore Schiap and was muse to the painter Jose Maria Sert, whom she stole away from his famous wife, Misia. She drowned in the Rhine, which was as tragic as it was glamorous. Mdvanii came to me in a dream (yes, the actual asleep-in-bed kind) in early 1987. I think her inspiration came from some far away place out in the Laniakea Supercluster, the Milky Way, or the Perseus-Pisces Supercluster that sent some profoundly deep cosmic messages. I just *had* to do this doll. It was stronger than I. I was so fully drawn to this concept and her creation that I had no choice really but to do her, despite the terribly difficult and costly aspects of the production.

She was launched in 1989, on the anniversary of the French revolution, at Liberty in London. She was ten and a half inches tall, made out of resin with a powder pink Caron skin tone. Lala and I precisely drew her body. I wanted a classic 1950s fashion doll scaled to proper human proportions with a Russian physiognomy like my adopted mother's. She was to have a somewhat stylized form and face, not too realistic. Though she wore fashion, little gowns and suits, I wanted her always to be stylized and not too realistic looking. I did not want fussy little clothes imitating too realistically real scale clothes. I felt that would take away from her charm as an "object of contemplation" as we called her at that time.

René Gruau drew her portrait and we used his artwork for all the Mdvanii packaging. Even her Alexandre de Paris wigs were illustrated on the box with the famous Cocteau drawing personally made in the 1960s for Mr. Alexandre, a close friend to the famous artist back then. I had high standards regarding her wardrobe and it took endless trials to arrive at a quality I was satisfied with. The adventure of miniaturization was a true challenge, even for the French workers and artisans, who all said that it was much too small, but finally, the dream came true. Perfectly fitted jackets, fully lined clothes (including the sleeves and the pants), and even seamed stockings, with woven labels just like all haute couture clothes, each hand-numbered. Unlike the radiantly smiling Barbie, she joined the leagues of drop dead chic women who seemed utterly aloof, introspective and vaguely troubled by *ennui*. She did not smile. I finally had achieved the Anti-Bourgeoise, Yin-Yang self-portrait I always wanted.

Presented as an intelligent and cultured European woman with a mysterious Russian ancestry, Mdvanii was anatomically correct, and implicitly bisexual. She had a lover, not a boyfriend, and several at that. Her favorite authors were Marcel Proust and Françoise Sagan. I wrote her first catalogue with a humorous tone evocative of 1950s and 1960s *Vogue* reviews of French fashion shows by Diana Vreeland. The catalogue had illustrations by the American portraitist Clyde Smith, known to be the first illustrator of the 1960s Barbie books. Clyde came to France several times and Bettina Graziani modeled her famous poses for him, which gave Mdvanii her unique fashion spirit. Bettina Bergery gave Mdvanii her *esprit* and blessing. Many of the things Mdvanii said were quotes from conversations she had with Lala and I. It was all so thrilling and fun.

Mdvanii took everyone by surprise. She was so far away from everything that existed back then. People in art did not understand her. Companies wanted a commercially produced version. The average doll collector found her horribly expensive, even though she was not *that* expensive at $500 to $3,000. But very soon, many people in the doll world and art world caught on. At first the art crowd was smaller, but it grew rapidly and today it is these collectors who outnumber the doll collectors. Nonetheless her audience grew fast, considering that she was a hand-made doll with a very limited run. Sometimes the wait for a doll was not just weeks but months. And yet nobody ever complained, such was the excitement of it all.

We opened a Schiaparelli-inspired gallery called Mdvanii Boutique on rue de Cherche-Midi, a street filled with high-end anti-quaries, art galleries, the House of Paco Rabanne, and a very famous bakery. On the door was a shocking pink BillyBoy* door pull (in the form of my fetish Goon motif, which was a representation of me as a soul floating in non-linear time and space) and on the window was stenciled "Luxe, Poupées et Volupté," a paraphrasing of the famous Charles Baudelaire poem *Les Fleurs du mal* in the verse from Invitation au voyage. The shop was comprised of the front gallery and an office with a workshop in the back. The gallery was entirely shocking pink and made to look like a circus tent with shocking pink fabric (old stock from the House of Schiaparelli I'd been given a decade before) draped over the walls and ceiling, an homage, of course, to Schiaparelli's circus collection of the 1930s. A garland of shocking pink and violet silk flowers hung all around the room. The floor was carpeted in vivid shocking pink wool. There was a suite of lovely Atelier Martine furniture and custom pieces inspired by the real ones and lacquered shocking pink. Every day I sprayed the air with a Schiaparelli perfume, not only her famous Shocking, but also Sleeping, S, Flippant, Zut, and even the rare Si and Snuff scents from the 1950s and 1960s. I played a recording of the Henri Sauget song "Si" sung by Juliet Gréco playing on repeat until one of the workers begged for it to be stopped. I told him that I was trying to brainwash everyone in the studio with this endless repeated "Si" and he did not doubt me for a moment.

One of the very first Mdvanii limited editions was named *Homage à Schiaparelli.* Presented in a deluxe gift set box, she wore a black suit with embroidered lips as pockets, a shoe hat and, what else, a miniature trompe-l'œil bow sweater! In this limited edition of twenty-five she came with a miniature reproduction of Man Ray's famous painting of a pair of big lips in a mysterious clouded sky called *A l'heure de l'Observatoire, les Amoureux* hand-painted by Lala.

Over the years, many fashion details and references to Schiaparelli were adapted to Mdvanii's scale. One, Mademoiselle Mdvanii (a larger version of the doll) called *Le Bœuf sur le Toit* was a reproduction of Schiaparelli's famous suit with Dalí-inspired lamb chop embroidery and matching lamb cutlet hat. Mademoiselle Mdvanii *Never Too Thin or Too Rich* is a reproduction of the Schiap skeleton dress. *Le Fétiche de l'Attente* is another Dalí and Schiaparelli collaboration: the lip suit with shoe hat. There is even one Mademoiselle Mdvanii named *Shocking à Rebours* whose sheath dress is made from a patchwork of Schiaparelli fabrics—lingerie bags from the 1930s—that I recycled.

In September 1992, *L'Officiel* magazine ran a sixteen-page article and a fantasy cover of the magazine with Mdvanii on it titled "L'incroyable BillyBoy*." It featured my fashion collection, the Surreal Bijoux and our Mdvanii doll dressed for the occasion in haute couture. She was presented as the "Mascot of French Haute Couture" and posed in miniature interiors that I designed with antique doll furniture and a few custom-made Chippendale reproductions made by experts from England. Precious jewels from Chaumet to Harry Winston were included. The article included a picture of Bettina Graziani dressed by Adeline André in a Surreal Bijoux creation with astrological stars and small smiling faces, in a sly reference to Schiap. We made a limited edition Mdvanii doll exclusively for the magazine. Bettina was quoted saying:

> When I met BillyBoy* he interested me right away. He is not like everyone else. First, physically, he is a strange character. He was dressed in the maddest way. Some zebra long johns. While some look at him with defiance, BillyBoy* totally endorses his eccentricity. He is a genuine creator in advance on everything. He was the first to invent his style of baroque costume jewelry. His creative originality is backed by an

amazing knowledge and a superb sense of humor. Billy had a baroque intelligence but a keen eye to find what's good for him. His eyes are like radars. He is a great worker. Even if he has created for himself a universe in which one steps into like a theater, he never acts by random chance. His obsessive passions die out quickly because he devours them like a carnivore. Of course, he can be unbearable, capricious, but he is never banal. Billy is not the kind of mind to settle down in life and to carry along masses of memories behind him. This is in that that he is fascinating. He likes change and has the courage to say it.[2]

It was a stunning article that exaggerated my talents, but this was how Paris functioned at the time. There was no Internet and the only thing available was the old-fashioned press. My friend Edmund White, the man who invented the term "gay author," wrote a wonderful text for an exhibition of my photos of Mdvanii that was shown for three years throughout France in the FNAC photo galleries. Norman Mailer's wife, Norris Church, had an extensive collection of Mdvanii at that time.

Mdvanii and the fourteen characters in her world had a lasting impact on commercial dolls of the time. They all seem to have turned into *parisiennes* with Paris-inspired clothes, names, and small gloves, turbans, stockings with seams, and little cocktail handbags, which were sadly lacking back when I started Mdvanii. They were actually nonexistent back then. Most of these dolls caught on to these leitmotivs sometimes as much as twenty-eight years after Mdvanii came on to the scene. She also inspired a strange new genre of young gay men creating their own artisanal dolls. Some have their own charm but nothing is as *KAPOW!!* as Mdvanii. There has yet to be a true rival made, because their creators seem unable to grasp the thing that makes Mdvanii "Mdvanii." I occasionally ask Lala when someone will create a truly original fashion doll and he always replies the same way: "It will be a long, long wait."

For various reasons, I started to lose interest in Paris. Less than a year later, in 1993, Lala and I left Paris for good, leaving the fashion world behind us, or so we thought. We arrived in Trouville on the Normandy coast with a wonderful Dalmatian dog named Vico, who literally fell into our laps the day we left Paris. A new life was starting by the sea. I got to see Françoise Sagan on a more regular basis and saw Marguerite Duras nearly every day as she was my neighbor. The first house we rented was practically on the beach. For Lala, it was heaven. Surreal Bijoux was on hiatus, a relief for both of us. Though we would never stop creating jewelry for private clients, we would act as artists and not as a business, much to my delight. A page had been turned and there were absolutely no regrets. The glorious, historic Normandy seashore washed away any last doubts. Lala and I had the amazing luck to know a type of Paris that has since disappeared. It was the very last moments of the old rules of manners, chic, and socializing. Schiaparelli was an electrifying subject because everyone knew exactly who she was and what she did. They had anecdotes about her. She may be more known by name now, but she has been reduced to a few iconic images and cliché ideas. The people we knew back then were a mixed bag, from the super famous to the unknown, yet all had one thing in common: they were interesting, if not fascinating. I am not at all nostalgic for those years, I am thrilled to have lived them, but am equally as thrilled everything has moved on and forward. I would not want to try to re-create those heady moments now. Lord, no! As the Countess DeLave says in *The Women*, "it was fun while it all hung together."

CHAPTER 16

. . . AND MANY MORE

never liked being called a designer even though I created art in the form of fashion and jewelry. I hated to call myself anything, even an artist, because it seemed both too restrictive and too evocative a word. I admired the people I loved who happened to be designers or artists, but could I do it? At the same time, I couldn't help but think of the many designers that I believe were truly artists who are now neglected by history. Like Paul Poiret, Marimekko of Finland, the unsung Jane Regny (who created fabulous youthful travel clothes and sportswear in the 1920s and 1930s), or Daniel Gorin, who made delicious lawn party frocks in the late 1920s. For every Balenciaga or Chanel or Schiaparelli there are a thousand other talented haute couturiers to rediscover, document, and bring forward. As a result, one of my goals is to promote and research the creative careers of as many of those unsung heroes as possible.

One of the true creators of elegance was Madame Grès, who also designed under the name Alix Barton. She was already a legendary figure by the time I met her in the late 1970s. She continued to make extraordinary clothes into the 1980s, but hardly anyone seemed to buy or wear them. Her fashion house just never seemed to have enough money. Surreal Bijoux was across the street from her couture house on the rue de la Paix, so I saw her regularly in her stark and elegant atelier, at the local café, and often over lunch. She was a discreet and refined old lady who always wore a turban. I photographed one of her last fashion shows and her last official portrait with Mme Claude Pompidou. Mme Grès asked me to pop by to show her some of my photos of the fashion show. I entered the building and climbed the stairs to find the place deserted. I waited and waited but no one was to be seen. It was August and practically everything in Paris closes down for the month. I wandered around and even checked the other floors. Still nobody. Just when I had run out of floors to explore, I accidentally found the staircase to the attic. I said to myself, what the heck, and climbed the stairs only to find Mme Grès, clad only in her 1940s shrimp pink fitted girdle and a black silk turban, draping a minutely pleated strapless gown on a Stockman mannequin. Mortified, I muttered my apologies and backed away down the stairs, my face surely a vivid red. A few minutes later she came down, fully clothed. As if nothing had happened she said to me with a smile, "How hot it is today!" Sadly, Madame Grès died bankrupt and alone in a seedy suburban retirement home. There was quite a scandal, though, as her daughter led the world to believe that she was alive for another two years after her death. By forging her mother's signature on letters, she managed to dupe journalists, curators, and friends alike, for reasons we shall never know.

Haute couture was already a dying art form in the 1980s, and the days when designers could impose styles on the public was also headed toward oblivion. It was then that I understood that the rising emphasis on branding would be the final deathblow to the entire concept of custom-made fashion. Though haute couture still exists today, it has become almost invisible. Fashion's highest form has become so mythicized that it is no longer a living thing, but a great ghost hanging over the heads of the public, who are only interested in the various legends. I believe social media and the Internet have fueled this—with today's ability to say and show more, we learn and see less. A pet peeve of mine is the way people mistakenly call fashion "couture" when what they mean to say is "haute couture." The word "couture" means sewing or a seam in a garment. One cannot escape the lack of true knowledge today. This is why you see the same stock images of Schiaparelli's shoe hat and the lobster dress reproduced in books, with no mention about the rest of her work. Does anyone ever see the *prêt-à-porter* clothes from her Place Vendôme boutique in the 1960s? They're equally fascinating, but absolutely unknown. If you do find a piece, most likely online, it's often from some unknown dealer with an overhyped provenance and unaffordable prices. These items are sold to be worn in today's marketplace, which is almost sinful now in my eyes. In a way, I have become those people who once asked me if I felt remorse wearing the historic clothes I collected. It's only because as a mature man I see now that once worn and damaged these clothes will be gone forever. History will disappear. I ask myself, if the teenage BillyBoy* were magically transported into 2016, would his approach to fashion be possible? I doubt it. In fact, I am sure it would be completely impossible to build a collection of the caliber of mine today. Absolutely impossible. The halcyon days of finding Vionnets and Schiaparellis on the dirty blanket-covered ground at the Puces de Vanves are over.

And yet, the world abounds with novices and so-called collectors. Information has blurred into what Norman Mailer called "factoids" in his 1973 biography of Marilyn Monroe. All you need to study fashion history today is a computer. I think the number of people who are serious scholars striving for historical accuracy is, and has always been, extremely small. When I was beginning this path, I hauled myself to the New York Public Library or the

Beaubourg and Louvre print documentation departments to look things up in books and albums. I made appointments with curators in museums all over the world to see collections of all sorts. This took a huge amount of time. To find facts from first-hand sources, like rare books and original documents held in museum collections, took months of planning and work. Now, it's a click of a mouse. I also read endless vintage books on subjects that are foreign to the majority of people, collectors and dealers alike. Who remembers Bruyère and Augustabernard? What about Mme Agnès's über Art Deco life and chapeaux by Mme Suzy? Who can really explain what *bolduc* is or what a *midinette* is? It was my duty and calling to learn these things and it has taken all of my life so far to skim the surface of this knowledge. I am far from a complete and truly satisfied student of the subject, yet to be fulfilled with the great wisdom passed down to me from the Fashion Gods, Goddesses, and astute luminaries I have known. I still have a lot to learn. Really, quite a lot!

When the Internet emerged as a resource, paradoxically, I saw a whole new and wonderful way to collect. At first, it seemed like the space age wonders promised during the 1960s had come true, and I thought I would love it. However, the ability to communicate instantly with people both near and far away has not been a joyride at all. I am regularly staggered by the claims people make online, like selling American-made Schiaparelli hats from the 1960s as "1940s Surrealist masterpieces" or common novelty prints by anonymous artists of the 1950s attributed to Christian Bérard or Marcel Vertès offered for sale as an unlabeled Schiaparelli from the 1930s. I am often fascinated by the immense greed of people. For example, offering a 1960s Schiaparelli licensed parure (or better yet, "demi-parure," which means nothing in French) for four thousand dollars. Some sellers seem so greedy and so badly informed that I have an almost morbid fascination with the lengths to which they'll go to hype a piece. Today, with so many economic problems throughout the world, I have no idea who'd buy a licensed hat, or even a genuine haute cou-ture hat for thousands of dollars. I always say to my family, "If I don't buy it nobody will." I believe this is, though I say it mockingly, some-what true. These over-priced pieces stay perpetually unsold, floating in the ether as permanent fixtures, waiting for the sellers to get some sort of reality check. Despite these grievances, I have still shopped my guts out on the Internet and have made many wonderful acquisi-tions that I most likely would not have found prior to its invention. I have found museum-quality pieces in addition to many fascinating details about my favorite subjects and collections. For example; I only recently discovered that Raymond Loewy and Associates, the world-famous industrial designer of the Art Deco/Streamline/Modern era, partnered with Schiaparelli. They conceived and engineered a design for a sensationally modern plastic wig stand that came in a box with the classic Loewy layout and graphic design.

Regarding collecting in general, I can only offer this simple advice: Never make what you love into a real business. I could never become a real dealer or merchant of vintage haute couture. I'd have a much-reduced collection if I thought about money when in the delightful endorphin-filled state of buying a new piece. I have had my collection for over forty-two years, at times at great cost because storing, moving, and dealing with these objects is a very tedious and time-consuming endeavor. It is like having another child at times. But this is of no consequence at the end of the day because it has given me such pleasure and has been worth every cent I could afford. Our own son, Alec Jiri, sometimes asks me to do something with him and if I am busy he'll ask me if it's with his other brothers and sisters, meaning my collection. Collecting couture clothes is an elit-ist activity for the most part; if you really cannot afford to pay the prices that these items sell for, you should not really endeavor to collect them. My advice also has always to not buy things which you cannot easily afford or for speculative investment. This is singularly the best advice I think I can give any potential collector. Sure, you can attempt to compete with the big boys and try to have the ne plus ultra of a collection quickly—you will have insurmountable debt. Or you can get the great deals, sniff out the iconic pieces being sold by unknowing sellers, flea markets, rummage sales, and junk shops. Use your instinct to find unclaimed treasures yet to be "rediscovered" which is pretty much what happened in my case. Though it seems a very precarious way to collect—in terms of numbers—you still achieve the caliber of things you desire. But don't let the lust for beauty in your eyes and heart become greater than what you have in your wallet. Beauty is everywhere and there are fabulous things to collect at any price—and I don't necessarily mean Beany Babies, or vintage Camembert cheese labels. They may have charm, but distinguish weird and quirky from genuine beauty. Even "collectibles" are questionable. I wouldn't want to be the guy who spent a million dollars on Andy's kitsch cookie jars. Nor would I want to be the one who buys many thousand dollar vintage Barbie dolls at crazy prices only to discover their plunge in value. There are much better things to buy in this world, trust me. Remember, I bought them when they were essentially worthless. I have two unopened shipping boxes of the 1959 Number One Barbies in pink boxes. Barbie doll collectors will know what this means. I bought them for one hundred dollars on Mott Street in Lower Manhattan in 1976 on my way back to Europe for another educational tour. I always seemed to collect things long before they were fashionable and when they had no monetary value. I also set the trend for some of them to be collectible, it's true, but money is such a tedious thing to deal with, especially when you are obliged to do so with undistracted attention. I was too busy enjoying these objects to really deal with the value. When they become so valuable, I lost interest. It was just the nature of my cycle. I assume each person's cycle of collecting is different and unique to them. My collection was usually complete by the time their trend kicked in. I collected my objects of desire in advance, which made it extremely easy compared to doing it now. The best things may even come to you as gifts, as was my case. This is the true richness of a collection, the relationships. In my case, the gifts I was offered were always a surprise, but I think those generous friends knew I would pass them forward into history as was my wish. Also, my mortality will oblige me to do so, in any case. I couldn't bear to be eternally on earth, with more and more possessions. Sounds like hard work and a collection should have a firewall in terms of work. One should ideally work hard, very hard, but always keep in mind what really counts: the love and the relationships. It will never be the objects in and unto themselves. I have spoken essentially in this book of all the happy encounters I have had, but I have also seen the most merciless, unscrupulous, and ruthless things from unethical collectors. For me it was seeing the zombie-like horror of human nature. These kind of collectors seem to make collecting all so pointless. Materially, at least, it does have a finality. One day I hope I will be able to place each collection in the most appropriate place I can find for it. Also, regarding value, this is the reason why I never endeavored to collect Rembrandts or early Picassos or tried to compete with those who have world-class collections of those masters. It's out of my budget. Odds may suggest one can find at least one in a junk shop, that two would be unheard of and three . . . well, forget it. What kind of collection would that be? How much fun would one have to forfeit, stuck with one lousy inestimably valuable thing and that's all. And for what, exactly?

There has been an increase in the number of museum shows dedicated to the subject of fashion since I began collecting. It was so exciting to anticipate the content and visit these exhibitions. It was as if the world had finally woken up to the historical importance of haute couture. In the USA, at the Metropolitan Museum's Costume Institute, there were wonderful shows under Vreeland's guiding spirit called *The 10s, the 20s, the 30s: Inventive Clothes 1909-1939* (1973), *The*

Eighteenth-Century Woman (1981), and *Dance* (1986). During this era, the shows they put on at the Met were truly splendid and I was regularly thrilled at how these professionals staged the shows.

Today, however, I feel there is a lack of passion in many museum shows. When I saw *Alexander McQueen: Savage Beauty* in 2011 (via a guided Skype tour) at the Costume Institute I thought there was hope. It was a brilliant exhibition with stunning displays. The show made a great point about Lee, who was a friend of mine, and his unique vision of the world and perception of beauty, as dark as his vision may have been. The accompanying book was lavish and well written. Like an old dog that hears his master's whistle, my ears stood up and I really paid attention to the show. But times have changed drastically since Diana Vreeland and Yvonne Deslandres roamed the earth, two rare and brilliant dinosaurs that made sure history's narrative was maintained at the highest levels. Diana may have used a twentieth-century Chanel necklace on an eighteenth-century gown in an exhibition, but at least she knew what it was and why she had done it. She did it for the "pizzazz!"

I have to confess that contemporary museum shows about fashion sometimes make little sense to me. Often a good or even rarified subject is simply dumbed down in the hopes of creating a blockbuster that caters to popular culture and an audience that cares very little for accurate history. But the nature of haute couture is elitist and really for the most erudite audience, so understanding and presenting it, in my opinion, requires more than a certain basic knowledge of the past. In order to make any meaningful sense of the material one has to explain elitism and privilege and the huge differences between classes of the past. One has to explain that they really rarely mingled. If you assume the public does not have this knowledge, then you have to spell everything out clearly and completely in a didactic way to make it understood. There are enough misinterpreted factoids and misinformation in the world already, and once they're there, they stay forever, endlessly repeated as distorted truths. I would love to see more clean-cut historical facts in exhibitions, and I am sure there is a way to make it exciting. The show at Les Arts Décoratifs called *Déboutonner la Mode* (Unbuttoning Fashion) featuring my friend Loïc Allio's collection of important European (mostly French) buttons that were acquired by the museum in 2012 is a good example. The curators showed precise and absolutely perfect displays of buttons with concise histories. That's what museums are for: to altruistically educate the masses. I realize that regular blockbusters are needed to keep the coffers filled, but I cannot agree with this bizarre new method I see as a trend throughout the world concerning museum shows of fashion. It's very hit or miss. I think that museums have been put on this earth to preserve and present the truest version of history as possible, not dress it up like a circus elephant and parade it around and whip it to death. I don't believe that the primary goal of museum exhibitions should be to dazzle their audience.

And what of Schiap? How do I imagine someone of her inclination and inspiration would fare in the fashion world of today? I know that the last year of her life she received a great deal of publicity in the most prestigious newspapers and magazines around the world. She simply hated almost everything in fashion at that point. She claimed to have hated the way her granddaughter Marisa Berenson dressed, even though, as one of the most famous fashion models of that era, she wore the chicest things. Schiap expressed this in often highly dramatic terms and looking back on it today, she seems outrageously camp. It's silly to imagine what Schiap would say now, but I can't help but try. She certainly would have felt flattered and very pleased about the various exhibitions in her honor all over the world (though she probably would have felt they were long overdue). She surely would have loved all the new technology available to create materials. Maybe she'd have a blog. I am not sure she'd have liked the punk era, but perhaps she'd have tried her hand at blue jeans, which she was apparently very interested in at the end of her life. I suspect she'd have hated the "in your face" sexuality of clothing today. Marc Jacobs's white boxer shorts and a lace dress at the 2012 Met Gala would undoubtedly have disgusted her. Schiap loathed vulgarity as equally as she did the creation of bad fashion. The sloppiness seen in fashion now would surely have angered her. Just before she passed away she expressed, in no uncertain terms, her enormous dislike for the Raggedy Ann styles of the early 1970s. She loathed untidiness in all and any forms. It was quite funny that she already thought people dressed too sloppily for her taste in the 1930s! She thought that a man wearing tweed in public to a dinner was the height of inappropriateness, so you can imagine how she'd have felt about the styles of today, even though quite a bit of them stem from her original ideas. But this is all just a fantasy, and the imagined musings of an enamored *passionné*.

Although the world of fashion and collecting is so utterly different from when I started, I would not like to see the old ways of the world return. When I began this path, the idea of collecting fashion was practically unheard of, but it has since become a phenomenon for better or worse. Haute couture has evolved into popular culture in a new way that has changed the way clothes are perceived. I, too, have evolved. I am over my desire to be a 1920s flapper, a 1930s siren, or a boogie-woogie bugle boy. They are all inside my heart and soul now, along with my ever-feisty Anti-Bourgeoise woman. She lingers just as strongly, just as vividly, but I no longer need to wear all the outer trappings to make her feel alive and well. Love has cured me of the need to dazzle and bewitch with clothes, though I still, on the odd occasion, will pull out and wear that old satin Schiaparelli hat with the golden bug on it. It has become a dear old friend to me and "she" still makes me laugh quietly to myself. Mephistopheles, in Goethe's *Faust*, says "You suprasensual, sensual suitor, / A woman leads you by the nose," and in my case, it surely can be said to be true.

PART TWO

"The eternal feminine draws us onward."

—Goethe

"In order to be irreplaceable, one must always be different."

—Coco Chanel

CHAPTER 17

ELSA'S CHILDHOOD

The fact that Elsa Schiaparelli's 1954 autobiography, *Shocking Life*, was written in a witty third-person style tells us something about the woman herself. In it, the Italian-born designer relates the tragicomic story of her christening in Rome. The episode seems right out of a Luis Buñuel movie and begins with her family in the immense and intimidating St. Peter's. She describes her father, a man of almost fifty, as looking like a wise old scholar with his gray beard. Also present are her thirty-five-year-old mother; ten-year-old sister, Beatrice, a classic Roman beauty with long black braids; and Schiap's nurse, who wears colored skirts and plaited hair and who carries the baby Elsa in her arms. The group proceeds to the priest, who inquires about a name for the child. This is the moment that we learn that the much hoped for boy, who would have had an inspired name drawn from Schiap's father's studies of Middle Eastern texts, including the Koran and *The Thousand and One Nights*, has turned out to be an inconsequential girl, in whom they'd lost interest, and therefore they'd failed to consider a name for her. After a period of embarrassing silence it is the nurse who speaks first. In the vast echoing church, she offers her own name, Elsa. Throughout her life Elsa Schiaparelli would be met with a series of challenges and struggles, both personal and creative, yet she'd always overcome them in some form or another. One door closed as a window opened, as the saying goes. The first thing I probably learned through Schiaparelli was exactly this. One only goes forward—setbacks and disappointments are only momentary and with time, fall away from the emotions like scales of a snake. Nothing, even the bad things that may befall us, are carved in stone. Things change and always we go forward. Schiap thought her name was the least appropriate one for a quintessential Roman woman, as she thought of herself when she was a young lady. She duly noted that being christened Elsa was the beginning of something immense for which she was destined, but not to be gained with an easy win.

Schiaparelli came from an illustrious and distinguished family. Her mother's family, part Scottish in origin, were aristocrats from Naples descended from the Dukes of Tuscany. Her father, Celestino Schiaparelli, came from a lineage of well-to-do conservative Piedmontese. Schiap portrayed him as an extremely cultivated and amazingly modest man, a solitary and reserved person who in general did not like people and tried to avoid them as much as possible. He was a dean at the University of Rome and a researcher in Oriental languages, notably Persian, Sanskrit, and Arabian. He had a wonderful collection of coins and used to exchange them with King Emmanuel II of Italy, also a seasoned and passionate numismatist.

At thirty-four, Celestino had been appointed by the King to head the magnificent Lincei Library of Rome, now the Italian Academy of Science. The Library was housed at the Palazzo Corsini in the Trastevere, the most Roman of the city's districts as well as the oldest. In her book Schiap evokes the pungent yet pleasing scent of the magnolia trees, the ambiance of a well-to-do family of title, and the things which most usually would concern such a family: education, history, and family. Celestino Schiaparelli was given one of the palazzo's resplendent apartments to live in with his family. It was in this classic Renaissance-architecture building, which counted Erasmus, Michelangelo, and Queen Christina of Sweden (who lived there in self-imposed exile for thirty years after abdicating her throne) amongst its illustrious guests, that Elsa Luisa Maria Schiaparelli was born on September 10, 1890. According to Bettina Bergery, "Elsa grew up in a palazzo filled with incredible things, colors, textures, and the turn-of-the-century grandeur of an aristocratic household . . . Her childhood memories were invested into her fashion collections. The place itself was staggering. She'd be shown treasures of the Renaissance by her father, wonders such as books of mythology and priceless medieval manuscripts that her mother donated to the National Library in Rome after his death, much to Schiap's almost bitter disappointment."

Her father's family also included a famous astronomer, her uncle Giovanni Virginius Schiaparelli of the Brera Observatory in Milan, who discovered the association between comets and meteors. There is a rather imposing public monument, a sundial actually, with an elaborate, realistic full figure of him in Savigliano, Italy, where he was born. He was also the first to observe what he thought were "channels" (natural formations) on Mars which, due to poor translation, was written as "canals." This led people to believe there was actual life on the Red Planet. This error was discussed so much that a worldwide myth arose erroneously crediting him with having discovered life on Mars. He was very fond of Elsa and used to hold her up to his great telescope. She later said that he was quite sure that Mars was inhabited by humans who harvested their crops. Most likely, though, he said this to amuse the young Elsa, who was naturally led to flights of fantasy and romanticism. He informed her that she had the constellation of the Great Bear on her face, referring to beauty

marks that could be read as star signs. The adult Elsa retained a special attachment to that group of stars, and would use the design for
a brooch in onyx and diamonds that she wore as a good luck charm.
Star motifs, the zodiac, and constellations proved to be a constant
inspirational theme throughout her career and even in the decoration
of her interiors. You can see this marvelous brooch on her in a 1940s
photo of her and Salvador Dalí that shows just how prominently
it figured on her dress. It was quite huge. It was most likely that
this large brooch came from one of her early inspirations. She set a
precedent in haute couture costume jewelry (and the many licenses
for it) inventing large non-classical jewels made out-of-scale and in
non-noble materials like plaster and papier-maché. Her father's cous-
ins, Luigi and Ernesto Schiaparelli, were remarkable personalities as
well. Luigi was a historian and an expert in paleography who created
the Schiaparelli Foundation. Ernesto was a famous archeologist who
not only discovered the Valley of the Kings in Egypt, but was also the
only person ever allowed to remove an entire tomb and its contents
back to his country. He created the Museum of Egyptology of Turin,
and the Museum of Cairo is full of his finds.

Elsa loved to go up amongst the rafters of the house, where
her mother kept her wedding dress and her old clothing. Attics are
always magnetic playgrounds for children, and little Elsa was no
exception. She used to spend hours there on her own, trying everything on. She was enchanted, as any little girl would be, by of all the
dainty undergarments, the once-fashionable "tailleurs" made from
sturdy materials and conservative-style dresses of exquisite creation,
trimmed with yards and yards of hand-made laces and embroidery.
She was enamored with the delicate blouses with those rigid whale
bone stays in them, necklines trimmed with rare handmade laces
and an effusion of romantic embroidery. These were matched to
tiny-waisted, bustled long skirts in a wide range of vivid colors that
all intrigued and surprised her, because her mother had very sober

tastes. Her mother never attended, though she could have, the court functions her husband's social position garnered, simply because etiquette demanded a low-necked dress, something her conservative father would never have allowed. Little Elsa had a special fascination for the white and cream colored quilted padding, often made of homespun horsehair and a rigid sort of canvas that women, during her mother's youth, used to create the mode of the day, known (depending on the country one lived) as "faux culs" and "bustles," which emphasized the derrière. She'd dreamily hold one up to her bosom in order to emphasize her own young silhouette. Elsa thought this was a very charming fashion and she still thought this in the 1950s, when she wrote her memoirs. It is a little known fact that it was Elsa Schiaparelli who essentially invented the padded brassiere, the padded bodice, and the idea known commonly as "falsies." She had a fascination for human morphology and this was so famously reflected in many of her fashions, her most famous perfume bottle, Shocking, with its scandalous Belle Epoque form. Schiap remained true to her first tastes, and it's very much apparent when she reminisced much later in life.

Infancy behind her, she was still made to wear tartans with black velvet collars, and for walks, a large brown hat trimmed with a wide yellow bow, which made her feel like a caged animal to gawk at in a zoo. She compared herself to a monkey. At some point, her mother decided that she was old enough to receive some pocket money, and she was granted a modest monthly dress allowance of fifty lire. Though not that much at that time, it was a lot for a clever girl to work with if she had aspirations to be fashionable. It only took some ingenuity. One can imagine how young Elsa managed to use her flair and ingenious ideas to make the most of the small amount. She used a principle, later known in the industry as "separates," to combine simple, well-cut blouses trimmed with all sorts of decorative devices and embroidery matched with different kinds of basic skirts, which gave the impression that she had a lot of clothes.

As a young child and a teenager, Elsa hated all the various schools she was sent to. The authoritative and unintellectual teaching methods of these religious establishments were not adapted for her curious and creative mind. They were simply dreary places she equated to jail cells with severe discipline, places where asking questions was forbidden. She could not stand to learn things that she did not care about, so she revolted against a system that sought to curb her imagination. She was not interested in what she was taught, and, though she could learn quickly, she just as easily forgot her lessons. She had a peculiar dislike for mathematics and always found herself with the lowest test score in the class. This total incomprehension to grasp figures was to last, as Schiap admitted, all her life.

When she was thirteen, she had a revelation: she loved to write. It came as a shock, an overwhelming physical sensation that she felt from top to bottom. She started writing poetry. By then, her father had resigned from his library activities, and the Schiaparelli family had moved from the Palazzo Corsini to a much smaller apartment in a house on the Piazza Santa Maria Maggiore. It had no mysterious attic to dream away in, no garden blooming with heavy-smelling camellias, and no room to be alone. So she built herself a hideout with a chair and a table and placed a huge Japanese screen around them. It was an Age of Romance hideout! There she stayed, possessed, writing for hours upon hours, as if in a trance amongst endless reams of paper. The adult Elsa, though a successful designer and businesswoman, admitted that she had never since experienced such a feeling of freedom and complete pleasure. She often confided in her older cousin Attilo, her astronomer uncle's son, an art critic who owned a fine collection of paintings and who shared with her a great complicity. He read her poetry and took the book to a publisher called Quinterri in Milan. Without knowing the age of the author, the publisher soon agreed to publish it and was even more surprised when he discovered that the author was not even an adult. The book of passionate verses was called *Arethusa*, after the nymph who guarded a fountain of forgetfulness in Homer's day. The young Elsa dedicated the book with these words:

A chi amo
A chi mi ama
A chi mi fece soffrire[1]

Welcomed by the critics, this sensual bombshell of a collection from the precocious teenaged poet was excerpted in newspapers all over the country and even abroad, notably in German and English publications. Naturally, the whole thing scandalized Elsa's family, who felt it was all a terrible disgrace. Her father refused to read her poems and shipped her off to an ultra-severe convent in the German part of Switzerland, where she fell ill and eventually went on a hunger strike that seriously threatened her life. The daughter of the Italian prime minister, who happened to be in the same convent, agreed to be her go-between and brought a message to Schiap's father when she was called back to Rome. After having read the letter, Ernesto Schiaparelli rushed to the convent, looked at his daughter severely, and without a word brought her back home. The attempt to force her to reflect upon her sins and extinguish a too passionate personality was a total failure, one that lasted exactly ninety-nine days.

By the time she was eighteen, Elsa was going to the theater and the opera with her father and attending concerts and recitals. She started to write articles about music. Though she did not have the technical knowledge and these articles were not meant to be critiques, she expressed in them her sensibility and non-conformist approach to the subject, and a few of them were published. She was tempted for a while by a career as an actress. But a career on the stage? Yet again, this would have been unthinkable and considered a disgrace by her conservative father. She consoled herself by sneaking into the

University of Rome (she was not yet old enough to attend lectures) for a course on philosophy, and she loved it. She started learning about Spinoza, Bossuet, and the Confessions of St. Augustine, which would remain her book of prayers for many years.

A wealthy Russian, whom she found very ugly, began to court Elsa. He'd come to visit after dinner to sit by the table and gaze into space. Her parents liked him but thought she was still too young for a suitor. After several months, he retired his courtship but kept sending her passionate letters, offering her all his possessions, including his late mother's jewels. Schiap would say, in her coldly ironic tone, later in life that it was really the only time a man gave her something of value. She could not avoid, however, falling in love several times more, notably with a handsome painter whom she discovered later already had a fiancée. She then fell madly in love with another young boy from the south who would come for the day from Naples just to see her, and would send her a huge box of tuberoses each day. The tuberose is considered in the language of flowers as "dangerous pleasures and voluptuousness." Her family was scandalized by these bouquets but young Elsa was mesmerized by the innuendo of the gesture. Again, later in life, this floral note is the one she used predominantly to create the perfume Shocking, which was made even more wickedly sexual when accompanied by the highly erotic Vertès drawings. Her family rapidly put both romances to an end. Hoping to be through with her unfortunate adventures in love, Schiap tells how she went through a phase of going out with a variety of boys just because she found that sophisticated and that social etiquette allowed for it. She did it just for the simple fact that she found it amusing. Much the way a noble heroine from the Middle Ages would have her intrepid knight wear her colors, Schiap would make them wear a mauve tie or handkerchief, her favorite color at the time, to announce to those interested that she was being courted by them. But when her Russian suitor came back, Elsa's parents finally approved the idea of the marriage. Too much pressure was suddenly put upon her though, and she felt cornered and desperate. Luckily, destiny had other plans for her. In 1913, a friend of her sister's, a woman who had married a rich Englishman, wanted to adopt children and asked Beatrice if she knew someone willing to come to London to help her. She was offering to pay the fare, so the twenty-two-year-old Elsa jumped on the opportunity. Escaping the marriage and moving away was a golden opportunity for her. As she left Rome behind, she thought to herself: "This is going to be for ever! There will be no coming back!"[2]

CHAPTER 18

ELSA AS A
YOUNG WOMAN

E n route to England, Elsa stopped first in Paris with some family
friends. As soon as she set foot in the Gare de Lyon, she knew
that Paris was the place she was going to live, perhaps forever. After
the majesty of Rome, she was immediately overwhelmed by the romance of the quintessentially Parisian train station. A humorous anecdote marks her debut in the *Tout-Paris*. By chance, she quickly met
a family friend who invited her to a ball at the home of the famous
Paris socialites, the Henrauxes. She did not have a dress, so she went
to the Galeries Lafayette and bought four yards of dark blue crêpe de
Chine and two yards of orange silk, quite a big extravagance for her
means. She draped the fabrics around her body and made a sort of
Zouave ensemble, with a sash made of the orange silk. What was left
of the silk, she fashioned into a turban. Her ensemble created quite
a sensation! But when she had to dance the brand-new tango, which
she did not know (*that* sort of dance was not taught in her fashionable dancing class in Rome), she bravely went for it and had great
fun until the movement maneuvered the pins out of place, and the

whole outfit began to fall apart. Her courteous partner, who danced her off the floor to another room just in time, graciously rescued her from total embarrassment. Her first ball and indeed her first haute couturiere's mistake, as Schiap recalled it.

Elsa arrived in London soon after and then reached her destination, which was a nice, comfortable country house, not at all like the millionaire's palace she'd been expecting. She met her good-willed hostess and found the children charming. It was clear, however, that she would not stay there for too long, and she escaped as often as possible to London. Her stay in the bucolic countryside in the ordinary role of nanny was to change when she met her future husband at a lecture. It would also dictate her future destiny.

At a lecture on theosophy in 1914, Elsa met the Count Wilhelm Wendt de Kerlor, a part-Breton, part-Swiss, and part-Polish theosopher, who was described once as a persuasive but inconstant Theosophist. She listened to him, spellbound, and rather boldly for a woman in that era met with him after the lecture. They talked for hours and seemed to be in complete communion. This was the age of enlightenment for the beginning of the twentieth century. So many women felt somewhat emancipated, and more and more were into spiritual, artistic and unconventional endeavors. Elsa was no exception, apparently. The next morning, they were engaged! The wedding was very simple and took place in a stodgy registry office. Her family, who surely found the idea of such an elopement highly unacceptable, rushed to prevent the marriage, but arrived too late. It always struck me that the way she herself describes this marriage implied something rather more earthy than spiritual; in the 1950s, when she wrote about it, it was a coy way to say they had relations. If this were the case, Elsa was quite the bold young woman for 1914. After all, she did write an erotic novel as a teenager. When Elsa got back from her wedding (at least Wendt was a gentleman) to a small house that her new husband had rented for them, she found that, like a wicked sorcerer's hex, seven mirrors had been smashed in the house. She never knew how it happened, but could not help but see this as a doomed beginning, a message written, literally, on the walls.

Sadly, her family's late attempt to prevent the marriage may have been well founded. Count Wilhelm Wendt de Kerlor was hardly what he claimed. He was born simply Willie Wendt, and it was over many years that he adopted several aliases, one of which was de Kerlor, which he eventually legally registered as an assumed name. He was never a count and in fact had no connection whatsoever to the aristocracy. In addition, he had no medical training, no degree or doctorate in anything, let alone science or philosophy. When questioned by an FBI agent years later, he told them he used the title "doctor" only to add prestige to his name, brushing it off with "It's done all the time in Europe." He was jailed at one point in London for telling fortunes without a license and was eventually kicked out of Great Britain. It was at this time, during the 1910s, that he came to America and settled in New York City, where he operated several businesses from his apartment. He was considered a ruthless self-promoter and without any remorse or shame. He earned money by giving lectures and writing articles on pseudo-scientific subjects. He claimed to be a psychological investigator and was hired as a private detective on two murder cases. He was, to his credit, an astute learner and perhaps ahead of his time in recognizing the importance of documenting the crime scene and preserving evidence. However, his value as an expert was diminished greatly by the naive and half-baked conclusions he drew from the "evidence" he gathered; he once testified before a Grand Jury that he could "see the face of the murderer in a drop of the victim's blood." The FBI investigated both Willie Wendt and Elsa as Communist sympathizers in the 1920s after they were observed at a number of Bolshevik gatherings in New York. He was even suspected of breaking into the home of an agent to find out how much the government knew of his activities. That is likely why Schiaparelli distanced herself from him and took back her own maiden name in the mid-1920s, dropping the title of Comtesse rather quickly. He was a disgrace and a fraud.

When Elsa met and married Wendt, the First World War was underway. Elsa did not really know where she belonged and felt as if she had no roots, an impression reinforced by the fact that her husband was distracted and feckless. The new couple decided to go to Nice, France, where some of her husband's family had lived. They rented a flat overlooking the gardens near the sea front. Things did not go well; she rarely saw her husband return from wherever it was he went during the day. A few times, feeling idle, she'd go off to Monte Carlo to the casino with a bit of money and lose it immediately. Without a penny left after one of these escapades, she was sent back to Nice with a railway voucher bearing the words, "With the compliments of the Casino!"[1] Schiap must have learned her lesson, for she never approached a gambling table again. She restricted risk-taking to other parts of her life.

The Comtesse de Kerlor enjoyed the Riviera, however, her husband saw no future for himself there and decided they should go to America. They arrived in New York in the summer of 1915. They settled in a smart hotel near Madison Avenue, but the situation was not very encouraging. The couple had been living on Elsa's dowry since their marriage, and it was not very large. Her husband, always rather vague, had no career ambitions of any kind and their financial state was not getting any better. Elsa noticed too that Wendt seemed physically unable to cope with the pressure of New York. Increasingly surrounded by infatuated women acting like giddy schoolgirls, he fell under the spell of dancer Isadora Duncan, who "marked him as to be won."[2]

On November 11, 1918 the Armistice in France was finally settled, but for Elsa, the struggle for life was becoming more acute every day. She discovered she was pregnant. One night she had a vision of being visited by her father, who sat near her as if to give her hope and courage. The next day, a cable arrived announcing that her father had died at the exact moment she had had her vision. In her memoir she would reflect "in the realm of love everything is possible. Possibly, at the moment of death, we are granted a last wish before taking the next step in our destiny. Is the body, upon reaching the wilderness of the end, allowed to stop and look back for a second at the most loved person in need?"[3] Elsa thus lost the strongest attachment in her life at the same moment she was getting ready to give life.

She gave birth to a girl named Maria Luisa Yvonne (around 1919–1920 though the exact year has never been verified) who was to be known as "Gogo." Willie, before disappearing from the picture, gave her, or rather tagged on as an afterthought to her birth certificate, the name of Radha, in memory of the goddess who had brought manna to Buddha under the banyan tree.

Titled, but penniless and alone, without even the money to buy a pram, Elsa went from hotel to hotel with her daughter in her arms to find a place to stay. A woman alone with a baby was not acceptable at any decent hotel at the time, but she eventually tricked her way into one. Gogo slept in an orange crate.

Poverty led Elsa and Gogo from New York to Boston to Washington, from Florida to Cuba, and eventually to Greenwich Village. She tried everything—from being an extra in a movie, to selling antiques, to doing translations, to reading ticker-tape for a Wall Street stockbroker (with disastrous results due to her complete lack of knowledge on how the ticker tape machine functioned) in order to make ends meet. For a short while, too, she worked at the American Relief Association, headed by future President Herbert Hoover, which was raising funds to feed ten million starving Russians. Her small income was earmarked entirely for the care of Gogo and Elsa was literally starving at times. How could she go on, husbandless and without skills? Life was bleak and unbearable for the Italian aristocrat in exile. Schiaparelli notes that memory fails her about the particular period. "I was to experience gnawing, black hunger, relieved only by occasional fruit or sausage from the coffee stall where the bus drivers used to go. I became so utterly depressed that I no longer wanted to go on."[4] Despite the dire misery of these times, the struggling Elsa, who had no news of any sort from her husband, never lost the strict code of morals of her upbringing, which prevented her from the age-old professions that women without any material wealth resorted to: prostitution and gold digging. She says this in her book *Shocking Life* in a much more subtle way, though the meaning is the same.

Was what happened next a sign from her faithful guardian angel, who had already saved her several times from those numerous childhood misadventures where she almost perished? One night she found a twenty-dollar bill on the street. She promptly ordered a steak dinner. The next day, she used what was left of the twenty dollars to buy a few nice "objects" she'd noticed in a pawnbroker's window. She then resold them for twice as much in some fancy shops uptown. Though doing such small-time antique trading was never a regular source of income, this independent antique dealing allowed her to struggle through, and at least get some food on her table on a somewhat daily basis.

Fatefully too, that summer, a young American woman named Blanche Hayes (wife of famous lawyer Arthur Garfield Hayes) rented the house next door to Schiap. Mrs. Hayes found her neighbor pleasant, artistic, and intelligent. They sympathized with one another and became close friends.

About this time, she also met an ambitious Polish woman, Ganna Walska, who had a naughty habit of only marrying millionaires who'd support her career as an opera singer. She had an exquisite beauty but unfortunately her incredible looks were as extreme as her lack of talent—she was tone-deaf. This may have been an exaggeration and just gossip. Walska wrote an amazingly lucid autobiography explaining her side of the story about her talent, even mentioning Schiap. When the singer was invited to perform in Havana, she invited the Comtesse de Kerlor to assist her. Elsa, happy to have a bit of warm weather, accepted. She loved Cuba; however, Walska was literally booed off stage by music-loving Cubans, so they made a hasty trip back home. Having had no success as an opera singer, but with great fame as a result of her beauty and her scandalous divorce, Walska created her first perfume, called "Divorçons" (or "Let's Divorce"). Much like her singing career and her marriages, the perfume had a very short existence. Years later, the singer acquired the Théâtre des Champs-Elysées in Paris and Schiaparelli often was invited there, much to her embarrassment, as she could not save herself from occasional fits of laughter due to the unintentionally comic recitals. Nonetheless, this did not prevent the opera singer from becoming a client; years later, Walska's vast and sumptuous wardrobe, which included many important Schiaparelli garments, would be donated to the Los Angeles County Museum upon her demise at age ninety-nine.

Also around this time, Elsa re-met Gabrielle "Gaby" Picabia, wife of the artist Francis Picabia, who was to play a very important part in her life. According to some accounts, Gaby was on board the steamship L'Espagne, on her way back to the USA when she first met Elsa and her husband, the glamorous Comte and Comtesse de Kerlor. Elsa reminded Gaby then of a languishing Burne-Jones woman. Gaby noticed immediately how astute Elsa was, how well-informed she was about the arts, and that she could speak intelligently though not for long periods in perfect French and somewhat picturesque English about the Fauvism, Cubism, and Futurist art movements. This was considered rather an accomplishment by Gabrielle, who had lived in the nucleus of these movements in Paris before the First World War.

In 1919, estranged from her artist husband and in dire need of money to raise her children, Gaby was returning to the USA to sell her Paris fashions, notably those of Poiret's rival and youngest sister, Nicole Groult, a then-famous name in French fashion whom Gaby had met through her husband. The clothes Gaby wore seemed extreme to Americans, but they gave her the reputation of being very sophisticated wherever she'd be seen. Although she tried very hard to succeed at selling the overly stylish Groult frocks, she had trouble drumming up a clientele in the USA. Nicole Groult, like her flamboyant brother, was working in the ultra-sophisticated French modern style, and these clothes had a unique aspect to which many Americans did not relate. The life of an American woman of elegance was very different from that of a French woman, especially a chic Parisian woman. Gaby began to ask around for advice and help from friends. An elderly American doctor friend told her he had a new patient, a well-born Italian woman with many contacts who might be able to help her find some clients. It turned out that the well-born Italian woman was the Comtesse de Kerlor, née Elsa Schiaparelli, whom Gaby remembered with pleasure from the Atlantic crossing so many months earlier. They were brought together once more.

Elsa, no longer using the title of Comtesse, seemed thinner, and her romantic, nostalgic aspect had hardened into a decisive, straight-to-the-point stance. No longer dressed elaborately in refined Poiret inspired artsy frocks, she cut her flowing hair short in the latest style, waved slightly across the head and adopted the sharp, almost curt manner of the liberated women of the post-World War I period. Chic as she had become, Elsa was living in a cheap hotel and was struggling. Mme Picabia took pity on her and asked Elsa to work for her. Gaby kindly shared her room at the Brevoort Hotel and even found a nursery for little Gogo.

Through Gaby, Elsa met French artist Marcel Duchamp, who came to New York in 1915, and stayed until the end of the war. Gaby's ex-husband, Francis Picabia, Arthur Cravan, and Duchamp were the voices of Dadaism. Elsa also met the famous and revolutionary American artist-photographer Alfred Stieglitz, who had a gallery called Photo-Secessionist Gallery at 291 Fifth Avenue. Stieglitz put out an ultra-modern magazine called *Camera Work*. Through the magazine, the American photographer Edward Steichen, who was brought into Paris fashion by Paul Poiret; a young Man Ray; and Baron Adolf de Meyer were also included in this burgeoning group.

Duchamp, Stieglitz, and the other avant-garde artists in New York all seemed to be eking out livings while expressing wildly radical ideas on art and culture. It was less than a decade after the landmark Armory show of 1913, where over three hundred European and American avant-garde artists scandalized America and created a riot of frantic controversy in the art world and the public at large.[5] Never before had the "grand public" been so aware of what was happening in the world of art. Old ideas were rapidly dissolving and radical new ideas were playing a major role not only in the arts, but in the lives of people of the times.

In New York Marcel Duchamp had already renounced painting and signed the first of his shocking "ready-mades." This is when Schiaparelli came to be amongst them. They were enchanted with Elsa's personality, and she soon found herself part of the inner circle of the group of eccentric artists. She was allowed to study some of these artists' work, and Baron de Meyer, who later, as they all would, worked for her, let her borrow and rummage through his vast archives of this new type of impressionistic photography to satisfy her enormous curiosity about modernism and everything that inspired it.

Man Ray would publish, sadly for posterity, only one issue of a review called *New York Dada*. But he, along with Marcel Duchamp and Katherine Dreier, also created a brand-new concept, a promotional organization called *La Société Anonyme*. Its exclusive goal was to emphasize and promote the newest and most advanced aspects of their art, which was more and more being called "modern art." Schiaparelli was engaged by Man Ray to make up the mailing lists of possible members and to make arrangements for the first meetings and exhibitions. It was a great revelation to the soon to be world-famous designer.

This experience amongst these artists broadened Schiaparelli's sense of artistic direction and helped her cultivate a sense of the core ideas of modernism. But as for the practicality of everyday life and earning a living, the business relationship between Elsa and her friend Gaby was not working out so well. To Elsa, Gaby seemed unambitious, too modest. Schiap saw things on a much grander scale and demanded a broader range of fashions than Mme Picabia had available. Schiap wanted to do more spectacular promotions, which were beyond Gaby's means. Whereas Schiap had patience and the power of persuasion, frustratingly Gaby did not have these characteristics, which Elsa saw as necessary to sell ultra-chic and ultra-expensive French haute couture. Finally, as a result of Elsa's great determination, the original collection of Groult clothes was sold. Gaby Picabia went back to Paris, but their relationship was far from over.

After Gaby left New York in the early 1920s, Elsa saw her ex-husband for the last time standing on a street corner in Manhattan. She had not seen him for ten months. Panic-stricken and breathless, she hailed a taxicab, hastily leapeded in, and left her former partner without having exchanged a single word. At this time, Elsa was desperate and still struggling; things seemed to be getting worse week by week. Her hotel bills were mounting so she had no other alternative but to write home to her mother, now a widow, and ask for help. When the small allowance arrived, she was able to put Gogo in the care of an old nurse in a cottage in the woods near Stamford, Connecticut, believing that the fresh air and calm, clean surroundings would be good for her. On Patchen Place, in

Greenwich Village, she took a tiny apartment so small she had to stand on the bed to dress.

After the war ended, a wild and woolly counterculture of the avant-garde in all the arts and crafts was blossoming in Greenwich Village. It was a beehive of creativity, and Schiap was surrounded by artists, writers, intellectuals, actors, poets, and generally bohemian people, with whom she socialized. By spring of 1921, Stieglitz (who was just starting to do fabric prints with his photography) told her about the latest advancements in color movie film photography, new experiments that appealed to her sense of the modern. Schiap got a few roles as an extra in some films being made in a New Jersey studio. (The intensely bright film lights nearly blinded her, though, which contributed to her near total moral discouragement.)

Around this time, a friend lent her a cottage, well provisioned and cozy, in Woodstock, New York. At the time, it was an artists' retreat, and it was there that she met an Italian tenor from the Metropolitan Opera. He was miserable in an unhappy marriage, and the two found some measure of happiness in each other's company, that is until his wife showed up shrieking and threatening divorce on the grounds of adultery. When he died quite suddenly, shortly thereafter, of meningitis, Schiap dealt with all the formalities of the funeral, while the wife, who normally would have been responsible for these arrangements, mysteriously disappeared.

During the cold winter of 1921-22, Gaby Picabia returned to New York with the latest Nicole Groult haute couture creations, and despite past differences, hired Schiaparelli again, knowing her charm and intelligence would always be an asset to her. When Elsa and Gaby returned to Paris briefly, Elsa supplemented her small allowance by selling from home other Paris fashions consigned to her through Mme Picabia's influence. Sadly, this venture didn't work out; the clothes were too expensive and the operation came to a halt, much to Elsa's disappointment.

By 1922, Elsa had been in New York for over three years and things had hit rock-bottom. Visiting Gogo, who was about fifteen months old by now, Elsa realized that she could hardly walk. She was diagnosed with infantile paralysis—polio. It would require expensive treatments of operations, plaster casts, and crutches that would last for ten years.

It was then, as Schiap recalls, that Blanche Hayes took a hand in her destiny. Mrs. Hayes, after having finalized her divorce in Paris, was reluctant to go to France alone, as she had little knowledge of the language. Considering that they got along well and that Mrs. Hayes had a substantial private income, she offered for Elsa to come to Paris as her guest. So they sailed together with little Gogo in tow in June of 1922, to Elsa's immense relief. One of the first things she did was to start her own divorce proceedings, which went through with amazing ease, since there was no ground for contestation. Exit Comtesse de Kerlor: she was now officially Elsa Schiaparelli again. Of these hard but unforgettable times, Schiaparelli said: "If I have become what I am, I owe it to two distinct things—poverty and Paris. Poverty forced me to work, and Paris gave me a liking for it and courage."[6]

CHAPTER 19

ELSA IN PARIS

O nce Elsa and Gogo had arrived back in Paris, Gaby Picabia invited them to live with her until things picked up. Blanche Hayes and her daughter Lora lived at a nearby hotel. Through Gaby, Elsa found a French doctor for Gogo who suggested the child live with his family so that she could have daily electric physio-therapy, which was beneficial to her condition. This arrangement was very good for both mother and daughter. Gogo lived with them for several years, and developed a close and loving relationship with the family. Schiap's allowance from her mother, who was happy to have Elsa and her grandchild back in Europe, covered the expenses of Gogo's care. Elsa visited her mother in Rome with Blanche and Lora, but had no intention of staying there. Although living with her mother would have solved many financial problems, she had found her freedom and wished to hold onto it, even if it would remain a struggle. She had a destiny to follow.

Back in Paris, Elsa took an old-fashioned apartment with Blanche near the Eiffel Tower on the Boulevard de La Tour-Maubourg. She ran a simple household: she was not far from Gogo, and she had the means to engage a cook and a maid. During the ensuing months, she enjoyed a cultural life of theater, opera, art exhibitions, and concerts, but she found herself wishing to diminish her dependency on Blanche. Gaby introduced her to an antique dealer, and soon, she was attending antiques auctions and going to antique shops in Paris and the provinces. It was a matter of only a few months before she was going off on her own to start a small business. Just as she had in New York, she used her keen eye and astute knowledge to shop for antiques. And again, thanks to an introduction by Gaby, she negotiated a good sale of her now-deceased father's coin collection, which helped with her divorce payments as well as Gogo's treatment, which was slowly showing results of healing the little girl.

Her alliance with Blanche Hayes meant that Elsa was surrounded by the American colony of Paris. However, she truly longed to meet French people and other foreign expatriates. Gaby again took notice of this, and introduced her to the fading Dadaist scene of Paris. Elsa renewed her friendship with Marcel Duchamp, and became acquainted with Francis Picabia, Tristan Tzara, and many other poets and artists. Man Ray took her to the fashionable hangout Le Boeuf Sur le Toit (The Steer on the Roof). The cabaret-bar started as a restaurant named Le Gaya, on rue Duphot. Business was slow, and allegedly someone suggested that the owner, a solid provincial man called Moyses, should contact the French writer Jean Cocteau. Moyses explained to Cocteau that he had a very good jazz band, which was not very appreciated by his clients. Cocteau's response was typically forthright: "Change your clientele." Cocteau came and played drums with Georges Auric and Darius Milhaud. Jean Wiener was at the piano with his partner Clément Doucet. They soon met with great success and Le Gaya exploded. Moyses moved the restaurant to the rue Boissy-d'Anglas. Le Boeuf sur le Toit, sometimes called the Nothing Happens Bar, took its name from a Brazilian song, which

Darius Milhaud and Jean Cocteau arranged and choreographed into a pantomime act. It was performed in 1920 by the famous Fratellini clowns, dressed in Raoul Dufy costumes and Guy Fauconnet masks.

The space was decorated in black glass with an iridescent glass ceiling. Raoul Dufy lithographs were hung around the room and a collaborative painting by Francis Picabia with text from his friends named *L'Oeil Cacodylate* was displayed behind the bar. One could read the diverse contributions, such as "Sadora loves Picabia with all her soul," "I love salad. Francis Poulenc," "I have nothing to tell you. Georges Auric," "My heart is beating signed Valentine Hugo."

Late at night, Wiener and Doucet's piano playing would yield to the jazz orchestra, which drew couples onto a crowded dance floor. Erik Satie, a member of the group of young composers referred to as Les Six, was a regular. Satie utilized the sounds of modern life in his compositions: typewriters, lottery-wheels, movie set clap-sticks, factory whistles, ocean liner, and car horns. It was the musical equivalent of the work Schiaparelli was soon to unleash on fashion and the chic world at large.

On any given evening, one might find Prince Jean-Louis de Faucigny-Lucinge, Edward Molyneux, or Prince Georges Ghika, who financed several Surrealist films and was married to the Belle-Epoque beauty and courtesan Liane de Pougy, the Vicomte de Noailles. You might also run into Fanny Ward and Rudolph Valentino drinking champagne with singer Yvonne Georges. At the next the table, the Comte de Beaumont, Princess Bibesco, and gossip columnist Elsa Maxwell would sit alongside Picasso in his red sweater (Schiap owned one of his paintings that she felt was an allegorical portrait of her) and the Honourable Mrs. Reginald "Daisy" Fellowes, heiress to the Singer sewing machine fortune and one of the most famous fashion leaders of the time. Nancy Cunard, the extravagant English beauty and heiress to the Cunard shipping fortune, and the Princess Eugene Murat were there too, both with their black lovers They both dressed in Chanel (who was also a regular patron), but eventually discarded the designer in favor of Schiaparelli clothes. Even Bettina Jones and her husband-to-be Gaston Bergery frequented the nightspot. In the 1980s, when I asked her about this period of social frenzy, she told me:

> There was a time when I went to Le Boeuf nearly every night . . . it was always filled with the chicest people of the time . . . between my tongue and those sensational clothes [by Schiaparelli], the place practically revolved around me. Schiap's clothes always were certainly a plus, she was the one who really made clothes sexy again . . . they revealed the lines of the body; they were shapely and had low necklines and could be backless or body hugging. Going to Le Boeuf in her clothes was always so much fun.[1]

Bettina left a distinct impression. As Boris Kochno wrote, "what a sensation Bettina was, she was like some enchanted being, always so radiant and so bewitching, and always dressed impeccably and with that Schiaparelli daring, which few women could pull off."[2]

At the same time, Paul Poiret launched his innovative open-air nightclub called L'Oasis, in the garden of his fashion house. He gave lavish parties under the inflated dome of his outdoor ceiling, a true innovation for the time, reviving pre-war stars such as Yvette Guilbert. He also hosted musical reviews, theatrical productions, and film projections starring Charlie Chaplin, Buster Keaton, and Harold Lloyd. Poiret used everything new that fascinated him to create an ambiance of luxury and gaiety. Knowing that his old friend Picabia's wife Gaby needed money, he asked her to play hostess for him in the summer of 1922. Alas, she had only one tattered old evening gown from before the war. Elsa perked up and offered to make her a gown. It was very simple in its design, but Poiret took note of it and asked to meet the designer. Elsa recalls how she met Poiret, whom she considered a great artist. It was her first visit to a true *maison de couture* and she was mesmerized. Driven by pure desire, she dared to try on a sample from his most recent collection that was draped on a display. It was a magnificent coat made out of black velvet with bright stripes, lined in blue crêpe de chine. Poiret saw her trying on the lavish coat and from afar admired her as she paraded back and forth in front of his big Atelier Martine mirrors. He saw how she admired it and caressed the fabric. He suggested she buy it as he thought it looked as if it were made just for her. Schiap, embarrassed, said she could never buy such a luxurious coat as it was surely too costly and besides she'd have nowhere to wear it. With a typically Paul Poiret grand gesture he offered her the coat as a gift, saying elegantly she should not concern herself with money. With a gentlemanly bow, he added that she could wear anything anywhere.

She was overwhelmed by the gift. Soon, she had an extensive wardrobe from her generous benefactor. The two became close friends, all due to his admiration of that first dress of Schiaparelli's he had seen on Gaby. Elsa kept all of the clothes he gave her until she was very old and said in her memoirs that when she wore them she appeared as if she reigned like a supreme fashion leader. Dressed in her own clothes she said she looked like her own "ugly sister."[3]

Paul Poiret had four children: daughters Martine, Rosine, and the youngest, Perrine, as well as a son, Colin. I befriended both Colin and Perrine in the early 1970s, and Perrine gave me a number of her father's designs, including some that belonged to her mother, Denise. One of the highlights is a 1919 dress made out of Raoul Dufy fabric. Perrine was quite a character. In the many discussions we had about her father, she shared with me splendid stories of his art and his character, and she also often spoke about his friendship with Schiap.

I recall her coming to see us regularly, them deeply engaged in conversation or laughing and having fun. They really appreciated each other's company, and when my father had financial difficulties, it was Schiaparelli who came to his aid . . . At one point, he was in deep financial trouble and she'd rally all the designers around to give him help. But not in a humiliating way . . . she was so elegant and so devoted to him. I know how much he appreciated her work . . . She wore his clothes and he was very pleased by that, he said she wore them to perfection. I remember her as a highly chic woman, with an allure which was unique unto itself. She had charisma and he loved people with personality and charm, of which she had plenty. He always said that she took up where Poiret had stopped. When he was no longer in active business, he felt her work was a natural continuation of what he had established; she took it further and made it evolve. This was quite a statement from him, as he felt he had invented everything in fashion and that there was not much left to innovate. In a way it was true, he did initiate so much, but she brought it all forward, building on his ideas but for a whole other generation of fashionable women.[4]

Perrine was always polite but slightly curt in her personality, so it was quite unusual for her to say such kind things about Schiaparelli.

With Poiret as a source of inspiration, Schiap decided to make another attempt at haute couture and design simple dresses for herself. Even though she still lacked even the most basic of sewing skills, she had a certain vision in her head, a very clear idea of how she wished to be dressed. Blanche Hayes recalled watching Schiap cut out some grey cloth, without a pattern, on the dining room table. Schiap proceeded to make a full-length coat for her, lined in printed silk, with a shawl collar in long-haired fur to hide the defects. It proved to be a great success, and many friends complimented Blanche on the stylish little number.

For Schiap, dress designing was not a profession but an art. She writes in her memoir, that fashion is not like the other arts, which once completed remain intact in their integrity, like a painting or a book. She thought fashion had to constantly move and change. However, she was met with discouragements concerning her decision to undertake the life of a couturier. A charming yet condescending man at the well-established house of Maggy Rouff told her she'd be better off doing vegetable gardening than being a fashion designer because she had neither talent or technical knowhow. But Schiap felt a need to express herself, and relished the opportunity to take a chance.

After the success of the coat and the rejection by nearly all the other fashion houses of Paris, a wealthy American friend of Blanche's asked Elsa to act as her guide to the fashion houses of the City of Light. Naturally, Schiap wanted to bring the friend to a Paul Poiret show, so she asked Gaby Picabia to call the designer's secretary to request good seats. It would also be Elsa's first experience seeing a *défilé de haute couture*, having only visited the atelier's salon on her past visits. The show was a veritable extravaganza of vivid colors and it cemented her lifelong admiration of Poiret.

Poiret was long-dead by the time Schiaparelli wrote about him in her memoir, but she took special effort to express her debt to him and honor her mentor with respect and love, something she acknowledged as rather rare. By the time she was middle-aged she felt and expressed often in the press and her book that fashion was lousy with all the vices and jealousies one could imagine. People in her métier took pleasure in the failures and losses of others and easily forgot kind gestures from the recent past. I read all these reflections in Schiap's own words when I was a teenager and have never forgotten them. They would always come to mind, almost comforting me, when I was in a situation where I was the subject of someone's insanity or jealousy. If Schiap had to endure such cruelty, I certainly could.

It was sometime around 1925 that a hand knit sweater worn by an American friend, which had what Schiap called a "steady"[5] look, caught her eye. It was notably different from Chanel's fashionable machine-knit sweaters and Patou's Art Deco inspired sweaters. Although it was drab in both cut and color, the knit was somewhat elastic and rough in texture, features that were inspiring and attractive to Schiap. She saw the sweater as being barbaric, like a fractured idea of a sweater. It was nervy and had panache in its insolence. Furthermore, it didn't seem to lose shape as quickly as other sweaters. She learned that this was an Armenian style of sweater, and it would prove far more important than its humble qualities would suggest. As Janet Flanner wrote in 1932, "Her entry into dressmaking was an accident . . . She happened to design a black-and-white sweater for herself, because, being Roman, she was addicted to black and white while other women were, at the moment, addicted to sweaters. This new note of chic melancholy, of Italian *morbidezza*, in the line of sports wear was hailed as a happy novelty by her friends."[6]

Schiap approached a few Armenian women to discuss the sweaters. One woman, whose name was Aroosiag Azarian (née Mikaëlian), whom Schiap called Mike, was an Armenian refugee from the Turkish massacres in East Anatolia. Azarian lived in England and happened to be in Paris on holiday when Elsa found her. Azarian explained her role to me in 1984: "I proposed her designs, new types of stitches . . . It was the other Armenians who executed the pieces of the models which were ordered, and I was in charge of the fittings on the clients and the sewing up of them."[7] The first trial sweaters were ugly and unsuccessful but they eventually hit on the best adaptation of her design. Schiap scribbled a few cubistic designs for Mike and the other women to adapt, and very quickly came up with her famous crude bow design, a *trompe-l'oeil* in black and white with a tweed effect, on a sweater that ended at the natural waist. This element was a departure from the doctrines of the *garçonne* look, with its dropped waist. Mike agreed to temporarily delay her return to England, where she planned to become a nurse, but ended up staying until Schiap's death many years later. The two women developed a symbiotic and very close working relationship built on trust, patience, humor, and mutual understanding. Faithful until the end, Mike said that at the outbreak of the Second World War, "I wanted to enlist in the army, as a nurse; Madame Schiaparelli had me come to her and she said to me, 'Mike, I need you too much.' So, I continued to work for Schiaparelli . . . until 1954!"[8]

Schiap wore the sweater to a luncheon, where all the fashionable women immediately noticed it and wanted one. Later on in life, she liked to quip something to the tune of (and I am paraphrasing a letter I have) that her professional life and career, like the sword of Damocles, hung from a thread (as the idiom goes). That first sweater, worn by all her friends, became very popular, and brought yet another friend of Blanche Hayes, a certain Mrs. Hartley, into the picture. Mrs. Hartley wanted to invest in a French business and, inspired by the success of Schiaparelli's sweater, persuaded her to produce a collection based on the new concept of women's sportswear. In the latter part of 1925, Mrs. Hartley bought a small dress-making establishment called Maison Lambal, located near the Place Vendôme on the corner of the rue Saint Honoré and rue du 29 Juillet. It is difficult to convey just how many dressmakers there were in Paris in the 1920s, but suffice it to say, it was quite a tribute to the talents of Schiaparelli when, in January 1926, *Women's Wear Daily* devoted an entire feature article to Maison Lambal's sportswear and daytime ensembles. The collection was widely viewed and considered quite successful. Sadly, however, Mrs. Hartley soon grew bored and realized that continuing to finance a dressmaking house with a designer who had as grand a vision as Elsa Schiaparelli was way beyond her modest means. Callously and rather abruptly, Mrs. Hartley decided to close down the house.

But this time, Elsa was not discouraged by the turn of events. Emboldened by her recent success, she opened her first establishment in January 1927, in an apartment at 20, rue de l'Université, near Saint Germain-des-Prés. Her first collection of sweaters, called "Display Number One," was spread out on tables in the apartment and held up by hand to show clients. They were startlingly original, and rooted in the Cubist/Art Deco look of the era. They featured floral motifs on the shoulders and geometric grey-toned graphics, rendered in combinations of metallic thread and wool knitted together, along with cardigans bordered in grosgrain ribbon. Scarcely a month after the collection was shown, *Vogue*, always sniffing out the latest and newest, devoted a page of photographs to Elsa's designs. Elsa showed the sweaters with front pleated crêpe de chine and flannel skirts, a bit longer than the current mode. She paired some with scarves and sport socks that matched the motif of the sweater. In May 1927, she made two- and three-button blouson jackets, hand-knit and edged in grosgrain in various shades of grey. She designed more pullovers and skirts to match the blouson jackets. By August 1928, she was firmly anointed as the ultra creator of hand-knits. It was proclaimed that "she belongs to knitted sweaters, or they to her."[9]

The *trompe-l'oeil* sweater with the bow knot was copied all over the world, especially in America. Schiaparelli had accomplished something rather notable. She had transformed the sweater, a prosaic garment meant to keep one warm, into a stylish accouterment for the fashionable woman. Drawing influence from her circle of artistic friends, Schiap integrated the concepts of Cubism and Surrealism into her design and in turn brought an awareness of the movements to a much broader audience. The humble sweater had become a modern work of art.

Her first export order, from a buyer from Strauss in New York (though there is some debate if Macy's or Lord & Taylor placed the first one), was for forty sweaters and forty skirts to match. Schiap's enthusiasm yielded an immediate "yes," without pausing to wonder how she could possibly make so many in a fortnight or even what the skirts would look like. She scouted Paris and found, with the help of Mike, enough Armenians to knit the sweaters in color and in black and white, and a local girl with sewing skills to help with the skirts. In November 1927 the wholesale buyer of fashions for William H. Davidow Sons Company, who also bought the original models and the adaptations of modernist designers and artists such as Sonia Delaunay and Erté, announced that he'd be the exclusive distributor of Schiaparelli sweaters in the United States. Many of these clothes were sold with a label that reads "Adaptation—Schiaparelli 4 Rue de la Paix, Paris." In my collection I have quite a number of Schiaparelli garments labeled this way, including a Tango-orange draped blouse and a black bouclé wool coat with draped leopard collar and cuffs that was worn by actress Joan Bennett. Elsa's sweater had become so popular that American copyists were making versions in mauve, green, shades of blue, and the original black and white. The November 1928 issue of the *Ladies' Home Journal* published a knitting pattern of Schiaparelli's sweater without even citing the designer's name. Schiap had entered into the mainstream.

Janet Flanner in the *New Yorker* called it the "chic melancholy"[10] look. Schiap's first advertisement in French *Vogue* in February 1928 was a quarter-page, a simple black block of square white lettering. The same month, the *New York Sun* remarked that Schiaparelli was showing more designs: dresses, bathing costumes, shantung seaside ensembles, and tailored jackets featuring geometric patterns and futuristic shapes and buttons. The British magazine *Liberty* raved about her asymmetrically striped sweaters in its March 24, 1928 issue.

Schiaparelli formally established her company on December 5, 1927, with Charles Kahn as a silent partner. Kahn was a businessman notable for his involvement with the department store Les Galeries Lafayette and the fashion legend Madeleine Vionnet. Schiap chose Kahn from amongst her many other offers, because he was French and this was, for Schiap, an important detail. However, just one year after her famous "Display Number Two," she bought out her partner, using a tiny detail in a clause that allowed her to get out of their contractual agreement. She already had a better offer from the Rothschild Banque de France that would finance her enough to be major stockholder of her own house. She would remain the sole owner until the end, something quite unique in the world of French haute couture.

She then hired a certain Monsieur Meunier as her heavy-handed and pragmatic accountant. He tried in vain to prevent her from squandering money on profitless ideas and materials. She also persuaded Michèle Guéguen to leave Jean Patou and join her team as a saleswoman; Guéguen later became director of the house. Yvonne Souquières, her private secretary (of whom Schiap said that she should be named Faith as she was so loyal to her), was brought on around the same time. This group would all remain Schiap loyalists until the end.

Now Schiap needed a suitable space for her new business. The apartment was cramped and she needed to expand. She moved into new quarters on January 1, 1928. It had a salesroom, a workshop, a salon, and a Jean-Michel Frank furnished room. It appeared elegant, although it was really just a garret at 4, rue de la Paix. On the front door a sign in black and white read: "Schiaparelli, pour le Sport." Her family was scandalized that she would use their name for trade purposes, and friends still exclaimed that nobody would be able to pronounce it; but Maison Schiaparelli rapidly became a very popular place to find fashionable sportswear.

As she did not have formal training in garment construction— she merely knew what she'd like to see in the cut of clothes—Schiap simply invented articles of attire and built her ideas from instinct inspired by everyday experiences. She always said she'd never invent a dress she herself would not wear. Her clothes were based on the principles of the architecture of the body, and on her memories of the beauty in her surroundings as a child. Her early fashion dictums decreed that the body was never to be lost or overlooked in all the fuss of design—the body was like the frame in all architecture. The more you paid the body homage, she felt, the more the dress took on its powers and strengths. Clothing has no life and transforms into a living thing only when it is worn. Sometimes it becomes a great thing of beauty. Pragmatically speaking, she felt that fashion more often than not becomes just an object of no consequence or worse, a pitiful or grotesque exaggeration of what the wearer wished it to be.

By the end of the 1920s, the rampant copying of French fashion was becoming a serious problem for industry professionals. Although Schiaparelli originals were sold in shops like Wanamaker's department store and the Know the Hatter shops, there were more copies being sold as the genuine article on the market than the real thing. The high fashion designers of France needed solutions. It became important to impose a system where foreign buyers could buy only one model that they would then be allowed to copy in their workrooms (not in France) and sell as originals. Meanwhile, French buyers were not authorized to make copies at all. They were required to purchase the quantities they needed for resale directly from the fashion house. Schiaparelli's highly publicized designs were amongst the most copied and became a topic into and of themselves.

It is interesting to note that around the same time, Schiap started to work with her first *fournisseurs*, the suppliers of various notions and accessories. One of them was the Maison Ardor, owned by Victor Greidenberg and René Le Marchand. In 1928, Le Marchand, a sixteen-year-old orphan, started as a sales representative at Ardor. He was passionate about buttons and their creative potential. Maison Ardor buttons and creations were very novel, combining materials like glass, plastic, bronze, mother-of-pearl, resin, and leather in unusual ways. One example is a small steamer trunk-shaped button, covered in leather, complete with a miniature leather belt and buckle!

They made a disembodied leg complete with a shoe with a big ribbon bow as garter, a hand with wings similar to that in the Schiaparelli perfume ads of the year they were shown, a Punch and Judy theater with dangling puppets, zany harlequin masks, marching toy soldiers playing horns, and entwined swans in bronze, all of which I have in my collection. But amongst the most spectacular creations by the artisans Maison Ardor are jumping harlequins (to be differentiated from the Jean Schlumberger versions).

At this time, François Degorce was also making things for Schiaparelli. The Maison Degorce was founded in the nineteenth century as a diverse jewelry company, and by 1938 they had begun showing their most original costume jewelry examples, notably pieces made from gilt bronze and laiton (brass), to the haute couture houses. The jewels they did for Schiaparelli include a gilt chameleon lizard lined with white strass with ruby red eyes. They'd come up with prototypes (like all the artisans and suppliers) and from them she'd choose the ones she wished to commission to go with her clothes. Some of their earlier creations for her include a carved mother-of-pearl panther's head, various hands (also similar to Jean Schlumberger's), owls, bouquets, a griffin's craw holding a small round object, accordions, and anchors.

These baubles clearly show how familiar Schiap was with Dadaist and Surrealist motifs. Links to specific works by artists such as Tristan Tzara, André Breton, and Dalí, as well as Meret Oppenheim, De Chirico, Magritte, and even Picasso, are echoed in miniature in these notions. Schiap was in tune not only with the art, but, by making jewels using their leitmotivs, she transcended their artworks and created entirely new versions on a small scale. Her jewels should be considered as important as any work by the modern artists of that period, regardless of the medium. One must bear in mind, though, as in all haute couture, that creation involves a team of drapers, cutters, knitters, fabric makers, graphic designers of fabric, and many other unsung heroes. These people contribute important aspects of the final garments, hats, or accessories. As for the jewels, unlike the licensed pieces which are masterpieces of fashion style, quality, and technique, they are created in small quantities by hand in ateliers in Paris and should be thought of as collaborations. Invented by these artists and *fournisseurs*, they were endorsed when Schiaparelli waved the magic wand of her approval over them. She was a maestro. She had the final say, as she altered and changed elements so that the final result was true to her vision. When Alberto Giacometti sculpted a brooch, ring, or bracelet for her, for example, it was a "Giacometti," but also a "Schiaparelli," as her vision contributed to its creation. They share the title of the final object by technique and concept. It is the final product, the œuvre that was the Schiaparelli sensibility, that is important.

After only five years in business, Schiaparelli's influence had grown to an all-time high. This elite standing allowed her to reintroduce a revolutionary style that Paul Poiret had promoted for years without much success, called the *jupe-culotte*, a divided skirt. In the mid-1920s, active women realized that these garments were very useful for sports and cars, aspects of more dynamic lifestyles. To heck with what their boyfriends, husbands, or even the Catholic Church might think! The separation between the legs, although discreet, was often pleated, paneled, or folded over, to create a skirt-like silhouette. Most manufacturers, though, thought the idea too avant-garde for their customers. Stoke Poges, the golf expert, in England wore them, and Chinese-American actress Anna May Wong wore them when traveling. But in the spring of 1931, Schiaparelli brazenly wore them in public in London while on a trip to buy tweeds. There was no subtle pleating or folds. She wore outright short, flared blue pants of skirt length, with an eccentric jacket with metallic clips, a matching belt, a spotted jabot scarf, an Anita Loos hairdo by Antoine, and a tight cap. With her owlish eye make-up and short, gauntlet-like gloves, she looked as if she'd landed from another planet. The British press had a field day insulting her outfit, saying, that it was hardly feminine and obviously a lesbian style of dressing, a concerning accusation at the time. In 1928, the now-iconic lesbian-themed novel *Well of Loneliness* by Radcliffe Hall was published and subsequently banned in many countries including England. This scandalous sartorial dustup sealed the fate of the *jupe-culotte* as a symbol of aggressive lesbianism. It was considered a smack in the face to proper Christian feminine women worldwide. Despite the initial scandal, the garment was quickly adopted by American women, who wore it at home when receiving guests.

The eccentric artist and lesbian Hannah Gluckstein, a.k.a. Gluck, did not help matters concerning the controversial situation of the jupe-culotte when she had her "men's clothes"[11] made at Schiaparelli upon the urging of her lover, Constance Spry. Needless to say, Gluck wore the style in the most worldly and aristocratic circles. She favored men's pants by Schiaparelli in white, but wore a pleated black chiffon jupe-culotte when she was in a more feminine mode. It is interesting to note here that although most of the time Gluck was indistinguishable from a slender young man, she painted exquisite portraits of women, many wearing Schiaparelli clothes. In her biography of this extraordinary artist, Diana Souhami wrote, "One of her best portraits . . . was 'The Lady Mount Temple,' dressed by Schiaparelli in the absolutes of black and white."[12] Lady Mount Temple not only commissioned Schiaparelli clothes, but also has the distinction of being the first woman in London to paint her nails red with Schiap nail varnish.

In September 1929, the American silk manufacturer Cheney Brothers asked Schiaparelli to do a set of no less than eight different beach pajamas using their brightly colored silks. The *Women's Wear Daily* advertisements bragged about the "Staccato motifs" of the new collection, the "colorful lines, dynamic and moving," which, they said, reflected the "elan and liveliness of modern life." This collaboration was a first, not only for Schiaparelli, but for fashion in general. It displayed Schiap's driving ambition and successful commercial strategy, and American manufacturers' motivation to work with French designers. It was a smart collaboration for Cheney Brothers to work with the most advanced and daring of fashion modernists, and to follow the direction of the current modern art movement. Perhaps it was the first time that fine French modern painting was linked, in a roundabout way, to commercially made fashions. The manufacturers did a great deal to make the name of Elsa Schiaparelli known, even though at first Americans still persisted to claim they couldn't understand why a French haute couture designer had such an un-pronounceable Italian name. By now, not only were Schiaparelli fabrics available under license, but her patterns became available as well. With a bit of needlework talent, an ambitious and style conscious lady of less-fortunate means could wear Schiaparelli.

In November of 1929 Elsa Schiaparelli returned to the United States for the first time since 1922, when she had left in shame and poverty. She went for three weeks to supervise the latest collection of Stewart and Company in New York. It was predominantly a sportswear collection, intended to dress the woman who played golf and tennis, sunbathed on chic beaches, and drove fast cars. Many of these items drew their inspiration from one of Schiaparelli's best friends, Comtesse Gabrielle de Robillant, who accompanied her on this business trip and also acted as the ideal model. The collection featured innovative elements like rubberized wool mixed with silk for a raincoat, and black patent leather mixed with rough natural linen for a flying outfit. Schiap's very new and peculiar mixes of materials were considered hugely chic and very practical, as well. New customers followed one after another: the famous bright young thing Nancy Cunard, Daisy Fellowes, Anita Loos, and the scintillating and highly visible Josephine Baker. *Vogue* and French *Vogue* both published images of socialites wearing Schiaparelli in 1928. Marlene Dietrich and Greta Garbo wore Schiap too. Bettina Bergery recalled Garbo's visits to Schiaparelli: "Garbo would come in and sit and watch a défilé. . . . She did wear the gowns and the hats, but not the eccentric ones. Schiap even did a hat with her profile, but the thing she'd order the most were sensible pants outfits and tailored suits in plain colors."[13]

In my piles of Schiaparelli memorabilia and documentation, one of my favorite things is the stack of invoices, and two in particular to a Mrs. E.H. Reynolds from 1928. Mr. and Mrs. Reynolds were on a European trip and were staying at the Hotel Chatham, as one invoice mentions. They list her various purchases of cravats, a belt, a dress, and several sweaters, including one decorated with a gazelle and African native. These early documents are precious in a collection, noting precise models and prices for haute couture directly from Schiaparelli so early in her career. Over the years I have found a number of them, each a precious footnote in history, and an ephemeral, intimate testimony of Schiaparelli. I love these small details, both as a collector and an historian. I feel the same way about buttons and the House of Schiaparelli pencils I have that are cream lacquered with her facsimile signature in Shocking Pink. They were *there*. These tiny little objects, which otherwise have no value or meaning, were a witness to a whole career and life.

CHAPTER 20

"SCHIAP" 1929–1933

I can remember not so long ago a penthouse on Park Avenue.
With a real tree, and flowers, and a fountain, and a French maid.
And a warm bath with salt from Yardley's.
And a little dress that Schiaparelli ran up.

—*Gold Diggers of 1933*

B etween 1929 and 1930, Schiaparelli's designs became even more daring. The Art Deco style, the slouch, and the straight-line beaded dresses were relics of the past. *The Paris Times* said in February 1929 that Schiaparelli was "one of the rare creators."[1] Finally, Schiap made her new move. As she later said in her autobiography, *Shocking Life*, "Up with the shoulders! Bring the bust back into its own, pad the shoulders and stop the ugly slouch! Raise the waist to its forgotten original place! Lengthen the skirt!"[2]

Schiaparelli worked out multiple variations of the hand knit sweater, knitting with large needles to create a larger gauge to give the garments a diaphanous effect, sometimes removing the collars and cuffs. Soon she was producing knit bathing suits with anchors, stars, and linked hearts integrated into the fabric. These were mostly inspired by manly tattoo designs, and chic women longed to wear them. The sweater that had launched her career began to incorporate a range of motifs, including African motifs. The latter would influence the early work of Salvador Dalí, although it is unlikely she had any real contact with the Spanish artist at that time. She modeled the skeleton sweater herself and its white knit ribs and collar bone received quite a bit of attention from the press, some scornful, but most wildly enthusiastic. It also won the acclaim of those enlightened to Surrealism's ideals, especially the Parisian artists themselves. Bettina Bergery had introduced Schiap to Dalí, and recalls that "he'd seen her Surrealist sweaters . . . and thought, even before meeting her, that she was a Surrealist. She had a Surrealist artist's mind and she had the nerve to actually wear her sweaters."[3] It was art, fashion, society, and entertainment all in one sweater! Schiap pushed these ideas to extreme limits with an unprecedented nerviness. According to Eileen Agar, one of the few female Surrealist artists, the women artists of this period dressed "with panache . . . Our interest in appearance was not the result of our desire to please men, but more so an attitude of life. The association of a Schiaparelli dress and the propos or the scandalous behaviors was only the transposition of the postulates of Surrealism in public life."[4] In Carolyn Burke's biography of photographer Lee Miller, Man Ray's revolutionary muse and model, the author suggests that Agar omitted the fact that Schiaparelli clothes simply excited these artist women. Fashion had certainly not seen anything like them.

In due course, the Armenians, headed by Mike, had their own workrooms and sweaters and knits were fitted on clients individually and adapted to their particular body shapes. Besides the "Armenian stitch," Schiap and Mike came up with other unusual knitting formulas, including one they adopted from a complicated wool example from the seventeenth century. The results were so extraordinary that stores, clients, and the press impatiently awaited each item. Despite all these innovations, eccentricities, barbaric motifs, and new proportions, the *New York Herald Tribune* was laudatory: "Comfort, perfect suitability, and undeniable smartness are qualities not often happily united in garments really designed for sports, but all Schiaparelli sports clothes are admirably adapted to the use for which they are made."[5]

With the advent of aerodynamic advancements and the first Boeing 247, air travel was all the rage. Up until 1934, Schiaparelli's collections related to the flow of air and modernistic progress: Typhoon, Bird, In the Wind. Schiap began designing flight suits, some in vividly bright colors in addition to her now firmly established black and white combinations. They suited both the female pilot and the fashionable lay traveler. She made one for her friend the Comtesse Gabrielle de Robillant, and both were featured in a *Ladies' Home Journal* article called "Smartness Aloft." The ensemble was made of thick, rough, untreated linen and pinched in at the ankles. The cuffs and front were decorated with patent leather in the style of real airplane pilot's suits and the upholstery of private airplanes. Eclair brand zippers were on the wrists, pockets, and collar. Schiap accompanied the outfit with a knit hat by her friend and client the milliner Agnès in black and completed the look with surprisingly masculine shoes. An understated suit in dark jersey was designed to be worn under the outfit so that a lady could alight on terra firma and emerge from her gear elegant and chic.

Amongst the most famous of flying ladies that Schiaparelli dressed was Amelia Earhart. Schiaparelli recalls a strange, hard-to-believe story that could have changed Schiap's fate considerably:

> She used to come to me very often and we became very good friends. Besides her courage and her skill, she was a most remarkable and wonderful woman, not without a peculiar beauty of her own, and vastly modest. When I visited her in the small American cottage where she lived in peace between adventures, she, her husband, and I discussed at length our taking the next trip together. I was all for it, but some business duty kept me from doing so. She went alone

and met her fate alone and disappeared into nothing, leaving no human trace by which to remember her.[6]

Moving from the air to the sea, Schiap's beachwear also continued to be daring and superb. Her spring 1930 collection featured three-piece cotton beach ensembles, with sleeveless coats lined in terrycloth and beach bags that turned into beach towels. There were black towels and pajama outfits in rough linen or light handkerchief cotton with gold borders. Several beach ensembles had ties that wrapped several times and ended with a bow-tied knot. These wrap-a-round dresses, inspired by aprons, were very popular with importers because one did not have to be overly concerned with the sizing of the garment, so retailers could make easier sales. There were two-tone wraps accessorized with enormous, floppy straw hats, and impudent backless swimsuits. *Vogue* reported in 1930 that Schiaparelli's cleverest beach costume, made in four shades of tussore, consists of four half-dresses, each with one arm-hole, and tied at one side like an apron. The ties of one half pass through slits on the other half, and both tie on the same side. These may be made in any color combination. She also was one of the first couturiers to invent all the coordinating accessories—crêpe rubber sandals, hats, and bags that matched the ensembles. She used exciting color combinations: pale blue and cherry red, orange and yellow, dark blue and violet.

The fabrics for these beach ensembles were equally unusual: heavy crash linen, buck linen, shantung, and moussa tuslic (a spongy wool). But especially interesting was her use of Rodier upholstery fabric and terry cloth yachting upholstery. I have a beach jacket in my collection dated circa 1930 that is an excellent testimony of her often-subtle genius. It is made out of a red and white quadrille terry cloth fabric that was primarily used for upholstery on boats. The pattern was considered quite modern in its grid-effect, and both Theo Van Doesburg and Piet Mondrian concurrently utilized similar patterns in their paintings. The jacket's pocket marks one of the first times that a zipper was used as decoration in a haute couture sportswear collection. There are isolated examples of the zipper being used in specific couture accessories, but it was Schiaparelli who incorporated it into clothing that went beyond pure functionality. When I showed Cecil Beaton this jacket when I visited him one summer in the 1970s at Reddish, he called this jacket "the absolutely first example of the zipper used in high fashion."[7] It also has plastic lined pockets, which are another perfect example of Schiap's early use of synthetics in haute couture.

The first Schiaparelli furs appeared around this time as well, but she did not limit fur to trims and linings like most of her contemporary haute couturiers. She faced a long scarf with fur and turned up one end to make a muff. There were fur wraps and sports coats of rabbit, sheared and dyed wild colors like bright blue and blinding oranges and yellows. She also made fox or astrakhan "horse collars" that could be slipped off and on that created a riot of press. Bettina Bergery explained them as "rings of fur, just slipped about the neck, purely fantasy, and so elegant. They were called horse collars because they resembled them, but no horse ever had such a divinely chic accouterment, of that I'm sure."[8] Meret Oppenheim, the Surrealist artist, supposedly made only one accessory for Schiaparelli, a metal bracelet covered in fur with a matching ring. One evening Oppenheim was sitting at the Café de Flore with Dora Maar chit-chatting and the subject of fur came up. The always opinionated Pablo Picasso had been saying at that moment "just about anything could be made of fur," to which Oppenheim quipped back, "Even this saucer and that cup," and then joked to the waiter, "Waiter, a little bit more fur!"[9] This otherwise banal remark led Oppenheim to realize her most famous art work in 1936 called *Le Déjeuner en fourrure* (The Lunch In Fur)—a cup, saucer, and spoon covered in fur, now in the collection of the Museum of Modern Art in New York. The bracelet that sparked the idea is a large band of brass covered in fur. It is a unique and sublime work. To see it isolated and unworn evokes the poetry of Surrealist artworks and rivals Oppenheim's renowned piece in presence and poignancy. There is a monkey fur handbag by Schiaparelli in my collection that originally belonged to Bettina Bergery. Bettina claimed this may also have also been designed by Oppenheim, who, according to Bettina, collaborated with Schiap until 1941. The last remaining family expert on her work says this is questionable, however.

Schiaparelli reached another landmark with her evening dresses. The first, in a seductive pitch black, was a huge sensation world-wide. In her autobiography Schiaparelli explained that it was the first evening dress with a jacket. It was essentially the most pared down ensemble of its times, devoid of embellishment, just a plain black floor-length sheath of crêpe de Chine dress, matched to a white crêpe de Chine jacket with sashes that wrapped around the back and tied at the front. She referred to it as a creation of the starkest simplicity and the most plain-Jane of gowns possible. She said that this simple invention was exactly what was needed at that time in fashion and that it proved to be the most successful dress of her career.[10] Another Schiap dress, stunningly photographed by Hoyningen-Huene for *Vogue*, was made in a heavy black ciré satin that tied around the waist and ended in a bow-tie knot on the side. I am very lucky to have a similar gown in electric blue from the same collection that was given to me by Comte Henri de Beaumont and that originally belonged to his aunt, Comtesse Edith de Beaumont. The dress is cut with Schiap's unusual asymmetric darting, which gives the deep décolleté bodice a plunging cowl neckline in the back. The skirt falls asymmetrically, voluminous on one side, clinging on the other. The natural waist adds to the completely sensual way in which this dress moves from the hips, with very liquid waves. This is a very early instance of a treatment Schiap would use throughout the 1930s. It was photographed on Bettina Bergery at the chic nightclub Au Florence and she claimed that it earned her a reputation as a femme fatale. The gown was empowering, and not only as a fashion statement. Bergery says, "It made you very aware of being a woman, vulnerable and also powerful at the same time, a new sensation for women, showing off your body that way."[11] It seemed that regardless of what type of garment Schiaparelli devised, it would innovate, shock, and draw attention. She had innate talent, she was outspoken to the extreme, and she threw aside every possible convention. She was an artist.

Tweeds accompanied the sweaters for daytime. Her use of rough tweeds in women's fashion was unprecedented. The material was associated with peasant weavers and generally used for rugged men's hunting clothes. Schiap used tweed in many ways and often in unusual colors. Some looked like stringy rag rugs. Another, which she designed exclusively for *Harper's Bazaar* in 1929, had an open weave bouclé in a strict blue and brown combination. She had already shown tailored ensembles in her Display Number Two collection in two thicknesses and weights of tweed, amazingly interwoven with reversible jersey. Two years later, *Vogue* said her tweeds and woolens embodied "a strong sense of color . . . a bold attack on fabrics."[12] Textile manufacturers released a silk fabric that imitated rough wool that year, which Schiap immediately put to use in beach pajamas and coatdresses.

To match all of her unusual fashions, Schiap entered into one of her first licensing agreements with the Westcott Hosiery Mills. She sponsored Fabrimode, revolutionary new colorful hosiery. An advertisement from the March 15, 1930 issue of *Vogue* shows a glamorous portrait of Elsa Schiaparelli and describes stockings that resembled crêpe chiffon, rough sports crêpe, shantung, and her much publicized tweed. It was a daring fashion idea.

That same year she also developed a collection of jewelry, necklaces and bracelets made of Prystal, a relative of Bakelite, multicolored wood, and zigzagged Triolet jewels in Galalithe and silver. Many of which, though not all, were designed and made by Elsa

Triolet, the Russian-French writer. Others were designed by Etienne de Beaumont, of which I have several that were given to me by his nephew, Comte Henri de Beaumont, and a variety of other artisans, including Maison René Lalique, Maison Ardor, and Jean Clément, who made eccentric jewels unlike anything ever seen before. They were more barbarically tribal and artistic and intellectual than anything called a jewel before Schiap.

The year 1931 marked the appearance of even more interesting and unusual cuts in her clothes with provocative, signature Schiaparelli details. It just seemed to never end. Her spring collection featured her first sequin embroideries on evening gowns. The summer styles were inspired by the *Exposition Coloniale Internationale* that opened in Paris that May. Edward Steichen photographed an exciting new Schiaparelli innovation in evening attire fashions for the June 1, 1931 issue of *Vogue*, the so-called hostess pajamas. The ensemble, modeled by the Comtesse de Zoppola, consisted of a short gold brocade jacket with bow-tied front flaps paired with bouffant pants in orange crêpe de Chine. Schiaparelli wore the same outfit at a presentation of her friend Madame Agnès's hats. Aside from the exoticism elements, this collection contained some of her slick modernist looks. *Vogue* wrote, "The conventions of cut held no restraint for her, rather they were something to be ignored in her avoidance of the banal."[13] Suits had jackets without collars, vests had a trompe-l'oeil crisscrossed effect, and a wooden soldier silhouette introduced padded shoulders with an emphasis on the natural waist. The same year, Schiaparelli revived her jupe-culotte for tennis champion Lili de Alvarez. The rather sober skirt had the British sports spectators and press howling with outrage. But those skirts, flapping on the court, were the embodiment of ultra-chic.

In March 1932, Hoyningen-Huene photographed actress Ina Claire in a chevron-printed Schiap dress and jersey gloves, coyly posed with a tiny cocktail glass and winking at the camera in sly amusement. On her head was the famous Mad Cap, a stretchy tube-like knit cap. The actress's endorsement of the hat created a veritable fashion frenzy. It became such a success, Schiap recalls in her auto-biography, that she eventually regretted designing it. It was seen absolutely everywhere, from the chicest uptown stores to the smallest shops in out-of-the way places all over world. She said, "From all the shop windows, including the 'five-and-ten-cent' stores, at the corner of every street, from every bus, in town and in the country, the naughty hat obsessed her, until one day it winked at her from the bald head of a baby in a pram. That day she gave the order to her salesgirls to destroy every single one in stock, to refuse to sell it, and never to mention it again."[14]

In her 1932 collections, Schiaparelli introduced her first apron-dresses that closed in the back, a design element she'd use many times in many different ways. Bettina Bergery remembered the peculiarity of the closures as "mechanical and severe . . . The sheer contrast of the hardness of the clips to the softness of the clothes, and the texture of the new fabrics, was very new."[15] She also showed her first epau-let shoulders for winter that year, with a very famous model called Hotchacha, a navy blue corduroy coat that proved to be a big hit with American buyers. Hollywood designer Adrian also started to use her approach to shoulders that year when Joan Crawford, who already wore Schiap clothes in publicity stills and in films, demanded he copy this new Schiaparelli silhouette for her. British *Vogue* said that her wooden soldier silhouette "transforms you from head to toe."[16] In the film *Je te Confie Ma Femme* (1933) you can see Schiaparelli's use of faggoting to enhance this effect. In the film, actress Arletty (Léonie Marie Julie Bathiat) wears an exaggerated version, created with the use of squared-off, undulated panels applied to the shoulders, with a peculiar neckline appliqué topped off with a pillbox hat. The overall effect is startling! Her football player-like shoulders were as advanced as fashion had gone at that time.

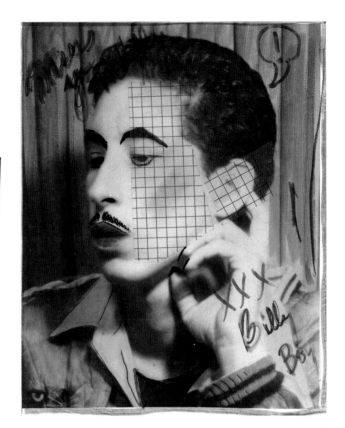

LEFT: *This picture of Calvin Churchman and me was taken around the time that I first met him and understood that love was not at all what I felt for my then-boyfriend Christopher. Calvin was for me a great genius and an inspiration.* RIGHT: *This is a photograph of me, aged fourteen, taken in a photo booth at Penn Station in Manhattan on the encouragement of Andy Warhol. Warhol kept the photos and a week or two later he told me to visit him and he handed me a stack of prints. I scribbled on nearly all of them in magic marker, adding the newly discovered (for myself at least) Letraset grid pattern.*

This Polaroid was taken in our home after a huge party we threw for our friend Myriam Schaefer, who was Jean Paul Gaultier's main designer at the time and who is now known for the iconic handbag she did for Balenciaga as well as her own eponymous collection. On the eve of a trip to Moscow, the party lasted until eight o'clock in the morning. Everyone of the Who's Who of Paris attended.

This photograph was the marquee image for the 1980 Danceteria fashion show of my work acquired by the Union Française des Arts du Costume (UFAC) at the Musée du Louvre, selected personally by Yvonne Deslandres. The Lobster tuxedo is now in the collection of the Costume Institute at the Metropolitan Museum of Art, chosen by Diana Vreeland and Paul Ettesvold.

This gown from 1936 was given to me by Marlene Dietrich, whom I befriended in the mid-1970s. She told me enchanting stories—many of which are not suitable for this book—and gave me some of her clothes, including this gown: a white ribbed Ottoman silk blend coat-gown. The decorative full-length zipper is plastic, which was an innovation of Schiaparelli's dating to 1935. The Bakelite bracelet, with initials "E.S.," was owned by Elsa Schiaparelli, though it is not by her. It was given to me by Schiaparelli's daughter, Gogo.

A sophisticated Schiaparelli evening gown of red satin covered in sumptuously grand ecru appliqués of lace dating to 1939. The unusual cut, with a mutton-leg—effect sleeve, has a remotely Directoire feeling. The Schiaparelli Colbert blue gloves were meant to be worn with the gown, as was the necklace of cut stones and glass on a black taffeta ruban by Gripoix (all the same date).

An amazingly cut "Frolic Purple" 1938 evening ensemble with a weighted train, draped on one side. It is made from moroccan crêpe and velvet. The belt is two-toned and made of three triangular panels, also draped on one side. The silk velvet jacket is fitted with large crystal buttons at the waistline. The two cherub brooches by Jean Schlumberger were given to me by Sir Cecil Beaton. The ring in gilt mesh beads by Jean Schlumberger is called the "Forget-Me-Knot," and was inspired by Victorian jewels and the tradition of tying a bow around one's finger so as not to forget a loved one. The Schiaparelli hat in the shape of a mask is in parlor pink satin. The handbag is an envelope pouch in gilt mesh lined in cream-colored satin by Schiaparelli. The gold kid leather gloves are labeled Schiaparelli and are haute couture, not the Fownes license agreement from the United States.

Petrol blue velvet mechanics overalls, made for strolling on a boardwalk or afternoon lunches on the beach. Two front pockets are the only decorative motifs. Made for and worn by the honorable Mrs. Reginald "Daisy" Fellowes, 1929–30. Matching booties by André Perugia for Schiaparelli in suede. The shaggy mohair jacket has Bakelite buttons and is from the same year and made to go with this ensemble. Elsa Triolet made the necklace in Galalith ovoid shapes, 1931. This tricot knit hat is among the famous knit hats made by Schiaparelli at the beginning of her career, from the very early 1930s. These types of hats inspired artists such as André Breton and other surrealists. It was photographed by Man Ray on Schiaparelli herself and once belonged to her.

Bettina Bergery, apart from Lala and my son, Alec Jiri, was the closest person to me in my life. I saw her nearly every day from the late 1970s until she passed away in 1991. We ate dinner with her most regularly and often she came to my house (and then with Lala, our house) and we just hung out. Looking back it seems rare that a 20-year-old was hanging out with an octogenerian. It was very "Harold and Maude" when I think about it now, though at the time I never thought of the age difference.

Radical, too, were the colors that Schiap was using. Hues like
Sang de Boeuf, Groseille, Beet Red, and Cardinal Red were matched
to outfits in contrasting colors such as vanilla white, chocolate brown,
and inky blues and blacks. "The colors of the clothes were the same
found in modern paintings . . . Poiret had made successful contrasts
with his artistic clothes, but when Schiaparelli made clothes, they
were much more sexy and svelte, the colors made each elegant lady
look like the fashion drawings of the time,"[17] said Bettina Bergery.
It is at this moment that the Schiaparelli palette begins to take on a
confidence that would continue to develop throughout her career.
I have many pieces from these years; all you need to do is look at a
book on modern painting and look up a year and you can see that
the palette of the modernists was identical to the colors Schiap used.

An advertisement in *Vogue* in August of 1932 announced a new
Schiaparelli-sponsored artificial silk, now known as rayon. In fact,
she promoted it so successfully that it was the first synthetic to be
widely used. She built an entire collection of the elastic rayon *crêpe
ribouldingue*, some of which had a crushed effect or a goffered "tree
bark" effect called Mélodie because its raised designs looked like
musical notes. Filochard looked like jasper or gabardine. Another
new synthetic fabric was a *peau d'ange* jersey called Jersarelli, a
play on Schiaparelli's name. It was a deeply crinkled, fine-ribbed,
reversible synthetic crêpe, brilliant and shiny on one side and matte
on the other. (Jersala, or Jersela, was synthetic silk jersey with a
satin-like finish.) The April 1932 issue of *Harper's Bazaar* said her
fabrics were "nothing short of thrilling, for she is a law unto herself
in such matters." At the London première of Noël Coward's *Words
and Music* in October of that year, Schiap caused a commotion by
wearing a gown made of a deep mulberry red Jersala. The back was
completely exposed, with a wide and squared-off *décolleté*. In a nod
to her American clients' experiences with Prohibition, the silhouette
was named Clandestine and the gown called Speakeasy because the

ample pleats in the back created a space to conceal a whiskey flask.

These flasks are connected to one of the more bizarre Schiaparelli incidents in my life. In the early 1980s I was leaving a dive bar in the Marais where I'd just enjoyed a few drinks with friends. I preceded down a dark street and out of the shadows jumps an old man in his seventies or eighties. He wasn't a bum, but he was not a gentleman either. He asked me for a cigarette, so I opened my cigarette case and handed him a Balkan Sobranie in shocking pink. He looked at it with some hesitation, and I assured him to it was a really good, normal cigarette. I then took out a lighter and lit it. He told me, "You know, you're the fifth person I've asked for a cigarette and nobody gave me one." I replied politely that it was no trouble. He proceeded to take out a leather-covered flask with a small gold signature on it that I could not make out. He unscrewed the cap, which doubled as a shot glass, poured some whiskey in it and handed it to me. I downed the hard liquor. When I was handing it back, the glint on the flask caught my eye, and I asked him if I could see it. He said yes, a bit surprised. I turned toward a distant streetlight and saw stamped on the leather "étui Schiaparelli" in gold. I simply gasped! "Where did you get this?" I asked. He told me he had had it since he was a young man. I explained that name meant a lot to me, and asked if he would consider selling it to me. He was a bit reluctant, of course, maybe even suspicious, but I waved 200 francs at him, which was quite a tidy bit of coin back then, and set up a meeting in front of the Lancel shop on place de l'Opéra the next day. He got a brand new flask and I was in seventh heaven.

Schiaparelli continued to sponsor many types of products and began to license her name. As early as 1930, she had licenses for jewelry and modernist buttons that were available in North and South America. These early buttons were hand-made in Paris by the same artisans who made her haute couture buttons, most often by Jean Clément. I have one set that is made to look like cats and they are presented on a card imprinted with her name. I have a very big assortment of mesh haute couture jewels, too. I love the way Schiaparelli used metallic mesh and chainmail to make everything from clothes to purses and jewels, transcending the material's form by shaping and draping it as if it were cloth.

In 1932, the Schiaparelli establishment expanded by two more floors to house the four hundred employees in the eight different workshops that were required to make the seven to eight thousand garments sold that year alone. Thérèse de Caramen-Chimay's office was under the stairway, as space was restricted even in these new quarters. "Pour la ville" and "Pour le soir" were added to the black and white sign outside. Jean-Michel Frank made up the salon to look like a boat interior, with white walls outlined with black and bright colors. Heavy naval rope was hung against the walls to display scarves and sweaters and the wool to show the range available. There were black patent leather curtains, simple black wood furniture, and multicolored rugs. A map of the Basque coast, painted by Jean Clément in green and blue against a white moleskin background, was on one wall. The shop was furnished with pieces purchased at the Jean Désert company liquidation sale. By the time Frank decorated the place Vendôme salons, his style (and Schiap's) had become a bit more romantic, but somehow remained severely modernistic. Like Frank, Schiaparelli played on contrasts, rough and smooth, shiny and matte, thick and thin materials. The harmony between the two ultra modern designers resulted in stunning visuals that had a great effect upon foreign buyers, especially Americans. The saleswomen, wearing little black dresses that resembled schoolgirl uniforms, sat behind black school desks. Despite Schiaparelli's use of bold color, she was still a tyrant when it came to her use of black, using it on nearly everything, including the delivery van she acquired and marked with white letters: "Schiaparelli—Pour le Sport—Pour la Ville—Pour le Soir."

Schiap had also moved her personal home base from her rue Barbet-de-Jouy apartment to a blvd. St. Germain apartment.

Jean-Michel Frank also designed the interiors in stark, black-and-white-themed rooms, accented with patches of bright color. There were rubberized chairs and glass-topped tables, black distressed wood furniture, parchment furniture, curved lacquered low tables and exotic fur rugs on the floor.

To celebrate her new place, she invited over a group of friends that included, oddly enough, her rival Mademoiselle Chanel. According to Schiap's memoir, Chanel "at the sight of this modern furniture and black plates shuddered as if she were passing a cemetery."[18] The heat of the summer transferred the white rubber to the seats of the guests' clothes, and Schiap joked that they looked like the trompe-l'oeil sweaters that had paid for the apartment's furnishings. Chanel referred to Schiaparelli condescendingly as "that Italian who's making clothes." Schiap, in turn, alluded to Chanel as "that dreary little bourgeoise." Edna Woolman Chase, editor-in-chief of *Vogue*, recalled an incident between these two strong personalities of fashion where "[Chanel] nearly ripped a Schiaparelli blouse off the Duchesse d'Ayen in an attempt to rearrange it more to her liking."[19] She went on to explain that one afternoon Horst and Schiaparelli were about to have lunch at the Paris Ritz when Chanel walked in. Chanel, always friendly with Horst, smiled sweetly and asked her friends to go on in for lunch while she stopped to chat with him. He rose to speak to her, which turned out to be a major mistake. Chanel stood talking to him for an entire hour, completely ignoring Schiaparelli, who one can imagine was turning her famous shade of shocking pink. Horst broke the deadlock as he glanced at his watch, murmured his regrets, and hurried away without any lunch to an appointment at his studio.

Even though she was a designer of haute couture, Schiap still took into consideration the economic depression that was beginning to have an impact in France. Many of her clients were Americans who had a diminished need for extravagant wardrobes and endless amounts of clothes. She believed in practical, multi-purpose clothes and, in the same way that Frank believed in simple, functional furnishings, often made of the most humble materials. Frank also collaborated with many of the same artists as Schiaparelli, like the Giacometti brothers (whom he essentially discovered and spurred to go on to become sculptors), Dalí, Christian Bérard, Alexander Rodchenko, and many others. Schiap was called an "architect of clothes" by *Vogue*, contrasted to Frank being called "a fashion designer for the home." It was often said her clothes were strict, clean, and angular. After her wooden soldier silhouette, she was accused of de-feminizing women, taking away the cozy, comfy part of femininity. Frank was accused of stripping down rooms to the barest of essentials, making them hard and angular at times, but often using feminine, soft materials.

Meanwhile, customers continued to come in droves, so many that in March 1932 Schiaparelli rented another small place at the back of the building to be run independently of the main establishment. It was simply called "Schiap" and was the first of her famous boutiques. One could find ready-made clothes and accessories at reasonable prices, beachwear, the now famous pajamas, sweaters, bonnets, suits, separates, and costume jewelry. Against one wall was a showcase with big glass pickle jars decorated with eyelashes made of paper or feathers, red lips made of leather, and all sorts of knit hats, feather boas, and scarves. That same year, Janet Flanner wrote a lavish profile of Schiaparelli in the June 18 issue of *The New Yorker* that touted her as the ne plus ultra of modernity. Such success in five short years, all from scratch.

In November, Schiap opened her London salon at 36 Upper Grosvenor Street. It was the usual kind of house you find in London, quite narrow, with four stories. She had the entirety of English high society as clientele. Schiap has said she deeply felt the contrast between the masculine city of London and the most feminine city, Paris. Due to this combination, Schiap felt as if she were exploding with ideas like a bright display of fireworks in her mind.

In keeping with her attraction to new materials, she developed a keen interest in British textiles. She visited all kinds of factories in England and Scotland, notably the Isle of Skye, and the house of Duncan MacLeod of Skeabow where some of the most striking tweeds in the world were made. In Scotland, Schiaparelli saw black sheep for the first time. Of her experience, Schiap recalled later in life just how much she'd learned and that her hosts were so charming and kind to her that she'd have stayed with them much longer if it were possible.

Her summer collection of 1933 reflects this British Isles influence in its textiles. A startling afternoon dress was made of string lace. Fresh-looking seersucker Scottish jackets were matched to sober skirts. Capes, with interior cords to keep them in place, were shown in fabrics like the Irish tweed and Irish Vale of Avoca dyed in the wool. The predominant colors were Eel Grey and Mussel Blue mixed with yellow, brown, and dark pink.[20]

In February of 1933 Elsa sailed across the Atlantic to New York for a vacation. It was her first trip back since 1929. She had not planned to work, but found herself giving a lecture at a luncheon given by the Fashion Group of New York. Dressed in a large shouldered coat with a prominent collar trimmed in monkey, and a circus hat atop her neatly coiffed head, she spoke about the latest trends for shiny cottons, the chic of broad padded shoulders, and pants for women (she disapproved of women wearing pants in the streets, but encouraged them for home entertaining, gardening, or country walks with family and friends). This lecture, so confidently delivered to the dumbstruck fashion faithful crowd, was of great importance. Schiaparelli was taken seriously by the fashion world, so seriously that she managed to make women wear lamb chops on their heads with complete confidence and pride a few years later.

Schiap continued to innovate in her designs of the early 1930s, creating a spiral-pleated matelassé gown with an optical illusion effect and maintaining the triangular shape in suits that she called "trays" and "shelves." Dresses were svelte and body hugging, but incorporated contrasting references to male attire that added another level of sexiness. "By keeping men off you keep them,"[21] she said. Her style incorporated every sort of masculine detail, as best seen in a menswear-style dinner jacket covered in sequins that appeared in *Harper's Bazaar* in March 1931. She also referenced colors of the military working class men's uniforms, giving them names like Granite Grey and Cathay Blue. Redingotes were transformed into severe, stylized hostess gowns and smart cocktail coats. One particular coat from 1933, in thick tweed in off-white cream, was cut exactly like a French eighteenth-century coachman's coat, with classical pockets and rather large hooks for buttons. Many years after acquiring this coat, I discovered that this particular button is most likely based on a series of sketches by Meret Oppenheim. Several other Schiap accessories, like a purse with hand-shaped closure and a porcelain hand that encircles a boutonnière, also resemble Oppenheim's illustrations.

"Found art" is a Surrealist iconographic term and staple of the movement. It uses Victorian romanticism of the disembodied hand and other body parts. The hand, and its shadow companion the glove, played a big role in the accessories of Schiaparelli. My friend Eliane Bonabel, who created the cage-like structure of the doll mannequins for the *Petit Théatre de la Mode* of 1945–46, collected hand motif objects. I had asked her about her predilection for these surrealist objects and she explained:

> In the early 1930s, the first rise of Surrealism in fashion occurred, which coincided with the Victoriana craze of the same time. Although the Surrealists like Dalí and Man Ray saw this motif as a Surrealist symbol, it had been used for centuries in the decorative arts. Schiaparelli had used them a lot over the course of the 1930s, but she wasn't the one

who brought it into fashion, it was shown in other designers'
collections, as well.[22]

The appearance of hand-shaped accessories in Schiaparelli's
fall 1934 collection coincided with the fifth edition of the *Minotaure*,
which had come out in May 1934. The illustrations of suggestively
posed hands in an essay by Georges Hugnet called "Petite Rêverie
du Grand Veneur" ("Small Dream of the Great Huntsman") may
have inspired Jean Schlumberger to create brooches for Schiaparelli.
In a photo made to illustrate the book of poems of writer Lisa
Deharme, *Le Coeur de Pic* (*The Woodpecker's Heart*) published in
1937, we see what appear to be the Schlumberger hands. He also
designed a brooch of a hand holding a rose and a matching belt of
two clasping hands. He said that brooch was one of the most famous
Schiaparelli pieces he ever created. In 1935, Man Ray photographed
hands painted by Picasso in trompe-l'oeil Schiaparelli gloves. His
obsession with hands appears in his portrait of Schiaparelli, who
uses wooden mannequin hands in place of her own. Elsa's own com-
mitment to the theme extended to her perfumes, which came in a
Jean-Michel Frank–designed plaster hand called "Le Beau Geste"
(The Handsome Gesture).

CHAPTER 21

1934

The year 1934 was a particularly interesting year for Schiaparelli. There were collections called Stormy Weather Silhouette, Typhoon Line, the Bird Silhouette, and Fish Silhouette for the evening. The Cone Silhouette was also included for that year and we cannot forget the Indian Silhouette. That year it was all about Backward, Forward, Upward, Downward! The lines of her designs looked as if they had been blown back or blown forward, the breast and waist went north and the length went south; everything was lengthened and elongated. Her imagination picked up speed and landmark innovations started to snowball.

Time magazine featured her on the cover that year and among the many compliments in the article, the most telling is that "Madame Schiaparelli is the one to whom the word 'genius' is applied most often."[1] Despite her reputation for the extreme, her clothes made a lot of pragmatic sense and were what women wanted to wear, including American women. Schiaparelli's immense success in the USA was linked to the way that she managed to design for any woman, regardless of her physical flaws or imperfections. It was a genuine chic achieved through thoughtfulness and an emphasis on pragmatic aspects of life like health, fitness, and practicality. She stood by her belief that quality and not quantity was key to dressing well, and she did not talk down to women with restrained budgets, an unspoken custom in some haute couture houses. The general consensus was that her brand of French chic was the ultimate in sophistication: smart, modernistic in its functionality, and clever in its new use of fabrics, textures, and colors, with many truly surprising innovations with the cuts and drapery. It also was the most international of the new styles coming out of the Parisian haute couture, and that spoke to women all over the world. Schiap's designs were different from the ultra snobbish, extremely chauvinistic clothes that Parisian designers felt were for the wealthy Parisian woman and no one else. This attitude of democracy was rather new, even shocking to the haute couture establishment, and the Chambre Syndicale de la Haute Couture often battled with Schiap over the rules she flagrantly ignored at times.

Naming colors, a predilection of the Second Empire period under the Empress Eugenie, became a Schiaparelli hallmark, for example: Stratosphère Purple, Astral (a greyish-blue), Cocotte (a light cherry pink), Petit-Pois (a "new" green), and Gris Foncé Chaud (a deep hot grey). To compound these frivolities, new fabrics appeared in these wild colors: acetate moiré, un-crushable rayon Cosmic net (a new double layered tulle), Feather wool (a long-fiber wool tipped with black or silver), Capricorne (a knitted rayon which could not be distinguished from wool), and Treebark, (a fabric that resembled its name). The latter was launched in August 1933 and was used extensively for several seasons. When I acquired a number of Daisy Fellowes's clothes they included some extraordinary Treebark gowns from 1933. Another cloqué fabric from this time was called Bigamie (of all things!), which was a crêpe made with bands of raised stripes.

Cellophane velvet and glass fabrics were, however, the innovations of the year. Cole Porter even included a reference in his song "You're The Top" (1934), as one of the ways to compliment someone you loved by saying "You're cellophane!" The glass fabric was a sensation, and although it perplexed the press, it thrilled the clients. "Schiaparelli's innovation, which caused gasps of amazement when first unveiled to the public gaze, has been perfected for general use now, and appears in a number of evening gowns and jackets in vibrant new colors of the modern mode"[2] came over the wires for general release. Mrs. Harrison Williams of New York had the distinction of buying the first glass dress ever sold, in Encre de Chine taffeta.

Another glass ensemble used variegated colors in a glass jacket that was worn over a black evening dress made of a dull, heavy crêpe with raised figures. The jacket of glass was held to a normal waistline by a transparent belt in the same material. It resembled Pyrex, but was paper-thin. Another evening ensemble from spring 1935 was comprised of a stiff, pale blue satin evening gown that was shown with an apron of Rhodophane worn over it, accessorized with many diamond bracelets and ropes of pearls. The fashion for crystal rings, earrings, and diamonds of 1933–34 was undoubtedly influenced by the new vogue for glass fabric. Lalique created a striking frosted glass bracelet for Schiaparelli, as well. The sculptor George Fite Waters called it "The New Art."

Towards the end of 1934, Schiaparelli produced two publicity-generating products. For the *Tribune in America*, she created an apron and all proceeds of its sales were donated to the Fresh Air Fund. This multi-purpose apron could be converted into a blouse for the hostess in the kitchen who must suddenly greet guests. It was rubber on one side and silk crêpe (available in several colors) on the other. The wearer could pull it up, attach it at the neck, and reveal the crêpe side; when dropped down, the rubber side was exposed and it became the perfect kitchen garment.

Her other product left a lingering legacy. Schiaparelli launched the perfumes Salut, Soucis, and Schiap (formerly known as S; the name was reverted in 1961). There were marvelous advertisements for the scents in *Vogue,* photographed on a black background with Schiaparelli's butterflies, a holdover motif from her painting days, gently lighting upon the bottle. The insects were made by Jean Clément. Another shows the bottle balanced on an automobile tire, of all things. Salut (which translates to "hi there!") was an evening scent with a top note of lily of the valley. The 1935 advertisement described it as "quintessentially exclusive. Reveals, accentuates and reflects personality." It is very interesting to note the emphasis on personality, a decidedly Surrealist manifesto concern. Soucis, which translates to "worries," is a very peculiar name for a scent. It was a delicate sandalwood fragrance, not unlike the 1970s essential oils found in hippie shops. Soucis was sometimes presented in a heart pierced by an arrow and touted as being subtle, discreet, and remarkably balanced. Schiap, well, Schiap just means Schiap, outrageous and chic. The ads, some of which featured a full-page Man Ray portrait of her, said equally tantalizing things: "For out of doors—Riding, golf, motoring and tennis are some of life's daily activities to which Schiap gives new charm. The sports-girl will appreciate this frank and refreshing perfume." Indeed, the name Schiap itself evokes to me witty repartee by a gorgeously dressed woman and sounds like the crack of a whip!

The scents were housed in trapezoidal bottles and boxed in tweed-pattern paper wrappers within rectangular cork boxes designed by Jean-Michel Frank. I cherish all the boxes and bottles I've collected, the most dazzling being the Roi Soleil, which belonged to Schiaparelli and was given to me by Gogo. The Beau Geste hand, in plaster, given to me by the actress Arletty, and the lily in plaster given to me by Marlene Dietrich figure in my collection as metaphysical objects now. I do not collect all the bottles and packages as a general rule, however, because there are simply thousands. I have the most significant and the most unusual examples, like the lamps made from Sleeping bottles used in the Schiap boutique. Paulette Laperche managed the perfume company even after Elsa Schiaparelli's death. It eventually employed forty people and did two million dollars in business each year. Allegedly, it was prevented from expanding because of the difficulties in obtaining the basic ingredients; Schiap would not hear of changing them or settling for substitutes.

1934 also marked the first year that Schiaparelli gave fashion shows just for hats. The most humorous ones had veils that covered the mouth, but left the eyes exposed. Two that were christened François Villon and Louis XIV, each with a silhouette that recalled the era of their names, had a great impact. A policeman's visor, called Riot, was a particularly successful hat that evoked the provocative and occasionally cynical Schiaparellian spirit. We find this aspect often in Schiaparelli's work, and it is perhaps a reflection of her personal outlook on life, the true element which makes creation of any sort transcend boundaries and become art. Evening hats reigned as well. Sequined styles worn with long dresses were considered fashion news. It's important to know that in 1934, the French Cour d'appel de Paris ruled that women's hats should be considered works of art and should be legally protected with copyrights and trademarks. According to *Women's Wear Daily* the judgment included a clause that said, "It is undeniable that the hats created by the high fashion houses participate, with their forms, their volumes, their lines and their colors, the same savoir-faire found in painting and sculpture. Such hats are in all evidence veritable works of artistic creation."[3]

The fashion shows were due in part to Schiap's newly established millinery salon. Previously her troops of Armenian knitters crafted her hats, along with friends and colleagues like milliners Suzanne Talbot and Madame Agnès, who were both noted for their extreme, avant-garde creations. The first creations to come out of the salon as purely Schiaparelli were velvet berets, a French classic that in the hands of Schiap featured bright-colors, corduroys, and, later, felt versions with upturned brims. There is an excellent photo in my collection of Bettina Bergery in the new rooms, where Madame Marcelle was the modelist. She said to me when I showed it to her in the late 1970s, "The first marvelous hats she did with Madame Marcelle were so fresh and so youthful and so sexy, not fussy like hats were at that time . . . Schiap's hats were stark and clean lined and so flattering for a head."[4]

The soon-to-be famous milliner Simone Mirman began her career in Schiap's London salon. I had the pleasure of meeting her several times early on in my passion for Schiaparelli. She was known to rework a hat to suit a face: "If your features are even, you can wear a small hat even though your face is large. A small woman can wear a big hat in spite of all the warnings against it; but it must be in proportion to her size. She should never try to wear a hat to make her look taller. She'll fool no one about her size that way."[5] Mirman headed the hat department on Upper Grosvenor Street until it closed in 1939. When she left, Schiaparelli, in her typical kind manner to employees, gave her the contact details for her English clientele. This would prove invaluable for launching Mirman's own millinery career.

It is only fair, as my soul contract with Schiaparelli came about from the encounter with one single hat, that I give special attention to this very important aspect of her career. Over the years of my collecting and research up until today, I have come across amazing testimonies of her peculiar genius for hats. I could fill a whole museum's room with just her hats. When I was still a teen, every Schiap hat I discovered in old fashion magazines simply lit my mind up with fire! I made endless scrapbooks of photocopies when I used to go to the New York Public Library, so many that the lady who made the copies (as you could not make them yourself) got to know me. The Louvre, which was just about to get refurbished, and an almost brand new U.F.A.C. had a small library where one could research. It was a field day for me, discovering all these wonderful hats. The pages of hats intrigued me the most in the official books of Schiap designs, each painstakingly rendered by Drian for every collection starting as early as 1933. Sometimes my husband, Lala, and I like to imagine how wonderful a display of all her hats would be and all the ways that we could stage them. Would they be paired with the clothes of each era, or displayed whimsically in a dreamy millinery landscape or fantasy boutique of pure, extravagant Surrealistic elegance and chic?

As chic and glamorous as the last half decade had been for Schiap, the next five years were to be a veritable blaze of creativity for the House of Schiaparelli, even more imaginative and successful than any before. How could she have known that for decades and decades after those years she would become the definition of Surrealism in high fashion and that her name would be immortalized well into the twenty-first century?

CHAPTER 22

1935-1940

Or give me a new Muse with stockings and suspenders
And a smile like a cat
With false eyelashes and finger-nails of carmine
And dressed by Schiaparelli, with a pill-box hat.

—Louis Macneice, from his epic poem "Autumn Journal"

(stanza XV, 1939)

Schiap recalls in her memoir that the year 1935 was such a busy and creative one for her that she wondered how she got through it all. On January 1, 1935, Schiaparelli completed her move from 4, rue de la Paix to 21, place Vendôme. Schiap was driven to make this ambitious move because of a desperate need for more space, despite the Depression. As of 1935, French haute couture showed a more than two billion franc deficit. Unemployment in the trade had been practically unheard of among the artisans furnishing materials and supplies, but by 1935 over ten thousand people in the field were out of work in Paris alone. Schiaparelli, however, was moving into a ninety-eight-room mansion. Few changes were made at 21, place Vendôme to accommodate the salons, ateliers, and offices of the establishment. Like all the others at place Vendôme, the historic façade of the building was built by Jules Hardouin-Mansart at the end of the seventeenth century. Schiaparelli turned down Poiret's house at the Rond-Point des Champs Elysées in favor of this site, remaining "faithful to her original district."[1] The severe Art Deco lettering of her logo also started to evolve to be extremely reckless and automatic looking. It evoked the Surrealists' fascination with trains of thought, unedited and flowing without deliberate direction, that often gave birth to a string of unrelated ideas. This form of Surrealism was baptized "automatic-writing" and provoked many an intellectual mind during that period. Schiap's grand-looking penmanship looked like it was signed with a drippy brush. This signature would henceforth be used on everything.

Schiap invented an elaborate new boutique where her ready-to-wear clothes, accessories, perfumes, and all sorts of frippery were displayed with panache. It also housed the Dalí transfigured stuffed bear that he had given her in reference to the moles on her cheek. Bettina Bergery dressed it in an orchid satin coat and covered it with costume jewels. The extraordinary Jean-Michel Frank undertook the decoration of the space. He installed a gilded bamboo cage for the perfume department in 1937 and engaged the Giacometti brothers to make gold-leaf columns with Surrealistic shells for lamps and other plaster furniture and decorative devices. Frank revived rough white linen *fauteuils crapauds*, literally "toad chairs," which were made modern yet subtle in their new conception, paring nineteenth-century ideas down to their fundamental lines with unexpected materials like straw, plastic, and suede. One settee eventually had a constellation print on it. There was also a heavy red swag trimmed in gold braid down the staircase that was notable enough to appear in a Cecil Beaton illustration for the March 1935 issue of *Vogue*. Schiap once sarcastically implied that her archrival Chanel was "so ashamed, she has to sneak into the Ritz from the back entrance" in order to avoid walking past Schiap's elegant house of fashion that was located next door to the hotel's main entrance.

The entire ambiance was startling and ingenious, the perfect backdrop for Schiaparelli garments. This was a time when photographers were forbidden at fashion shows, and artists such as

Bérard and Dufy, Eric and Vertès, drew the collections at the *premières.* The sensational showings of the collections were attended like the long-awaited opening of a highly anticipated play or opera, and were repeated up to three times a day, and, on certain occasions for very special and privileged clients, at a moments notice. The openings at Schiaparelli's salon were not quiet shows of garments on severe models, with lifeless expressions and stiff gestures as in other houses. There were music, lighting effects, dance steps and grouped tableaux, stunts, jokes, and even animals matched to the clothes.

The models were dressed head to toe in Schiaparelli, with matching hats, gloves, scarves, jewelry, shoes, hosiery, handbags, and maybe an umbrella, walking stick, or even a bouquet. Elsa, knowing her value, refused to sell just a few of the elements of a number in the collection, the client had to order the entire ensemble, accessories and all, or order nothing, unless of course, you had special permission from Elsa herself. Thérèse de Caraman-Chimay quoted Schiaparelli in one of her first press releases saying, "The search for an overall effect is so instinctive with her that details seem natural. A painting is not beautiful because of the treatment of one tree, and the attraction, although made up of details, is as indefinable as the charm."[2]

Schiaparelli's tight control of her aesthetic also extended to the windows that over-looked the place Vendôme. Bettina Bergery had a special gift, a *je ne sais quoi* for dressing the windows; according to Schiap she "made them the laughable, impudent, colourful last-born of the *quartier*, upsetting every tradition."[3] Soon, Bettina was given Schiaparellian figures for her displays. The house mascots were two eighteenth-century Pandora dolls, almost human size and made of wood, named Pascal and his passive wife Pascaline. They were shown in every conceivable esoteric setting, completing Bettina's surrealistic visions. Later on, a life-sized wooden donkey called Bimbo was added, complete with an exotic and gaudy Sicilian harness and saddle. This pet appeared in the Marcel Vertès ads for Shocking as early as 1943. Bettina also decorated the boutique windows, but had limited resources because Schiap was always a little stingy about spending money on them. Bettina recalled her work on the windows:

> Elsa allowed me to do absolutely anything, no matter how crazy . . . we had fountains and we had satin frogs covered in jewels, we had mises en scène and tableaux always showing the full outfits . . . there was always a theme which recalled the collections. The circus-themed collection had carousel ponies and confetti, the Forest collection had practically an entire forest installed in them . . . it was all very amusing and very glamorous. I loved doing the windows and felt it helped make Schiaparelli's a remarkable place, a must-see place for anyone visiting Paris. Dalí always gave me ideas for the window though he never did one himself. He suggested I use lobsters made of wax when the dress with his lobster was in the collection . . . and snowmen, polar bears, straw dummies and many other Surrealistic compositions. He always suggested extremely unrelated objects compiled together to make a little scene. It was a lot like his own Surreal exhibitions where he'd even occasionally include something by Schiaparelli, like the Shocking pink ski cap which covered the face entirely and was somewhat sinister looking.[4]

In Schiap's home there were two more wooden life-sized doll-like statues, named Mr. and Mrs. Satan. I had the pleasure of meeting these two formidable creatures at Gogo's house when I would visit. Schiap had acquired them in Edinburgh, but on separate occasions. Mrs. Satan first; Mr. Satan followed two years later. Once established in her space, she says, "They receive guests with enigmatic smiles and snapping eyes . . . They both have sinuous bodies shaped like an S—and hoofs instead of feet. As at the Fontana di Trevi in Rome one can put a penny in his hand if one wants to come back. Most people do."[5] I always did! They certainly must have looked upon me with great favor, as I was always so lucky concerning Schiaparelli.

The 1935 season started with a fashion show radio broadcast to America. She called the silhouette Celestial, and it featured pleated dresses and dress-saris. One had an astrological print of the Great Bear constellation, her personal touchstone. Perhaps she felt, in order to inaugurate the new place Vendôme salon, she should pay homage to her star sign for good luck. A clever Sherlock Holmes could have predicted the upcoming fashion tendencies by looking carefully at an April 1935 *Vogue* photo of Schiap in her office. Discreetly placed at hand's length was a small jade Buddha. There was a strong Oriental influence. The year before, the Princess Karam de Kapurthala had visited Paris for the first time. Madame Grès recalled to me how she and Schiaparelli found inspiration in her beauty and dress, with Schiap focusing on "the embroideries, the colors and the details . . . the chic was in her baroque usage of the Indian lavishness."[6] Furthermore, Schiaparelli won the stunning princess as a client, who "wore her Schiaparelli clothes everywhere that was fashionable in Paris and Europe."[7] The Maharani ordered twelve ensembles for herself and an entire wardrobe for her three-year-old daughter.[8]

Gowns from that collection had harem pants, or India trousers, underneath. Heavy rose-colored silk satin, so heavy that it could have stood alone, and dull rayon and grey silk crêpe, were used in strapless gowns. Some had long lamé scarves that could drape to the floor or attach to the arms via loops for a dramatic sweeping effect. She also created sensational sari dresses. The first Schiaparelli ensemble illustrated by Christian Bérard in *Vogue* was a sari of plum chiffon with orange underneath. Also, in 1935 Persia became Iran. The Shah Reza Pahlavi allowed his subjects to wear western clothes and banished the veil for women. Schiaparelli designed a cape called Thousand

and One Nights in black *berbère* wool lined in Parlor Pink taffeta. Embroidered with gilt and pink lamé threads, it was lavishly spotted with flowers and leaves in mottled reddish pink glass. It was worn with satin fingerless gloves. Jean Cocteau illustrated the ensemble for the July 1937 issue of *Harper's Bazaar*, where it was referred to as the Sentinelle cape. This illustration provided the inspiration for a 1950 photograph by Henri Clarke for *L'Album du Figaro* with Bettina Graziani as the model. Clarke told me that Schiaparelli was extremely intimidating to work with, that even when photographing one of her designs from before the war, she would make sure it was done correctly. In fact, it was not uncommon for the press to send prints of the photos they wanted to use to Place Vendôme for her approval before publication.

Her winter 1935–36 collection was revolutionary in many ways, as politics had entered into fashion. On September 29, 1935, the Associated Press wrote, "While the world is divided between kingdoms, republics, and dictatorships, and European statesmen weigh the problem of threatened Italo-Ethiopian war, Schiaparelli has launched both royalist and republican clothes." To commemorate the Silver Jubilee of George V, she offered royal blue and imperial violet clothes. For the Left, red French Revolution capes matched with Gallic rooster-crest caps. In order to show her anti-fascist feelings, she made a black evening gown in the form of an Ethiopian warrior's tunic with trousers of purple velvet, to honor Emperor Haile Selassie. A Venetian-inspired cape was a classically Schiaparellian reaction to the *Exposition de l'art Italien de Cimabue à Tiepolo* that opened in May of that year. It was made from an exclusive Schiaparelli fabric called le Simoun, a wrinkled silk taffeta by Bianchini. It was a hit, with a surprising political ramification of its own. Kathleen Cannell observed in *The Christian Science Monitor*, "Schiaparelli launched what you could call Democratic fashion. Before, if two women found each other wearing the same outfit, it would be followed by a rag-picker's war and they'd change couturiers . . . [now] they would amuse themselves in deciding who was the chicest amongst them."[9]

A small Surrealist revolution was about to occur that year in Schiaparelli's fabric, too. After a trip to Sweden, Schiap brought back the idea of a newspaper print fabric after seeing old women at the market selling fish wrapped in newspapers twisted into funny hat shapes. Back in Paris she asked Colcombet, the most daring textile maker, to produce a fabric made from clippings, even the sarcastic ones, about herself that she had gathered and pieced together like a puzzle. "But it will never sell!" exclaimed the terrorized man. Schiap stubbornly insisted, and she was right. It sold thousands of yards and was made in all sorts of colors. It was used for hats, beachwear, linings, blouses, umbrellas, and parasols. This avant-garde fabric also recalled Surrealist and Dadaist collages, as well as paintings by Braque, Picasso, and Kurt Schwitters. This fabric allowed textile designers to realize the extent to which they could go in creating strange and quirky prints.

The print became a thrilling and visionary fashion influence, and not only for women's clothes. Johan Colcombet wore a tie made from it in May 1935, artist Jean Dunand wore newsprint suits for the inaugural crossing of the Normandie, and Dalí was photographed wearing a dressing gown version while painting. A portrait of pilot Amy Mollison shows her newspaper scarf tucked into her Schiaparelli suit. Dolly Wilde, the eccentric niece of Oscar Wilde (and fan of Schiaparelli's most eccentric fashions) would be memorialized wearing a scarf in the print in her 1951 biography by Natalie Clifford Barney.

The fabric also was the cause of scandal. It all started rather innocently. Cecil Beaton did one of his usual "Fun at the Openings" sketches for British *Vogue*.[10] He showed many of Schiap's accessories, including the newspaper material hats, but he did not reproduce the material exactly. Instead he invented his own clippings. One headline said, "Vogue wins Bérard, loses Huene to the Enemy" referring to Christian Bérard and Hoyningen-Huene's swaps at *Vogue* and *Harper's Bazaar*. Most disturbingly, he replaced Schiaparelli's head with a picture of Hitler and penciled in "dirty Jews." Beaton was eventually fired from the magazine in January 1938 after having, again, penciled in anti-Semitic phrases illustrating an article about New York society.

Other less scandalous prints included a telegram gown which, with the same humor as a *New Yorker* cartoon, exclaimed, "All is well, mother-in-law in terrible shape." For Daisy Fellowes's book, in a flattering gesture to her ultra-important client, Elsa created a print that included the title, a sketch of the author, and pen and ink illustrations by Vertès. She also had the map of Normandy and frolicking pigs printed on crêpe for late evening supper suits. (I own a number of these ensembles, some from the wardrobe of Daisy Fellowes.) Schiap offered flower prints in primary colors and hallucinatory kinetic dots rimmed in contrasting tones.

Schiaparelli continued to incorporate the latest technologies. A variation on her glass fabric, called Spunglass, was shown as a collared dome cape over a Cosmic dress. There also was an unusual "oak-cork" crêpe. Discs, hatchets, and hearts of Lucite appeared on gold metal mounts with handles encased in Perspex, also called Prystal. Belts in cellophane had alphabets scribbled around them, were painted with animal crackers, or had a valentine edging of cellophane that was pierced so finely it looked like lace. "You felt like you just jumped out of the future when you wore her clothes, the materials were so extraordinary," Bettina Bergery recounted.[11]

Not everything was a success. Schiaparelli's so-called Eskimo collection was one of the few pre-war collections that bewildered more than amazed, with designs that made the wearer look bulky and over-clothed. One coat, for example, had details such as forearms shielded by gauntlets of husky fur that made the wearer look like an ice-hockey goalie. Hands were gloved in suede-lined fur gloves as thick as those a truck driver might wear, but American *Vogue* still called them the most exciting accessory of the year.

In 1933, Harry Houghton, of the Canadian branch of the Lightening Fastener Company, gave Schiaparelli ten thousand dollars to promote their plastic zippers on her clothing, which she did in 1935. When the collection launched, it was big news and a hit with the foreign buyers. But there was one minor setback. Schiap discovered the clothes could not be shipped to America, because, for reasons previously unknown to her, an agreement between France and America stipulated that French-made zippers could not be imported. The zipper controversy reached the size of a political issue and eventually, after a few days of hair-tearing, the zipper dresses were at last allowed into America. After the first collection, the Eclair zippers were replaced with versions from American manufacturer Talon. For her London clothing, Schiap used the Lightening Fastener, and for the Parisian clothes she kept the Eclairs.

Zippers were put on every conceivable garment, both as decoration and function. They could transform a garment. A dress with a zipper down the back could be worn zipped up for a casual dinner or down to create a formal evening gown. They showed up on country skirts, formal attire, sportswear, bathing suits, and pockets. They were placed on hips, sides, fronts, sleeves, pockets, wrists, and diagonally across the front of a dress or gown. Ski and golf suits had zipper pockets. Dresses, such as the magnificent cream shantung one in my collection with four bright red leather-tasseled plastic zippers, used them purely as decoration—as they do not open the pocket. One can easily imagine how exciting it must have been for a woman at the time to wear such a creation. The zipper was in the zeitgeist of the time.

I learned about Schiaparelli zippers all over the world. Charles James, who I knew from the days when we both lived at the Chelsea

Hotel, told me, "There was no designer who was young who in some way or another was not inspired by or fascinated by Schiaparelli—no one could simply say they didn't like her work except maybe Chanel."[12] I think that might be the first thing James ever said to me. I had the chance to ask him about zippers because I knew he had used them as early as she had, and even perhaps earlier. His astonishing Taxi dress (so-called because it was so easy to put on, it could be done in a taxi cab) had big Schiaparelli-inspired external hooks, but he designed other dresses with zippers that spiraled around the body. He said Schiap's use of zippers "was very much known in the world of haute couture, you read about Schiaparelli using them in the fashion magazines, who raved about the zips. I'm sure my using them preceded her use of them. At first, I was pissed off, I thought she copied me. Maybe it was in the air of the times, though." It was very unlikely Schiaparelli copied James's rare use of the zipper, but designers tend to think they are the ones who reinvented the world, and anecdotes often show this aspect of fashion rivalry.

Sometimes the modernistic zippers Schiap used were made a bit more baroque and had tassels of real garnets, pearls, dangling charms, bells, and other peculiar things. Bettina Bergery recalled with amusement "a zippered dress with a flashlight on it, you'd turn it on returning home from the opera . . . another zipper had a pencil attached to it on a chain, to write notes on special calling cards in a special pocket on the dress, you'd use that when you'd be in a nightclub . . . to pass on a note making some remark on so-and-so's dress or how bored you were . . . everything imaginable hung from [Schiaparelli's zippers]."[13] Bettina said often that the idea to use zippers came to Schiap from Aldous Huxley's novel *Brave New World*. In sync with Huxley, she used them often in the most bizarre, futurist ways. A burgundy red velvet dress from my collection has two dangling Bakelite elephants on the pull of its glaring white Talon zipper. The appliqué pockets on the front are edged in zipper just for the effect. The use of them there, though practically useless, is simply wonderful and very funny. She used them as if they were simply a trim. This in itself is wonderfully modern and fascinating as a fashion detail. A baby blue Viyella blouse, also in my collection, is astonishingly modern. Demure and short-sleeved, it has a slick transparent Lucite plastic zipper up the front. I find that the soft with the hard, the smooth with the textural fuzziness, make this a sensational garment. When I acquired it as part of a very large collection of Daisy Fellowes's wardrobe, I found this piece a particularly good example of the genius of Schiap. In that one blouse, you have her story, a story of contrasts. Like Schiap's character, it features elements that are at odds with each other.

Then of course there is the famous Schiap treatment of buttons. Her buttons echoed the most oddball things: crayfish, coins, birds in flight, safety pins, paper clips, spinning tops, lollipops, fish hooks, padlocks—she even used buttons that looked like shoelaces. There were buttons engraved by *pyrogravure* (wood burning), as seen on folkloric souvenir boxes, which Clément devised for her. Strange surreal innovations appeared in lieu of buttons, such as kerchiefs through holes (and square holes for that matter), all sorts of huge industrial chains, used both horizontally and vertically.

The spring 1936 season brought a long and lean silhouette, with lavish decorative ideas. Some of her jewels were filled with perfume, and the clothes included men's flannel shirt-coats (buyers thought they were as important as Chanel's little black dress, destined to become a fashion staple), shirt-style raincoats, and lots of gadgets like gilded chains to lift dresses. The main theme was a strange association of wild horses and the composer Chopin (the 100th anniversary of his birth was that year). Surrealism was still very evident in the winter collection, as seen in a plaster hat in the form of a mask with long, curled, red leather eyelashes and white lips. Her continued focus on this artistic style begs the question: Did

Schiap consider herself a Surrealist artist? She certainly utilized the ideas faithfully right through to the end of her career. Schiap's mid-season press release from that year, written by Bettina Bergery and Hortense MacDonald, mentioned that models numbers 419, 435, and 500 were "after Salvador Dalí."[14] His painting from the same year, *Jour et Nuit du Corps,* shows a pointy shouldered, bright Schiaparelli blue ski suit, with a plastic zipper down the front, with four roll-up blinds to expose the nude body underneath. Was this a Dalí an homage to Schiaparelli or a Schiaparelli-inspired painting by Dalí? One can only guess.

There were handbags in the form of birdcages, others that looked like beach balls and were in rubberized multi-colored silk, gold hearts on gold leather straps for the wrist (with matching brooches by Jean Schlumberger), and mailman's sacks, which introduced long, long straps on bags. One particularly odd one from an earlier collection was made from monkey fur to match Schiap's Perugia boots! The first example with this new look was given to me by Bettina Bergery and is even now quite peculiar and very chic though totally not politically correct (of course). Schiaparelli bared the toes when she introduced the Perugia-made shoe, which the April 1936 *Harper's Bazaar* described by saying, "The astonished foot . . . is wearing Schiaparelli's curious lattice-work elastic suede sans buckles or buttons." Around this time she did velvet bowties for shirts, showed Viennese-inspired petit point and gros point luggage, and vests that caused quite a stir in the fashion world. *Harper's Bazaar* wrote, "And Schiaparelli's brand new idea; hand-embroidered petit point for a waistcoat. On this one she puts buttons made of gold coins, like the silver coins you see on Austrian Tyrolian jackets. An idea for the needleworkers." That season she matched stockings to dresses and put kerchiefs on the heads of ladies in her evening gowns. There were no boundaries anymore for Schiaparelli. Odd associations of fabrics, styles, and accessories, all with some sort of Surrealistic leitmotif, were now long-established hallmarks. She tossed convention completely to the wind! The next five years were to be considered by some future scholars of fashion as her *Age d'Or*.

Schiaparelli's key to surprise and amusement in her accessories. There were triangular umbrellas, one in raffia and another in thick twill. Brooches were in the form of everything, including gingerbread pigs, baby elephants, fruit, vegetables, fish and crayfish, horse-drawn Roman chariots, and birds (designed by Bérard and executed by Jean Clément). There were brooches in the guise of lanterns that actually lit up, just like the famous Schiaparelli handbag whose interior was illuminated when opened. (It is interesting to note that the same year artists such as Dalí fixated on things that lit up.) This strange, almost mythical handbag is rare, and so far, there are no examples in either museum or private collections. The bag in question was simple and harmless enough from the outside but when opened revealed a sophisticated gilded metal interior. It was absurdly fitted out, with places for lipsticks, a swing-out mirror, and myriad pockets. Illuminating the interior as well as the face when the mirror swung out, there were two lights inside the bag for which one lights up the outside coach lantern, it is decorated with chiseled etchings attributed by some handbag dealers to Salvador Dalí though that is incorrect. These sketches depict Surrealistic women; one is the goddess of day and the other of night. These handbags were possibly manufactured for Schiaparelli around 1938 in Germany by the L.F.W. Straeter company. Straeter called them "Lite-on," and gave them international patent numbers. But these numbers originate not in the USA—as stated—but in France. The manufacturer later exploited this patented element and sold it well into the 1960s on bags of its own design. People often mistakenly attribute those bags to Schiaparelli.

More weird gadgets with sexual innuendo were made. One cannot forget her particularly strange "passion thermometers." This gadget was perfect for an era when sex was predominant in the minds of society.

Romance, contrary to sex appeal, was also in the air. A lot of the Surrealism played out in small details, most notably in the accessories. Cameos were surprising on sportswear; dangling hearts by Jean Schlumberger were decidedly nostalgic. Bracelets made of letter wax seals and charms, charm bracelets in pewter, ceramic vegetables on raffia cords, and plastic fish bracelets designed by Bérard were available. All these touches were ironic statements that contributed to the Surrealistic aspect of Schiaparelli's work in general, and I believe create an argument in favor of calling her work an "oeuvre." Clément's raffia bracelets and necklaces have a particular appeal for me. I have the bracelet with vegetables and several other ceramic figurative necklaces from this year, including a necklace of lily pads and flowers with the most hilarious closure made of a teeny frog.

Vertès illustrated Schiap's gloves with fingernails for *Vogue*. They were worn first by Bettina Bergery, who claimed she inspired Schiap to make them. She loved to tell me the story:

> I always wore the most eccentric of [Schiap's] gloves, I had several pairs of the ones with cat claws, which she said were inspired by me, as she often felt my 'cat's tongue' could spread like fire the most vicious of gossip. She thought I needed claws to accompany my temperament. At a formal dinner once, wearing the black gloves with gold claws, I was sitting near Marie-Laure (de Noailles) and Schiaparelli. Schiap said to me I should 'just tear the eyes out of the young lady flirting with Gaston and just get it over with.' Schiap said I was like a nasty cat when I was jealous, so she made me those gloves.[15]

She was not the only one to wear them and be inspired by the gloves, either. Eileen Agar, friend of Roland Penrose, the British Surrealist artist, spoke to me about them in London in 1988:

> When I saw them I instantly knew I had to wear them. I used such imagery in my earliest work, there were hands in my work as early as 1936, such as the portrait of me called *Photograph of the Artist Wearing Her Ceremonial Hat for Eating Bouillabaisse* . . . you can see how hands and hand themes were important for me . . . so I went to Schiaparelli and bought the gloves. They were expensive, even if I had a special 'artist's price,' but oh-so-chic . . . I wore them often and felt very elegant in them, they had that certain thing that was in the air at the time, which everyone understood and appreciated. Schiaparelli was so clever, such a genius she had . . . I wore other things of hers and the all were so unique . . . and unaffordable . . . you had to be rich to be elegant and artistic in those days.[16]

Jean Clement created the nails and delivered them through the supplier's entrance to the ateliers. There they were carefully applied to the simple black gloves one at a time. Other Surrealistic gloves included ghoulish veins.[17] Some featured lines on the palm, ready to be read by a fortuneteller, others resembled monkey paws, and one pair had clear windows to show lacquered fingernails. Leather gloves had gilt horns on the back that evoke the cuckolding wives in Italian folklore. She offered long satin and velvet mittens for evening with multi-colored tulle. Silk jersey styles were available in electrifying colors, like neon blue and acid green. Surrealistic effects included gilt embroidery that imitated a zipper from the top of the hand to the bottom. Other gloves had jagged trompe-l'oeil rips on them, sometimes covered in shocking pink rhinestones.

Belts had hollow daggers that each contained a comb and a lipstick, others had strange pockets on them or a policeman's billy club that contained a pencil for bridge. Some belts were aluminum, others braided patent leather, others lacquered string.

Hair ornaments, the ultimate female accessory, were still present at Schiaparelli's, but they were unlike anything that had adorned the hair since the eighteenth century. They were romantic and peculiar, with historic references but in new materials that made them totally modern. Plastic hair combs could look like anything but combs and inspired a revival of this accessory. There were beaded ones with matching bracelets by the Maison Lesage that looked like cornucopias, geisha girl hair pins, carnival masks, entwined baroque leaves. A gilt metal comb designed by Jean Schlumberger with a Rococo/Baroque swag of birds, fruit, and flowers that was attached to a long, spiraled conical form that could hold a fresh flower or piece of ivy on the head of some privileged, elegant woman.

I found my example of this comb at a shop owned by Madeleine Castaing, the famous decorator, who I have known since the 1970s. She was mad as a bat and known for wearing a tight rubber band around her head that pulled the loose skin back in order to give herself a cheap facelift. She covered this configuration with a pageboy wig. On her face, she painted oddly shaped lips in the 1920s manner, with Clara Bow style highly rouged cheeks, and long painted eyelashes just like in her famous portraits by Soutine. She drew eyelashes on under her eyes like a doll, in straight spaced little lines. If anyone else did this they would have appeared utterly out of their mind, but because it was the great Madeleine Castaing it was bemusing and respected. I don't think she realized that the decades had passed, and I am convinced she lived in the 1920s in her mind. For that alone you had to like her.

As a very young girl Madeleine was a famous silent screen film actress. She was the equivalent of a French Mary Pickford. She married and soon became known as a famous art collector and artist's muse and she started to make up her face to look like the paintings. She was close with Modigliani and Soutine, who did many famous paintings of her like *La Petite Madeleine des Décorateurs* in the Metropolitan Museum of Art's collection. She and her husband knew everyone from Henry Miller and Maurice Sachs to Erik Satie, Blaise Cendrars, André Derain, Jean Cocteau, Marc Chagall, and Pablo Picasso. They had an extraordinary collection of paintings from these masters of early twentieth-century art. She also became a famous decorator and was pretty much the go-to person when you wanted über chic, costly antiques and bibelots. It was considered the ultimate honor to be invited into her apartment. It looked like a film set, quite flawless, with a hugely eclectic group of antiques, put together simply by their similarity in colors. Her country house, though, was even more of a privilege be invited to, as it was considered the absolutely ne plus ultra of French taste. She was famous for her use of panther as carpeting and black lampshades. She somehow, with her bewitching taste, made Directoire and Second Empire look totally modern.

Madeleine was notorious for her shifting prices. When you expressed interest in something at her divine shop, the price would soar into the stratosphere. When I was in my late teens and early twenties, I had to use a complex system of feigning interest in other things that she would give out-of-this world values to. Then I would pretend to be vaguely disappointed in order to buy what I really wanted. It was a challenging but exhausting endeavor that sometimes took an entire day's worth of chatting and listening to her amazing spiels. Sometimes it worked, but even when it did not, her stories were mesmerizing. My Schiaparelli comb took no less than fifteen hours to negotiate down to a reasonable price. She went into a song and dance about nineteenth-century hair combs, which she claimed that piece was, while I listened for an extra hour. I loved this exchange in a perverse kind of way, listening to her embellish and exaggerate the gorgeous things she had in her shop. It was especially amusing when she was entirely off the track with her invented explanation for an item. My hair comb by Schlumberger and the story behind its acquisition still amuses me to this day, in spite of the tedious process it took to get it.

The Schiaparelli fabric prints of these years were more Surrealistic than ever, with images of postcards, playing cards, birds, a Jack-and-the-beanstalk print, telegraphs, and La Crise patchworks. The latter appeared to be darned together Li'l Abner-style and was a perfect reflection of the Depression's misery. The world's wealthiest women were now dressed in custom-made French haute couture clothes that looked like they were made from leftover bits of fabric. Decades in advance of the punk rockers of the 1980s, Schiap took anarchist camp with a touch of cynical irony to one of its furthest limits.

Schiap made an important trip to Russia that November for the Sample Fair of the Fashion Industries of France, accompanied by Cecil Beaton and her American publicity manager, Hortense MacDonald. The Russians adored parachuting at that time, and it in turn inspired Schiap to break away from her evening silhouettes of flared, bias-cut skirts with a natural waist to create the Parachute line. The new line shifted the waist up in Empire style bodices with natural shoulders and skirts that were seamed like a parachute. A tiny bolero jacket was offered to accommodate the high waistline. Another accessory was a parachute bonnet that looked like a child's pleated fan in white cotton, topstitched in red, and tied with red ribbon.

While in Russia, Schiap was asked to design a dress that newspapers claimed Russia's forty million women could wear. She designed a plain black dress similar to the style she loved to wear on a daily basis. To top the ensemble she offered a loose red coat lined with black, fastened with large, simple buttons, and a knitted wool hat that every woman could easily copy. The coat closed with a zip and had a concealed pocket. The Soviets eventually rejected this as an invitation to pickpockets in streetcars. This was also when her now famous "Impossible Interview" appeared in *Vogue*.[18] It featured a caricature drawing by Miguel Covarrubias with Soviet Premier Joseph Stalin and Schiap suspended from parachutes with other parachutists in the background. The cartoon depicts Schiap's idea that French fashion will be eventually imitated and assimilated into the wardrobes of Russian women, and that their natural desire to be pretty and smart will be stronger than any Soviet ideologies. In the end, Stalin asks her to cut the strings of his parachute because the idea is too much for him to accept. Schiap's trip to Russia caused scandal and controversy at home, too, with some very unpleasant and negative criticisms about her political allies, who included Bettina Bergery's husband, Gaston. Her trip was thought of as an aside to Bettina's husband and his political stand of the time and she accepted the offer upon the insistence of her friend. Rumors followed that she was closing her London branch in order to open one in Moscow. Mrs. MacDonald and Bettina demanded the press retract such rumors and unfounded gossip.

The Current Events collection followed the Parachute line. Salvador and Gala Dalí, Edward James, and Louis Bromfield were amongst the Who's Who of Paris elite at the opening. It was the moment of the Front Populaire in France, so Schiap made rabble-rouser hats and cravats with long Revolutionary streamers. It was also the accession of Edward VIII and she came out with Coronation velvets and furs, with hats based on the royal crowns. Her well-known coat and suit with drawer-pulls was a collaboration with Salvador Dalí that was based on his painting *Venus de Milo of the Drawers*.[19] The jacket was made from navy blue velvet and had five drawers with plastic drawer pulls. Underneath was a blouse of wrinkled sky blue taffeta woven into ruched bands. The conical hat was navy blue with a hemmed brim and grosgrain ribbon. The coat was accessorized with a hat with a black plastic crown. In Cecil Beaton's strange and eerily lit photograph of the clothing in *Vogue*, a model brandishes a copy of the June 15, 1936 issue of *Minotaure* whose cover, by Dalí, features a female body in a suggestive pose with the head of a minotaur, a drawer instead of breasts, a lobster spilling out of her stomach, red claw-like nails, with another small drawer at the ankle and keys and bottles adorning her legs. These are all themes that Schiaparelli also explored in her work. She also used this drawer motif after the war. The Dalí-inspired Drawer Pull hat in bright orange or yellow felt, complete with a bronze beaded knob, is hard to date. My story of this hat is very odd. One day in 1989, I came home to find a handsome stranger in my house. He had been welcomed by Lala, who believed he was an old friend of mine. I said to this dashing young man, "Hello, may I ask why you are here?" He told me that he loved Mdvanii and wanted to meet me. Over the next few days we became good friends. His name is Bill Black and he is an actor and film editor—we have the same initials. I also found out he had the same Schiaparelli hat. I said, "How and where did you find it?" to which he said, "I found it on my birthday about ten years ago." "That's odd, so did I, I found mine about ten years ago, on my birthday." I was not surprised to find out that we were born on the same day in the same year: March 10, 1960. The oddest thing about Bill was his strange story of being abducted by some sort of alien, and to this day when he passes under a streetlight it blows out. I have witnessed this and found it very strange indeed. I always wonder why we had met. He graciously gave me his Schiaparelli hat shortly thereafter. We've been friends ever since.

There is a now-iconic powder compact that looks like a New York City rotary pay phone dial that the world pretends was designed by Salvador Dalí, although it most definitely was not. It was originally shown in the July 1935 issue of *Harper's Bazaar* magazine. The original showed signs of Dalí's influence in the 1935 design, but surprisingly the manufacturer (at least according to his family) didn't even know about Surrealism and Dalí when he made it. When Dalí worked with Schiaparelli, which was only a few times, it was extensively written about in her press releases. The Dalí collaborations were duly noted in the house list for clients and buyers with their model numbers and a full description. I conspicuously used my compact on an occasion at a dinner in Paris with Dalí in the 1970s, but he was hardly even aware of its existence and only feigned a vague interest when I told him it was by Schiaparelli. He took it in his hands, examined it, and found it mildly amusing. That was that.

Through many years of research I discovered its true origins. As with most pre-war Schiaparelli accessories, it was manufactured by a family-owned atelier (which was in this case a very small company) headed by an *artisan fournisseur* named Bollack. They were expert metal and enamel workers, known for high-quality, small-sized fashion novelty accessories. This little workshop held the patent rights to the compact, as it was the custom for artisans to patent pieces they felt might be successful. Not all artisans had the possibility to ensure this fussy legal procedure. The compact started out as a haute couture piece made only for the season of 1935, made exclusively for Schiap with each and every one manufactured by the Bollack atelier. An agreement authorized her to subcontract an American-made copy for sale in the USA, to be sold as genuine Schiaparelli, but at a lower price so import charges were not included in the price. However, some stores chose to import the French version while other stores, perhaps not as high end, chose to sell the less expensive model. There was a market for both, as snob-appeal played a great factor in the buying and wearing of French haute couture during this period until the 1960s. I met with the heirs to the Bollack ateliers and inquired if they had any knowledge about how the compact came into being. They told me their grandfather made metal fashion accessories and the idea had come to him after seeing the use of telephone themes in popular culture, which was linked to the art of the era.

The original telephone dial powder compact, enameled in black (or cream) on both sides, is hand-made and marked "Déposé Tous Pays" (Registered Model in All Countries) and it came complete with a swan's down puff. Despite the attempt to prevent copies by including its patent label, it was mercilessly copied in rather bad reproductions up until the 1970s. It's exasperating to see these copies, many made in the USA, sold by American dealers and on-line as authentic ones as they bear little in common with the original in terms of quality.

After the first two originals of 1935, the story gets very complicated as far as which are considered authentic (only two of them) and which are unlicensed reproductions made long after the patent expired. In general, copies from the early 1950s are unusually strange colors like red, green, and blue, and were made usually from brass and tin sheet metal stampings (called *estampés* in French). Most copies found are by Stratton, a famous compact manufacturer in the USA from 1935 until the 1970s. Bollack also made the fish that lit up, the passion thermometer, the traffic signal brooch, and a number of other novelty accessories that were used by Schiap during the second half of the 1930s.

1936 brought another important muse into Schiap's life, in the form of a plaster cast of Mae West. The bust was quite small in reality (only twenty-nine inches tall) and by the American artist Gladys Lewis Bush (1897–1954), with exaggerated proportions and rather kitsch in nature. It led to the following year's debut of Schiaparelli's most famous perfume and fetish color, both influential and full of mystery and excitement. Schiap was supposed to design costumes for a movie called *Frivolous Sally*, which was re-written and re-named *Sapphire Sal* by Mae West. Schiap writes, "She had sent me all the most intimate details of her famous figure [and] for greater accuracy, a plaster statue of herself quite naked in the pose of Venus de Milo."[20] Upon seeing West's outrageously bosomy and curvy proportions, her first reaction was "How shocking!"[21] History was made though

I am convinced what she thought was shocking was the kitsch aspect of the relatively inelegant statuette. The perfume, with its supposed Mae West curves, was named Shocking.

Mae West's plaster bust and the silhouette also inspired the artist Leonor Fini who, in collaboration with Schiap, modeled the perfume's bottle on the form of a Victorian dress dummy. It was garnished with multi-colored glass flowers (by Lesage) and a tape measure scrawled with the scent's name hung around the neck. It was sealed in red wax stamped with Schiap's lucky "S." White lace was enameled on the dome packaging and it was all on a Shocking pink and gold plinth. The stopper was in the shape of a dressmaker's pin. An overwhelming number of articles appeared after the perfume's release that proclaimed enormous enthusiasm. "She uses 'Shocking' as her new term to describe that elusive quality which in the past has been sometimes known as 'It.' This year, if one wants to be smart, 'Shocking' is the word to use when discussing a glamorous woman, an amusing revue, or exciting personality."[22] Leonor Fini also confirmed its success, "Everyone wore it . . . Bébé [Bérard] used to dowse his whole body and even his beard and his dog Jacinthe with it. The G.I.s bought it in droves after the war, and it remained successful up until, well, they still make it I believe!"[23]

As for the name and color, Schiap wrote that it had flashed before her eyes. She wanted something impudent and full of life and evoking the East, not the West. "A shocking color, pure and undiluted." Christian Bérard and Jean Clément, whose genius for color were well established by 1937, are generally credited for developing this pugnacious shade. In his foreword to Palmer White's *Elsa Schiaparelli: Empress of Fashion* Yves Saint Laurent wrote that "she alone could have given to a pink the nerve of a red."[24] It was particularly effective in wool, taffeta, and satin, but long after Schiaparelli's retirement, it covered absolutely every surface requiring a color, from baby prams to cars and even buildings. There was even a sexy, *clin d'oeil* lingerie bag, in shocking pink satin edged in lace, in the form of ladies' panties with Schiaparelli's scrawling signature embroidered upon it. It has become part of the lexicon of color, historic and forever. The *Vogue* editor Bettina Ballard, in her 1960 autobiography, said, "Shocking pink was an invention of Schiaparelli and a symbol of her thinking. To be shocking was the snobbism of the moment, and she was a leader in this art."[25]

The Mae West form also contributed to the most shocking aspect of the bottle, which was that it had breasts. This also led to Schiap's invention of "fake breasts," padding the bosom, which was considered an incredible taboo. Diana Vreeland remembered, "A dress I had of Schiaparelli's that had fake ba-zooms—these funny little things that stuck out here . . . All I can say is that it was terribly chic. Don't ask me why, but it was."[26] Schiaparelli wrote about these first falsies. She explains how the hourglass silhouette mesmerized some of her girls, particularly the ones who did not have bosoms. She recalls a funny anecdote about a girl who had decided to be more provocative and used falsies, but ended up looking like she had four breasts after they slipped over the course of the evening. The woman was Bettina Bergery. She mused in her memoir, "Dalí absolutely loved the padded bosoms, and he was particularly thrilled to hear of my mishap . . . he said I had had a Dalí experience . . . and that he could have orchestrated it." This was the beginning of the falsie. The most modern were called Very Secret and they could be blown up with a straw to the ideal shape. It must have been quite hilarious back then, this whole preoccupation with breast size. I cannot emphasize enough how sexual innuendo, bordering on out-right sexual shock treatment, was such a very important aspect of Schiaparelli's clothes and thinking in general. The word Shocking was not by any chance vague. She genuinely did shock polite society on a regular basis.

From all this padding came the Hourglass silhouette, which was achieved the old-fashioned way by using bodices with boning and padding to dramatic effect. Broad, square shoulders, tiny waists, and rounded, accentuated hips, achieved in long evening costumes by bias-cut skirts which flared out at the knee. Another way of creating this effect was with longer jackets, with hip-accentuated peplums, matched with narrow sheaths or very, very short boleros with small waisted full-skirted gowns. It was very innovative and seen only briefly in this 1937 collection, before appearing again in 1947 with Christian Dior's New Look. Roger Vivier, the famous shoemaker and great friend to Dior, who designed many shoes for his collections said, "It goes without saying that her late 1930s fashions were an influence on him, the romanticism and also the shape of the dresses, the fashions they called the 'New Look' so obviously came from her pre-war fashions . . . although he'd never outwardly admit it, he'd obviously drawn greatly upon it. She had done 'Dior' before Dior and he did not like that."[27]

Probably the best-known ballerina-length dress was the one with the Dalí-inspired lobster and parsley print on white organdy with a bright orange (sometimes bead-encrusted) corset yoke. Sache, who translated many of Schiap's prints into reality, manufactured the fabric. There is a fantastic anecdote about Dalí and the dress that Bettina Bergery confirmed. "Oh yes, that's absolutely true, Salvador was determined to smear mayonnaise on that dress. He thought it was some sort of erotic paranoid expression. He and Elsa argued about it even. He said he was the artist and she replied that *she* was the artist, and her clients would have none of that, regardless of how art-y it was. He sincerely wished to do that, but he also adored to provoke anyone anywhere."

A full-length version was in Mrs. Wallis Simpson's famous trousseau. Cecil Beaton told me in the late 1970s that the dress was lengthened because "she had thick ankles and the shorter length was not becoming or flattering but as it was determined to be one of the most talked about dresses in the world, she was determined to have it in her trousseau, she knew it would make great press for her and the wedding."[28] His photo of her in the April 25, 1937 issue of *Vogue* is on the grounds of the Château de Candé and shows her standing in the garden, gathering blossoming branches, lobster evident in its entire splendor. During the same conversation Beaton also told me, "She looked particularly ravishing in those shots. I did several. To get the angle of that hatchet face right was no easy feat . . . The lobster dress photo was a great success for me, and for her and for Schiaparelli."

I had the chance to make the acquaintance of the Duchess of Windsor, as a teen in the mid-1970s. I found her very genteel. As I was a very young man she treated me with vague politeness in a very aristocratic manner. She had a rather chilling way at times, but other times she struck me as someone who'd love to just kick off her shoes and do the boogaloo. In my diary entries of the time, I wrote: "The Duchess of Windsor is very nice, (I think), she was severely dressed today with a lot of make-up . . . long Man Ray-ish lips, a bit like Diana V. but not as amazing, they remind me of the Vertès lips on Schiap ads . . . She said she 'adored Schiaparelli' and was sad she had died a few years ago . . . She said that for her the lobster dress was one of Schiaparelli's most amazing creations." Bettina Bergery told me that Wallis had been a client of Schiaparelli's long before her marriage to the Duke of Windsor, but said, "She was so difficult with the fitters, who'd sometimes come to me in tears."[29]

Despite the many Schiaparelli clothes Wallis had worn over the years, it was the lobster dress that seemed to be the most sensational and the most publicized. Other magazines showed the lobster dress in illustration form. René Gruau told me, "I remember the drawings I did of the Duchess of Windsor's trousseau for a fashion magazine. We were allowed to go to the House of Schiaparelli and draw a mannequin posing it, and I'd add her profile on to the drawing at the end. Then I did the famous lobster dress—it was such a novelty, and after the whole affair, the scandal and then, finally, their marriage, the trousseau was seen by the whole world and that Schiaparelli dress was immortalized, it was in every magazine. I was very pleased to have had the chance to sketch it and have it published."[30] The lobster print was also done on cotton for beachwear, which sold like wildfire to many of Schiap's private clients. Not too long after the success of lobsters on clothes, a number of different manufacturers in the USA made clothing with this crustacean sprawled across it.

The autumn collection themed Paris 1937, was based on the *Exposition Internationale des Arts et Techniques dans la Vie Moderne* which was held in Paris on the Trocadéro, in front of the Eiffel Tower. According to author Claude Arnaud, it was during this time that "Cocteau took advantage this way of his downtime to sketch motifs for Elsa Schiaparelli themes to the fury of her rival, Coco Chanel."[31] The collection included an evening gown that featured a lady's profile on the left sleeve with gleaming blonde bugle bead hair flowing down the sleeve to the wrist. The ensemble was completed by Cocteau's famous signature with his rakish star. Another Cocteau ensemble included a stunning redingote, embroidered by Lesage, of a trompe-l'oeil vase composed of two rose crowned faces in profile by Jean Cocteau. It was immediately identified as a Schiaparelli master-piece and widely covered in the popular press. It used the phenom-enon of pareidolia, the effect of seeing faces in places they are not intended, like in clouds or in a stain on wallpaper. This concept was greatly admired by the Dadaists and Surrealists. There is another piece related to Cocteau but the story has been incorrectly told for decades. There is a one-of-a-kind brooch in my collection, of which there are hundreds of counterfeit copies out in the world. It is often referred to as the Cocteau Eye brooch. The counterfeits are circulat-ing amongst collectors, who think it is an authentic one. The fake was manufactured by Patrick Retif and sold in the Louvre museum gift shop in 1984. It has been presumed, much later in the mid-1980s, that this eye-shaped brooch was a Schiaparelli jewel. In a certain way it was for a brief moment, as Cocteau drew it for Schiap for fun. It (the 1980s counterfeit) even appeared in Florence Muller's book on haute couture jewelry, which is particularly unfortunate as I told her this story thirty years earlier.

Bettina Bergery attempted to get Schiap to use the brooch in a collection around 1937. It was made in prototype form either by Cocteau or in collaboration with one of the artisans, most likely Jean Clément. It was worn in the subsequent collection's fashion show. According to Bettina Bergery, "Schiap was wild about it."[32] This apparently enraged Cocteau and he decided he'd no longer wanted it to be used as a Schiaparelli accessory, although officially one could say it was supposed to be one. So it seems the House of Schiaparelli never offered them to clients as a Schiap jewel and only one unique example exists, which is in my collection. The Musée de la Mode et du Textile had Patrick Rétif, a Parisian costume jeweler, reproduce it as a Schiaparelli brooch for the museum's boutique. He used a press photo of the one in my collection in L'Express magazine. Oddly, the photo was reversed and reduced in size, and not knowing what it was made from Rétif made it in slush cast metal and the resultant piece is backwards and a much smaller. It has nothing to do with the House of Schiaparelli since it was not made or sold by her. Those who bought the item in the museum's boutique have a reproduction of something which is not by Schiaparelli and not even by Cocteau since it's made incorrectly and not in the original materials.

It was no wonder that with the success of the Cocteau-designed ensembles for Schiaparelli. Chanel, who was also a close friend of the artist's, would be furious. In the first presentation of them, exuberant shouts of "bravo!" were belted out in the booming voice of Christian Bérard. Bettina Bergery told me, "If he liked the show he made remarks in a loud voice. His enthusiasm was immense and everybody was caught up in it. I am quite sure that many ideas became popular and sold well because Bébé kept on repeating 'C'est divin! C'est divin!' Schiaparelli claimed that when this supremely Parisian artist shouted during her shows it was a definite seal of approval, and it was true, he was a fashion judge and jury of the times all unto himself. The coat was a huge success, in fact, instantaneously, the moment Bébé saw it."[33] Other important evening looks from that year are the Pagliacci trousers in yellow taffeta and orchid satin coats with balloon sleeves seen in a dramatic Man Ray photograph for *Harper's Bazaar* and the now iconic Dalí collaboration Tears dress, which has the optical effect of having been ripped all over. It had a cleverly devised head wrap that was appliquéd with waving organza tears to further the illusion. It even had ruched fingerless gloves in pink to match its colors of violent violet-red-purple, bright blue, and shocking pink, all outlined in black.

The somewhat startling, and quite novel Neon fabric of that year spoke to Schiap's fondness for glaringly vibrant, violent colors. The shock value alone was chic, but when made into clothes with simple lines, trim and tailored, the effect was dazzling. There were prints of huge pansies in yellow and mauve around which was scrawled "Toutes mes pensées sont à vous," a line from Germaine Beaumont's *Lettre à Delphine*. Butterflies in every conceivable size, arrangement, and color were used for the summer collection. Some were textured in three-dimensional embroidery and appliqué. Some were very large, in contrasting neon colors, while others were realistic, photograph-like images. The theme of captive beauty was so dear to the Surrealists and so poetically manifest in that collection. In the *Life* magazine article, the dress ordered by the Duchess of Windsor for her trousseau says in its caption, "Colored butterflies printed on blue crepe are characteristic Schiaparelli touches on this evening gown designed for the Duchess of Windsor. Over it, an evening coat of navy blue horsehair lace. Blue is the Duke's favorite color."[34]

By December 1937, *Women's Wear Daily* was raving about "Schiaparelli's Famous Bolero Silhouette" as one of the "highlights of the season," and that the hats were as important as the clothes themselves with emphasis on the buttoned cushion version.[35] Some of these were black with shocking pink buttons. The one Bettina Bergery wore was black taffeta with two plastic wings, all in deep navy blue like Schiap's own. Dalí created designs for some details, such as buttons in the form of a chocolate tidbit covered in bees, an example of which he gave me as a young teen. We also find the iconic Shoe hat in this year. It was inspired by Dalí's 1933 photograph of his wife, Gala, in their home at Port Lligat wearing a shoe on her head and one on her right shoulder. In Schiap's presentation, it was worn with a suit embroidered with lips, with Bakelite lip buttons. This hat has remained one of the best-known creations of Schiaparelli. From this collection I have an all-black crêpe-and-velvet collarless jacket with lip-shaped pockets appliquéd to it. I also have a simply amazing Schiaparelli evening bag of this year made of Bakelite and felt which has the same red Bakelite lips, exactly shaped like the buttons, on it.

Dalí's wife Gala wore the hat, but Daisy Fellowes had the nerve to wear the entire ensemble perfectly and to much acclaim. Bettina Bergery recalled that "Daisy wore it in Venice . . . it was the most talked about hat ever, besides maybe Marie-Antoinette's coifs at court. It was truly something else to see her so nonchalantly wearing the shoe hat."[36] It sparked a bit of rivalry between the two women, and Bettina recounted that Dalí said Gala was jealous, but Gala said to me directly, "I wore it better than her. I was Dalí's creation, she could not wear it as only I could."[37]

Despite what the artist's wife may have remarked, Mrs. Fellowes was the epitome of the Schiaparelli type. By this era, she was diamond hard, severely elegant, boldly arrogant, and while she wore frills and flowers, tulle and butterflies, she was as cool as ice and knew she was the absolute leader of haute couture fashion. At least this is the impression she has left to posterity. This attitude is best summed up in a Marcel Vertès sketch of her with the shoe hat on her head, yawning behind a Tannhäuser program. Only a woman of such confidence in her place in the hierarchy of fashion could pull it off with such élan. But, despite the fact that Mrs. Fellowes was touted as the only one who had the nerve to wear it, the hat was worn by the famous, the fashion elite, and socialites throughout the world, sometimes in a subdued and more abstract form.[38] The bright shocking pink heel and sole was sometimes substituted for a discreet black felt. Nonetheless, according to *Life* magazine it "almost stopped New York traffic."[39]

The Lamb Chop hat and matching cutlet-embroidered suit covered in minute multi-colored mirrors was completely Dalí, recalling the painting of Gala with bacon on her shoulder and his rotted meat obsession of the late 1930s. "Dalí painted me with meat many times, he was obsessing on it and wanted me to wear it, so I did. Schiap embroidered meat on jackets for me and I wore the hat. I looked very well in it,"[40] Gala Dalí bragged. This meat-inspired hat created a riot of press at the time but Schiap defended this absurdity by saying, "I like to amuse myself, so I do so through some of my creations. If I didn't I would die."[41] The amount of press on that one hat alone is staggering. One Associated Press article includes a photo of a real lamb chop. "To keep you from eating the hat and wearing the chop, the bonnet and meat are shown close together."[42] It was recalled with rapture, enthrallment, and annoyance for years to come. The publicity for these two hats would follow Schiaparelli for the rest of her life and beyond.

The accessories were all variants of her Surrealist and playful themes: a huge bee brooch with plastic wings, articulated metal millipedes brooches, over-the-ear earrings and single earrings, gloves with jeweled rings or embroidered gold leaves, the amusing Toujours Fidèle dog-shaped cigarette case. One large straw hat had a powder puff and a mirror in the brim, a rather Surrealist place for a vanity. There was also the "slightly mad looking"[43] Sunbeam brooch by Jean Schlumberger with gilt rays studded with rhinestones. Thousands were sold throughout the world. Schlumberger said that "the sunbeam brooch used to be an ornament on a piece of furniture . . . it's something from the nineteenth century. Schiap instantly loved it." He also noted that Schiap was not always fond of the fact that his name was associated with the piece. "Madame Schiaparelli felt it was her creation as it was she who turned what would seem to be rubbish into something chic . . . it was infuriating but I do, now, see her point. Without her behind me I would never have succeeded. I would never have been noticed, the Sunbeam brooch was a great triumph for us both."[44]

Sleeping, Schiap's next foray into fragrance, was born in 1938. A heavy, sugary scent with top notes of vanilla, it came in a Baccarat crystal candlestick with a candle flame taper, and a cone-shaped candle snuffer. Its coordinated color was Sleeping Blue: a powdery, periwinkle shade of blue bordering on teal. "It lights the way to ecstasy," claimed the 1939 Vertès-drawn ad. It was called "Schiaparelli's own interpretation of a night perfume—caressing, intoxicating, lingering."[45] One could not make more sexual innuendo than that. It may not be a coincidence that Man Ray's painting *Le Beau Temps* of 1939 has the same candle and candle snuff as a head of one of the figures in the painting. Perhaps the theme was inspired by René Magritte's 1930 painting entitled *Dreaming Key*, in which the image of the same candle has a caption "Le plafond" (the ceiling). In due course, there were many versions of this perfume, and eventually a lipstick in a tube that was a trompe l'oeil, half melted candle. It was an archly witty and rather genius perfume concept from beginning to end. One Sleeping gift set came in a box representing an eighteenth-century drawing room with two doors that opened with keys hidden in the bottles. In another, a royal canopied bed in quilted grey satin, entirely hand-made, accommodated two snuggling bottles. And in another, the gloved hand of the Statue of Liberty held the candlestick taper aloft. Three miniature bottles nestled in a cradle of New York and others were cuckoo clocks which when opened a bird popped out and cuckooed! One was a music box that really worked, with two little bottles of Shocking that turned slowly around, going inside a little house flanked by two miniature doll house-sized potted plants in pink, the roof enscribed with "Shocking de Schiaparelli."

Nineteen thirty-eight yielded four collections that are probably the best known of her career. The year began with the frantic Circus collection, shown in February, followed by the lovely Pagan, Zodiac, and la Commedia dell'Arte (or Harlequin) collections.

The Circus collection had a million novelty effects and evening bustiers fitted to gowns, which resembled bareback riders' corsets. There were flared boleros with motifs of prancing dogs and horses, grey elephants, spotlit acrobats, tents, and clowns. A black crêpe sheath with soutache and trapunto padding was topped with a miniature hat that looked like a gold snail atop yards of black organdy veiling. The epitome of the Surreal was a skeleton dinner dress marked with embroidered ribs and spinal column made in trapunto quilting. The dress also echoed the era-defining expression "You can never be too rich or too thin," attributed to many famous women, notably Wallis Simpson, Dorothy Parker, and Babe Paley.

Marcel Vertès wrote in his 1944 book *Art and Fashion*, "Even the graveyard must yield up a fashion fillip, so stylized skeletons, big as life, appeared, appliquéd to evening dresses. The buyers sent off enthusiastic cables to New York: 'SURREALISM! GET WINDOWS READY FOR BIG SPLASH!' Publicity directors took up the cry: 'Surrealism! The newspapers will eat it up!'"[52] Immense, billowing balloon gloves in Bérard and Vertès circus prints of clowns, the Surrealist credo "Attention—wet paint!" was printed on dresses and "tent" veils that covered the head as if a miniature tent collapsed above it. The Vertès drawing depicting a merry-go-round with over-sized rabbits, steer with pink collars, swans, gilded chariots, and other fantastic images of childhood was printed on silk chiffon, crêpe, and satin, on both turquoise blue and bubblegum and shocking pink back-grounds. A ballerina-length flared dinner dress with short sleeves was made from the pink silk gauze in this print. A photo of Schiap in a civet fur coat shows her draping the fabric next to the gown on a model. The scene depicts a fashion show at Schiaparelli's filmed in her salon. One of the most rare garments from this fabric is a dress-ing gown made in the satin turquoise print that was made for Bettina Bergery and is now in my collection.

The collection featured many waist-length, fitted evening jack-ets that dipped in points at the front like pre-war silhouettes; the so-called Eton jacket-style. The simple white wedding dress in this collection was Schiaparellized by its veil of tulle embroidered with electric blue bugle beads, which achieved a look slightly terrifying, like wet Surrealistic hair wiggling down the head in the manner of the Medusa. There were slim harem skirts and low-cut décolleté devel-oped in printed crêpe de Chine, trailing circular capes that introduced extra flare at the center back and only fastened high at the front. One was in pink satin embroidered around the shoulders in the pattern of a giant gold charm bracelet. Evening coats were very slim, belted, and Chinese in suggestion with full slit sleeves with contrasting bor-ders falling to the floor. For daytime, circus-theme prints ruled as well: snails, balloons, and deranged-looking clowns.

The collection had many suits with short hip-length fitted jack-ets, which accentuated the high neckline of the blouses. Besides the jackets, some center front-buttoned gilets, some with Dalí-esque dresser drawer pulls, had elbow-length flared capelets attached, some in the peculiar material named "gayac." Suit skirts had fine crushed gathers around a higher cut waistline. Some suits were

made of mattress ticking and one was entirely backwards, with buttons, pockets, lapels, cravat, and brooch all on the back. This utterly
Surrealistic suit was cunningly drawn by Vertès and perhaps sums
up the psychology of the times.

The hats of the Circus collection were many and sublime. A
pointy pink sequined clown hat matched a cocktail suit buttoned with
clown hat buttons. Bérard's illustration of this hat is one of the most
reproduced images of 1930s and Schiap's work. There was a highly
publicized inkpot-shaped hat of lacquered straw with a quill dip-
ping into the ink. As if these bold hats were not enough, the sublime
became ridiculous when Schiaparelli put a life-sized hen in a round
straw hat on the head, and not discreetly, as it was on the cover of
Vogue. Extremely tall multi-colored feathers like a circus pony's hat
that tied on with ribbon, a hat that had as its decoration a clothespin
in the center, a wildcat hat, crushed clown toppers, some with bug
adornments, (particularly dear to me and my collection), and lots of
Pagliacci shapes in felt. Poke bonnets were shown in magazines with
a brooch of Schiaparelli's head and bust made by Giacometti. They
were very long and narrow and some were simply tiny, jeweled felt
pillboxes attached to scarves that tied around the neck. There was
a monkey's hat in red felt with a set of tall green feathers drawn by
Vertès. Model 96, shown in the April issue of *L'Officiel de la Couture–
Paris*, was an oddly shaped raffia hat with an outfit described as, "a
charming seaside frock, blue striped with white, in 'Gaucho' twill
woven from 'Flesa' from Coudurier, Fructus, Descher. The *soques*
and amusing raffia hat form an original ensemble—by Schiaparelli."
The "soques" are matched to outrageously high wooden platform
shoes that tied with large ribbons up the leg in the ballerina-style.
One trim, body-hugging dress had large Surrealistic buttons and a
hat that swings out into space like a peculiar amorphic form. Also
shown was a beret with lengthened brim, pushed up at front and
slightly up tilted in back pre-dating Dior's use of it in the 1950s.

Accessories included more vegetable jewelry and Etienne de Beaumont jewels in enamel and gold metal in the form of three-piece rings that took up the entire finger as well as the nail. Floral sprays in big false stones made up an enamel Dahlia brooch that matched the gowns printed with huge dahlias. It was described in a press release as "an enchanting evening gown in 'Organsoie imprimée' from Ducharne. The back was made in mauve chiffon, which formed a long sash in front." There were the famous masked and muzzled foxes by Schlumberger, cherub-adorned lanterns, and fish that lit up. Metal brooches with fluorescent paints designed by Jean Clément looked like Pagliacci clown heads. Ads throughout America, such as one in the October 15, 1938 issue of *Vogue*, show exotic Schiaparelli jewelry on an African sculpture. Who else but Schiaparelli could get away with such an association? She once again reminded the world that she was largely inspired by art.

Fields, woods, and countryside unfolded in every detail of the Pagan collection.[46] Insects were omnipresent and accessories were embroidered with bunches of wheat, oak leaves, and flower petals. Botticelli was referred to everywhere. Foliage was wound around the waist of chiffon-draped gowns. Nymphs and naiads were printed on evening gowns. Capes looked as if they were designed for Robin Hood. Carnations and cornflowers covered a lavender blue gown inspired by *La Naissance de Vénus*. A satin bolero, half pink, half yellow, had apple blossoms and wooden strawberries.

This was also the year and collection of the famous Rhodoid necklace (now in the collection of the Costume Institute at the Metropolitan Museum of Art) with insects all the way around it made by Jean Schlumberger. Individual insect pins were arbitrarily sewn on lapels, hats, and belts. It was called Collection Caviar[47] in magazines and shown with gold leaf necklaces, fern brooches, and leaf-covered hats. For Schiap Schlumberger also made a bracelet with leaves and ladybugs, a necklace of gilt frogs interspersed with emerald-green drops of glass, and ladies' cufflinks shaped like life-sized baby frogs. The pair in my collection was a gift from Diana Vreeland. Once I went to see Jean Schlumberger and he told me that making all those bugs and insects took an eternity, as one necklace could have up to thirty of them on it. "I must have made thousands of them. We had to get them all done within just a few months between the collection and the delivery of the clothes to clients. It was exhausting and a lot of work, but we laughed and laughed sometimes, to think these brightly colored metal insects were the height of fashion."[48]

Every conceivable type of flower, fruit, and leaf was somehow embroidered, made into jewelry, or applied to the clothes. Buttons are closed-wing grasshoppers and these were made into brooches as well. Gleaming green grasshoppers perch on gold-leaf bracelets while red acorns sprout on silver lamé. Jewelry by Etienne de Beaumont included more striped enamel flowers, a strange strung series of faceted colorful buttons, and simple strung necklaces of garnets with rhinestone teardrops. Mine were a gift from Comte Henri de Beaumont who was a great and close friend of mine since the 1970s. Belts were chains of tortoise shell or green leaves being eaten by caterpillar-shaped clasps.

Roger Vivier, the man who invented the stiletto high heel shoe and many other courageous shoe designs was a friend of mine throughout the 1970s and 1980s. He told me he did some of his first designs for this Pagan collection. "When I was quite young," he told me in 1982, "I started to do a few designs for the haute couture, Schiaparelli accepted some of them . . . some were in cloqué fabrics imitating the feel of moss, others were in very deep colored suedes, one pair had a leaf entwined at the vamp. I considered it a real success for me to do these designs and I felt as if I had really reached the top."[49]

The breathtaking Zodiac collection of that year, with its astronomical and astrological motifs, was truly splendid. There were a tremendous number of details and innovations; everything glittered and it had the most interesting little design details of stiff horsehair and metallic mesh evening wraps. Naturally, there were prints of the constellations, but Schiap also showed jackets embroidered with mysterious signs and shooting stars in shiny threads, emphasized with sequins, beads, and rhinestones. Fabrics for evening tended to be shiny lamés and iridescent *tissus changants*. There was also a lot of silver and gold, midnight and sky blue velvets for daytime ensembles. Clément created a necklace of polychromed aluminum illustrating star-studded constellations, and golden button cufflinks of Galalith clouds punctuated by a tiny glass star. "Collection Caviar: Schiaparelli's necklace, a constellation of galalith stars in all the acid colors of hard candy"[50] was another necklace of clusters of stars that Gala Dalí wore bare-breasted in one of her husband's Surrealist montage photographs. The necklace sat center stage, so to speak.

The Louis XIV *Roi Soleil* embroideries adorned capes whose linings were button-quilted like a nineteenth-century English sofa. Jackets had a series of pockets in the form of Sèvres porcelain *cache-pots.* Bettina Bergery said, "They were devised by Lesage . . . so utterly amusing, such clever pockets and they were truly sublime, I felt like a living artwork when I wore it. At the time, this irony and playfulness mixed with such arrogance and historic reference was the absolute height of elegance . . . Schiaparelli invented this type of elegance."[58]

There were mirror-embroidered jackets for evening, coats of moiré fabric, high-buttoned boots, hoods of fur, and the famous handbag that lit up (supposedly designed by Salvador Dalí, although unlikely). Colors were inspired in their names: Mauve Aérostatique, Soot Blue, Saltwater Green, and Cameo Pink. All these reflected the Surrealists obsession with neon and phosphorescent colors.

Finally the Harlequin or Commedia dell'arte collection closed the fashion season chez Schiap in 1938. Italian Commedia dell'arte was at its best, thought Schiap, when shown accompanied by the music of Scarlatti, Vivaldi, Pergolese, and Cimarosa. Every style of patchwork, in beads, fabrics, leathers and in startling Italian colors were used in this famous collection, which was evocative of some Surrealist paintings (1939's *Le Beau Temps* by Man Ray shows geometric forms in acidic colors with checkered motifs indicating clothes). Lots of pink, mauve, red, orange, blue, and yellow, all outlined in black and white were worn with Frolic, Schiap's new purple lipstick. Gowns had asymmetrical details—one black moiré dinner dress featured one puffed shoulder, one flat, a puff at the back of the knees, and a puffed pocket on one side. Day suits were bicolored, half in Hudson seal, the other half in black wool. Everything had masks. "Granted, they may be as useless as a fan, but they are altogether charming and they belong to now," Schiap decreed.[51] I have a great many pieces from the mid-to-late 1930s in my collection. Seeing them in person is the only way to understand the splendor of these clothes. The way they were worn, how they were put on the body is particularly fascinating, aligning with my ideas behind Surreal Couture.

Summer 1939's collection showed the enhanced shape of the body, long fluid dresses and gowns, with draped bustles for the evening. There were pale evening jackets with Louis XVI or Chinese-style Lesage embroidery, as she'd shown earlier, though this time more elaborately developed. This was probably due to Schiap's new client, Mrs. Hui-Lan Wellington Koo, the Chinese Ambassador's wife. The designs alluded to more genteel times. Some of the prints were by Jean Peltier and Suzanne Janin, his wife, who designed exclusive fabrics for Schiaparelli for the Ducharne fabric company. One of them was in the Vertès style, evoking Mae West's silhouette, another was of swallows carrying love notes with wax seals on a chain of romantic little blue flowers.

Pink and black were the major color themes and practically every *frou-frou* accessory, like a zippered bag in tulle and sequins and a heart-shaped and lace-trimmed sachet, was in this combination.

Accessories included gloves with fingers trimmed in wrinkled lace and dark necklaces in moiré ribbon with dangling coins, acorns and other bibelots. Schiap had Perugia make a pair of evening sandals in blue kid piped in gold which had three revolving balls under the instep based on the design of a roller skate. Prints were of red ladybugs, lilies of the valley, zebras, green beans, hands joined as if in prayer, and a Chinese refugee child's rendition of angels. The last gleaming salute to the Paris that everyone adored came at the Beaumont Ball, but war loomed months away.

On September 1, 1939, at 5:45 a.m., without the formality of actually declaring war, Adolf Hitler ordered the Luftwaffe to bomb Poland into abysmal submission. France and Great Britain immediately declared their involvement in the war and braced themselves for a Nazi onslaught of Blitzkrieg attacks and the demolition of Paris. Paris dolled up in its battle dress. Monuments were covered in sandbags, anchored balloons loomed in the Tuileries, and a state-issued gas mask was on the shoulder of every French citizen and school child. Orphans, memorably illustrated by Bérard, were evacuated to the countryside with nametags around their necks. Sugar, tobacco, gasoline, and coffee were immediately hoarded and then sensibly rationed. The black market flourished, and all the smart Parisian ladies and society matrons, newly servant-less, stood in lines at the bakeries, butcher shops, and dairies. Imagine the novelty, the disorientation, the humiliation—or perhaps the elegance—of doing one's own shopping! Fashion suddenly became a bit more practical. *Vogue* described Schiaparelli's "Two ensembles with 'poches commandes' [pockets for what you order] in gray wool and green wool."[52]

Five months before the invasion of Poland, in April, Schiaparelli showed her autumn 1939 collection. The theme was music and it featured more conventional motifs and silhouettes (although Surrealism, irony, and wit did not disappear overnight). Keeping a gay enthusiasm and positive outlook seemed the obvious thing to do in reaction to the tensions that had been building across Europe. The entire Musique collection is superbly embroidered with musical instruments, musical notes, and sheet music, as if Paris's mondaine women sang and danced their way into the war. The gowns were long and slim with fitted tops. Skirts were slightly flared and jackets were long in front and gathered in the back. Day suits and sports pants have bouffant hems. Many coats and jackets were trimmed with bells. Accessories include belts and hats with music boxes that play tunes like "Rose Marie, I Love You." The Musique collection had every conceivable allusion to music: tambourine and piano-shaped and piano key buttons, musical note embroideries and prints, stoles trimmed in little bells, and even singing birds. Musical instruments of all sorts became brooches and necklaces, many by Schlumberger.

For winter 1939–40, Schiap launched a much more practical collection called the Cigarette silhouette, streamlined and softened by bias cut pleats. In this collection, we see some pockets in the shape of moneybags, more aprons on dresses, bouffant hems, and long, tubular jackets discreetly draped in the back. The English Guardsmen who marched in Paris on Bastille inspired hats with chinstraps. Accessories were typically Schiaparellian, little *bottines* of fur with buttons, and bracelets in leopard skin. Velvet three-quarter length gloves in vivid colors were worn with bib necklaces of coins.

On August 28, 1939, *Harper's Bazaar* editor Carmel Snow wrote a sinister report from the Paris offices at 15 rue de la Paix:

> To those of us who are in the fashion business, Paris is a city seen in the bleak rains of February or in the sultry heat of August, a city jammed with buyers—frantic, amusing exhausting, and glorious. Today I see another Paris. In this last week it has become, almost overnight, a city deserted. The taxis have disappeared from the streets. All the telephones are

cut off. You can walk for miles without seeing a child. Even the dogs—and you know how Parisians love their dogs—have been sent away. No one who has been in Paris these distressing days of suspense will ever forget the silence of the city or the courage of the women of France. As man after man is mobilized, these Frenchwomen go about the work of their daily lives without a trace of hysteria. It is not a moment of mass courage but of individual heroism.[53]

She describes the lights out on the Champs-Elysées and the hushed silence. She spoke of the enormous new prices of the dresses, the cancelled orders, the over-zealous perfection the French couture individuals were putting upon themselves, making sure fittings were as perfect as possible. She also spoke of how pillows were used for soldiers in the grand hotels to assure their comfort as much as possible, with sofa cushions provided for the other guests. She mentions how different it was from the First World War when the atmosphere had been gay and lively and enthusiastic. She mentions many of the artists who were drafted, and the gloomy melancholy of the situation. At the end of her article, she says:

If the war lasts a long time, there will be much work to be done there and wheels must begin to revolve again. It is quite possible that some of the dressmakers may stay open or resume their work once more. I am glad to be here in Paris during these days of suspense. It is a great privilege. My respect and admiration for these women with whom I have worked for so many years is unbounded. Their courage is something I shall never forget.[54]

The last important collection Schiap was able to design before the total outbreak of the Second World War was her Cash and Carry collection for spring 1940, shown in October 1939, which emphasized several new ideas. Surrealism died a hard death as the economical use of less fabric felt practical and pragmatic. There was a military theme of bandolier briefcases, some even created by the clever use of cutting the pattern directly into the jacket, which created a trompe l'oeil of the real thing. Flared and belted coats, suit jackets, and washerwomen dresses that could be transformed with an apron effect. There were practical things like raincoats in milky white waterproof fabric, jackets that closed with dog leashes and chains that were shown with cunningly small hats with big bows. The first air-raid clothes were in plastics. One white coat could apparently, withstand the effects of poisonous gas. *Women's Wear Daily* said that these air raid suits were practical and elegant in any emergency. They were shown with enormous handbags that could hold a gas mask and a miniature medicine chest, as well as make-up and other feminine sundries. The first dresses Schiaparelli devised for emergency laundering could drip-dry and came in colors such as Maginot Line Blue, Foreign Legion Red, Trench Brown, Aeroplane Grey, and still, of course, her Shocking Pink and Sleeping Blue. Although the black school desks were only half filled with *vendeuses*, there were no tailors, only three mannequins, and most of the clientele was fleeing, Schiaparelli still put on a brave and innovative show.

The silhouette of many of the dresses was that of 1872, the first year of the Third French Republic. Long skirts with muffs, draped front aprons, and attached pockets alluded to nineteenth-century romanticism. A marked waist and a draped, pleated, or full front evoked a fashionable lady of the Third Republic. That last year was not all drab reality as one might imagine. The clothes were quite elegant considering the circumstances. Schiaparelli's work always focused on the practical, which, if one recalls, is how she began her career in fashion. She did air-raid suits in phosphorescent fabric, Lastex elastic waist skirts for "the fat years and the lean years," and day dresses that turned into gowns by means of a string which let down cleverly hidden lengths of the skirt. One evening ensemble of cape and dress could be transformed into an overskirt when tied around the waist. As fastenings became harder to find, creative closures became even more necessary as button-makers were immobilized. As gas was rationed, bicycling became the only mode of transport for most people and over eleven million bicycles were registered by 1942. Schiap's chic culottes were a modest alternative to blowing skirts, and her off the face hats with forehead bands assured the wearer wouldn't lose her hat when bicycling. Skirts had enormous pockets and dresses had yet more "built-in" muffs to protect against the cold while standing in long lines, which also recalled nineteenth-century fashions. Gauntlets for evening gowns suggested military or gladiator arm protection, but strangely they were made from Victorian mercury glass shoe buttons. Handbags were actually baskets, painted black and lined in silk, a necessary innovation as the leather bag makers, like the button-makers and most of the men working in couture, had been drafted.

The last prints to be made featured rationing schedules on them: "Monday-no meat. Tuesday-no alcohol. Wednesday-no butter. Thursday-no fish. Friday-no meat. Saturday-no alcohol, but Sunday-toujour l'amour." (In reality, these were the words to a popular Maurice Chevalier song). Another print had cartoons of clothing with the number of ration coupons needed to buy them. The background was a sea of 66's, the total of the number of allotted coupons. Another was a drawing of typically French windows with green shutters locked shut, a frightening image of the war soon to come. Schiap used collections paid for with coupons to raise money. The total sum of several garments was paid for in advance in exchange for tickets that could be redeemed for clothing and accessories at a later date. Schiaparelli also designed a uniform for the Salvation Army, a blue outfit with a red collar and a blue apron. Even the hats took to the war: the flat colonial style ones and the Bali straw boaters had, like so many boarded up mansions and deserted private homes, "slip covers" that could be removed and washed if necessary.

Schiaparelli showed fitted mermaid silhouettes, using FormFit corsets in her summer 1940 collection. According to a press release, the Scissors Silhouette was "breasts high and separated, waistline intriguingly slender, hips trimly tailored" according to Formfit. Dresses were draped with pleated hip treatments. Jet-black embroidered boleros accompanied evening gowns with plunging necklines. One of the most famous was drawn by Leonor Fini and featured in nearly all the magazines. Diana Vreeland told me "it was one of the last evening dresses to come out of Paris and it was widely publicized . . . we have it in the collection in pink and in the 1960s, on a fashion story for *Life* magazine, it was photographed amongst many of the great classics of fashion we have."[55]

But then came the *drôle de guerre*, known in English as the Phony War. Paris was not bombarded or attacked and the Parisians used their tin gas mask cases for every sort of function, from lunch pails to mail carryalls. Meanwhile, the non-war continued throughout what Winston Churchill called "the winter of illusion." Fashion buyers from foreign countries, with great determination and exposure to dangers, shortages, rations, and bitter cold, came to see the collections. Debarking from the ocean liner George Washington, they brought parcels of food, checked into unheated hotels, dealt with endless minute unpleasantness in order to see the shows. *The London Daily Telegraph*, noting the fact the French carried on with showing high fashion despite war, wrote, "Do the Parisians know that their country is at war?" *L'Officiel de la Couture* wrote in March 1940, "There is so much youth and character in the models one feels their creator must have taken pleasure in creating them." The war hit home for Schiaparelli when, on June 10, 1940, the radio announced that Mussolini would ally with the Nazi regime, and stab the French right in the back. Unable to bear the shock standing up, she dropped to the floor weeping inconsolably.

The effect of the war on everyone and everything was evident throughout. *Vogue* editor in chief Edna Woolman Chase wrote an introduction to Schiaparelli's next collection saying, "the needles of Paris have been suspended, temporarily we hope, by the fortunes of war. And for the first time in memory, an autumn mode is born without the direct inspiration of Paris. For the first time, the fashion center of the world is here—in America. How long the isolation will last, no one knows."

CHAPTER 23

THE WAR YEARS

When Schiaparelli made the decision to leave for America, her move motivated some people to ask Schiap how she could have left Paris at such a time. She answered with this quotation from Dante's *The Divine Comedy*:

> *In the middle of the journey of our life*
> *I came to myself in a dark wood,*
> *where the straight way was lost.*
> *Ah! how hard a thing it is to tell what a wild,*
> *and rough, and stubborn wood this was,*
> *which in my thought renews the fear!*
> *So bitter is it, that scarcely more is death.*[1]

The situation was extremely difficult and, after a lot of pressure to leave, she returned to New York for the duration of the war. Before doing so, she had her now world-established fragrance Shocking packaged in a box that represented a cage containing a bird of peace, "Shocking Sings of Hope."

In August 1940, the Nazi regime announced its intention to transport, step-by-step, piece by piece, the entire Parisian textile, haute couture, and ready-to-wear industries to Berlin and Vienna. The president of the Chambre Syndicale de la Haute Couture Parisienne, the couturier Lucien Lelong, and his deputy Daniel Gorin, were vehemently opposed to the idea and somehow managed to convince the Third Reich powers to let the industry remain in Paris and be ruled by the Vichy government. It's not really clear how they managed this, but they were able to delay the ultimate upheaval until the war ended. But in the Registry of Commerce archives in Paris, it appears that, in accordance with the September 27, 1940 Nazi-imposed law, all commerce owned by Jews would have to be clearly marked with yellow panels outside.

Schiaparelli wrote a poignant article in the September 1, 1940 issue of American *Vogue* entitled "Needles and Guns," describing her escape to the United States after time on the front in France. In this article, she talks about how "we fought to keep the great French dressmaking industry alive." She is photographed in a turban and she describes her dress with a hand-written note shown with the photo that reads, "I left Biarritz with only three dresses, and this is my favorite—severe black silk. The collar, the cuffs of my gloves, and my stockings are all of white crocheted cotton. (My glasses are chained to the gold vanity-box.) E.S." She also describes being asked to design a uniform for the Salvation Army in Paris. She discusses at length her struggles to produce under such difficult circumstances something practical and pragmatic, yet elegant. She focuses on the ingenuity essential to survival. Regarding the last collection, she stresses, "The showing was a remarkable demonstration of the spirit of France at this moment . . . and under this terrific stress, some creators made better designs than they had ever realized were possible." The article establishes her last designs as splendid, as the Schiaparelli dresses depict all the grandeur of Parisian elegance at its height during what was described as "the eclipse of Paris."

In the offices of Schiaparelli Perfumes, Inc. in the United States, located in prestigious Rockefeller Center, Schiap designed a wardrobe of twelve outfits, and a number of hats and accessories, which she had reproduced by various New York manufacturers of finer women's clothes. She also authorized them to be sold throughout the country with special labels that cost a dollar each. The sums raised would go to a fund administered by the Quakers for unemployed Paris fashion *arpettes*, the workroom girls who picked up the pins.

Schiap had an arrangement with the Columbia Lecture Bureau to lecture across America. She created eighteen sportswear outfits with the intention that they could be copied and sold at affordable prices throughout the country. She also did a collection in collaboration with Bonwit Teller, after the boat carrying her most recent collection and these sportswear outfits from Paris was torpedoed. The October 1940 issue of *Harper's Bazaar* showed Schiaparelli in their workrooms. Despite the fact they were very lovely, these clothes were not made with the same panache and quality of her French haute couture. Consequently, she was not fully satisfied with the collection.

When Schiaparelli finally commenced her lecture tour, "she plunged west into the heart of the United States for what she afterwards referred to as the biggest love affair of her life—with the American people."[2] On October 8, 1940 she told the *Harvard Crimson*, the daily newspaper of the Harvard University, that the long, loose jackets that had been adopted by young women took the place of the big coat, down to the knees, traditionally worn exclusively by the male students at the chic east coast universities of the USA. In St. Louis, she was greeted by at least 20,000 people who were eager for news about France. She showed her 1939 fashions, which still made news with their novelties. Schiap even made them seem like sensible wartime pragmatism. She was at the zenith of her fame and considered the most famous designer in the world. During her stay, Schiaparelli won the coveted Neiman-Marcus Award, a distinction given to leaders of world fashion by the famous Dallas, Texas luxury store.

During the war, after her successful conferences in America, Schiap really had very little to do with fashion *per se*. She had many offers to design and direct new ventures in dressmaking, but she admitted that she could not have accepted any lucrative offers to design or consult for any fashion whilst she was in the USA. She said she had an obligation to remain aloof especially from anything that seemed like haute couture because it would place her in a position of vulnerability and could have been considered a traitorous threat to France's greatest creative industry. She also would have been in a very false situation where she'd be unable to justify herself. Therefore she stayed clear of moneymaking offers in the fashion world of the USA during the war.

However, Schiap participated in a number of charity events and donated her time to volunteer work. She was often in the news for one reason or another. For example, on June 4, 1941 she was part of the jury of the First National Sewing Contest at the Waldorf Astoria Hotel in New York where she spoke about the need to protect France and help its children. She also organized artistic events to raise money. One such effort was the Surrealist show that she put together with a number of other displaced socialites and celebrities from Europe.[3] The show included works by Marcel Duchamp, Max Ernst, Picasso, Kurt Seligmann, and Matisse, among others—all close friends of hers since the 1920s. The catalogue for the exhibition is a masterpiece in itself. Titled *The First Papers of Surrealism* it has a cover by Marcel Duchamp, pierced with holes and tinted yellow to highlight a photograph of cheese. It reads: "What is there in our time that creates the condition favorable for this persistent and magnetic domination? It is perhaps that Surrealism exists in the very lives of a people functioning

in a power age, inherent in the fabulous unreality of living in a shock-
ingly real period; that it is embedded in the fantastic implications
underlying the bald mechanistic aspect of that age?"[4]

Against the advice of her American friends, connections in diplomatic circles, and the pleading of Gogo, Schiaparelli decided to return
to Paris to check in on the condition of her businesses. On January 4,
1941 she took the *Siboney* liner from Jersey City, carrying only one
suitcase and a parcel package of 13,000 vitamins destined for distribution in the Free Zone of France by the intermediary of the American
Friends Service Committee. However, at a stop-off in Bermuda, a
British customs agent confiscated what he'd called "contraband" (the
vitamins), under the pretense that it was forbidden to transport food
products. The navicert, the British governmental certificate that normally should have avoided the search and seizure of the package and
authorized the vitamins' distribution in the Free Zone of France, had
not worked. The strange set of circumstances became known throughout Europe and the situation was turned into a German propaganda
tool despite the fact that the incident was quickly resolved when
Schiaparelli arrived in Lisbon, where the Ambassador to Great Britain
organized the transport of the vitamins to the French Free Zone.

When she returned to Paris, Elsa Schiaparelli found herself in an
awkward and uneasy situation. Germans and Italians considered her
Italian and the pressure on her was increasingly intense. One day, the
American minister asked her to call at the embassy. He informed her
that he and his staff were leaving in a few days and he strongly suggested Schiaparelli go with them. She understood perfectly that she
could do little by remaining in Paris and that her staff, given her current situation, would be safer without her, but she was still extremely
reluctant to leave. The reasons for her to leave increased as days went
by. The minister told her she was foolish and in genuine danger. Her
family was in Italy, her daughter in America. The minister put a visa
on her passport, which she wisely kept on her person at all times and

told her he had a secured place ready for her on his special train. Her stay in Paris was brief and by the beginning of May, she returned to Lisbon, thanks to the help of American friends in the diplomatic services, notably Gaston Bergery. She had left her house of fashion in the hands of Louis-Arthur Meunier and her secretary, Yvonne Souquières. She left Lisbon on a Pan American Airways flight on the Dixie Clipper with forty other passengers and arrived in New York on May 25. This time she entered the United States with an immigrant visa, not as a tourist, so she could apply for citizenship, which she refused to do. In the course of a British stopover just prior to her final destination the British interrogated her about her relations with the Germans and her activities in the United States. The transcript of these interviews would be the beginning of what would become a large, confidential secret service dossier on her activities throughout the war years. The Ministry of the British Economic Services labeled Elsa Schiaparelli a suspicious agent and possible spy or collaborator between May 1941 and October 1944. While no official charges were brought against her, the unfortunate incident over the vitamins made her suspect throughout the war and even after.

Following this denunciation, Elsa was placed definitively on the British blacklist. Certain conflicts within her London-based perfume business didn't help matters either. The English company bearing her name reproached her for not giving them the perfume recipes that, according to them, should have been given to the company. They also felt her royalty payments should have been suspended until the recipe was handed over. Finally, the British refused on several occasions in 1943 to grant her visa to enter the United Kingdom to work for the assistance of the Medical and Surgical Relief Committee. In their refusal of her applications there was constant reference to her supposed anti-British sentiments. Elsa Schiaparelli could never understand why she was so poorly treated by a country she considered her second home.

The Schiaparelli house of fashion was placed under Nazi administration as of February 1942 and in consideration that the major shareholders, Charles Kahn and Charles Blumenthal, were both Jewish, the house fell under the evil auspices of the regime. Elsa Schiaparelli, attempting to evade these eventual prejudices, named herself the president-director general in May 1941 before her return to New York for four years. She would retain the title until January 21, 1946.

Irene Dana ran the house in Paris in Schiap's absence.[5] The clientele was mainly comprised of the black market "new rich," also nicknamed the B.O.F.s, because of their newly acquired wealth in selling *beurre* (butter), *oeufs* (eggs), and *fromage* (cheese).[6] There were also conspicuous mistresses of German officers, some highly paid prostitutes, and the remaining French stars and non-Jewish French elite. The list of Schiaparelli clients was mysteriously absent when the Nazi regime requested to see it to check the Jewish clientele. Some couturiers decided to close their businesses rather than accommodate the regime, as did Vionnet and Madame Grès, whose house and name were literally stolen out from under her.

The running of the salon was, at best, difficult. Dana ran it from 1940 until 1945 with the *premier tailleur*, René. Together they designed things "in the manner of" according to Bettina Bergery, but in reality the clothes were heavy, conspicuous, awkward, and caricature-like. The first season without Schiap, the team basically re-visited the Cash and Carry collection using the André Drian sketches in the model repertory books as inspiration.[7] One interesting thing to note is that the labels during these years are undated. The last collection actually designed by Schiap was dated, but the following season, when she was in the United States, the team waited for her return to date them. No one expected Schiaparelli to remain abroad as long as she did, and the longer she was absent, the less the collections looked like her work.

People in the know said the Paris haute couture clothes during the German Occupation were generally ugly and unflattering, and forcibly made by the fashion houses under great restraints and personal crises. The clothing deliberately made the clients, who were mostly despised by many of the fashion houses, look grotesque. They wanted the German mistresses and prostitutes to look like what they were: unwelcome and often parvenu invaders. It was said that when a German officer's wife once asked "Why are the clothes so ugly?" a salesgirl replied, "They suit you perfectly." Schiap recalls it in another way in her autobiography; "When a German asked one of my salesgirls: "How would the hats be if we were not here?" she answered curtly: "Very pretty."[8] The haute couture industry had to continue to keep Paris alive, to keep people working, and somehow to keep people's humor about them, but the aesthetic of the clothing truly reflected the twisted state of the world. The clothes were to change slowly but assuredly due to the various shortages and needs. Each war seemed to liberate women just a little bit more as reflected in their fashions.

At the beginning of the war the dresses were relatively the same proportions as the pre-war clothes, but with rationing and politics, little by little the silhouette changed.

> The enormous bulky look of the shoulders, the tight waists, the very short skirts that billowed like a kite when bicycling, sometimes exposing ultra-practical pants, and at other times leaving nothing to the imagination, the short gawky coats called "les Canadiennes," the complicated hair-do high in the middle of the head and loose to the wind at the back, the clog shoes that made the prettiest foot appear as shapeless as if women were club-footed, the hideous headgear, tormenting, heavy, and unbecoming—all denoted a Paris convulsed and trampled but still possessed of a sense of humour,

and intent, in order to defend its real inner self, on putting up
a front that purposely skirted on the edge of ridicule.[9]

Things at Schiaparelli's would not change overnight. Shocking
pink embroidered padlocks by Lesage were somehow less humorous
than the first time they were seen. The famous Ex-Voto leg necklace
on knit blue collar (knitted by Mike Azarian in 1941) in my collection
was shown with model number 23. This small print ensemble for the
afternoon with squared cap sleeves featured a plastic Eclair zipper on
the side of the knee-length skirt and on the back of the blouse and was
topped with a flower-sprigged *canotier* style hat. One ensemble had
a typically nostalgic but sinister black horse-drawn carriage embroidered by Lesage. A suede waistcoat from 1943 was embroidered to
look like a medieval book of spells complete with seals. By 1943–44
dresses were very short, the hemline falling almost right at the knee,
partially due to cloth rationing and but also due to the shorter styles'
deliberately intended un-flattering form. The French couturiers were
increasingly deprived of materials and workers and their disgust for
the occupying enemy was heightened to an extreme.

Hats were in abundance in frou-frou tulle and black lace that
covered the face, some dotted with paillettes or felt dots. "La Ligne
en Hauteur" (the line going up, giving height) showed wildly high
hats of dark blue straw. Explosions of flowers and poufs of feathers were perched dramatically on the head. All sorts of formerly
unheard of materials for hat making, like strips of rubber bicycle
tires, recycled men's shirting, wood, and rope, were used. The wartime years saw a huge variety of hats suitable for any face shape,
hairstyle, or personal preference. Throughout the war, on both sides
of the Atlantic, elaborate creations full of almost euphoric fantasy
were matched to the somewhat dreary utility fashions, which were
brought about by rationing. In fact, at the onset of the war the only
items not rationed were hat makers' materials. In France, hats were

nicknamed *pièces de résistance*, not only implying that they were the best feature of the outfit but also as a witty reference to the fact that were no restrictions in regards to materials for hats and a slight against the Nazi occupation. These headpieces were often built up and extravagantly high on the head. At Schiap's "a little hat of black tressed paper formed a catagan knotted with a white ribbon"[10] made from recycled newspaper and was painted with house paint!

Pants on women became another issue during the war. By the end of the 1930s, stores in the United States imported certain models and they continued to be seen on various celebrities and at home on ultra-sophisticated women. However, as the war carried on, the practicality of pants became too important to ignore and women adopted them to great success. The Vichy government saw it as a threat to basic feminine instincts.

The French movie star and actress Arletty, in an article called "For or Against the Woman in Pants," made a studied declaration against them: "Women who have the means to offer themselves boots and coats are unforgivable in wearing pants. They surprise no one and this lack of dignity is simply proof of their bad taste."[11] Her opinion was backed up by that of a minor couturier named Marcelle Dormoy, who said, "I am against pants which have nothing feminine about them. They don't allow the natural charm of women to show. I don't mind them as lounging pajamas. In any case, you can be sure that none of the couturiers will present pants. We are too concerned about the elegance of French women." This was a purely opportunistic propaganda ploy. Later, in the 1980s, Arletty gave me another take on the subject: "I loved Schiap's pants, you could live in them if you so wished and depending on what they were made from, you could wear them from morning to evening. During the war, it was still considered very racy, a bit lesbian looking and unfeminine, but they were glamorous and had a sort of provocative aspect which men loved. However, I was always looking my best in Schiaparelli's dresses, they suited my body better than pants, despite their comfort." Well, only idiots never change their minds!

Pants, at this point, were hardly the main issue in French haute couture. Just dressing in high fashion was difficult and complicated. Beginning as early as July 1941, clients had to have a special card to access the collections, which strictly limited the number of models shown. The quantity and quality of fabrics and trims were also regulated. Every French citizen had ration tickets: 100 points per year to dress. To get a new suit, you had to give 30 points and bring in at least one used suit in exchange. On the other hand, those with the special client card could get an entirely new wardrobe for only 15 points, with the stipulation that 5 percent of the price would be given to the Caisse de Secours National, a precursor to social security. Even if the fabric was rationed, the quantities allowed to the haute couture was not limited to the official 30 percent of its needs of 1938. This was contrary to other sectors of the fashion industry. In 1943, the haute couture business was allowed enough fabric to satisfy the demand of fifty thousand regular rations even if in reality the clientele was not remotely even half this amount.

By February 1943, Joseph Goebbels, Reich minister of propaganda, ordered all the Parisian fashion houses to be closed, but Lucien Lelong, head of the Chambre Syndicale de la Haute Couture, managed to convince the Germans to allow the houses of fashion to continue their activities. This way Lelong directly saved thousands of French people from forced labor in Germany and also prevented untrained Germans who did not even speak French from coming into France and taking over the work of the famous French fashion houses.

On August 25, 1944, the Allies liberated Paris and the *American Journal* had a front-page open letter from a reporter who had gained access to Schiap's house. It gave news of her staff at rue de Berri, who sent their greetings to her, and from the place Vendôme, as well. Thrilled and moved, Schiap wished to immediately return to her

Paris home and her house of fashion. Not long after this article was published, while she was still in New York trying to obtain a permit to return to France, she was confronted by a self-appointed tribunal from the Chambre Syndicale de la Haute Couture. They were in New York attempting to revive trade activities between the two countries. At their request, Schiaparelli was omitted from their organized activities with the fashion magazines. She was subjected to a mock courtroom scene at the St. Regis Hotel and accused of collaborating with the American Garment Makers Union during the war to promote American fashions, which to their eyes, were greatly influenced by the Schiaparelli style. She flew into a rage, asserting that she had done nothing but stay out of fashion. She showed them speeches from her 1940 lecture tour in which she stated her opinions that high fashion could only be truly created in France. After this unfair trial, they finally admitted that she had been faithful to France. It was an unpleasant shock to be so shabbily treated by a French Union of which she had always been a major supporter. From her accusers she perceived a prejudice that she felt for the rest of her career, and their words, "It was easy to be in New York during the Occupation," disturbed her deeply. She was bitterly hurt as she had indeed been faithful and acted in a noble way during her stay in America that had gone apparently unacknowledged. I have always thought this was simply jealousy, rearing its ages-old head.

On October 5, 1944, Irene Dana showed a collection that ended with a number called Liberation, a full coat in blue moiré over a white dress with big red panels. This "Schiaparelli" collection was not well received by the American press, who said the collection was too eccentric and too luxurious for the still war-ravaged world. In the November 15, 1944 issue, *Vogue* printed an open letter from Lucien Lelong in reply to these hostile rebukes in the American press. He stated that the collections in question were not destined to be shown or sold to the Allies, but were meant for Parisian women and dressmakers in the provinces. There were still many problems finding materials to make clothes, as well as the many more pressing problems that Paris had just after the war, notably gas and electricity shortages, not to mention scarce food and water. Despite all the difficulties and even with a small demand from some foreign buyers, it was still rather impossible to re-commence foreign export. The distribution of all of the production of French haute couture was absorbed by the country and besides, the exchange rate would have made the price of French-made fashions four times more expensive than the prices of 1939.

Schiaparelli, although not speaking about fashion ideas, voiced her political opinion, yet again, concerning Italy immediately after the war. "Italy's Surrender Thrills Her, Noted Stylist Wants Mussolini Tried," read the headline in the *New York Times*. In a long and complicated interview with Gertrude Bailey she said she felt that the Italian people were essentially democratic and that they should have a war trial of Mussolini. Not to "execute him as quickly as that, she said of the possible verdict, I think he ought to be made to realize what great harm he has done to the world." In an effort to be diplomatic the article claimed, "She wants to work 'with all my strength' to help bring the Italians and French people together, 'because they are people who live the same kind of lives. They should be friends.' Her gold dangle bracelets chimed as she gestured her big hope. They were all that remained of her bizarre accessories on an otherwise trim, tame navy blue suit."

Later on I recall Bettina Bergery saying in conversation in regard to the war years that Schiaparelli "was the last person on earth to support Fascist or racist ideas or be unfaithful to her home and country. She never could understand why she was so shabbily treated during the war and after. She was very hurt by what the press accused her of and the way she was treated during the years she was in America."

CHAPTER 24

POSTWAR 1945
LE THÉÂTRE DE LA MODE

French miniature mannequins in the Théâtre de la Mode, now
enlivening the Whitelaw Reid mansion at 451 Madison Avenue,
illustrate many delightful current Parisian fashions and in the com-
posite they demonstrate the solidarity and effectiveness of the French
couture. For when one sees a group of creative artists, individual to
the core, pooling their talents as a unit, the sincerity and directness of
the effort make for a memorable achievement. Perhaps this solidarity
of the French couture was intensified during the Occupation, when
under the skillful guidance of Lucien Lelong, then president of the
Chambre Syndicale de la Couture Parisienne, it was held together in
Paris in the face of unbelievable difficulties. However that may be,
the lessons learned through these experiences have not weakened
but rather strengthened the spirit of those whose abilities have given
substance to French fashion and the Théâtre de la Mode flowers as a
symbol of their persistence.

This now historic Théâtre de la Mode exhibition was conceived
of as a vehicle to raise funds for war victims and to utilize the talents

of the French haute couture. It began immediately following the Liberation of Paris. Monsieur Raoul Dautry, President de L'œuvre de l'Entr'Aide Française, spoke one day in front of Monsieur Lucien Lelong of all the money he needed to carry out his task of national rehabilitation. M. Lelong assured M. Dautry that he could count on the assistance of the Paris dressmaking and millinery world. They simply needed to find the sort of event most likely to excite public curiosity.

The idea they came up with was a gala where little dolls dressed by the haute couture houses would be exhibited and sold. They felt that the occasion lent itself marvelously to one of the oldest traditions in the French dressmaking industry. Up until the First Empire, dolls were used to share news of the latest fashions. They were dressed in scaled down clothing, with accurate hairstyles and undergarments. One can only imagine, in the long ago past, how the arrival of these dolls was eagerly awaited in provincial castles and foreign courts, so that society ladies could learn about Paris fashion.

Because of the wartime shortages of fabrics and raw materials, as well as the unbearable restrictions of the German Occupation, it would have been impossible to stage a grand event. The idea of using miniatures seemed the most reasonable and practical way to raise interest and awareness of the industry's comeback. For some of the traveling shows in the collection, farmers and laypersons offered what materials they could, like chicken wire from their coops. One Swedish gentleman even melted down a big part of his copper roof to contribute to the funding of the project. The doll makers gratefully accepted these contributions.

This unprecedented event gathered the entire world of pre-war Paris fashion designers (except the self-exiled Chanel). Established names like Lelong, Ricci, Patou, Rouff, Worth, Manguin, Paquin, and Piguet joined newcomers such as Balmain, Carven, and Fath. The milliners, cobblers, jewelers, *paruriers*, and *métiers* of fashion were not excluded, either. These fashions were presented on a new type of wire mannequin created by Eliane Bonabel, with heads sculpted by Joan Rebull (Torroja) out of plaster and painted to look like terracotta. The fascinating effigies were displayed in sets designed by artists such as Jean Cocteau, Christian Bérard, Boris Kochno, André Beaurepaire, Emilio Terry, Louis Touchages, Georges Douking, and Georges Wakhévitch. The dolls startled some. Madame Carven, whom I knew very well, told me they were lovely, like strange sculptures, but not at all doll-like and very difficult to dress. Making clothes for a wire shape is not easy or inspiring—but they persevered.

The House of Schiaparelli created a few models, designed by Schiaparelli, including a dress in yellow crêpe printed with a tiny black motif of the place Vendôme. It had kimono sleeves and a tight waist with a scarf-belt gathered in the back, and was worn with long black gloves and a little black straw hat. Another model wore a long evening gown with a fitted bodice and long sleeves in pink satin. The flared skirt was formed by several bands of colored satin edged and sewn together by a jagged seam, almost like a jaunty patchwork, a nod to a gypsy-style skirt. The dress's shoulders were studded with real diamonds by Van Cleef & Arpels, with a matching diamond belt and diadem. Gloves were by Faré and the shoes by Casale. The doll was displayed in a set designed by Christian Bérard. By great luck, I have a few of the Bérard panels used in his set that were recuperated when the show was sent to America. There was also a Schiaparelli suit in turquoise crêpe, its jacket fitted with yokes forming epaulettes coming down the back and gathered in a belt around the waist. It was worn with a little black straw hat with a bias of turquoise crêpe knotted in the front. It had long yellow gloves by Faré and an umbrella by Vedrennes. It was in an André Dignimont set, as was the dress in yellow.

The Théâtre de la Mode was an enormous success. It traveled the world and was greeted by hundreds of thousands of visitors and acknowledged by royalty, ambassadors, and celebrities. It was launched with great fanfare in England, Sweden, and the United States. The corresponding catalogues are fascinating to read, and offer a generous insight into the noblesse of the human spirit and the aesthetic and spiritual motivations of artists during depressed times and moments of social crisis.

Years later my friend, the American photographer David Seidner, photographed some of the remaining dolls for an exhibition celebrating the "rediscovery" of many of the dolls in 1985 at the Maryhill Museum of Art in Goldendale, Washington, where they had remained, forgotten, for forty-four years. They had been stored in the museum because it was too costly to ship them back to France after the American tour. I was invited a few times to see him shoot. It was a great experience to watch David compose his photos; he was so thoughtful with the dolls, lighting and posing them as if they were living creatures. It was then that I realized just how talented he was. When shooting a Schiaparelli one, I must have looked awestruck. "I bet you'd like to walk out with this one, huh?" he chided, which made me laugh a lot. I admire his photos of the dolls for Susan Train's book and I cannot find a single imperfection in them. Back when they were new, these little figurines of the Théâtre de la Mode were extraordinarily influential. Similar models were used again in a number of other fashion related exhibitions in France until the early 1950s. I was able, with great luck, to find some for my collection, along with various other documents, such as original drawings from the first two shows. I also had the great pleasure of being friends with Eliane Bonabel and André Beaurepaire, who was only twenty-one when he designed a very elaborate set done in his inimitable Baroque style.

Schiap finally arrived back in Paris in July 1945. Although it has been noted that she did not write one single word of thanks to her faithful employees, those loyal workers who saved her house from being closed, she did, without being asked, immediately double their wages, which had been frozen since the beginning of the war. Schiap tried to get back into the swing of things quickly, but the first few collections, according to some people in the fashion world, seemed as if they were very out of step, still rather late 1930s looking. She said, "I was still a dreamer and I continued to have a vision of women dressed in a practical yet dignified and elegant way, and I thought of the ancient wisdom of the Chinese and the simplicity of their clothes. I made flat dresses with sloping lines, easily packed, easily carried, light in weight and becoming to the figure."[1]

"Schiaparelli brings color back to fashion!" were *Vogue*'s words in the first issue published in post-war France.[2] The colors were naturally blue, white, and red, those that represent the French flag. From this collection I have a necklace, created by the now highly-collected Louis Rousselet firm that was known for making haute couture costume jewelery in a very unique style of molten glass and gilt filigree metal. Though they are known mostly for the creations made for Schiap's rival Chanel, they made jewels for many other houses including, at the dawn of the post-war era, the House of Schiaparelli. The 1940s started a trend of large, sculptural cuts in her work that had begun in the 1930s but did not really develop to the extreme until 1949. Schiaparelli also brought back her usual contradictions of materials. As early as 1946, asymmetric panels and bustiers were seen, as well as uneven lapels, and asymmetric jackets where one half was longer than the other. Pockets of large proportions were put in unusual places. Felt jackets had lavish gilt embroidery and could be worn with corduroy slacks. There were severe modernistic, synthetic coats trimmed in rare furs. There were pockets at the knee of a day dress, the hip of a jacket had one side ten inches lower than the other, and a beach outfit was simply a huge square with very, very big pockets. One coat had a strangely placed pocket from which hung a long chiffon handkerchief. She'd use fabrics such as Tergal, Nylon, and Cracknyl for coats, sun suits and swimwear, and Pluvionyl for light, crease-resistant, and waterproof dresses, hats, and coats with matching handbags and umbrellas.

One of the most exciting new aspects to her work was her collaboration with textile makers in Switzerland. Although she had been doing this since the pre-war period, her name was associated now with the actual manufacturers, whom she acknowledged in advertising and photo credits. I discovered very useful information by chance. When I was quite young I had the great pleasure to know Madame Andrée Brossin de Méré, the textile designer of great acclaim. She was famous in the haute couture of Paris for her work with Givenchy, Dior, and Saint Laurent. Her prints of cakes, tomatoes, lettuce, and a trompe-l'oeil of braided hair for a Givenchy headscarf are famous. I often visited with her to hear tales of fabric, lace, and the humorous things she had created in Paris.

At a 2007 symposium organized by Glamour Engineering founder and curator Michelle Nicol, I met Tobias "Tobie" Forster. "We have had a mutual friend," this incredibly congenial gentleman said to me. It was at this moment, he recalled, as did I, the many happy moments I spent with Madame Andrée Brossin de Méré. He told me how she spoke to him about me, which made me even more nostalgic. Eventually he told me about his family firm who worked closely not only with Madame Brossin de Méré, but directly with Schiaparelli, as well.

This firm was Forster Willi & Co., which was founded in 1904 and has been a family business ever since and is based in St. Gallen, Switzerland. Mr. Forster took over on October 1, 1963 and ran it with great success, though he is now retired. Conrad Forster, his father, invented cotton organdy in the nineteenth century by putting cotton muslin through a chemical process that made it transparent and stiff, and thus created an entirely new material that would be used in high fashion designs. Schiaparelli used it often, as it was still a fresh and beautiful material for her even as late as the 1950s. The firm also made wonderful guipure lace.[3] Guipure is one of the specialties of St. Gallen. Some Schiaparelli models were made using his fabrics, which are amazingly well-documented in their truly marvelous archives that start in 1943. Here are two examples:

Picasso, summer 1949: a strapless, full-skirted dance dress in an unusual machine stitch of abstract design.

Schiaparelli day dress, summer 1949: a transparent organdy embroidered with baroque designs of flowers, cinched waist with black belt and simple pie-pan hat attached with a simple white ribbon, transparent, elbow-length gathered gloves. Unusual most-likely Perugia pumps.

I wish I could list them all!

Another important French fashion publicity vehicle also occurred right after the war. November 1945 marked the debut of *Elle* magazine, founded by Helene Lazareff, Françoise Giroud, and Jean Chevalier. It was geared to the younger generation and the very new way of making, buying, and wearing haute couture. It specialized in fresh, more youthful looks for women and pioneered so many things that we now take for granted in women's fashion, like short, simple hairstyles and ready-to-wear clothes. The debut cover showed a model in a tobacco brown colored Schiaparelli suit and Directoire style hat and scarf, holding a live tiger cub. I guess a bit of that old world Marchesa Casati chic was still the norm. One can only hope it didn't end up as a muff.

Schiap played with proportion in a fabulous and strange way throughout the post-war 1940s. These were her "architectural" years. She made a hat that looked like an enormous paper boat and a fashion magazine remarked that it wasn't a boat, but a hat in white toile that the designer made for the burning sun." Another looked a little like a lampshade in tiered organdy. Others were tight, asymmetric cloches that hugged the head; one had a visor with a hole for the eye to look out of on one side. Another had a woman's profile, with a diamanté eye and eyebrow brooch that was designed by my friend Maxime de la Falaise for Schiap in 1949, or so she claimed. (Bettina Bergery maintained that Maxime hadn't designed this particular hat.) There were many new stylists engaged at Schiaparelli's and whoever actually had the idea for the profile hat is incidental.

As Pierre Cardin recalled to me, he worked briefly for the House of Schiaparelli, for only two months somewhere around the beginning of 1945 as an assistant designer.[4] Monsieur Cardin had little to say about Schiaparelli to me besides a few banalities, which was rather surprising to me. Finally, in 1984 or so, still reluctant to discuss Schiaparelli with me but no longer tight-lipped, Cardin recalled that she was impossible sometimes, quite a personality, terrifying, and incredibly chic. He was glad to have had the experience but was soon to work for Dior—he was asked by Dior himself to work there—and then he created his own house. I wish I knew which pieces he worked on.

The winter 1945 collection, still under the direction of Irene Dana, featured soft collars that jetted forward and large, square-shouldered coats with full skirts and short, bouffant sleeves. The soft lines of the dresses, full in the front and around the hips, were shown in the traditional bright Schiaparelli colors, although many of the fabrics were of a questionable quality. (Some were made by Coudurier-Fructus-Descher, and other materials came from Rodier and Remond.) Most of the colors were tarnished and somewhat dreary, however, as if all the world's colorists were creating on a cloudy, somber day and using mud instead of water for their *aquarelle* palettes. The Gruau drawings seen in magazines in 1945 showed her styles: sharp silhouettes, drapery on high hats, and cinched waists. One even showed a woman holding an Art Nouveau statuette and claiming the "Modern Style" was back. Dalí, who wrote extensively of the importance of that first incarnation of modernism, must have been quite pleased.

The collection was designed after the restrictions on cloth per garment had been re-defined and the prices brought somewhat under control. American buyers didn't come to see the presentations that year, but their French representatives did, although the prices were still unaffordable and delivery uncertain. However, the high cost didn't bother the remaining wealthy Parisian clients at all. In fact, the new fiscal laws made it advantageous to buy.

But selling was not the foremost preoccupation for the haute couture industry. The main motivation was proving that Parisian chic continued to reign and that the creative spirit was still alive and well within France's industries. French luxury would not be usurped or replaced by any other countries' fashion styles. There were still a few occasions to wear evening attire in 1945, where designers showed their most creative ideas, but sumptuous balls and stately formal affairs seemed to be, for the time being, something from the past. In addition, many of the models could not be copied in America, Great Britain, or South America due to the lack of materials. Even if the press had attended the fashion openings, photographs were not permitted until April 15, to avoid private clients running into copies. The Chambre Syndicale thought it best to arrange the schedule to benefit the private clients more than the buyers and retailers.

But Schiaparelli tackled the new era head on. In conversation Bettina Bergery recalled Schiaparelli as being as practical as ever. For air travel, taking into account the thirty kilogram luggage limit on a transatlantic flight, she designed a straight, shoulder-to-hem "Constellation" travel coat and a matching travel bag that was instantly applauded and another coat with "suitcase" pockets and a "commuter's bag" with two huge flaps on either side. She claimed that she made an entire trousseau of clothes in a special air travel bag weighing less than ten pounds that included a reversible coat (which could be worn day or night), six simple dresses, and three collapsible hats. She considered this collection the natural answer to the lifestyle that the jet-setting, post-war woman faced, though she felt the whole concept was too ahead of its time. The collection was one of the most intelligent ones she ever designed, and although it garnered publicity, there were no sales. These ideas recall her 1929 collection and the "Smartness Aloft" essay with its chic but practical clothes for air travel.[5] Even when applied to a new generation, it was still too far in advance.

She noticed that women insisted on looking like little girls with short skirts and Mary Jane–style shoes, even though childhood ended decades before. These women had "built-up faces that looked as if they had cried 'Stop!' to death." Logic, she thought, was "out of fashion." As for the mood of that time she said, "Love and fidelity turned on the spin of a wheel. Companionship, leadership, creed, all were forgotten."[6] Schiap continued with her concepts of feminine beauty in spite of the after-effects of the war. Her nouveau riche customers were probably disappointed when she said, "I want to make clothes for women to live in, not parade in."

She solemnly admitted in her autobiography, that maybe she had rusty wheels and she found out soon enough that they no longer had their axles in the center. Her fashions, she admitted, were not at all accepted and were considered eccentric in the high fashion milieu. The vibrations of the world, she felt, were out of sync and the workaday monster, which she scornfully referred to as "utilitarian," had taken hold in England and France during the war, and had completely taken over.

The first postwar Schiaparelli-designed collection was finally shown on September 13, 1945. She claimed that she started where she had left off in 1940. The winter 1945–1946 show had Directoire hats that romantically tied under the chin. Gowns in Scottish taffetas were strapless. The suits still had a fitted look with shoulders rather large and square. Collars went all the way up to the chin with the heads sometimes topped with high-colored *postillion* hats. There was a definite French Restoration period style to the clothes, a look back to another time after a great political upheaval. The clothes were cocky and arrogant, mannish and contrasting, a bit arcane and very sophisticated, but when combined in an ensemble, feminine and romantic. In the *Vogue Liberation Album* for January 1945, there were seven examples of Schiaparelli's clothing. The advertisements for "Sleeping" suggested awakening from a long slumber, and the ads for "Shocking" featured a nomad returning home to the place Vendôme with a large bottle of the perfume under her arm. I see a general theme of rebirth.

The summer 1946 collection was largely influenced by Indochina, which was on the verge of a war of independence with France.[7] Schiap showed long, straight-cut coats with multi-colored embroideries and introduced the "Vieux Beaux" print: a romantic and cartoonish rendition of the old boulevardiers of the Belle Époque era. They looked quite a lot like Vertès's style, with that rakish, breezy style he was known for, though these prints were not by him. Illustrations in *L'Art de la Mode* showed cap-sleeved short dresses in a blue and white print fabric by Racine with large poke bonnets of the same material that attached to the dress like a hood.[8] These were notably feminine and amongst the more successful models. By autumn Schiaparelli was interested in contrasts, short little jackets with embroideries in rayon and cotton, worn with little linen afternoon dresses and monochrome colored evening dresses.[9] Evening gowns had jagged edges and hats and headpieces matched the blouses of suits.

For Winter 1946–47 Schiaparelli proposed custom-made dresses with false bustles worn with jackets and as well as svelte afternoon jackets and dresses with draped hips gathered in the back.[10] Coats and suits with sloped shoulders brought back a sort of slouch that hadn't been seen since the early 1920s, the same style that Schiap had once reacted to so violently. The clothes were padded, with full coats that had big, wide low pockets and undulating hemlines. The closures featured her Surrealistic buttons, a regular expectation that were considered little artworks. They were still used as a clever detail to relieve the severity or simplicity of a garment.

Button makers throughout the world are eternally indebted to Schiap, as she launched a multi-million dollar industry, which remains strong today. They created copies of her designs, calling them "whimsies," and the once-Surrealistic notion only reserved for the elite finally reached the mass population. In order to profit from her own influence, she created a license to make buttons in North America in the 1930s, but she would not profit as much as the mass-producers whose buttons were sold in every "five-and-dime" in America. Some of her licensed buttons were metal-rimmed photographic scenes of the Arc de Triomphe and the Eiffel Tower. These were covered with thick transparent celluloid and are avidly collected today by American button collectors. Another set, infinitely harder to find, are those manufactured by La Mode buttons, made in France for export by the very same makers of the buttons for her haute couture collections. They came on a card presenting, in one example, a set of red and black cat heads carved into what appears to be a resinous Galalith or Bakelite type material with the heading printed on the sample card, "Introducing Cat's Heads by Schiaparelli."

New colors and materials for 1947 included golden tweeds. Palettes of deep shades of mauves and greens, light blue like the eggs of robins, and a red like their breasts (called *Rouge Gorge Rouge*) were used in solid colored knitwear and satins with hints of black. The red-breasted robin, according to old wives tales, is a bird sacred to the gods that oversaw peaceful households. Interpreted by Lesage, she kept watch over her eggs with especially lovely embroidery that included feathers, chenille, cotton, lamé threads, sequins, beads, and silk threads in no fewer than ten different colors. This little treasure of embroidery was found on the inside of a pocket! It is amazing how Schiaparelli's color palette evolved in the same way as a painter's. Unlike many other fashion designers, she was a leader in this regard. Her palette was immediately copied by the ready-to-wear clothing makers all over the world, referenced in advertisements for lipsticks, nail polishes, home furnishing fabrics, house paints, and even automobiles. Her colors were always so poised, so studied, never a glitch or glaring color in the collection, even if some were completely indefinable. This was surely something to do with her collaboration with Jean Clément, a master colorist himself. Rumor claims that he was the one who came up with shocking pink. From hats to hosiery, from the ensemble to matching shoes, everything fit into her season's palette. Even the interior of her *maison de haute couture* had colors matching the season. In August 1947, she re-decorated her by-then legendary boutique.[11] Never one to remain stuck to the past, she amused her clients with new decorative ideas and again, giving them her newest colors to linger in while they chose clothes.

The spring 1947 season, with its pink and black-themed clothes—a now familiar leitmotif—had a jet embroidered *tournure* dress and sleeveless jackets.[12] The general look featured padded sloping shoulders, cinched waists, and a rounded padded bustle in the rear. For her summer 1947 collection, Schiap announced a very peculiar and tightly wrapped "Mummy Silhouette."[13] Only God in heaven can know how she came about those strange tubular straight dresses with spiraled ribbons. Maurice Tabard, the enormously talented photographer, did a strangely surreal photo of her "Robe-Colonne" for *Album du Figaro*. Looking like a wrapped up mummy, the model gazes dreamily off to the left of the image, clutching ruffled satin gloved hands to her face as if having a metaphysical experience, maybe one of those Dalí-fueled orgasms that my friend Ghislaine de Boisson, a Schiaparelli house model, told me about. The lighting is startling in Tabard's unique style. Tabard expert Pierre Gassman noted that Tabard was the master of lighting. His photo of the Schiap dress is a perfect example of his work. The model looks like she is a Madonna in rapture.

A new perfume concept called "Le Roi Soleil" debuted in a sophisticated bottle designed by Dalí in 1946. It was created by Baccarat (as were all of Schiaparelli's fragrance bottles) and was in the form of a sun with a face represented by birds supposedly modeled after Gogo as an adult. However, there is no evidence to support this claim, nor did she mention any information about that rumor when she offered me her mother's own bottle of the perfume. Over lunch at the St. Regis in New York in the mid-1970s, Dalí recalled how the bottle sparkled and shimmered in its shell case. He mentioned the drawings he did for it as "marvelous."

The bottle rested on a stepped base that vaguely resembled the collar of a king's ceremonial robe, but it also looked like the sea. It came in a blue-grey colored metal clam shell-shaped container that was lined in Sleeping Blue velvet. The whole image represented life and happiness. The presentation color was a yellow-gold and naturally Dalí did the advertisements of Louis XIV as "Le Roi Soleil." The drawing for the ad was lovely and fresh, and not typically Dalí in style. Schiap also did scented oils for the body, face, lips, and eyelids called, "The 4 Essential Oils: Shocking Radiance" that came in square bottles with a Dalí painting printed on the front of each one. Some of the dresses in the fashion show of that season were presentation dresses for "Le Roi Soleil" perfume and the models in the fashion show carried the elegant flacons. One dress looked like it was a gold bullion sack, drawn about the hips with a drawstring. One of the house models that presented the new perfume was named Lud. "Lud worked only for Schiap just after the war, I think around 1946. She was stunning. Absolutely stunning. I often did shots of her for *Vogue* in the Schiap clothes, but [at] the openings, she had such a chic way of presenting the clothes," Horst explained to me in the 1970s. *Vogue* editor Bettina Ballard wrote of her:

> Lud was the great star Russian model of the moment, of whom Horst took many of his greatest pictures. She was ruthless with herself, having cut off part of her breasts and thighs for a better figure. We would never put too low a dress on her because the plastic surgery had been badly done and her nipples pointed up-ward. Lud would look over the dresses, choosing what she wanted to wear leaving the rest for the other girls. There was no point in trying to put her in anything that she didn't like—she would throw away the picture by posing badly. She rarely smiled, except for Dilé, who could get through to her, or for Horst, with whom I suspected she was in love. After the war I found her thickened and saddened, showing clothes for Schiaparelli with her husband in trouble on a black-market charge.[14]

"Le Roi Soleil" was considered a masterpiece of the perfumer's art and the elite raved about its deluxe bottle. However, it was an extremely expensive perfume, and the luxury version's bottle and package were unaffordable to most people, even the newly wealthy post-war Parisians. It solicited comments from the ultimate snob, the Duchess of Windsor, who called it "the most beautiful bottle ever made" and that it "displaced the Duke's photograph on the coiffeuse."[15] Eventually the scent came in other, simpler bottles, as did most of the Schiaparelli perfumes.

Schiaparelli went to London on October 1, 1948 to convince the English women they should wear the new longer-length skirts shown in Paris, which provoked a protest against the British government's restrictions on fabric. According to the law, the longer length skirts were a useless luxury and a waste of fabric in a period of strict rationing. Paradoxically, in the USA, Catalina Swimwear company made the interchangeable and multi-changeable bikini by Schiaparelli. The restrictions of fabric were not an issue because it was so small. The suit starts off so brief and tiny that it would be indiscreet to wear in public. However, as it evolves, it covers just a bit more each time, finally emerging as a somewhat socially acceptable bikini, which was already controversial for its exposure of feminine flesh.

In 1948, everything seemed very romantic at Schiaparelli's house, which brought in, amongst other silhouettes, the "Riding Habit Line," the "Dandy Look," and the very narrow "Arrow Silhouette."[16] A Richard Avedon photograph for *Harper's Bazaar* inspired by nineteenth-century style portraits used a classic painted backdrop to showcase a luscious polka-dotted dress. It was described as "Schiaparelli's charmer of white dotted Swiss organdy, its skirt pulled all to the back and into a low pannier, caught with a bow of peach-colored organdy set six inches below the waist. At the front of the décolletage two points reach almost to the shoulders, as is the new way with strapless dresses, Schiaparelli's organdy hat."[17] The hat was enormous, of course, and the dress right out of an antique Parisian fashion engraving.

Fashion legends such as Diana Vreeland, Bettina Ballard, and Carmel Snow wore her clothes and understood them from a feminine point of view. They had first raved about her clothes in the press and seemed still to have a genuine enthusiasm and admiration for her work. For example, Bettina Ballard dedicated a section to Schiap's work in her autobiography, *In My Fashion*. Ballard explained that "her outspokenness during her days of fame was all part of the Schiaparelli shock treatment."[18] Schiap seemed to elicit very flattering and sincere reminiscences from her most famous clients. However, some of her fellow designers, and those who immediately succeeded her after the war, sometimes seem to hold back compliments in her regard.

Pierre Balmain, whom I knew, was falsely discreet in his regard for her with a lot of *sous-entendus*. For Balmain, Schiaparelli was never his taste; she was too artistic and clothes need not be artistic, only elegant. Molyneux was Balmain's mentor and he learned a lot from him. His career was the evolution of a classical style, he told me. I get the impression that Schiap's own personality—hard, nervy, and extravagant—annoyed some of her fellow fashion comrades and that they were tight-lipped about her for personal reasons, not so much in reaction to the work itself, although they make clear their dislike for it. As everyone who knew her has said to me, you either adored her or despised her.

If Balmain and Molyneux were good, albeit safe designers, their contributions to the grand chic of French clothes were not linked to any special line or construction that either of them had created, and certainly not to their use of beige, which Pierre Balmain talked on and on about to me. The importance of beige became a joke when I mentioned it to friends who knew how Monsieur Balmain could chew my ear off about how gifted he was with beige. The world's best-dressed women, including the most famous and celebrated ones, wore Schiaparelli clothes and in my opinion wore those overly "elegant" Molyneux and later Balmain clothes as a safety net. Perhaps they were suitable for going to a wedding or baby shower. Neither designer's work was of any particular brand of elegance that was of such a sublime sharpness as was Schiaparelli's. While collecting their clothes is important for history, none of them ever consistently created as remarkable or stand-out clothes as Schiaparelli. Dior has several famous designs, the most notable is his suit called "Bar." He was particularly snide about Schiaparelli in his autobiography. Also, Dior and Balmain seem to overlook her amazingly clean-lined clothes, her use of black and white and beige (yep! even beige!), her severely sleek designs based on use and comfort, and her extraordinary construction. Effect was one of the most important elements in 1930s-era French fashions and Balmain seems to have forgotten this as well. Trimmings were sometimes essential in creating dramatic or subtle effects, which Schiaparelli mastered without ever being gaudy. Also the use of embellishments during the 1930s gave a great many jobs to people. She used métiers that would have perished if it were not for her use of them. Most of all, Balmain seems to have over-looked that Schiaparelli was a master draper from the first collection onward. Her earliest designs were superior examples of the type of clothes he tried to endorse much later. Ballard makes an important point: "Balenciaga once said that Elsa Schiaparelli was the only real artist in the couture, which didn't mean he thought that art and dressmaking were good companions. Certainly she used color with the boldness of Picasso, and the drama that she produced with black was even more outspoken than that with colors, particularly her use of gold embroidery with black," continuing, in her words, with "they always had such sureness of line, such boldness."[19]

By 1947, Schiaparelli was inventing strange new things that were not so easily accepted as she tried to regain her foothold on a postwar style. Always chic and lavish, her clothes experimented with many new ideas like romantic flashbacks and historical references. Schiap's collections of 1947 and 1948 were always a great inspiration to me, even though fashion historians rarely discuss them today. The models shown for spring 1948 featured thin, slim lines interrupted only by drapery projected in the front, some of which was lined in fur. Many of the tailored jackets featured large pockets. She showed pearl embroidered organdy collars that fastened on the shoulder and worn over tight-fitting satin gowns.[20]

For summer Schiaparelli showed her "Amazone, or Riding Habit, Silhouette" with wasp waists and a natural shoulder line with a large puffed sleeve-effect.[21] "Faille puce," a taffeta created by Marcel Guillemin, was used for an off-the-shoulder gown with a *pouf* and

Scottish tartan in taffeta was made by Bianchini-Férier. One summer dress had a bodice imitating a strapless corset in ruched rose-colored toile by Martelli that was worn with a loose bolero, both trimmed in bands of ruffles. Her underskirts edged with ruffles and her *caleçons* (or bloomers) were among the many "revivals" mentioned in *Vogue* and *Harper's Bazaar*. The soon-to-be seen "'Impressionist' fashions" from Schiaparelli would be "marked by docile shoulders, pliant little waists, skirts hitched back from flat fronts, below-the-elbow sleeves."[22] These styles were shown in a romantic way, photographed in black and white and looking as though the photographs were taken during the Belle Époque. Body-hugging gowns with trains trimmed with bows were matched to light red stockings, which also matched her new lipstick, called "Stunning."

The autumn, 1948 collection emphasized the treatment of sleeves and had many variations.[23] Tight shoulders with width underneath were influenced by the look of the Second Empire, which was celebrating its 100th anniversary. She also included jackets inspired by clerical garments, with winged shapes at the elbows, straight skirts, and short drapery for the evening. The following collection for winter, 1948–49 showed conical afternoon and evening skirts with poufs, and coats with bat wing sleeves and storage pockets called "manteaux-sacs."[24] Long bouffant sleeves were removable on evening gowns and monkey fur boots, revived from the pre-war period, returned. Styles that Schiap had used much earlier seemed fresh again for a whole new generation of women wearing haute. Cloche hats were revived with great success, some in suede and side-tilted, others in velvet. I have several of these in my collection including one that was adapted for the American market in brilliant bright blue with a beaded "S" on the side. My assistant Jane modeled it for a photograph Patrick Safati and I did that appeared on the cover of *L'Express* magazine when I had my Schiap homage show in Paris. One can see the violet walls of my first apartment with Lala in the background.

In 1948, Schiap used Boucheron diamond buttons on the back of an Empire-style coat that had a soft, pleated tail cut in an unusually long and high proportion to the coat. Associated Press in Paris thought it was worthy of world news that Schiaparelli adorned her creations with *haute joaillerie*: "Schiaparelli shows in her new collection this short evening dress, it's formed with eight layers of tulle in yellow, orange, and navy blue. The bodice forms a corolle, the waist is grasped by a belt of black leather. A necklace and bracelet in spiral forms in topaz and diamonds by Boucheron adorns this bright colored dress."[25] She continued to work with Boucheron in 1949 as the jewelers of the place Vendôme were making a grand promotion of fine jewels.

"Zut," a new fragrance, appeared in 1948. It was named after the French expression meaning "shucks" or "darn." The perfume came in a rather odd-looking bottle designed by Vertès and described in the American press as "leg-art."[26] It was shaped like a Victorian dance-hall girl's lower body, to complement the "Shocking" bottle's upper portion. A spangled tutu has fallen to the ground, and the careless, maybe coquette little dancer would most obviously have said "Zut!" A saucy garter belt in "Zut" green satin hugged the bottle's box. It was all very sexy and funny.

"Zut" emerged as a great success. It reflected the romantic new clothes, with its nineteenth-century bottle and color. Its presentation color was Zut green: a deep, dignified medium-dark tone reminiscent of the darker tones of the impressionist palette and the Belle Époque's color scheme. The Marcel Vertès advertisements are pure magic—luxury, sexiness, and Schiaparelli elegance par excellence. Emulating nineteenth-century coquetry, licentious men, showgirls swept up in big strong mustachioed boulevardiers' greatcoats, and dancers running after a Nijinsky-like faun who'd stolen away the bottle, Zut was all sex and seduction. There was even a Schiaparelli men's tie printed with the Zut bottle all over it! *Oh la la!*

For spring 1949, Schiaparelli came up with yet more slimming lines, structured with drapery projected in the front and décolleté that stuck out from the bust.[27] Silhouettes for the evening were sheaths down to the knees until they spread out to the floor in a swirl of fabric. Fur basque tails on evening coats, and fur yokes trimmed in draped fabric were used. Many items of clothing, for day or night, had mink and ermine tails. Artist Eric drew Madame Schiaparelli wearing her animal tail trimmed garment, a large rectangular affair that draped over the shoulders and closed with peculiar François Hugo buttons (and now in my collection). Summer 1949 presented a return to some of her oldest ideas including the backswept "Hurricane Line," which took a backseat in the press because Balenciaga had just launched his "Blown-Back Line" to great success.[28] He obviously drew inspiration from Schiaparelli's 1930s "Stormy Weather" and "Typhoon" silhouettes. Topee and pith helmets were made of bamboo cane strips. I have an overblown hat of straw that is as large as a child in my collection. It has armholes so that it could also be worn like a bolero. It had a matching bathing suit that was featured on the cover of *Le Corset de France* magazine, summer 1949 issue. There were many simple straight dresses with tightly cinched leather belts with round saddle-stitched handles like those you'd find on luggage. *Paris Match* featured two full pages on the "Dress Without Any Seams."[33] This garment was light years ahead of what was happening in fashion and only now can we recognize the extraordinariness of this creation, something worthy of the great Japanese designers of today. From the Greek toga to those intricately draped dresses of Madame Grès, its modernism is timeless and this dress alone is a true masterpiece of twentieth-century fashion. Yet this was only one creation of that year. She also offered a beach costume that is a gigantic, and I do mean GIGANTIC, square garment worn as a peignoir in brilliant yellow. It is essentially two enormous squares with buttons down the front, with huge pockets, worn over a skintight black strapless bathing suit that also has huge white buttons down its front. The entire ensemble would be topped with a huge straw hat. It came with four pegs with which to pitch it like a tent in order to change in or out of the bathing costume. It was truly one of the oddest, chicest things of that year without a doubt. It was probably hard to wear in real life, but it looked wonderful on covers of fashion magazines and in sketches by my dear friend, the illustrator Dagmar who kindly offered me so many of her original Schiaparelli drawings, accessories, and clothes as well.[29]

The 1949 autumn season emphasized thin lines and natural shoulders, irregular bodices, necklaces in odd shapes, and pointed pendants.[30] Referred to later as the "Broken Egg Silhouette," everything was zigzagged and jagged. Gowns had what her press release described as "cracked eggshell" corsages and shapes were distorted, invariably looking wonderful in fashion drawings as they were highly graphic. Every dress seemed to have a zigzag, an edge, or a folded-over triangular flap, as if it were peeling off the lady. One asymmetric suit looked as if it were accidentally buttoned incorrectly. A number of garments had this effect. She made a trapeze-line coat that was completely pyramidal in shape, with one remarkable example featuring an incredible winged collar that stood out and up like an angry bat.

I mentally associate one of my best friends, Laurent Mercier, with this collection. Born in Switzerland, he was art director for Pierre Balmain haute couture in Paris, was Lenny Kravitz's stylist for many years, and had his own fashion label. He was also known throughout the Paris world of high fashion glitterati and the über chic nightclub scene as his alter ego, named simply "Dragoness Lola von Flame." His drag persona is simply one of the most unique creations I have ever known. It was love at first sight when our mutual friend Sylvie Fleury introduced us, and we have been very close friends ever since. Lala and I had the pleasure of discovering that he is quite possibly our best model for Schiaparelli suits of this era, the ones with small waists and padded shoulders. We call him "the *tailleur* girl."

Laurent has a way of posing that is simply perfect. He understands haute couture and instinctively knows all the references and exactly how to pose, and especially in a tailored suit. He's been a constant source of fun and inspiration for the photos of my collection. He literally made one of the 1949 "Broken Eggshell" suits from Schiap famous in the Swiss press with his dramatic pose at the Hôtel Le Palace in Lausanne. He and I both are somewhat mesmerized by the Schiaparelli looks of the late 1940s. Once, despite knowing what a purist I am when photographing Schiaparelli clothes, he put two Schiaparelli hats on top of each other because he thought it looked better on him! He almost got away with it until it dawned upon me what he'd done. I was in stitches laughing because he wanted to see if I'd notice. He has a way about him which is truly comic and makes everything so lively, and it took twenty minutes to stop laughing and arguing about it. He's one of the nicest people in the world and we all adore him at home. Discreet, demure, and understated as a boy, a she-panther femme fatale as Lola Dragoness Von Flame, he is also one of the stars of Thierry Mugler's *Follies* in Paris. The last name, "Dragoness von Flame" I baptized him with when one day I referred to Maxime de la Falaise as a Dragoness, this because she was so wickedly chic. We laughed so much about it that I decided it should be Lola's quasi-aristocratic "title" and then I added "von Flame" as his ersatz gotha last name. So that makes me his "drag mother" in a special sort of way. We always have a long string of fun and games when we see him.

The late 1940s house of Schiap was not all fun and games, though. An employee strike in Parisian haute couture in July 1949 took everyone by surprise. As a result, Schiap showed a rather unusual collection for winter that year. The motto of the collection was, "Sorry for the pins and needles and be kind not to pull the basting" and the headlines humorously complimented it by calling the collection "striking."[31] Schiap explained that because the sewing girls had walked out a fortnight before the show (some of them unwillingly but obliged to do so), she remained alone in the workrooms with the tailor and the *première*, while downstairs the saleswomen and the mannequins had stayed. She decided that the show would take place on the day and hour advertised, regardless of what happened. So everybody present worked in a fever for the huge challenge, in the best of moods. The *défilé* happened at the scheduled time and what a show that was! Some coats had no sleeves, others only one. Buttons were scarce, and there were certainly no buttonholes, for they were too difficult to make. The dresses had sketches pinned on them, pieces of material to show what colors they would eventually be. Stately evening dresses cut in muslin sprung to life with costume jewelry. Here and there explanations were written in a bold hand. Schiap said, "Certainly as a publicity stunt it was sensational. It was the cheapest collection I ever made but it sold surprisingly well. And it had its effect, for the next day all the girls were back to work."[32]

In 1949 Schiap made news with all her innovations and surprises, almost as if she had staged her own comeback. She received attention worldwide, especially in the United States. She represented the stateliness of the past, all the luxury and allure of the pre-war era, but also everything that was modern and sharply elegant. She resuscitated her original boutique idea and updated it severely, in both design and functionality. It was the era of boutique "separates," and Givenchy played a great role in this story.

Hubert James Marcel Taffin de Givenchy, born an aristocrat, worked for Schiaparelli during this time of rebirth in Paris fashion, roughly between 1947 and 1951. He started with designs for the haute couture collection, some of which were startlingly chic.

Looking at the Schiaparelli clothes from the early part of the time he worked with her, you can recognize the distinctive Givenchy style. Although Schiaparelli had utilized extremely simply cut clothes since the 1920s, with graphic and severe shapes, and had a sophisticated draping system based on very basic forms, she also was a master of embellishment and ornament. Givenchy, too, was clever with form. He so admired Balenciaga, and used very linear shapes with simple, graphic appeal. Although later in his own career he used adornment to perfection, such as eighteenth-century Saltambanque monkeys embroidered on an evening gown for the Duchess of Windsor and his *trompe-l'oeil* headscarves whose prints looked like hair in plaits, Surrealistic tricks were not so much his thing when he first started. For example, one evening bolero certainly bore a number of his trademark ideas. It was short and a bit longer in back than the front. It had the romantic balloon sleeves that would eventually evolve into the famous "Bettina blouse" silhouette. The high collar was long and pointed, also typical of the Givenchy style. This bolero was, however, lavishly embroidered in Lesage beadwork. The motifs, amorphous shapes, and multi-colored patches edged in gold lamé threads and re-embroidered with sequins, soap bubble glass beads, and dangling pendants of opalescent glass gave it a look of decidedly abstract art. One can only imagine that this embellishment was something Schiap devised for this bolero and that Givenchy, whose style was largely based on simplicity at that time, would have cringed at the extravagant ornament on the intriguingly sculpted basic shape of the garment. This, as Givenchy explained later in life, was the bane of his existence at Schiaparelli.[33]

He later designed boutique clothes for Schiap. Beautiful separates, such as skirts with large pockets that wrapped around the body. Simple organdy or cotton batiste blouses for day and two-piece gowns comprised of a bustier and an evening skirt. What now seems a very simple idea was, at the time, a fashion revolution, re-launched for the new era. He was also known for his charm. "I went to Schiaparelli's to sketch . . . but all I remember is meeting Givenchy, he was so enchanting," Dagmar wrote to me in 1988.

According to Mr. de Givenchy's biography, it was quite unprecedented for Schiap to have an assistant.[34] She did things alone; working in starts and stops, with distractions and temperamental outbursts on occasion. As soon as Givenchy arrived, he worked in a room next to the studio where all the fabrics were piled up. There he started drawing and sketching. However, Schiaparelli had no intention of changing her habits. Givenchy describes how she would open a book on Egypt and use a bookmark to save all the places where a photo or image would please her. Once she had finished reviewing the book, Schiap would call for her premier and command, "Make me a toile from that!" Stupefied at the sight of the reproduction of an Egyptian Goddess, the workers would nevertheless do the job without a single comment, often in a sort of terror or bewilderment. "The result was often a success," said Givenchy. "The 'toile' did resemble the desired original but produced often a dress which was unwearable."[35] It was at these moments that the unshakeable Schiap would intervene adding, ripping, changing, accessorizing without stopping, all the while telling extraordinary stories about her incredible life. "I don't know if her stories were true or false, but who cares? To hear her saying that she saw a sign in the fact that an earthquake made Rome tremble the day she was born was enrapturing."[36] Though Givenchy felt that Schiaparelli made him bend to her ideas much against his own will, he was always willing to improve his knowledge of high fashion and managed to cope with it. He had an excellent relationship with the workshop and with Elsa, who he found extremely difficult but always fascinating.

While Givenchy admired the smugly elitist, cosmopolitan, and traditional clientele, he had been thinking for a while about a way to simplify the wardrobe of the contemporary Parisian woman. Although he was part of the generation which saw the immediate success of the Dior's "New Look," he noticed that it was fussy, hard to wear, required endless fittings and one needed a wardrobe mistress to help put it on. Givenchy had the sense that elegant post-war women were aspiring to a simpler way of dressing even though it had not yet been proposed by any designer or house of high fashion. Schiaparelli had already had her boutique, which stocked her delicious ready-made clothes in it, but they were imposed fashion silhouettes or full looks and often required fittings. After the war however, the concept was changed and even further simplified thanks to Givenchy. A client could mix and match pieces and individualize her wardrobe. The same item came in many colors and fabrics, so truly unique outfits could be pulled out of them to suit the individual woman. They were also much more simplified cuts of clothes, easy to make and easy to wear. He also saw that the top floor workrooms chez Schiap held endless rolls of leftover used fabrics. He thought it was a waste and felt it would be a pragmatic and clever thing to simply use them up and make clothes out of all those unused though still luxurious materials. Scion of an old French Protestant family, he once said in a conversation it was the Protestant side of him that could not bear seeing such waste. This is where the concept of *séparables* (separates) was born. It was a new, functional chic that gave clients the liberty to choose the clothes themselves and the way to wear them. The separates were also much more affordable. According to the American *Vogue* editor Susan Train, "I'll never forget this immense young man, reserved and very handsome, who changed our lives. Thanks to him, we'd find accessories to enlarge and transform our classic wardrobes, as well as young and new clothes, at reasonable prices. . . . Hubert was the first to launch glamorous ready-to-wear, the famous 'separates,' and to come and discover his latest creations, on those ravishing straw mannequins, was always thrilling. The Boutique was an unavoidable address, the most pretty women of the time were always found there."[37]

Hubert de Givenchy, with his soothing personality, good looks, wit, humor, and patience managed to befriend Elsa, winning her over. She invited him to parties, dinners, receptions, and the aforementioned Italian Chianti and "spaghetti parties" in her bistro bar in the cellar. There he met society's stars like Francis Poulenc, Jean Hugo, Henri Sauguet (who created music for her perfume "Si," which was inspired by Chianti bottles and the ambiance in her bistro). He recalled that despite these stellar get-togethers, he remained with Elsa until everyone left and witnessed her loneliness and knew, as she did, that they would gossip about her but happily return upon another invitation to her home. He found this rather poignant. The youthful designer remembers going out with her, on one occasion, to see a Roland Petit ballet. Just before leaving, he noticed she had on one red shoe and one violet shoe. Embarrassed, he timidly remarked to her, "Excuse me, but I believe that you put your shoes on too quickly Madame" to which she coldly replied, "But my dear friend, that's real chic! You need to learn this because you haven't yet understood it."[38] Givenchy claims that it was a lesson he'd never forget.

However, it was not for very long, this new life. Eventually, after having met investors from America through Hélène Bouilloux-Lafont, Givenchy decided to make the move. He confronted Schiaparelli. "I am sorry, but things being what they are, I have decided to spread my own wings." "If you leave me you'll go bankrupt," she said, furious that one could defy her. Despite this almost damning curse, he left and became one of France's most distinguished and lauded haute couturiers. Schiap, however, never spoke a single word to him again as long as she lived.

When Givenchy finally did open his own house, Philippe Venet briefly succeeded him at Schiaparelli, but then he, too, went his own way. Venet, whom Givenchy met at the age of twenty-four and was

Givenchy's *âme-soeur* according to his private diaries, described the process to me in conversation: "She gave ideas always and I executed the canvas. She had several designers, not including Givenchy anymore, who left one month after I arrived. He used to draw all the sketches and she would use them, always with her interpretation. . . . She would change things like altering a green dress by having one of the sleeves in red, that's typical of the things she could do, or she would do buttons big as plates."

He further explained how clients would order the clothes as designed and that Schiaparelli did not care to change the models in order to please customers. It was more "take it or leave it." Venet noted that many of her clients owned several homes, and if they liked a red dress for example, they would always order four, one for each house. One could not travel with a gown folded in a suitcase.

For Venet, after the war Schiaparelli was still considered a good house, but she did not have the same impact as Dior or Balenciaga. For him, Balenciaga was the ideal, with his emphasis on construction; he tried to make the body look better as a figure. The house was searching for a successor, but Venet was not the one. He said to me, "Schiaparelli was an old relic, a huge Trojan horse of prestige and glamour, it was too much for me . . . I could never have carried off the grand old House of Schiaparelli."

In 1949, after the immense popularity of her *Time* magazine cover story, the newly formed and restructured American offices created seasonal collections adapted exclusively for the American and Canadian markets, fashions based on her haute couture but not exact copies. The resultant clothes where as extravagant and had as much panache as the Parisian clothes. Due to this enthusiastic new adventure, many licenses were created.

In my opinion, Schiaparelli licenses (and many designers' agreements of the sort) are of great historic interest. Licensed clothes and accessories are often overlooked by fashion history scholars who view them as "watered down ideas." Schiaparelli's extraordinary dominance in this field was not only good business, but also a way to bring her fashion sensibilities to the entire world, regardless of economic situations. The look, the style, and the freedoms these pieces brought to fashion are innumerable. That is why I have always been as enthusiastic about these pieces as the haute couture originals. The global and overall fashion statement is extremely strong and has influenced many generations, long after her retirement. Her colors entered into the lexicon of color charts, and her costume jewelry was perhaps more popular, in the true sense of the word, than that of her rivals like Chanel. Chanel's costume jewelry was only for the privileged and rarely available outside her rue Cambon salon. Schiaparelli costume jewelry exists in large quantities in thousands of different styles. It is widely collected and carries forth her legacy. So, in this regard, I felt it essential that I address at least some of the various and varied licenses she made throughout the world, largely in North and South America.

A 1949 *Newsweek* cover article entitled "Schiaparelli the Shocker" said that her August collection had reaffirmed her mastery and that she had multiple projects in view.[39] They reaffirmed her leadership in this field in contrast to "Dior and his immediate imitators, who are falsifying good taste with creations simply meant to attract publicity." Many features in the press drew attention to one particularly sexy number called "Forbidden Fruit," a tight, strapless ruched sheath dress with a pale pink trompe l'oeil of a brassiere in crystal drops, giving the impression of an embroidered bosom.

Wholesaler Henry Mandelbaum of New York was contracted to manufacture and sell to one prestige store in each city of the United States. These designs included suit and coat collars with shocking colors of blue, red, and yellow, and dyed-to-match fur collars and linings. Designs could be made longer or shorter, with a décolleté or not, depending on how they were buttoned. Coats continued to follow her "Pyramid line" with vast expanses of fabric creating literally a tent around the woman, often lined in bright colors or bright colored dyed fur.

The Givenchy era at Schiap ended at the mid-century mark. Through the intervention of designer and passionate collector Dominique Sirop, I acquired a few dresses and accessories designed by Givenchy for Schiaparelli and original drawings by Givenchy. I always had a real fondness for the Givenchy–era Schiaparellis, maybe because I met him and dined with him chez Bettina regularly, or maybe because they were so cleverly cut, with great structural details and shapes. They were very modern clothes, and they brought the Schiaparelli house right up into the post-war zeitgeist with gusto.

CHAPTER 25

THE 1950S

For a new decade there were naturally some new ideas. These years, as far as I am concerned, are one of the most imaginative and sculptural moments for fashions in French haute couture. This was true in general as the decade moved forward—Balenciaga, Dior, Fath, and eventually Givenchy experimented successfully with all new ideas. Schiap had, as usual, her unique perspective and in my opinion, the most extreme and the most detached from the mere discipline of dressing the body. These were the years that French fashions were an expression of art. If Balenciaga was the Picasso and Dior the Calder, then Schiap was the Jackson Pollack of the group. If the Schiaparelli post-war era of the 1940s saw very visionary cuts based on asymmetry and startling shapes, the 1950s saw all of her unique talents concerning color and texture juxtapositions, artisan details from buttons to accessories, and new perspectives on proportion brought together in most often extreme and very successful ways. Strangely, though, fashion historians have as yet to truly recognize and applaud the unique vision of this last decade of her haute couture. Though she'd make haute couture for only another four years, the decade opened with a blast of avant-garde pieces that baffled most people. Spring 1950 featured an almost unwearable but refreshing and certainly noteworthy collarless coat called Canasta and a suit designed by Givenchy called House of Cards which was so oddly cut it's hard to even describe. It consists of a burgundy velvet jacket with a wired hem that sticks out, making a neat little square to the side. It is embroidered with sequins in a wavy iridescent and opalescent optical design by Lesage. The skirt was wired to the same shape. So eccentric was this model that at a costume ball at which Schiap was a guest, her "beau," known as Mr. "H," wore the jacket along with the mask of a rabbit! Her hats of this season were nothing short of from another planet. There were hats indeed, but with holes cut out for the eyes. Some seemed right out of a crazy science fiction B-movie. There was also a wedding dress provocatively called Striptease.

The fabulous *Flair* magazine, published in America, often showed Schiaparelli clothes, such as a one-shoulder evening dress of night-blue shantung worn by Baronne Marguerite "Daisy" de Cabrol.[1] In the December issue there was a very interesting document: "Rough-hewn gilt metal bracelet. Schiaparelli copy by Coro, about $8." This implies that Coro costume jewelry was making Schiaparelli jewelry, for which I have never seen any other reference or advertising. Friedrich Ludwig (von) Berzeviczy-Pallavicini, one of the editors at *Flair*, was a friend of mine in the 1970s and 1980s. He was nothing less than a truly camp dandy, what a gas he was! I meet him through Horst and we lunched regularly at the Metropolitan Museum of Art. He told me all of his Schiaparelli stories, for example, how he designed a few prints for her scarf license. He pointed out that in the 1950 Christmas issue, in his drawings of Christmas trees, was a violet-tinted Schiaparelli tree with its Shocking perfume bottle shape. I simply adored him and all of his stories of Austria, the famous tearoom Demel in Vienna which his family owned, and all his chasing after young boys like myself.

A line of children's clothes, called Schiap-Bébé received quite a bit of publicity when Schiap's granddaughters wore them to absolute perfection. In *Vogue* we see them often with their mother Gogo, as in a November 1949 Horst photo: "Marisa and Berinthia Berenson, the daughters of Mr. and Mrs. Robert Berenson, photographed with their mother, the former 'Gogo' Schiaparelli. Here the beguiling little girls wear wool coats and bonnets designed by their grandmother, Elsa Schiaparelli; the color, her shocking pink, new to children's fashions." The smiling sisters appeared on the cover of *Elle* for Christmas 1953 in stunning red velvet Schiaparelli dresses, three-tiered with a huge cummerbund and bow in the back with very short pagoda sleeves.

By 1950, proportions had reached a final extreme. Hats were either tiny caps on the back of the head or enormous and strange shapes. Shapes were dimensionally odd, as seen in a completely triangular plush short coat with two and a half inch wide buttons that had strangely shaped enormities.[2] Romance was still apparent in the exquisite strapless white organdy dress with nineteenth-century style black embroidery that was modeled by ambassador's wife and socialite, Mrs. Barry Bingham. Another incredible and odd-looking silhouette was in slate blue and ruby red. With a shirred bodice full to the waist, the stole was lined in red with the most amusing detail of all, "Lips drawn with Schiapencil."[3] This was utterly the most innovative makeup idea of the year, the lipstick pencil, now a classic.

Schiaparelli created the Schiap-Sport label for her boutique. These pieces were made in the same workrooms as the haute couture and boutique clothes, and Givenchy and Maxime de la Falaise designed many with the old fabric stock. One particularly noteworthy item is a rib knit cream-and-navy striped jersey sweater, if that's what it could be called. It is entirely de-constructed with enormous shell buttons on the shoulders.[4] It predates Issey Miyake by nearly thirty-five years! Another item was a blue-dyed rabbit fur stole polka dotted in white, just one model amongst many oddly colored furs, "shortie" jackets, and fur linings she did around this time. There was a lamé-bound cellophane X-ray cardigan and sheath dress that went unnoticed by the fashion press, but was copied shamelessly by Chanel years later. Another Schiap-Sport dress was belted, ruby red velvet with only one shoulder, cutting across the neckline diagonally, elegant in its simplicity. Belts were in fishnet covered in fruits or made of shells or from leopard fur. Maxime de la Falaise claimed she did many of these Schiap-Sport designs, which were enthusiastically bought by many of her famous clients, including the Duchess of Windsor. "I used to wear a lot of things she made for the boutique, funny little things, jewelry, belts, accessories, they were always so amusing," the Duchess of Windsor told me.

It was through Maxime de la Falaise that I first purchased her mother's Fortuny gowns from the 1910s, all of which are without doubt the most superb examples known amongst collectors. Throughout our friendship Maxime offered me many bits and pieces of her remaining haute couture clothes from Balenciaga, Dior, and Yves Saint Laurent, with whom she was especially closely associated through her daughter Loulou. She kindly gave me accessories by various costume jewelers like Jacques Gautier, Roger Scemama, and Roger JeanPierre. There are also very eccentric Schiaparelli accessories and scarves that she claims to have designed when she was there. These crazy looking scarves are in fascinating cloqué fabrics, extravagantly long and in peculiar shades of orange and brown. This fabric you can see in a huge, truly bizarre looking cape photographed at the time. She also offered me a huge "thing" by Schiaparelli, some sort of negligée bag in satin and transparent plastic. Countess de la Falaise had a unique and devilishly chic sense of humor and always looked grand with her striking beauty and eccentric taste. I spent many, many hours with her, shopping at the flea market for the evil-looking antiques that she loved, like a painting of Christians being thrown to the lions or a vase with a hideous scaly dragon with horns and slit eyes wrapped around it. In New York, we frequently ate at the most snobbish restaurants around at that time such as Elaine's, The Four Seasons, Tavern on the Green, and Maxwell's Plum. We were occasionally joined friends like Giorgio de Sant'Angelo or a wonderful lady from Yves St. Laurent named Connie. Maxime was a deadly raven brunette with cruel lips painted blood red and arched eyebrows. She was "Old Skool" Paris glamour and hedonism mixed with a Downton Abbey disdain. As gay men often admire and are fascinated by camp, cruel women, she was impossible not to love.

In 1952, Schiaparelli launched her sensational perfume called Sport de Schiaparelli. It had originally been introduced in the 1930s and marketed as a unisex fragrance to golfers, tennis players, and aviator clients, but it did not fare well. The re-issue was bottled in an authentic G.H. Mumm et Cie Brut Champagne bottle approximately six inches tall, complete with cork, wire, foil![5]

With an accent on youth and newness, Schiaparelli made a pair of glasses, patented for their originality, inspired by the ever-so-fashionable Italian Vespa scooter. The Vespa was seen in the windows of her boutique in the 1950s, ridden by Pascaline (the wooden bride of Pascal, the house mascot) dressed smartly in a cardigan and pearls, buttoned breeches, and satin bottines. A Vespa also was seen parked outside Schiap's own house on rue de Berri and it would be noticed by the one-and-only Andy Warhol.

Apparently, in summer 1956, when Andy Warhol made his first trip to Paris, he sketched the one he saw in front of her famous abode. As she obviously still had an affinity with the latest, the newest, and the most youthful trends, despite the fact that she was, by then, part of the "old world, pre-war" school of French haute couture. "Oh gawd, when we used to go to Paris, we'd go to the rue de Berri to see if we'd spot her. After she died we'd still go down rue de Berri to look at the house and one day we went there and realized that there was some furniture being thrown away, and we found all this furniture outside. I really wanted that furniture, so [we] had to organize through the gallery, really quickly, a truck to bring it back to Fred's place or the gallery until we could deal with it," Andy once claimed to me in the mid-1980s.

I went to Fred Hughes's Paris apartment many times in the 1980s, not far from the Paco Rabanne boutique at the beginning of the rue du Cherche-Midi, which is also the street where Lala and I would open the Mdvanii Boutique. The pieces of Jean-Michel Frank's furniture that once belonged to Schiap were still in place. Beaten and worn, under the supervision of a huge and very spooky Julian Schnabel portrait of Fred Hughes made of broken plates, Schiaparelli's Frank furniture bore testament not only to Andy's and Fred's dedication to all things Art Deco, but also stood as a last sign of the great Schiaparelli. I thought it was quite fun to sit on the chairs that I knew Schiaparelli had also sat on. I felt an almost metaphysical sense of connection, that material things were as alive as I am. While I had felt this often in seeing her work—the strange and brief reassurance that the world made sense—I'd equally feel the intense magic being left alone in the salons of the place Vendôme. When Schiaparelli's house on rue de Berri was finally ripped down, I felt numb for several days. How could they tear down that amazing mansion, from which so much art and culture had come? I had never been inside it, but had walked by it for decades, paying homage in a silly romantic way. It made me happy to see it and when it was gone, I felt unusually sad.

The relics that Andy saved were enough to make me dream of all the beauty they represented. For me these old pieces of beaten up furniture were like seashells you take home from a glorious beach where you may have passed a summer in love. They were not significant in any way other than as a vestige of the beauty in the world. I spent many an evening in that apartment, reminiscing about all sorts of subjects, Schiaparelli included. I even made a short Super 8mm movie and cassette recording with Lala and Brigid Berlin, Superstar of Warhol cult film *Chelsea Girls*, commenting about those last bits of Schiaparelli's furniture. It turned out almost entirely incoherent in the true Warhol style. The fuses had blown out and the only light left was that of a few candles we could find in the kitchen.

I met Gogo through Diana Vreeland and Bettina Bergery sometime in the 1970s. I hadn't a clue what to expect from Gogo. She was my hero's daughter and I was a little bit shy. I found her absolutely delightful. When I moved to France I saw her regularly in her beautiful home. She was a very supportive woman, took interest in my artwork, and was a good friend to me. Her second husband was a charming, aristocratic gentleman named Gino, the Marchese Cacciapuoti di Giugliano, and was known as an actor and director. They often invited me to casual dinners in their home and often we ate spaghetti. It was Gino who made the spaghetti and the first time I had this simple but delicious dish with them Gogo said, "Oh, I see you know the correct way to eat spaghetti. Some Italians use spoons but it is so incorrect." Gogo and her husband had a great warmth, and were very down to earth despite her intensely mondaine upbringing.

But let's get back to Schiap. The year 1950 continued with more oddly cut Schiaparelli clothes. The coats were wacky. Buttoned in great big triangles or diagonally, it was all about the shape. Bettina Ballard, still a fashion editor in the early 1950s, wrote a feature article about this latest collection. It was about this time that Mancini, mostly famous for his beige-and-black spectator pumps and slingbacks for Chanel, also started to make shoes for Schiaparelli, notably the Chinese-inspired black lacquered wood slip-ons with an elaborately embroidered vamp. "She was very grand and very demanding, she had worked with Perugia and was used to that old world, pre-war service . . . she was difficult to please and asked for small changes, which were always long and complex sometimes to do," he told me in the 1980s.

The summer 1950 collection coats had short, bell-shaped sleeves, long pieces in the back to be draped over the shoulders like a shawl. Long gloves were impressively embellished or structurally exaggerated. There were accessories that paid homage to the holy year, like Cardinal caps and straw hats in the shape of bells with fringe and pompoms. The most outstanding colors were a deep red violet and a contrasting dark blue. The Richard Avedon cover of the July 1950 *Harper's Bazaar* captures this modern look. Shot in Taormina, Sicily, it shows Schiaparelli's striped linen headscarf worn with a white linen beach dress, crisp and blinding white, and accessorized with a brilliant red new lipstick by Schiap rakishly called Buccaneer.

Autumn of that year saw a stunning display of Schiaparelli's talent. There was an evening gown called Corps de Cygne (swan's body) in white and pink. And later, in her summer 1951 collection, a dress with violet pleats in the front. She often experimented with pleating during those two years. The influence was Venetian lanterns and delicate, vaporous folding and it was found in everything from day dresses to separates, in unusual materials and oddly contrasted colors. Horst told me about the photo he took of the dresses when we spoke in 1977: "Although I always like stark backdrops, the photo of the pleated Schiaparelli dress is a rudimentary backdrop, you couldn't get simpler. The colors were two tones of violet and the dress was so fragile and lovely, anything added to the pose or the photo would have done injustice to the image. *Vogue* wanted to exploit these new delicate dresses coming out of Schiaparelli. . . . the photo, I felt, was a success."[6] Her jewelry licenses were at the height of their success, particularly in the United States. An endless number of styles were sold in chic stores throughout the world, in South America and even Japan. Her hats were available in the USA in an extraordinary number of models, either imported or licensed designs made stateside. One shown in *Vogue* was "Schiaparelli's little Breton hanging, it seems, almost by a hair," which was worn so far back on the head that it was literally vertical in line.[7]

Ghislaine de Boisson was a model at Schiaparelli's in the 1950s (she was the fit model at Schiap's for Princess Margaret). "I wore Schiaparelli clothes quite a lot . . . a lot of the clothes were so fresh and so amusing, you could wear them anywhere," she told me during a chat in my ateliers in the mid-1980s. Madame de Boisson allowed me access to her personal photo album in which she is seen with Charlie Chaplin, Dalí, Bing Crosby, Zizi Jeanmaire, and on a camel in Egypt, always dressed in Schiaparelli clothes. Many of the photos in her album were the house shots she did for the Schiap boutique. One photo of her with French cabaret singer Zizi Jeanmaire and Bing Crosby shows the unusual way Schiap used English eyelet for the corsage of a simple belted dress with sweater jacket. When I showed the photo to Jeanmaire (who I had the pleasure of knowing) she said, "Yes, I wore many Schiaparelli creations, both on stage and off . . . and of course, when I did '*Mon truc en plumes*,' I had feather boas from Schiaparelli . . . her clothes were perfect, dazzling and so full of humor and elegance."

I also had the great pleasure of knowing Robert Doisneau, the extraordinary French photographer. Denise Sarrault, the 1950s model, who was particularly famous for modeling Givenchy's clothes, introduced us. We met because he wanted to do his first color fashion photo and somehow, I was asked to be the subject. In the photo I wore an Issey Miyake ensemble while eating a banana split at La Coupole in Montparnasse, Paris. After that photo was published, Denise and I were asked to shoot my Schiaparelli collection at the Musée d'Art Moderne in Paris for the magazine *Femme*. The resultant photos by Doisneau were superb and after that we had a friendly relationship. He told me many stories about post-war Paris and though he never really was a fashion photographer he did know Schiaparelli and was asked to do some photos for *Vogue*. In June 1950, Jean Babilée and Nathalie Philippart would dance together in a dance from *Swan Lake* before a benefit ball given at the Hôtel Lambert. Eight hundred people were invited to this ball, including Schiaparelli and many of her clients, such as the Duchess of Windsor and Marie-Laure de Noailles. "I did a few shots of Madame Schiaparelli and the costumes she had done for the dancers. Nathalie Philippart was in a white pleated dress with a huge pink bow from the previous collection of Schiaparelli with a swan headdress. Schiaparelli was a tough old lioness by that time, she intimidated me and I was petrified she'd not like the shots I had done at the Ball. But, it was not necessary to worry as she loved the shots so much, she had dozens ordered as photos for her press releases immediately after the ball."

Schiap's contribution to the mid-century modern look was called the Front Line Silhouette. It is exemplified by a suit, modeled by Bettina Graziani, which has a flat front achieved with a flat oval wood board slipped inside the front of the jacket and also features a rounded peplum with a huge arched pocket at the front. One set of buttons marches straight up the suit, the other set, on the diagonal. The Duchess of Windsor ordered this model but had the eccentric pocket removed and the buttons placed more symmetrically. Skirts became svelte, slit up to the knees and coats again were at their most pyramidal with eccentric collars. One short paletot in thick Mediterranean blue wool was worn over a thin, close-fitting black dress, which had a scarf-collar that slipped through a notch in front and turned into a muff. It was structurally very eccentric and wonderfully graphic.

The summer 1951 collection featured Ouatine, a cotton padding fabric. Long fitted capes were worn over skinny skirts. Camouflage dresses had different colors on the back and sides. There were sunray-style pleats on many of the garments. Huge sleeves, diagonally placed buttons on coats and jackets, and thin evening gowns with trains of rigid panels with a *queue de cheval* (ponytail) silhouette. Josephine Baker bought some of these gowns for her shows. The "ponytail" originated from Baker's famous version of the style, seen on her album cover and in her performances. Schiap was the first to use it in her haute couture show. A coat from this season in the private collection of designer Mr. Per Spook is notable for its beautiful chic cotton padding. It also has a painted-on white feather motif with a *Sang de Bœuf* red background. Mr. Per Spook said, "It was like a man's military coat, something you'd wear in the fields, but it was flared and the motifs of feathers, so humorous. . . . I wonder often how startling it may have been then, as it is still startling and it's more than thirty years later."

For autumn of that year, more innovations: Schiaparelli again emphasizes asymmetry, other aspects are cuts and stitching in the "X" shape. Draped décolletés are adjustable on simple dresses, and a flared coat of brilliant red is shown with a panther-skin hat worn way back on the head. A dress shown in the *Album du Figaro* had cuffed pockets low on the hips made of grey flannel. The dress buttoned up the front with a perky little collar jutting out in front. Its three-quarter sleeves ended with cuffed gloved hands. For the head, a flowerpot hat. There were folding hats and Roger Model-designed handbags that looked like golf bags. One had a zipper all the way around the ovoid shape with a perfectly round hole through it that created a self-handle. Huge earrings were studded with stones and Coppolo e Toppo sunburst brooches seen in *Album Figaro*. One of Schiap's big successes was the white English eyelet used for loose jackets without buttons.

One dress, from a series within the 1951 collection, was a very Issey Miyake-like creation. This cocktail dress is in bright green pleated silk faille taffeta. While it is sober, with large lemon slice buttons down the bodice, when the hands of the wearer were put though the armholes of the skirt it transformed into cocoon coat, like a lantern. It is utterly fabulous and very delicate. I acquired the dress from Dominique Sirop. I went over to his small apartment, a few streets away from my atelier on rue de la Paix, and exchanged a Paquin for it. I was simply floored when he showed me the dress because for me it represented the essence of Schiaparelli thinking. Simple, elegant, yet with a touch of strange. It's one of my favorite post-war dresses because its vision was light years ahead. It's like the deconstructed clothes of the Japanese designers of the 1980s, only three decades before they began.

The next collection, winter 1951–52, had a highly oriental-inspired feeling with Persian accents. The Shape Line was supposed to represent the rolling of sea waves and Givenchy was responsible for a long gown with a wired bottom, shaped to undulate like a wave. Schiap's Dolman greatcoat had secret pockets in the sleeves and was called wonderful by *Vogue*.Details included lace décolleté, buttons and clasps made of leather, wide belts in wrinkled suede, several layers of bowties, and full backs on evening gowns. In *Jardin des Modes* for January 1952 we see her famous accordion pleated, shocking-pink-and-black felt *cagoule* which has a vaguely science-fiction look to it.[8] "In the form of a paper lantern, this cagoule in shocking pink and black felt is maintained by a head-hugging band of black jersey and is prolonged by a plastron to protect the chest." This item received quite a lot of attention and Schiap even included a photo of it in her autobiography.

For autumn 1952, the collection again emphasized cotton.[9] Honeycomb piqué was used for a strapless Casino dress that buttoned provocatively up the front. Lala and I photographed the late Grafin Celia von Bismarck in one of these dresses in my collection. She looked like Grace Kelly in it. There are large supple coats in printed glazed chintz and the heart-shape is still present in the décolleté. Bettina Graziani modeled nearly every cover of the newly founded magazine *Elle* and one, photographed by Jean Chevalier for the October 1, 1952 issue, shows a typical casual chic Bettina pose, with immaculate makeup and a Schiaparelli sweater.[10] Bettina recalls: "The sweater was mine; I had bought it at Schiaparelli at a good price, the models had a reduction. It was so new, so modern, big and comfy and in a deep golden suede with knit sleeves . . . you could live in it. Jean just took the photo as I arrived in the studio, there was no preparation really." Jean Chevalier recalled the session similarly: "When Bettina arrived in the studio, she was expecting to wear some lavish gown or have to change into something else, but as she was so much what young people wanted, and looked perfect as she was, I did a few shots of her as is . . . and it ended up on the cover and a feature story in the issue."

Schiap's Cigale or Grasshopper Silhouette for winter 1952–53 had colors that were still bright, along with beige, greyish black and reds.[11] But she was also using turquoise, blue, orange, and of course, pink. Fitted silhouettes, slightly round hats inspired by the grasshopper shape and forms, necklines that sit away from the body, and peplums were all featured. A short while later in the season you have *après-ski* outfits, all the rage, with gaiters. Also skirts lined in fur, culottes down to the knees, and little fitted jackets with a thin band of lace at the waist.

An important fashion-related event which concerned Schiap in a way was realized by the Grands Magasins du Printemps held in collaboration with the newly founded Union Française des Arts du Costume (called U.F.A.C. for short) and the designers of the era from May 28 until August 14, 1953.[12] Schiap had donated the first part of a collection of her own designs and the rest in 1969. She also included all the season-to-season drawings. This key show by Le Printemps department store, with its fascinating catalogue, marks the first time contemporary clothes were shown with a museological intent by the City of Paris.

The summer, 1953 collection featured an emphasis on accessories, princess line dresses in thin jersey and thin wool skirts slightly flared for the day and in stiff bell shapes for the evening.[13] Coats in longhaired wool came in odd colors. Many of the things seen in spring had been adapted for summer: more sports outfits inspired by the British army uniforms, half-moon shaped décolleté, ample backs, and eccentric beachwear—including sailor pants with five pockets on a leg with each one holding a handkerchief of a different color. The "over the ear" earrings, not exactly new at this point, and chain bracelets with pompoms were some of the fantastic jewelry seen in *Vogue*. That February, Schiaparelli authorized the license to eleven manufacturers in the United States to reproduce models. This was in addition to a line of lingerie called "Schiaparelli Couture Lingerie," launched in 1951, which including peignoirs, stockings, nightgowns, and underwear.[14]

New season, new collection: For autumn 1953 there were; silk fringed coats, the braided beach glasses, evening gowns in cotton with floral motifs and fluorescent colors, especially her Si orange and an ultra version of shocking which resembled a 1960s Day-Glo pink.[15] The same month Schiaparelli gave her first menswear license in the USA.

In one of her last haute couture collections, Schiaparelli showed more princess-line dresses, without belts, worn with long coats whose sleeves reached all the way to the fingers.[16] There were ample skirts on ankle-length evening dresses, bowler hats, a lot of Coppola & Toppo jewelry, strapless corsages with jigsaw forms, and short coats of camel hair with elaborate closures and high draped collars. *Vogue* said in September 1953 that some of the "Paris Beauties" of the season were "the wonderful Schiaparelli wrap-around broadcloth evening dresses cut like very distinguished aprons." Schiap must have been displeased to see some of the Hubert de Givenchy dresses getting equally important pages (in fact more) in the same issue, notably his silk taffeta cocktail dress in polka dots, which seemed to make a particularly big impression in the press. Its simple, ingénue look was something he'd developed at Schiap while doing the boutique clothes and it could equally have been a Schiap dress in its shape and wittiness. There is also a wasp-waisted gown with voluminous sleeves embroidered with red roses and leaves.

Bettina Graziani modeled some Coppola e Toppo necklaces and bracelets designed by Schiaparelli's in-house designer Serge Matta for *Vogue* magazine in 1951. The necklaces and bracelets were meant to look a little like seaweed. They were photographed by Henry Clarke, who told me in 1980, "It was effortless to do the photos on Bettina, she just put them on, as if trying them on, looking out the window at something going on in the place Vendôme, I just snapped the shots, it was so easy, so elegant." Bettina said of the same photo, "It was just a quickly done photo, the jewelry was so lovely, so strange, you really didn't need to over-do the pose. . . . Schiaparelli told me later that it was one of her favorite photos." The necklace in this photo is in my collection, bought at Sotheby's, and previously belonged to the photographer John French's wife. Other extraordinary luscious pieces of jewelry from Coppola e Toppo were shown in Vogue on a regular basis.

When I moved to Switzerland, Lala and I became friends with Martin Leuthold and his partner, Peter Friederich. Martin is the art director of the embroidery house of Jakob Schlaepfer, which is an iconic name in the world of haute couture. Martin has shown us the machines they've invented to make the most amazing effects, what they do and how they operate. It's simply staggering to see. In the archives I've found many Courrèges and Ungaro embroideries using transparencies that the firm invented. What is so interesting is that though the haute couturiers create the garments, it is the embroidery house that creates the fabrics. When Schlaepfer comes up with an innovative new fabric, incorporating transparency with iridescent film, sequins, and gauze for example, the designer such as André Courrèges is shown it and perhaps chooses it for a garment. Many people believe, incorrectly, that the designer also designs the fabrics. This does occur, but rarely as it's so costly. Sometimes the fabric is the main aspect of the garment. A simple A-line shift would be unremarkable if it were not for the astoundingly original fabric, entirely covered in sequins or perhaps holographic. Just like with Schiaparelli, who had a perhaps larger role in which fabrics were made and used, it is a collaboration of the noblest intentions. The embroiderers are a bit French fashion's unsung heroes.

The early 1950s work of Schiap saw many new fabrics inspired primarily by artists. Some of the finest fabric designers worked for Schiap at this period and she allied herself with artisans outside of France, as she had done since the pre-war period with the same panache. Zika Ascher was a good friend of mine throughout the 1970s and 1980s. He can be considered the artist laureate of fabric for Great Britain, having introduced many of the elements now common in fashion fabrics such as shag fake furs and huge prints, strange mixtures of textures, and fabrics which, when brushed with the hand, change color. He worked with many of the same artists Schiap had worked with.[17] His huge silk-screened prints were revolutionary when he launched them: As he recalled to me, "Everyone was afraid of them at first. We couldn't sell one single order, but Dior came to my rescue, and soon after Schiaparelli started using them . . . It would have been one of our finest flops if Dior and Schiaparelli hadn't imposed them in their collections." In his Victoria & Albert show in 1987, the catalogue, written by Valerie Mendes, says, "Many fashion pundits disapproved of these large scale Ascher prints and predicted that they would not catch on. Dior first proved them wrong by using the silks with their enormous leaves and flowers for dramatic evening dresses. Schiaparelli followed and exploited these grand painterly designs to the full, as in this strapless, long sheath dress lavishly extended by a pleated side panel, which fell from the waist to trail along the floor."[18]

This particar gown was shown in the April 1952 issue of *L'Officiel* in a soft watercolor-like screen print, reminiscent of the eighteenth century, although very much in the style of the 1940s and 1950s as influenced by Bérard and all the amazing scope of artists that Ascher was working with. The print in the Schiaparelli gown was predominantly nattier blue, tilleul green, and burgundy red; the scale was fabulously overblown. Zika Ascher once said to me, "You know, I owe a lot to Schiaparelli, if it hadn't been for her support to artists before the war, which was such an influence on me, I don't think I'd have had the nerve to get so involved with so many artists . . . it became the thing we'd be best known for in the end." The Zika Ascher limited-edition artist's scarves are now coveted collector's items, considered silk original prints by these artists, as valuable and historically relevant as if they had been done on paper.

In 1953, Schiap did a collection called Caressing Line, which had shoulders descending almost to the elbows and armholes that began below the natural waistline. One such coat in my collection is in cream white brocade with an unusual bowtie closure in front. Hats were still original and amusing, such as a velvet cap with a point right down the middle of the forehead and a big round faceted jewel pendant that rests just a centimeter above the eyebrow line. However, the boutique was the main direction of the company, and the majority of Schiap's mentions in fashion magazines referred to the Schiap Boutique or Schiap-Sport line of clothes.

In 1953 American *Vogue* was still pure propaganda for French fashion and it showed her accessories more often than her clothes. "Her last years, it was like a firework display of ideas, a million of them, you couldn't say she shyly faded into retirement. She was like a wild horse, charging to the end, as exciting as the first days of her career," Bettina Bergery said to me in conversation.

Schiaparelli brought out a new perfume as well, called Succès Fou, or wild crazy success, whose concept and ads were designed by the French artist Raymond Peynet. The fragrance came in a green, opaque glass bottle shaped like an ivy leaf, within a heart-shaped box edged in gold ink. Some of the imaginative displays for stores included a place Vendôme column with a Peynet romantic couple seated on top.[19] Earrings dangled from Schiap's signature "S" in the form of the ivy leaf, which held sponges infused with the fragrance. Others were in the form of a chatelaine with a tiny ivy leaf-shaped glass bottle surrounded by a gilt ivy leaf hanging from tiny chains and dangling from a smaller leaf.[20] Schiaparelli and the place Vendôme salon were so famous by that year she had to publish postcards, which were sold throughout France and available, for free, at the place Vendôme salon.

In March 1954, Schiap announced a plan to greatly reduce her production of designs and concentrate on her private clients. Despite her enormous world fame, haute couture clothing business was losing money.

I had overcome great difficulties, enjoyed immense success, gone through abysmal depressions, and now I am to consider what all this meant this meant to me . . .

Thinking upon these matters, I realized that a circle had been completed, and that I could not follow the same road without falling into slavery; that I had to tear myself away from the place Vendôme which by then owned and claimed me too tyrannically and make an absolute change.[21]

CHAPTER 26

1954–1970

n 1954, Schiap spent a great deal of time in her house in Hammamet, Tunisia, writing *Shocking Life*. Her autobiography was as Surrealistic and stylistically peculiar as her career had been. Compiled from twenty-five years of press coverage, diaries, and interviews, its distinctive voice gives one the impression that Schiap wanted to leave a very particular impression of herself. It is essential reading for its look into the mind of a great fashion personality, one who defined and imposed the fashions of the twentieth century, and who was responsible for so much that we continue to see in the early part of the twenty-first century. Whereas Chanel invented the sober chic look of the bourgeois lady of Paris, Schiaparelli did the opposite. She invented the sexual woman in fashion. And as she matured, Schiaparelli's attire was not only seductive but outwardly, flagrantly sexy. From the beginning, her fashions could transform the woman of average or even homely looks into the *jolie laide*. Women everywhere, thanks to her strong leadership in fashion, had the chance to be seductive and alluring. As fashion journalist Alison Settle, editor-in-chief of the British edition of *Vogue* between 1926 and 1933, said in her book *Clothes Line* in 1938: "Schiaparelli, probably the most intelligent woman who ever designed clothes, said that the woman truly well dressed is, after her own experience, rarely a pretty woman. The woman who is naturally beautiful has it too easy, you see. Those who, less favored by nature (that's to say even not at all) must work to make herself seductive, to distinguish herself by her chic."[1]

Schiap decided to close her haute couture fashion business in 1954, although she left her boutiques open, thus ending more than twenty-seven years of creating the highest form of fashion. It was the end of an era although the septuagenarian Chanel hauled herself out of mothballs on February 5 that same year for her revival. It was a gesture meant to add prestige to her fashion perfumes, which she no longer owned. Would Schiaparelli take pleasure in the fact that Chanel's first collections were ridiculed and booed by the international press? "Schiap just laughed when Chanel came back . . . She found it ridiculous, more so tragi-comic, that Chanel was attempting to do fashion again . . . and those first collections were a complete bomb! She'd said to me ironically, 'The poor dear must need the money, what other reason would someone at her age do such a thing?'" Bettina Bergery told me.

One important point to make here is that Schiaparelli did not declare bankruptcy as people have written over the years.[2] She was inclined to save her perfume business by not milking it dry of funds in order to keep the house of fashion running. Haute couture, in her mind, had irreversibly changed for the worst. It was no longer what she had known and created for her "modern," youth-oriented eras. The contemporary way of living in those post-war times was so very different from the glory days of her success.

It came as a shock to the mondaine world and the fashion elite that Schiap was ending her haute couture business. Schiaparelli represented an era; she was an institution. Daisy Fellowes, once the doyenne of all that was glamourous, wrote to Bettina Bergery of what she imagined Schiap should now go on to do: "How awful for Elsa . . . I do hope a miracle will happen and it will become a wonderful perfumed library that will sell all the books of research by Bettina Bergery and the novels of Gaston Bergery and the fairy tales of Natalie Barney and the second childhood of Daisy Fellowes."[3] It was truly the end of an era.

Many autobiographies of great stars, socialites, artists, writers, and musicians speak of her. In *The Fashion Makers* by Robert Riley, a profile summarizes her career: "Schiaparelli, who practically single-handedly created the fabulously fashionable thirties. Her face crinkles with laughter; her tongue is racy; her eye still searches for the new artist even as it did in the days when Bébé Bérard sketched her collections with neon brilliance, Cocteau designed her prints and star-shaped buttons, Dalí painted a lobster rampant on the skirt of an organza dress."[4] Bettina Bergery wrote in an unpublished 1960s text for *Tatler* that the 1930s had become so fashionable again that after seeing the latest Dior, Ungaro, Patou and Yves Saint Laurent collections, she wished she hadn't given some of her "old Schiaparellis to the Musée du Costume. They would be so right for this minute."[5] Fortunately for me, she hadn't given away many and years later, after wearing them well into the 1980s, she kindly offered some of her Schiaparellis to me (as did her sister, Anne Fuller).

Schiap had played her role like a great actor in the history of French fashion. Her ideas have been incorporated entirely and absolutely into the styles that followed her retirement and long beyond. Once she closed her haute couture business, she concentrated on her perfume business and she continued to make exciting collaborations with artists. François-Xavier created jewelry and decorative pieces for her and Claude Lalanne designed a display for her perfume, Si. *Si,* in French has a triple meaning: it can mean "if," and in certain contexts it's an affirmative way to say "yes" or "of course." It is also the name of the seventh note in the music scale. The perfume was quiet a press sensation. Schiap, Italian by birth, marked her bottle with the Italian word for "yes" to confirm her desire for pleasure. It was designed to look like a straw-enveloped Chianti bottle with the wax of an orange candle dripping down it, just like the centerpieces in her candlelit "bistro" in the cellar of her house, where she entertained friends. The orange associated with the new perfume was as fluorescent as shocking pink and was called Si Orange. The perfume bottle had to be "uncorked" to be opened and was launched with a 45 rpm record with music by Henri Sauguet and sung by Juliette Gréco, the *boul miche* muse of Saint-Germain-des-Prés. The record was called "En hommage a Madame Elsa Schiaparelli, la Valse des Si!" with "La complainte du telephone," a typical Gréco song, on the flip side.

Henri Sauguet contributed a handwritten note on the back of the record cover: "Dear Elsa, how not to answer 'si' (of course!) when you ask me to present in music your new perfume, Si. I do it on the note 'si,' it's the seventh of the scale, we musicians call it the sensitive one. Here it is. It swirls, swirls, swirls all around the hundred ways that women have to say 'si,' in this *'Valse des Si'* that I am offering you, dear Elsa, to tell you too that if we love you this way, it's because we admire you. Si! Henri Sauguet, 1957." The song had only one word, "Si," which was sung over and over to the strains of Sauguet's enchanting melody. It was played frequently on the radio and was a huge success which, naturally, drew a good deal of attention to the perfume, resulting in many sales.

Schiap's hats had always been imported in the USA and authorized for reproduction by American wholesalers and retailers. But her hat licenses, begun as early as 1934, which were sold across America in mass-produced series, appear to be the complete archetype of what eccentric hats would be for each era. Schiaparelli hats were found in every fashionable store in North America and Canada. There were so many different models that it would be impossible to catalogue them. A journalist at the time implied that out of all the various eccentricies endorsed by Schiaparelli it was her extraordinarily varied styles of hats which had the biggest impact on the ladies all over the world. This Schiap believed was because a very beckoning hat could set a beautiful woman apart, whereas an attention-grabbing one or even an outright eccentric one became a fighting effort against the insecurity of not being pretty. Some hats from the early 1930s are labeled, "Authorized Adaptation Schiaparelli, 4, rue de la Paix, Paris." Others are marked "Authorized Reproduction Schiaparelli Paris, France." In 1949, she did a line of hats called Miss Schiaparelli for younger women and the collegiate crowd, and another called Schiaparelli Junior for young girls aged eight to fifteen.[6]

Schiaparelli hats are often un-datable. Some 1940s versions look like products of the 1960s and vice-versa. They incorporated every odd shape, material, color, and theme. Some looked like a human brain or a basket of carrots, a doctor's satchel or a spider web, a tressed coiffure or a thatched roof—one even looked like the famous Dalí painting of the women with a head made of flowers. They came to represent the wacky eccentricity of Schiaparelli and were parodied and spoofed everywhere. Fashionable women wore them and kept them for years, as they seemed never to go out of date. They were timeless. In fact, they technically have never stopped being made. Even after her death they were still made.

Collecting them in America as a young teenager, where her hats found a particular success, for me, was the most hilarious thing of all. The stories women would tell me, the ways they would be preserved in their shocking pink signature Schiaparelli hatboxes, sometimes faded, the silk paper around the hats lovingly kept. Each and every hat is a veritable work of art, an expression exclusive to the mind and idea of chic of Elsa Schiaparelli. A few examples: the Television hat, Snug cap, the straw braided hat pierced by a spike hatpin, the gold African peak with emerald drops (which she wore herself in a

Vertès portrait), the lobster basket with Dalí lobster-printed linen, the Skylarkers, which Schiaparelli said were to be "dashing, upward-and-forward-shooting," the Rooftop hats, the Hide-and-Seek hats, Cookie cutter hats.[7] All these eccentricities were worn with pride and elegance by fashionable women the world over. A Schiaparelli hat was even mentioned in Cole Porter lyrics. There were often parodies of her hats, such as those in the George Cukor film *The Women*.

Her fur coats were still the rage. There were dozens of different designs in many luxurious furs such as panther, ocelot, and Somalian leopard. They were available at dozens of prestigious department stores throughout America. Schiaparelli also created exclusive fur designs in Canadian ranch mink for various companies, including Mitchell Fur Co. Limited. Schiap began using what is now known as "fake fur" for jackets and even dresses in the 1920s and offered them in vivid Pop Art colors before this technique became the norm in the 1960s.

What is fascinating is the consistency of the "out of time" feeling of Schiap's designs. They're sometimes very baroque and Surrealistically-inspired and at other times, amazingly stark and modern. Without question, Schiaparelli hats are highly distinctive and always bore her touch and sensibility, regardless of the era. The colors, of course, were a veritable blaze of the rainbow, a psychedelic *2001, A Space Odyssey* rush of every vivid sensation a hue could give.

After the close of her couture house, she continued to design products for her many licenses in America. She still introduced very chic and refined fashions that were in the newest vogue, with an emphasis on youth, and gay, uninhibited freshness.

Gogo was involved in her mother's work by 1956 and originated yet more Schiaparelli myths. Bettina Ballard described her as "the only person who really counted in [Elsa's] life . . . a popular spoiled pet of both capitals [London and Paris] who, at the age of sixteen, traveled with her own pink silk sheets. Everything that either the mother or daughter did or said was news."[8] Gogo may have been the apple of her mother's eye, but when she attempted to use the Schiaparelli name in the late 1940s on an American license of moderately priced fashions called "Gogo Schiaparelli" (that included a line drawing of Gogo walking her dog Popcorn), her mother shrieked the house down. Once, during that debacle, when Gogo was walking down a Manhattan street, Elsa crossed to the other side to avoid speaking to her. That license was a brief and somewhat peculiar blip in the Schiaparelli story. Once the line disappeared, so did Schiap's anger, and Gogo returned into the fold of her mother's good graces.

Dolls called Go-Go de Schiaparelli were made with Schiaparelli-designed clothes and came in vivid pink boxes. The series included a teenage doll (in the popular Jill and Jan style dolls of the era) called Chi-Chi de Schiaparelli and another was an eccentrically coiffed ballet dancer called Tu-Tu de Schiaparelli. The 1950s Ginny doll obviously inspired the look of these dolls, but Schiap's dolls came with a vast array of designer clothes and a wardrobe case to carry them in. Another American doll, created in 1951 and named Honey by the Effanbee Doll Company, came with exact reproductions of Schiap's Paris haute couture, labeled "A Mme. Schiaparelli Creation by Effanbee." They were perfect down to the accessories and included eccentric hats, oblique closures on trapeze coats, and the Surrealistic raffia eyelash glasses.

Schiap also produced endless, absolutely endless, scarves in every conceivable color and print.[9] One example, from the 1950s, was a reproduction of an Atelier Martine print in pastel flower tones. Perhaps it was an homage to her late friend, Paul Poiret. Some were reproductions of Weiner Werkstätte designs. Sometime long after the Circus collection was shown, probably in the 1950s or 1960s, the Bérard drawings were printed on a scarf. One of the most provocative (and this is where we can understand why these days people say Schiaparelli was the first "punk" designer) was a series of scarves in very classic *pied-de-poule* check or other very classic prints. They were as sober as a Sunday morning, but spewed upon them in a random and very *décalé* way were funky splashes of what appeared to be, in trompe-l'oeil, ink! What would later be considered a punk leitmotif was a scarf from the early 1950s!

One notable anecdote about a Schiaparelli scarf was told to me by Emilio Pucci, who ran into her at a ski resort in the mid-1960s:

> I saw from afar, someone from behind with what I thought was one of my scarfs, the bright colored prints I was then widely known for. As I get closer and closer, I realize that the scarf is not one of mine at all and as I turn to see who was wearing it, it was Elsa Schiaparelli. . . . She looked at me and said something to the effect of 'Emilio, you are what's happening now, my scarf is by Schiaparelli scarves and it's perfectly in with what's happening now . . . so, of course it looks like your Alta Moda.' I was deeply flattered that whoever did that scarf for her license of scarves would use my work as a source of inspiration. Imagine, a Schiaparelli scarf that looked nearly identical to one of mine!

Another scarf story from the 1960s involves Andy Warhol in the 1980s, when I often shopped with him for antiques in Paris, London, and New York. In New York we went to the flea market, now famous but then just known to dealers and collectors, on 26th street. Stuart Pivar often joined us. Andy tried in vain to seem normal, but all the dealers knew who he was of course, but also who I was, so haggling was out of the question. Instead, I'd just decline buying something until they got the message that I was not a total sucker. I did pay through the nose at times because I simply wanted something that I felt was important to my collection. When you're a collector your only regret is what you don't buy, you never recall what you paid for something if it really brings you pleasure. Sometimes Andy and I would argue as to who would buy what, but he always kindly let me buy the pieces I really wanted. He'd remark on this in the so-called "diaries" Pat Hackett wrote for him for Crown Publishers, which came out after his death. "Went to the flea market and ran into Billy Boy . . . Billy Boy wasn't in a money-spending mood. They really see him coming and jack the Schiaparelli prices up."[10] One day, in the early 1980s, I wore a bright Schiaparelli scarf from the late 1960s to go to the flea markets in Manhattan with him. I remember him saying, "Oh, wow, she copied my flowers! The large flower printed on the scarf which did, in fact, resemble his flower paintings. I pointed out to him that the scarf might have pre-dated his paintings, to which he replied, "Oh, I must have copied her flowers, do you think Patricia Caulfield did Schiaparelli scarves? Oh, wow! I should do some new flowers of that scarf."

Even in the late 1960s there were still endless amounts of incredibly sexy lingerie and stockings available in the latest synthetics. Since the 1920s, Schiap had been both creating and licensing stockings and innovating with patterns and textures. If fishnets are no longer considered sleazy, as they were in the nineteenth-century (when they were worn only by coquettes and dance hall girls) it's thanks to Schiap. For her legwear in the 1920s, she put every wild color on God's given earth on ladies' legs, making them even more sexy by giving them equally peculiar names.[11] She transcended the banality of just covering the leg. Under her name, the stockings were cunningly displayed on statuettes: a French maid, a circus strongman with dumbbells, a bereted and smocked French artist with a saucy moustache and a palette. Some of these were made of plaster, others rubber or paper maché. They were used in chic stores as counter displays. Another clever stocking presentation was her signature Shocking Pink satin with Sleeping Blue accents umbrella-shaped holder. Trimmed in black lace and ribbons with her signature embossed upon them, these clever holders were made to resemble a Belle-Époque parasol. Inside was a note which read like a Dada poem by Tzara or Breton, "A 'SHOCKING' gift when rolled up tight, with SCHIAPARELLI STOCKINGS, right. NOW, to solve what seems a riddle: remove the handle from the middle. Loose the ribbon, spread the base, there you are, a LINGERIE CASE!"[12] These splendid and serendipitous pieces of Surrealism came in big pink boxes marked with her name and were sold in stores like Marshall Field and Company in the USA.

By the 1960s, Schiap's stockings went totally Mod, with optical patterns and textures, including a black pair with op-art graphic designs called Skap-Op, which resembled tattoos when worn and were very much like the tattoo body stockings Issey Miyake made in the late 1980s. They were also evocative, yet again, of her earliest designs from the late 1920s. Thigh high stockings from this era were called Hip Pose and came in clear plastic envelopes with stylized drawings resembling models Twiggy and Penelope Tree on the outside packaging. It was as if she had declared war on the conventional leg! The revolutionary Girdle Stockings by Schiaparelli were "to wear with self-holding leg band girdles without hooks, snaps or fasteners." Supp-Hose brand made some of her designs in stockings and ran ads which claimed, "In addition, the Schiaparelli label has been licensed to high fashion manufacturers of dresses, jewelry, scarves, gloves, lingerie, bathing suits, rainwear, bras and girdles, women's shoes, and children's wear." And, yes, the bras were very sexy—even sexier were the girdles.[13]

From the early days Schiap also had shoe licenses (when she did not work directly with designers such as Perugia, Massaro, and Vivier). There were feather or jewel trimmed slip-ons and, a bit later, the cork and leather mule wedges worthy of, again, a cheesecake pin-up girl. She did the famous slip-on Spring-O-Lators in gold kid edged in clear plastic, Lucite, or pony skin printed with fake leopard spots. In the early 1960s, she created ultra-spike stilettos in every color and material, from silver glitter to gold and silver brocade mesh. One pair of glitter shoes, which came in black, "bronze," gold, and silver tones were called, menacingly, Dagger, perhaps a variation on Roger Vivier's "stiletto." Nearly all the shoes that you can find now on the Internet that have the "Schiaparelli-New York-Paris" inscription in them were designed and made by the Jacques Levine company in New York, though they were based on models shown in Paris. Levine made these basics over and over in a multitude of fabrics and prints for what seems years. One can find the same shoe style in ten different treatments of materials (leather, cloth, suede, brocade, etc.) and in a variety of different colors.

Schiaparelli's name was also used on eccentric wigs and postiches, something she had promoted in the very early 1930s with hairdresser Antoine. They all had the Schiap touch, with names like Avant-Garde and Concerto some in extravagant colors like pink, green and blue, just like the Schiaparelli dolls of the 1950s.[14] She had a line of watches as early as the 1930s, and by the 1940s was doing "His" and "Hers" versions in stamped silver. I felt very lucky when I acquired the MGM star Ann Miller's Schiaparelli pendant watch. This watch, from the early 1950s, is a British heraldic form, with a lion and a horse in gilt metal. Schiap's watches were groovy and quite sensational objects, like a Lucite pyramid on a wide black patent leather band. Some were even modeled by Twiggy. There were many different pendant necklace watches with cameos and tapestry scenes of Watteau figures on the reverse side or made in streamlined space age shapes. One watch had a bracelet of Roman coins. Some watch faces did not have any numerals at all, just hands. Others were huge in proportion to the hand and had equally enormous numerals. Some had numeric words printed "Un, Deux, Trois, etc." or the numbers were simply backwards. The politically tumultuous 1960s saw the launch of Chain of Events at Schiaparelli, which was a series of watches with huge chains as bands and soldered watch inner parts as the outside of the watch. Advertising copy stated, "Time to plan for the busy times ahead. Whatever the action—in town or country—around the block or around the world, a Schiaparelli chain watch is very 'up-to-the-minute' fashion." The Schiaparelli Bambooty Collection of watches came out in 1969 and, as the name implies, had a bamboo theme to it, all matching her Asian-influenced ready-to-wear clothes available in the Paris boutique and department stores. My all time favorites of these watches include one from the 1960s which has a huge Plexiglas pyramid instead of a usual watch face. Another, on a Bakelite pole, is a copy of the classic public clocks on the rue de la Paix. The watch detaches from the base to make a pendant.

It is impossible to go on naming all the Schiaparelli licenses, which included endless numbers of eyewear in all sorts of fanciful Perspex and Galalithe cat-eye shapes, one of which had miniature awnings. There were wacky, coquettish umbrellas with odd handles and trims in bright colors and prints and there were baroque-looking jewel-studded metal pillboxes. Other products include her "fine hand-crafted leather originals designed by Schiaparelli" line of briefcases, French purses (as described by a brochure in the 1960s), clutches with fake Gobelin tapestry, billfolds, Pocket Secys, cigarette cases, sunglasses cases, Schiapettes, coin purses, and travel wear.[15] There were playing cards for bridge, endless paper patterns, envelopes, and invitations. For Christmas, one could wear Schiaparelli hostess aprons in frothy organza striped in pink and gold. Other items that bore the Schiap touch were elegant things such as desk organizers and stationery holders. The most astonishing and amusing items from Schiap were shocking pink, black, and gold brocade book covers, which had brass tips and closed with shocking pink ribbons. This way even books could be "dressed" by Schiaparelli! The ultimate thing Schiap designed was "Schiap-aire", a room freshener comprised of a bottle filled with Shocking pink perfume-impregnated crystals. So, let it be known, Schiap even designed air. These days there is a Schiaparelli-labeled pink leather iPad case. She would surely have liked that.

One could dress one's walls with Schiaparelli wallpaper, as well. She licensed upholstery fabrics with Schumacher and Waverly in New York that were wildly eccentric and vibrantly colorful patterns. They had images of huge flowers (called Fleurs Modernes and made from Bonded Glosheen cotton chintz), Parisian park chairs, roses, and hearts. Other patterns were Chansonette, which was a stylized rose pattern, and abstractions such as Surrealistic snowflakes edged with gold and Electra, which was an asymmetric arrangement of atomic age elliptical shapes in 1950s bowling alley colors of green, orange, and black. Another was a modernistic elliptical form called Mannequin, which had a tag telling the tale of how Shocking's perfume bottle was based on Mae West's figure. Some of the wallpaper designs were actual reproductions of Schiaparelli's own paintings of flowers and fruit trees. In 1961, she even sold cut crystal for the table: bowls, pitchers, drinking glasses, and ice buckets. These were advertised throughout America. Last but certainly not least, Schiaparelli shower curtains! Of course I have one in my collection, never used, thank god. I just don't know what to make of it still!

One of the most popular licenses was for the incalculable amounts of costume jewelry, made in Rhode Island, the costume jewelry capital of the United States. The labels for the jewelry claimed, a bit erroneously, "Designed in Schiaparelli's 'La Boutique' in Paris. Look for the signature on each piece." They all had evocative names such as Champagne Morning, which was a parure with a brooch nearly three inches across in grey and yellow stones. They were displayed in the shops atop bright pink and black satin pillows with Schiaparelli Jewels embroidered in the corner. These sets of jewels, which ran the gamut from Surrealistic shapes and figures to loud blasts of oddly mixed, glaringly-colored and contrast stones have all achieved a highly collectible status amongst a certain echelon of costume jewelry collectors in the USA.

However, most American collectors have an incorrect understanding of how licenses worked and how this applied to Schiaparelli. I found out early on that Schiaparelli licensed her name just before the mid-1930s for mass-production of costume jewelry and accessories to the David Lisner Co., which was also her authorized American agent and distributor for her French-made haute couture pieces. In 1949, the Ralph De Rosa Company produced Schiaparelli jewelry. Each American licensed collection had eccentric pieces mixed with the more conventional matched sets. In later years, the licensed jewelry began to lack the highly original look of the earlier work associated with the famous haute couture jewels by French artisans. Under her name, De Rosa designed chunky parures with prong-set, molded iridescent glass stones (called watermelon by collectors), "aurora borealis" rhinestones by Swarovski, or large faceted colored glass stones that were produced in the mid-1950s. The company used pot-metal, sterling silver, and gold-plated backings. Though Schiap retired from haute couture in 1954, the Schiaparelli license wasn't discontinued until sometime in the early 1970s. She sold the rights to her name and business just before she died, which allowed the American manufacturer to continue producing designs up until 1974. This jewelry is highly collected today, especially via venues such as Etsy and eBay, though many collectors mistakenly think Schiaparelli designed them. Schiap herself did not actually design these sets of costume jewels. Schiaparelli *approved* them, as she had with the hand-made artisan jewelry made for her haute couture in France. Alongside the artisan pieces, she also stocked her Paris boutique with the licensed pieces, importing them into France from the USA.

I would like to correct the myth that the misspelled oval tags on some pieces are fakes or copies. They were a batch of late-1960s, early 1970s pieces which were simply incorrectly manufactured by omitting a letter in her name. They were discounted but distributed on the sly by the manufacturers. These last pieces also are noted for their innovative and inventive styling, sometimes more elaborate than earlier sets and of a very high quality. Schiaparelli's haute couture jewels were usually unsigned. There are a few exceptions of costume jewelry, mainly post–World War II, that included the names of artisans on the pieces. In 1948, Lydo Coppola (married name Toppo), in Milan, designed pieces for Schiaparelli and in her case, these are marked "Coppola e Toppo." Lina Baretti (who may have collaborated with Leni Kuborn-Grothe Kitzbühel) and William de Lillo had their names on Schiap pieces, as well. There are many other unsung heroes who designed the jewels as far back as the 1920s. One of my favorites is Mme. Scapini, who was a close friend to Bettina Bergery and who did extravagant jewels, possibly in collaboration with both Lina Baretti and Leni Kuborn-Grothe Kitzbühel. These signed pieces are very rare now and are only able to be identified correctly by a few people who have the experience to recognize them. In the late 1930s, the licensed jewelry pieces were signed "Schiaparelli" in lower case block letters, like her Paris logo. This was used up until 1949, when the "Schiaparelli" name was engraved in script and sold as "Designed in Paris—Created in America." It is important to note that there is no such thing as "unsigned" *licensed* Schiaparelli costume jewelry from any period. None of the famous artisans associated with her haute couture jewels designed any of the licensed pieces, even though Schlumberger did make a name for himself with costume jewelry independently. Collectors should never accept these American-made unsigned costume jewelry pieces as the genuine article. *Never.*

Probably the most extraordinary and archetypal collector of Schiaparelli costume jewelry today is my very dear friend Paige Powell. The beautiful and witty Paige is an animal rights activist and has been deeply involved in the arts and with notable artists such as Warhol, Haring, Scharf, Clemente, and Basquiat. To me, she represents the ultra-sophisticated collector who uses Schiap accessories in an updated and clever way. Schiaparelli indeed brings out the most lovely of fantasies in people. Even today, she's making life just a bit more beautiful.

Schiap did not stop at clothes and jewelry for ladies. She made, and I collected, men's clothes, which I have worn since the day I discovered that they existed in the mid-1970s. As early as the 1950s, Schiaparelli sold men's hats, which I used to find by the dozen on Manhattan's Mott Street, where old Jewish haberdashers sold me their dead stock with delight. The men's clothing license agreement was signed in May of 1953 with Peerless Robes and Sportwear to produce dressing gowns and pajamas for men. I have a very amusing pair of pajamas with a map of Paris printed all over them.

She allied with the Bachrach Company to produce her luxurious ties. One of the modern art-inspired ads from the 1950s showed a Picasso- or Calder-esque line drawing of a headless man. The caption, in child-like scrawl read, "*Perdre la tête!" with an asterisk explaining that's French for "*To lose one's head." Another of the same genre was titled "*Bouillant de colère! *Boiling with rage, because nobody presented him with these magnificent ties by Schiaparelli."[16] These were drawn by the well-known Jean Carlu and depicted a very scribbly man with popping eyes and stream rising from his head, part of his body in a casserole of boiling water! Another ad, with its stylish cartoon of a father with his family, read, "Voila Papa! Schiaparelli does ties for men. If your daddy has recurrent nostalgia for the Ritz Bar, the place Pigalle, and the shops around the place Vendôme, you'll make him ever so happy with these. They are just what you'd expect from the rich imagination and gifted hands of Schiaparelli . . . witty, Parisian and wholly original in design and color treatment. In fine satin or twill, expertly tailored in tie flawlessly, individually boxed in Shocking Pink." But it's hard to believe that in the USA any average "daddy" would have "recurrent nostalgia" for such luxurious places in Paris, despite what the quaint, old-fashioned *New Yorker*-style cartoon implied. Schiaparelli was not doing what was considered the height of masculine elegance in the USA with these licenses. They were perhaps a bit too ahead of the times. Even the embroidered logo on the ties, a prancing poodle in a men's top hat, which was supposed to evoke masculine sartorial frivolity, may have offended a number of the McCarthy-era set of grey flannel-suited men. Yet they were extremely popular and a license which lasted for decades. In the 1960s the Burma company and Dunlap-Nadler's, the producers of her men's ties, went all out with wildly loud Pop-Art inspired ties in print styles made famous by Peter Max and psychedelia in general. Schiap did a license of men's jewelry, notably tie bars and matching cufflinks, and also stickpins, some quite precious and all packaged in red or pink boxes. They were considered a bit effete if not outright questionable in taste, though, and were not the greatest of her license successes. Truman Capote once told me, "Schiap, oh my goodness, what a divine thing she was . . . I wore some of her clothes for men in the 1950s . . . They were crazy . . . they had flowers on them and in sissy colors. I loved them."

The ties and jewelry were designed to be worn with her men's shirts. One particularly notable men's shirt is from the early 1950s and has a trompe l'oeil of a Roman gladiator's chest of armor. Others are in shocking colors, like lipstick red, bright yellow and pink, bright silver, and neon greens and oranges. Many were way too sexy for the average male of the era, but were still startlingly elegant. There was also a *West Side Story*–style sharkskin fabric, which was truly something someone from the Jet gang would wear if they'd had the means to buy such roguish luxury shirts. Sharkskin was a highly iridescent fabric that seemed to suit the younger generation's need for flash. By the Mod era, Schiap's men's shirts had become even more eccentric. These series of shirts looked like they were conceived for

Brian Jones or Mick Jagger. The men's sweaters, made in Italy in the 1950s and 1960s, were very James Dean in style and exquisitely made in a range of colors. Many had a trompe-l'oeil effect that echoed her earliest sweaters. One, a jersey knit in golden yellow and brown, had what appeared to be a sleeveless gilet over a long-sleeved sweater, over which was a scarf.

Schiap's men's cologne, which debuted in 1939, was called Snuff. The name was inspired by the tobacco, which was fashionable in the eighteenth century. It came in a cigar box, swathed in excelsior shreds, first as a pipe-shaped bottle and later as a stylized men's torso. The former suggested Magritte's painting *The Treachery of Images (This Is Not a Pipe)* from 1929, in accordance with his idea that "an object never fulfills the same function as its name or its image."[17] Schiaparelli's Snuff obviously evokes this idea, as the pipe-shaped bottle is not a pipe, but a crystal bottle, and the cigar box only a clever packaging, not a real cigar box. Also, the slang expression for oral sex performed on the male sex organ in the French language is pipe, which gives this perfume bottle a strong innuendo as well.

The spicy scent was a rage amongst the sophisticated men of the era. The ads by Vertès showed top-hatted cave men, very sexy and nearly nude, with virile, hair-covered torsos and a big club. It was advertised as being for "rugged" types and "for men with ideas," a highly ambiguous and suggestive slogan.[18] It was very macho and quite homoerotic. It was the first men's perfume, a rather shocking idea executed with Schiaparelli sexual aggression. It was a great success, like many of her perfumes.

"Oh God, I remember that scent so well, it was THE smell of gaydom . . . at cocktail parties, between cigarette smoke, you'd smell the sexy scent of Snuff by Schiaparelli," Brion Gysin reminisced. Painter André Beaurepaire, who was the youngest artist to participate in the Petit Théâtre de la Mode, confirmed to me in 1983, "Only Schiaparelli could get away with making a perfume for men . . . naturally, the idea, as good as it was, had to have a masculine appeal . . . the manly device of a pipe was perfect, and it was so much her style."

Years after she shut down her couture house, the Schiap boutique in Paris continued to prosper. Schiap gave a private cocktail party in December of 1958 to launch the newly re-vamped look and name, now simply Schiap, just like the very first shop of the 1920s. In some of her end-of-year personal and promotional calendars one could see photographs of the splendid chic of the shocking pink and black interior of the boutique with its severely modernistic furniture.

The boutique held many peculiar little accessories, elegant separates, and fanciful hats. With names like Twist, Jet, Bowling, Blue Pink, and Rosine, one can only imagine what the clothes in the Schiap Boutique looked like. In the large collection of original Schiaparelli house drawings and clothing I possess, the fashion seems sleek and stark.[19] It could be said that these clothes and accessories are mid-way between two styles. They evoke a sober, elegant young lady, an ingénue in the manner of the film *Gigi*. The silhouettes are trim, with clean-lines. With simple buttons, and often tailored, the clothes matched the structural hats. Yet sometimes the early 1960s boutique clothes were wacky, in the mood of early Pierre Cardin or Courrèges, with large color blocks, geometric boldness, and bright colors. As stylish and evocative as they were, these clothes were often over-looked at the time by the fashion magazines, but to my eyes they are an integral part of the Schiaparelli story.

Yves Saint Laurent wrote the preface to a book published in the 1980s on Schiaparelli by an author whom I don't find particularly well-informed, however, I must acknowledge that I regard Saint Laurent's contribution as one of the most poetic and most accurate essays on Schiaparelli ever written. I find in it a true sense of understanding for all of the elements that make up Schiaparelli the person, the artist, and the fashion designer. It's truly a superb text. It starts off with, "She slapped Paris. She smacked it. She tortured it. She bewitched it. And it fell madly in love with her."[20] Evidently, having known and dressed her, Saint Laurent was genuinely well positioned to write about her, and did so with obvious love and admiration. "Schiaparelli came to me right at the beginning when I opened my house. She was extraordinary and very intimidating. I could not believe I was making clothes for her, it was as if I'd been commissioned to dress the high priestess of haute couture. She had such a style, it was a challenge to make clothes for her. She definitely knew what she wanted. She always told me she liked my models. I knew she wore Balenciaga, too. That in itself was such a flattering thing for me, she chose a master and myself when I was just starting out," he recounted to me in the mid-1980s.

In 1969, at the urging of the Fashion Group of Philadelphia, Schiaparelli made a donation of the highlights of her career, seventy pieces of haute couture and a few accessories, to the Philadelphia Museum of Art. After seeing a tiny notice of this donation in a newspaper a few years afterward, I had the great fortune to see the entire collection and itemize it for my archives. The collection had been given to the museum with the intention of having it on permanent display, but this never happened. When I went to see the pieces, the people in charge went through a lot of trouble just to locate them. They seemed to be perplexed by my interest and could not understand why I was so eager to see them. I was left to my own devices in a barren room with these splendors for days on end. The pieces were eventually shown in a 2004 exhibition at the museum, but back in 1969 their value wasn't immediately apparent.

In 1973, upon the wish of Madame Schiaparelli, another eighty-eight of her garments and accessories were given to the U.F.A.C, thanks to the privileged relationship between her and Yvonnes Deslandres. This would be her second important gift to this museum. Schiap also donated the remaining albums of the Drian drawings and sketches (from the early 1930s through 1954), which could be examined by almost anyone who asked for years. Consequently, many pages were ripped out. It was only in the late 1980s that their preservation and protection was made a priority. I was very fortunate to have had access to them for my research and was able to precisely date many of the clothes in my collection, as well as uncover details about jewelry and buttons and hats.

The early 1970s was a very nostalgic era, with obsession for Art Deco and 1930s cinema. This feeling touched nearly every creative domain, including commercial venues and advertising. Fashions of the pre–war era and many obscure stars were "re-discovered" and appreciated again in their old age, such as Louise Brooks and Fred Astaire. It was inevitable, then, that people would revisit the grand epoch of French high fashion and the work of Schiaparelli. In Paris in the early 1970s an article appeared with a headline that said, "It's stronger than herself, in the middle of sentimental and amazing bric-a-brac, SCHIAPARELLI STILL DRAPES DRESSES IN SECRET!"[21] The in-depth, pages long article starts with the journalist being met at the door, by a houseboy. The journalist then goes on to describe every room. The house is filled with amazing things of all sorts, eccentrically displayed. The story describes multi-million franc paintings on the floor and dictionaries surrounding the television set. It goes on to describe Elsa in bed, surrounded by an array of exotic remnants of her extraordinary lifestyle and avant-garde taste. The journalist claims that despite being bedridden, in her better moments, Elsa still drapes and designs dresses. It's a very touching portrait and much more tender than the acerbic Schiap that one reads about in those last years of her life, when she clearly despised all the current trends and the lifestyle in general of the early 1970s. She was still a source of inspiration and awe at the end of her life, though. In 1971, Schiaparelli received a huge wave of publicity, appearing in many magazines and newspapers worldwide, in often witty and nostalgic articles. One such article was just titled "The Sloppy Seventies":

The Paris collections begin tomorrow, but Madame Schiaparelli feigns little interest. She is scathing about fashion today. "I call it a bad moment, not a revolution, that may still happen, but I hope people will come to their senses. I think that women like to be dressed up, this sloppiness is just a phase. Not that I am against modern clothes, I like pants. I used to wear them, and they are wonderful for traveling. It isn't a question of being old-fashioned but all this sloppiness gets into people's lives, the way they eat and general manners." Sloppiness is her favorite description of the 1970s. "Gypsy clothes just don't go with today's life. Getting on buses, shopping, driving cars is ridiculous with those long skirts. I always liked plain clothes, good blouses and skirts for the day."[22]

Nevertheless, by the early 1970s Schiap had recognized the interesting aspects of denim and all of its possibilities. She saw that blue jeans would soon be fashionable everywhere. In the November 1973 *Le Journal du Dimanche*, a French popular magazine, she was called (incorrectly) "the first hippie." "She was dying to try out jeans," said Gogo in the article, which claimed that she later brought her mother Levi's brand blue jeans from America. In one of the last interviews Elsa gave, she humorously claimed, "I'm a little annoyed with myself, I was a very bad influence," in response to the things she witnessed in fashion in the early 1970s.[23]

Chanel, Schiap's archrival and creator of the antithesis of her style passed away on January 10, 1971 at the Ritz hotel at the age of eighty-eight. Her fashions, though they had a slow and hard climb to be accepted in the first years of her comeback, had become acknowledged as a symbol of French luxurious chic. And what would Schiaparelli have to say about her passing? As Bettina Bergery said to me, "She [Schiaparelli] was very sharp tongued, borderlining on spiteful, but she was much too intelligent to have been vindictive concerning Chanel, I know she wasn't, we spoke of it once in a while, she disliked Chanel, but she certainly was not gloating about her death." Schiap, in regard to whom she admired the most after Vionnet, in her own words said "Chanel—she was a great girl and she achieved the incredible feat of doing the same thing for fifty years."[24] More in tune with reality was Comte Henri de Beaumont's observation expressed to me in conversation, "After the war, Schiap definitely had a low esteem for Chanel. For her, Chanel had betrayed France with her scandalous behavior during the war. I think by the end, she simply couldn't care less about that old witch Chanel, as far as I understood, the rivalry was all in Chanel's mind if there was talk of rivalry at all. Schiap was really above it all."

After a number of small strokes, Elsa Schiaparelli died in her sleep on November 13, 1973, in her home in Paris. She was buried in the Picard village of Frucourt. Mass was said for her in the Saint-Philippe-du-Roule church in Paris and at the Saint Thomas Moore church in New York. On her tombstone is her gilded signature. In March 1974, Paris *Vogue* ran a touching and long article paying tribute to Schiap. Written by Marisa Berenson, it was called "Schiap, My Grandmother," and featured photos by Marisa's sister, Berry, of a selection of Schiap pieces in the Costume Institute that were lent by Diana Vreeland. Marisa begins by telling the reader that she called her grandmother "Schiap" because she did not like being called "grandmother."[25]

In the very early 1980s, the owner of the House of Schiaparelli approached me to design for them, after the sadly unsuccessful collaboration a few years earlier with Serge Lepage (which I adored and found extremely beautiful). These clothes by Lepage and those made just after were labeled "Schiaparelli Atelier, 21 place Vendôme Paris." I was greatly encouraged by the new owners of the house, mainly by

Guido Sassoli de Bianchi, an Italian count and a man of great charm. I had a number of hilarious meetings with him, often with my friend and their fit model Sheila. The House of Schiaparelli showered me with gifts of perfume and accessories and all sorts of things. I wore the perfume for years and years, they gave me so much. I loved that I could casually stop by 21 Place Vendôme and look at the old documents and furniture: Pascal, Pascaline, and Bimbo, the donkey. I put most of the remaining documents in order and they graciously gave me documents for my own use. I received many letters and kind wishes from various members of the House of Schiaparelli for various shows I did. I also had a regular, lengthy correspondence with the house for various reasons concerning my research. Anke Carver's incredible thoughtfulness and kindness to me while in Paris during those early years of my research on Schiap was invaluable.

After the brief tenure of Serge Lepage, I received a letter from Gogo that stated, "Did you ever combine with Sassoli? His wife just produced a collection, all Italian made, with copies of Schiap found in the archives. The materials, it seems, are good. But really I wish you were in there pitching instead of a German debutante." It would have been a first for an old house to hire a very young designer such as myself. Over a number of years they made regular requests for me to become artistic director and designer, but I refused. Being a designer for a real fashion house did not attract me. I never wanted to make clothes in order to sell them. It seemed very dull to me. And when I thought of designers I'd met, like Chanel, they reminded me of the person I definitely did not want to be. Designers could be artists like Schiaparelli, but most were not. They made clothes. They made clothes as a business. I don't have much esteem today for the fashion industry, and just associating the two words together is something that I don't appreciate. It's not really about clothes anymore. It's all branding. It's all about the sale and the spectacular shows to make publicity. Not my thing at all.

Schiaparelli seemed to have an absolutely rigid and uncompromising way of looking at haute couture and all of its hierarchy. She remained true to herself and this was a wonderful lesson that I learned from her. I am probably equally as uncompromising in my work, which is good, but can also create enemies and problems. But so be it. As I have said all my life, "If Schiap could do it, so can I." I especially used these standards in my work as a haute couture jewelry maker and with Mdvanii (for which many have criticized me).

I was very busy preparing the Schiaparelli exhibition called *Hommage à Schiaparelli* in 1984 which was organized by the city of Paris and the Musée Galliéra. It included loans from the Met's Costume Institute in New York (the shoe hat), the Brooklyn Museum (the insect necklace), the U.F.A.C., and a few other museums. I was very enthusiastic about the whole project, which became more exciting every day. When the installation time occurred in the Pavillon des Arts in the center of Paris, the pieces I had selected from my collection could finally be put in place. My assistant Jane and Lala worked non-stop with me for the whole day and night before the vernissage.

The place was filled with everyone famous in fashion. The mayor of Paris, Jacques Chirac, and I posed for photographers with Gogo Schiaparelli and Marisa Berenson, who looked rather vivid in a shocking pink Chanel suit (as irony would have it). In spite of some flaws, the show was the first of its kind and everyone was quite happy to see the wonderful work of Schiaparelli. It was clear I had put Schiaparelli back on the map. The press the show and I received was enormous and came from all over the world, from Japan to Russia to South America. It seemed the whole of Europe found Schiap again through this show. It was the first time that some of the most iconic Schiaparelli pieces were shown in public since the war, like the Cocteau drawing embroidered coat and the telephone dial compact. Gogo lent a few pieces to the show, like a tartan gown and a pink-and-black harlequin-patterned opera coat, along with some of Schiaparelli's own Yves Saint Laurent and Balenciaga garments. My exhibition also inspired numerous other shows, as well as books and articles on the theme of Surrealism and fashion throughout the world for many years.

This *Hommage à Schiaparelli* show in Paris inspired my friend Stephen de Pietri, the exhibitions coordinator for Yves Saint Laurent, to design the *Fashion and Surrealism* exhibition at the Fashion Institute of Technology in New York City. I was a major contributor, not only of my own work, but also of Schiaparelli pieces. His designs for the Surrealism show would remain one of his most noted works after the perfection of the YSL shows throughout the world.[26] I met Stephen through Diana Vreeland. He was yet another acolyte of hers and I treasured him as a friend. He was so fascinating. Being an actor and a costume designer in his early years, he had a flair for the dramatic, and as a curator he was a perfectionist in his documentation and choices of pieces for shows. There are days I miss him so much, he was truly a marvel to behold, like a blonde-haired pixy, so delicate and refined with an equally refined, rather arch sense of humor and knowledge of fashion history.

A Schiaparelli retrospective was organized in 2004, based on the Philadelphia Museum of Art's collection of Schiaparelli. This show, called (what else?) *Shocking!* traveled to Paris and was combined with pieces, notably drawings, to make another exhibition. Decorator Jacques Grange, who specializes in twentieth-century decorative style, did the installation in Paris. A catalogue by the curator Dilys E. Blum accompanied the show. It was received with open arms by the fashion public. Most of the reviews were positive. Some articles said her clothes often were dowdy. I really do not agree with this critique at all. The exhibition had several pieces that were made for women of varying body types and the author of one particular article which accuses Schiap of this clearly had not taken into consideration the times, the desired effects, the social condition. Dressing in haute couture is not always spectacular. There were times historically where sober, plain dresses were extremely expressive of the times and very necessary for the way women lived, especially in Europe.

I agree with most of the points about her clothes the press made in general about putting the clothes in context with other designers as well as the politics and art of their times. A few of the remarks make for interesting debate, as well. A flat statement in one article claimed that she conflated fashion and art. This seems to be a bit dismissively generalized. An entire book can be written about that comment and, in fact, many books about this subject have been published since the 1920s, starting with Poiret's books on the subject of fashion as art and Marcel Vertès's now-iconic book *Art et la Mode*. I feel, without question, that Schiaparelli's clothes can be considered artwork even if they were not considered as such at the time they were made. This has happened with many varied things throughout history. In haute couture alone there was a time when fashion illustration and photography were not considered art. Costume jewelry and millinery were not counted among the noble arts, either. This is the fascination with the work of Schiaparelli: It opens up so many doors, and prompts provocation and reflection. The definitive Schiaparelli show—whether by myself or someone else—is yet to be done.

CHAPTER 27

ARTISTIC
COLLABORATIONS

I n the last years before the war, Schiaparelli was at the height of her collaboration with artists, artisans, and the craftsmen in the fashion industry, always supporting and encouraging anything new and mixing it with the luxury of the grand tradition of French haute couture. This was an essential part of her great genius and, I believe, the center of her success both aesthetically and historically. These collaborations also represented an achievement in human relations and spirituality. Despite the fact that she had a reputation for being difficult, Schiap, in my opinion, cherished human relationships and conformed very much to Eastern ideas of spiritual bonds. She was also, pre-war *the* single biggest client to the registered artisans of Paris.

One such association was with Albert and Marie-Louise Lesage and their embroideries. Albert Lesage had spent three years in charge of haute couture at Marshall Field while Marie-Louise was a *modeliste* at Vionnet under the name "Yo" for four years. When I'd hang out with Mr. Lesage, it took me sometimes a whole hour to focus on what he was saying because his atelier was crammed to the rafters with amazing things. I'd have to force myself to focus on one object. He found that funny. "Your eyes are taking over your mind, BillyBoy*?" to which I'd say, "Can you blame me, everywhere my eye rests there is something dazzling me." My eyes were burning from all the beautiful things scattered around the cramped room. It was haute couture heaven.

In 1924, Albert's parents decided they wanted a business of their own, so they bought the Maison Broderies from Michonet, who were the embroiderers for Napoléon III beginning in 1864 and did the lavish embroideries for Charles Frederick Worth's haute couture. I have a few Worth gowns and jackets which they did the embroidery for that are unbelievably elaborate, with ombré ribbon, chenille, gilt threads, and minute rhinestones set in silvered or gilt pronged settings the size of a pin prick.

Albert's son François showed me endless albums of documents in the house that enabled his father to familiarize himself with the techniques he used in the mid-1920s. He produced fabulous fringed work, geometric and stylized designs, and superb Greek-inspired things for Vionnet. Their business grew to proportions that became considerable competition for Rébé, the top embroidery house at the time. The stock market crash of 1929 eventually saw the end of these rich embellishments. Between 1930 and 1934 Lesage concentrated on beaded purses and bags, belts, and other small accessories. It was a difficult period for them, as well as for most of the trade.

I met Albert in the mid-1970s. I used to go with François to lunch around Hôtel Drouot where he'd point out things he was sure came from his family and I'd leave bids on them. At that time, you could buy dresses, suits, hats, handbags, gowns, costume jewelry, and other haute couture pieces when French auctioneers sold them in big lots. These auctions had rapid-fire rhythm, and within minutes you could have won an entire collection of French high fashion.

Years later, when I presented my Schiaparelli show with the city of Paris, François explained to me how Schiap started her association with his father. Schiap liked Albert Lesage because he would invent new techniques for her, but also revived eighteenth-century methods and trims. Most embroidery houses were much too conservative to even consider such innovations. For example, a lamé guipure was created for Schiap in 1936 after she had requested a dull finish on the gold lamé fibers. Lesage then wrapped each fiber in the threads of silk, producing a dull, yet iridescent thread, which could be made in contrasting or complementary tones. He revived *soutache passe-menterie* and the marvelous *bigoudi*, a thread wrapping technique in which the result is a soutache that is tapered on each end. It was usually found on eighteenth- and nineteenth-century military uniforms as borders and epaulettes. Schiap used his work in all of her famous collections. The Lesage level of quality and perfection of technique was quite impressive. Olga Rambaud, the *premiere* embroiderer with Lesage, executed all the Schiap samples. She could put up to three hundred hours into a small jacket. When Albert Lesage died in 1949, François came back from his American business and took over the firm.[1] James Galanos told me in a 1979 conversation, "We all regretted him leaving Hollywood, we really felt as if we had been working with someone so important in the world of French fashion, it was as if by working with him, some of his savoir-faire would rub off on our clothes, that he'd bring some sort of snob-appeal to the clothes."

After his father's death, François Lesage created designs for many houses but especially for Schiaparelli. He invented the funny watermelon embroidery for her in 1949, which was part of her Forbidden Fruit collection of that year, and also the last of her beaded hats, such as the one with a beaded "S." He did gowns embroidered with fur, gilded and silk threads, rhinestones, and crystal beads all in one design, such as the black silk velvet gown with thin straps. He had continued with all of his father's integrity and was able to work with Schiap in a similar way for years until she closed her couture salon in 1954.

In addition to the heightened focus on embroidery, Schiaparelli began to offer strange jewelry beginning around 1929. She fully embraced costume jewelry, as evidenced by the porcelain flower, feather, and ermine necklaces that appeared with many of the outfits. She often used Elsa Triolet's barbaric multi-colored wooden jewelry that featured strong colors. Triolet also invented odd, modernistic structures out of humble materials such as paper maché, porcelain, glass, and wire. She was a poet, writer, and staunch communist.[2] She wrote an obscure, little-known book about her early experience as an artisan costume jewelry maker called *Colliers de Paris* (Paris Necklaces) in the 1930s, which was not published until 1973. In it, she recounts the extraordinary relationships she had with Schiap and other famous fashion designers of the era, including Poiret and Chanel. She notes, incidentally, the irony of a Communist having to earn the means to go to the Soviet Union within the luxurious haute couture community. In this fascinating little tome, Triolet remarks upon the astounding fact that Schiaparelli, whose fashions were the most fabulously expensive and chic of all Paris, chose to use decidedly working class materials such as cotton, canvas, and raw wool, finishing them with straw belts and horsehair collars. Triolet's work, like that of Jean-Michel Frank, Schiaparelli, and other leaders of style of the day, transformed the concept of what was beautiful. In their hands, humble became high luxury.

One of the most famous "Schiaparelli" necklaces, was handmade by Triolet. The Aspirin necklace was made with incredible precision using unglazed porcelain *pastilles*.[3] I have several of these creations, as well as photographs of many of the other things that Triolet did for Schiap. Bettina Bergery was photographed in the Aspirin necklace by Man Ray and I am fortunate to have it in my collection. She was photographed in many other Triolet jewels for

Schiap as she personally loved them, including the spectacularly modernistic zig-zag necklace. The first Triolet piece to be seen in *Vogue*, under the heading, "Summer Accessories—to wear in town," was her Egg necklace for Schiap.[4] It ties on with thick black velvet ribbons. This is also in my collection. Another very successful model was made from coils of African glass. A stunning modernist piece was seen on Mademoiselle Elena de Mumm. It was fashioned from three concentric circles that fastened around the neck and was possibly inspired by African jewelry. It was imitative of the Dadaist motifs found in collage. Photographed by Hoyningen-Huene, Elena was lauded as a young modern and for her charm, culture, and talent, her startlingly classical beauty, and the fact she was a painter herself. "Elena was so daring, so beautiful, she rivaled Kiki de Montparnasse in avant-gardism and her clothes were the most envied around. . . . She wore so much of Elsa's clothes and Triolet's jewels. They had a magic when combined," Bettina Bergery recalled. When I first started collecting Schiap, it was these very jewels that thrilled me the most. After a few decades of searching, I had the good luck to get many of them.

The Triolet jewels were successful but the two Elsas were not without their difficulties. "My Elsa [Schiaparelli] would be angry that the other Elsa [Triolet] would show new designs to other couturiers before her. She wanted exclusivity and priority to her designs," Bergery said to me in conversation. Schiaparelli was not only demanding as to how the suppliers entered her establishment (the supplier's back entrance) but she'd make other hard-to-meet demands. Bergery continued: "Once Schiap gave Triolet an order for four dozen necklaces which had to be delivered within three days. It was physically impossible to do even if Triolet had the raw materials to do them. So, Schiap would scream at Triolet, who in turn would scream at her own suppliers of raw materials . . . And it all turned out fine, but with a lot of hair-pulling and accusations."

Another one of Schiaparelli's collaborations, as we have seen, was with the multi-talented costume jewelry designer Jean Schlumberger.[5] "Schlum" started his career as a jewelry designer sometime around 1935, with Schiaparelli. When she jokingly requested to see his costume jewels made from "junk" that he found at the marché aux puces the term "junk jewelry" came into being. At his home in Paris, he explained to me that Schiap had seen some of his diamond-studded and gold-encased Meissen porcelain flowers (the kind that decorated eighteen-century chandeliers) and summoned him to her office. "She hired me at once to make costume jewelry and buttons," he said to me in conversation. "She was so difficult—always demanding—but so very stimulating." He used Victorian castings and other things that he found at the flea market in Paris. In an early interview he mythified his work by saying, "It was by a chance walk through the flea market, a few years before the war, I saw, piled up on a tray, several dozen Saxony porcelain flowers which came from old chandeliers and I thought they'd make pretty clips. Mme. Schiaparelli heard of them and proposed to me to design for her costume jewelry. I had to look constantly for new and audacious ideas. This research I found within myself corresponded to a personal taste which was only confirmed when I passed over to real jewelry."

He did a riot of fantasy costume jewels before moving on to real jewels. One of his most beloved themes was the sea and for Schiap he did every kind of shell, fish, and starfish, all enameled and studded, many of which he later in his career he interpreted into real jewels for Tiffany's. I was able to collect most of these jewels from all sorts of sources, including not only the flea market, but also Arletty, Marlene Dietrich, Eliane Bonabel, Nadia George-Picot, Diana Vreeland, and Bettina Bergery.

In 1993, Hilton McConnico designed displays and the catalogue for a show of works from the collection of the Musée des Arts

Decoratifs in Paris called *Un Diamant dans la Ville*. The pieces were donated to the museum by Luc Bouchage, Jean Schlumberger's partner in life, upon Jean's death, along with several hundred documents and drawings. Schlumberger considered his drawings more important than the actual jewels because he felt "jewels can be taken apart, stolen, destroyed so it's the original design which really counts," according to Luc Bouchage.[6]

I met with Jean Schlumberger many times throughout my life. Luc and his close friends called him Johnny but I'd never dared to out of respect. I first met him in the mid-1970s through Gene Moore, the acclaimed window designer at Tiffany's in New York, but really got to know him in 1978, when I came to Paris. He and Luc both helped me identify many of the Schiaparelli pieces in my collection. When he passed on, Luc said Jean wanted me to have a tie pin in his famous "oxidized" silver and gold, studded with stars, and a few of the remaining prototype pieces for Schiaparelli costume jewels such as the mold used to cast the Schnerb bracelet he did, as well as the Dauphins. Jean had said his work for Schiaparelli was prolific and very inspiring for him. It was also difficult, because it was always a big undertaking to make many samples of each design. He worked for her from around 1935 to early 1940, though not exclusively, which annoyed her. He made spectacular pieces in 1938 for Schiaparelli. For the Circus collection, Schlumberger made clown head buttons and large ostrich brooches (though other artisans like Clément made the same subjects for jewels at the same time). For the Pagan collection, he made vegetable jewels, including bracelets with enameled ceramic eggplants, peppers, and carrots. There were also more singular pieces like earrings in the shape of ears, a plumed hat brooch, and a necklace with swans and bejeweled muzzles for real fox furs.[7]

A Schlumberger-Schiaparelli landmark were his cupid brooches which were pinned to lapels. Of their popularity in America, Schlumberger said to me, "Yes, those little angels sold like hotcakes,

the Americans even copied them and sold them for fifty-nine cents!"
He went on: "They were so famous that there was not one fashionable lady who didn't have a pair, I was pleased at first, but eventually
it came back to haunt me. Over and over again, Schiaparelli expected
each and every piece I did for her to have the same success. Some
had relatively good success, but nothing reached the level of those
cupids and the handheld rose pin. There were official Schiaparelli
copies made for distribution in department stores, but these were
not made by Schlumberger. It has been a challenge to understand
the exact story as to how they came about.

The Cupid clips were even represented in a painting by Picasso
in *Portrait de Nusch Eluard* (1937). The painting captured two versions of cherubs in different poses. It is interesting to study this painting by Picasso with particular regard to Schiaparelli and the cupids.
Roland Penrose, in his book *Picasso: His Life and Work* (1958), recalls
Nusch in the outfit depicted in the painting:

> With her usual taste for originality and elegance, Nusch
> made her appearance one day rue des Grands-Augustins
> in a black dress and new hat. On the lapels, there were
> two golden cherubs, and the top of the hat was decorated
> with a horseshoe. The pale and fragile face of Nusch, with
> its etheral charm and her simple and frank gaiety, seemed
> even more ravishing in the severity of this ensemble. Picasso
> remarked that the hat had the form of an anvil.[8]

Schiap's winter 1937–38 collection had not only the cherubs, but also
the hat in the Dans le Vent style. These clips were also immortalized
in photographs. Cecil Beaton wore one on his lapel in a self-portrait.
"I loved those pins, they were so amusing for the time. I thought
it was very romantic to wear them although few men dared wear
ladies' jewelry at the time. . . . I liked the symmetry in the double

self-portrait. . . . I wore them long after the fashion well into the 1950s . . . maybe even later," Beaton told me. Later on, just before his passing away, he offered me two that are now in my collection.

Jean Schlumberger, with the endless help of Luc, allowed me to photocopy his entire remaining collection of press books, which helped me immensely in studying his work for Schiaparelli. He said in 1984 that he kept the memory of "a willful woman, with a strong personality who had a sharp sense of up and coming talents." One of the iconic Schlumberger brooches mentioned earlier, the hand grasping a red rose, received an unusual amount of press all over the world in newspaper fashion sections. I am lucky to have several in my collection. Jean Schlumberger told me that it was probably over this brooch that the unspoken rift between Schiap and him occurred. She was extremely displeased that his name was used to promote the design because she felt it was simply a Schiap jewel. Though they continued to work together for about four more years, the relationship went from playful and friendly to decidedly colder. Each time a piece he'd made became successful, she'd drift further away from him.

It is important to bear in mind that during this era, it was rather unheard of that a *fournisseur*—an artisan who designed things for haute couture like handbags, shoes, or jewelry—was ever credited. It was not as if Schiap was particularly mean-spirited. In the hierarchy of high fashion there was the designer, for which the house was named, and all the rest were employed, whether they were salaried or outside artisans or workers of any sort. They had no right, in accordance with custom, to use their work as an occasion to make publicity for themselves, even if they were highly recognized within the inner circle of the fashion community of Paris. It was very rare that an artisan was well known enough in the trade to merit credit, though when it did happen, as with Roger Vivier and Mitchell Maer for Dior, for example, it was considered a huge honor that the designer bestowed acknowledgment upon the artisan. In the post-war period, it became customary to credit the more important makers and artisans in Paris but at this time, it was not standard.

One of the earliest Schlumberger pieces that I received as a gift were a pair of silver potmetal and rhinestone unicorns marked Schiaparelli, from the 1930s and made for the American market. Schlumberger said he'd made them as haute couture pieces and that they were molded later to be included in Schiaparelli's American line. He said the setting of stones was difficult and that he tried to avoid making pieces with them. Arletty gave these unicorns to me in the 1970s. We were having coffee one rainy day and I must have seemed mopey, as a friend of mine had just been killed crossing the street. As I told her about my loss, she just slid them over to me on the table as I sat there looking glum. She then just handed them to me and said, "Take these, you'll like them, they'll cheer you up. Unicorns are magical, you know." That immediately changed the atmosphere and as I resigned myself to the death of this dear friend, I felt as if Schiaparelli herself was sending me some cosmic message that he'd made it to paradise. During these early years of my life in Paris it seemed as if I was surrounded by an immense amount of kindness and generosity, especially from the friends around me. Arletty was a very kind person, very down-to-earth, and what kids today call, "keeping it real."

Other major contributors to the work of Schiaparelli were Alberto Giacometti and his brother Diego, whom I met in the last years of his life. Diego was quite a pip. Shy, and usually dressed in overalls or work clothes, he was a true gentleman and filled with modesty despite his talent and fascinating personal history. He shared information concerning his and his brother's work for Schiaparelli. He told me how they constantly argued over receiving credit, which was by now a familiar story. He also described to me collaborating with Schlumberger on materials and the modifications

Schiaparelli requested on certain designs: "We did a necklace of gilded pendants, like flames adding glass beads, upon the suggestion of Madame Schiaparelli . . . that was a nice piece, but we didn't really like putting beads with it." The Giacomettis also made a small bust of Madame Schiaparelli, which was worn as a brooch and made into a box by Jean-Michel Frank. Diego Giacometti offered me some of the now forgotten pieces, which touched and honored me deeply.

Other major collaborators included textile designers such as Colcombet, Ducharne, and Atelier Calisti. Jean Peltier and Suzanne Janin designed for Ducharne in the 1930s. Janin showed me many examples from the 1937-1939 period, which included textiles such as the Le Gai Paris and Le Bon Temps, Les Ballerines (which matched a button of a ballerina's single leg and tutu), one of swallows called Les Hirondelles, ladybugs called Les Coccinelles (which matched a Schlumberger bracelet), jam pots called Les Pots de Confiture, and one that matched Schlumberger jewels. Madame Calisti showed me prints in the early 1980s of romantic hands and little angels, rooster heads, of ostriches called Les Autruches and blackamoor heads on a blue ground that match a necklace and a blouse which was worn by Gogo in a lovely photo of her as a young woman.⁹ Nearly all of these jewels are in my collection.

Other collaborators, of course, include the many, many artists and photographers with whom she kept company: Christian Bérard, Marcel Vertès, and Roger Rouffiange, the illustrator who I knew quite well in the early 1980s and convinced to participate in my homage to Schiap.

Vertès was one of her favorite artists and is responsible for much of the most well-known Schiaparelli imagery, including portraits of her. He is considered an outstanding twentieth-century painter, printmaker, and illustrator. Having moved from his native Hungary to Paris during the First World War, he lived and worked in the famous Latin Quarter, where he quickly established himself as an important participant within the Paris arts scene, continuing in the footsteps of Boutet, Forain, Toulouse-Lautrec and others. The art of Vertès was highly evocative of all the most *avant-garde* of places: art galleries, haute couture salons, bordellos, the racetrack, the Ritz Bar, and the Deauville beach. He drew glamorous, languid portraits showing the mondaine and demi-mondaine worlds in a snobbish clash. Concentrating upon scenes of Paris street life, portrayals of women, and depictions of circus and cabaret acts, Vertès left a legacy of original lithographs and drawings that superbly capture the spirit of pre-war Paris. As it did for many other artists, the devastation of the Second World War forced him to move to the United States. Settling in New York, with his reputation as a great artist firmly established, he continued doing his Café Society portraits and paintings. Ten years later, he returned to his beloved Paris and spent the remaining years of his life there, painting until the end. I am lucky to have quite a number of original Vertès works of art, including the original advertisement maquettes for Snuff, Shocking, and Sleeping fragrances, some originally owned by Schiaparelli.

Jean Oberlé, a rather important and very much acclaimed artist of the pre-war era, (though much less known now), was also a favorite of Schiap. He had a delicate style, which has a naive charm reminiscent of eighteenth-century drawings. When Schiaparelli's remaining estate was sold at auction in 2014, I acquired an oil painting of a little boy selling violets and a portrait of Marcel Vertès by him. I hang these two next to a portrait of Paul Poiret that was given to me by Perrine, Poiret's youngest daughter. It seems like an odd circle that closed about me like a ring of love and grace.

Others of Schiap's collaborators include many photographers such as Horst P. Horst, Roger Schall, Man Ray, and Hoyningen-Huene, all of whom contributed superb images that brought her work to millions. Man Ray and Schiaparelli had a long relationship that dated back to her years in America. When she returned to

Paris, where Man Ray was then living, she rekindled their friendship. He claimed later that his New York photos of her were not the best portraits he had done of her, but that the Parisian ones were successful. By 1924, Man Ray was firmly established as a reputable and innovative photographer, and had contracts with magazines such as *Harper's Bazaar, Vogue,* and *Vanity Fair.* By the spring of 1930, Schiaparelli was photographed by him in her own styles, including the evening gown with a train/belt that she said was the biggest success of her career.[10]

The third and fourth issues of the Surrealist revue *Minotaure* contain fabulous Schiaparelli references and intermingled her presence with the avant-garde set of intellectuals and artists in Paris.[11] The Dadaist poet and writer Tristan Tzara illustrated his article, called "D'un Certain Automatisme de Goût," with three Man Ray photos of Schiaparelli hats.[12] One, with a top evoking the female genitalia, was called Savile Row, another, photographed on Schiaparelli, was called Crazy Coxcomb, and the Madcap was shown on Bettina Bergery.[13] The sexually suggestive shapes of the hats represented, at least to Tzara, the enflamed sub-conscious and sublimated sexual desires of women made highly readable in the world of fashion. This could be seen in Schiaparelli's work throughout her career. In the same issue of *Minotaure,* a portrait of Schiaparelli was used to illustrate his article "L'âge de la Lumière." Her head was superimposed onto a bust of white plaster, and was coiffed in waterproof lacquered wigs made by Antoine. She looks aloof and distant, yet incredibly chic. This jarring image, deforming reality, both in identity and literally, is a concept dear to the fundamental principals of Surrealism. In 1953, when Marcel Vertès made a Surrealist collage of Schiaparelli's various leitmotifs including dinosaurs and bird-sized butterflies, against a barrage of press photos of Schiaparelli's famous creations, this photo would figure prominently. *Minotaure* also showed her clothes in illustration form. I am lucky to have acquired, thanks to my son, Alec Jiri, searching the Internet, a collection of drawings of Schiap clothes complete with the cardboard envelope in which they were sent to Schiaparelli at her home on rue Barbet-de-Jouy in Paris.

Of course, no study of Schiaparelli would be complete without talking about her buttons. Never before had such intense thought gone into the prosaic notion of the button. Carefully carved and rendered, buttons on Schiap clothes were the final detail that made them genius, that last, little thing which made a jacket or coat not just a thing to wear, but a sculpture. The reality of Surrealism was epitomized by this concept of using these small sculptures. One man made the most thrilling examples from the pre-war period, Jean Clément. Schiap wrote that "he was a genius in his way, a real French artisan, who would work with such burning love that he was almost a fanatic. He would arrive at the last moment when we had given up all hope of having anything to fasten our clothes. There would be a smile of triumph on his face while he emptied his pockets into my lap, waiting anxiously for a word of praise."[14]

Jean Ubel, known professionally as Jean Clément, was one of Schiap's earliest collaborators.[15] His workshop, on rue des Gravilliers, was shared with the Francis Winter atelier. Winter also worked with Schiaparelli up until the 1950s, and is cited as the designer of her handbags in press coverage. Roger Jean-Pierre, who later founded his own workshop for parure, headed their atelier. He designed jewels for Dior, Balenciaga, and Yves Saint-Laurent, and eventually became *Président de la Chambre Syndicale des Paruriers de la Haute Couture.* The team also included Pierre Toulgouat, who started as a photographer. His model wife began working for Schiaparelli as early as 1932. She modeled the famous ensemble number "1045," which was comprised of a coat of "Setting Sun Pink" with squared shoulders and very pointy collar worn over a pale beige-yellow wool dress and a set of three braided scarves in beet red, pale yellow, orange or pale rust pink.[16] The outfit was literally a riot of color. In a Hoyningen-Huene photograph, the placid-looking Madame Toulgouat leans against a rustic Serge Roche piece of furniture in a sober blue spongy wool coat adorned with two blue foxes worn around the neck and under the chin, falling down the front with a knit hat and matching gloves by Schiap.[17]

On the rue des Gravilliers, there were numerous specialists who made high fashion accessories. The atmosphere was very art school-like and creative. In the 1980s I asked Pierre Toulgouat how Jean Clément came to work with him before the war. He explained,

> Rather by accident. At the time of the Depression, to survive, I oriented myself towards fashion photography. My young wife, American, whom I married in 1928 became a mannequin at Schiaparelli's in 1932. On my own, I did photo campaigns for the fashion shows, then I went to work for Jean Clément in 1934-35 and I stayed until 1937. . . . I did my own samples and then Clément would show them to Schiaparelli who would accept or refuse them; as a way of earning a living, it was pretty much come and go, but I couldn't complain.[18]

Another interesting testimony about Clément came from Roger Jean-Pierre, who started with Clément in 1934: "We'd give drawings of belts, buttons, each one of them, one after another, more and more irresistible, in shapes and materials that were 'impossible.' When Madame Schiaparelli had appreciated our propositions, we had to make them!" The atmosphere around Jean Clément wasn't always joyous. In fact, Roger Jean-Pierre was the official go-between as Schiap and Clément had strong temperaments. This led to arguments, which at times seemed irreconcilable. Jean-Pierre said:

> There were little moments of brooding and I had to calm things down a bit, take the edge off things. Each season

one had to refresh and re-new completely the collection of accessories, create new colors, that we'd submit, by paper, for the okay of Madame. Sometimes the atmosphere was even rather heated, tempers would flare. Once, she had sensed that she had hurt Jean Clément's feelings so very badly that she called Michèle Guéguen to "tell Clément I'm sorry, though I don't remember what I said or did"—apparently the closest thing Schiap would give resembling an apology. . . . [But] she was a veritable orchestra leader: she had the incredible art and talent of pulling from each person the maximum that they could deliver.[19]

Jean Clément engaged many people who would go on to make names for themselves in fashion besides Jean-Pierre, Model, and Toulgouat, and he worked for Schiap up until his death in 1949. But, as cited in this research, she also worked with many different suppliers. She created a little bit of confusion about who exactly designed the aspirin necklaces: "Aragon, the poet, with his wife Elsa Triolet, author of *Les Yeux d'Elsa*, designed necklaces that looked like aspirins,"[20] Schiaparelli inaccurately recalled in her autobiography. It was Elsa Triolet who actually designed and made them. Schiap continued on the subject of the buttons by explaining, "The man who does my buttons now [in 1953] is grand-nephew of Victor Hugo," referring to François Hugo.[21] Most of his buttons are signed with his name, though not all are.

These artistic collaborations are a very important aspect of Schiaparelli's career. Although, as mentioned earlier, it was simply "not done" to credit suppliers, Schiaparelli was one of the most adventurous designers to do so since Paul Poiret. She made an effort to encourage new talents and of all the designers of her era, she probably collaborated the most with artisans and fine artists. This concept of collaboration is what has inspired my own work the most, aside from Dadaism and Surrealism. For Schiap, it must have been difficult to deal with so many egos, though her anger can only be fully understood when put in context. As with my own collaborations, I was always credited and compensated so I can only imagine how an underpaid artist must have felt to go un-credited. Humans stay essentially human no matter what the era or social class.

EPILOGUE

I want to end this book with some brief stories about the many people I've known who in some way or another shared something special with me about Schiaparelli or helped me to understand something about her and about life itself. I can mention only a few individuals since my life so far has been filled with many fascinating people, each of whom has expressed many thought-provoking things about Schiap. Thanks to initial introductions concerning Schiaparelli, I often developed meaningful and profound relationships with people that transcended the subject.

It is quite evident to me that Schiaparelli's clothing innovations were often based on direct sociological needs and combined with the vision of a true artist. I think her clothes should be referred to as an oeuvre. They are beautiful and clever, of course, but they are a lot more than just that. Schiaparelli's deeply artistic nature also helped cultivate and inspire other artists of her generation and beyond, up until today. In fact, now more than ever. During her lifetime here on earth, thanks to her initiative through these collaborations, she was able to achieve highly evocative trends and artistic themes that still inspire us today. Her fashions and ideas influenced several generations of people and again, they still influence not just fashion but also lifestyle and a way of thinking. Today more than ever, people who are interested in her are able to understand her way of thinking. All sorts of things, including figural motifs in clothing, deconstruction, architectural shapes, and the use of new materials to create fascinating new clothes, come from her way of seeing clothing on the human form. She radicalized and changed how women were perceived within a social context. Most of all, however, I came to see that she was on a spiritual journey; she had a deep sense of humanity and the human pursuit of understanding the soul. It was thanks to her that from my many extraordinary encounters I was able to slowly learn about her work and come to appreciate it, in its entirety, as a body of work of metaphysical art. This helped me grow as an individual and as a historian because I was able to pass her message along in varied forms of communication: writing, exhibitions, and my artwork. Through the meetings with so many varied people throughout my life, I was able to define what art was, not only by conventional definition, but for myself personally. Through these encounters I was also able to see this great artistic achievement through a once humble medium and with materials not often associated with fine art, that is, prosaic clothes used for something that could be considered banal: dressing the human body.

Over the last forty-two years, I have had the opportunity to talk about Schiaparelli with many people, some mere acquaintances and some close friends, not all necessarily from the fashion world. I am glad to have contributed to the popularity of collecting vintage clothing, notably haute couture, and making Schiaparelli more known and, during the early 1980s, contributing to the great trend of "Surrealistic" themed fashions and accessories of that era and afterwards. One of the most memorable and generous people I've connected with over haute couture was Mrs. Jacqueline Kennedy Onassis. She helped me throughout my career in fashion by wearing my jewelry and was wonderfully instrumental in the publication of my book on the Barbie doll, which is a whole story unto itself. She urged me to complete this manuscript and we spoke about it up until the very last days of her life. Over the years, she told me many stories of her own fashions and their influence, especially her love for French haute couture and her belief in what she called "truthful elegance."

Mrs. Valerie Mendes, fashion and costume expert and curator at the Victoria & Albert Museum, became my good friend in the 1980s. We often corresponded about Schiaparelli and would see each other in London on my visits to the museum. I admired and appreciated her immensely. She had a great sense of fashion, a vast knowledge about haute couture and fashion in general, and a willingness to share ideas with me. We also shared an obsession with the basic black dress, something we could speak about for hours on end. She wrote perfect texts about Schiaparelli and immaculately presented her dresses in exhibitions at the V&A.

Another person who stands out in my memory from the trendy 1980s London scene was Hamish Bowles, the fashion journalist. I greatly appreciated his wry sense of humor. We talked about historic fashion, which he was keen and very knowledgeable about. We drank dry martinis while talking about Schiaparelli and who I should meet to help me in my research. Once in a while, as he started his own collection, we'd even trade garments. He once gave me a Schiaparelli for a Dior, which was fine by me. He had a great appreciation for Schiaparelli despite his predilection for the post-war designs of iconic couturiers like Balenciaga and Dior.

Also in London, and as equally elegant as Hamish, was shoe designer Manolo Blahnik. During a conversation about Schiaparelli at a dinner at Mr. Chow's, Manolo unintentionally became my Proustian madeleine. I had, on this particular occasion, the opportunity to tell him how, as a young teenage boy, I would see his bright-colored 1930s-inspired suede pumps with fur puffing out at the top and think how Schiaparelli could have done them. Just thinking about those shoes gave me the sensation of being that teenager again. The next day, he kindly sent around to my suite at the Ritz Hotel the very two pairs of shoes I had seen so many years earlier in his shop and that we had discussed. I added them to my collection and they allowed me to relive a bit those early halcyon days of my life when I discovered that looking for Schiaparelli was a magical, electrifying, enthralling, endorphin-induced happy time.

Tina Chow—artist and haute couture aficionado and collector—and I would linger for hours, either in London, Los Angeles, or New York looking at my collection, which inspired her to build her own. I remember so well when she wore a blue beaded Schiaparelli number to a party I gave at the Carlyle Hotel. She looked like a dream in it, and it still pops up in Internet searches for either her or Schiaparelli.

From Park Avenue and Broadway to Regent Street and Mayfair, from Brooklyn to Finland, it seemed everyone I'd encounter would eventually have something to say about Schiaparelli. Even Lady Diana Spencer, whom I had the pleasure to meet, spoke to me about Schiap.

Some of my memories are bittersweet. The last time I spent time with ballet dancer and friend Rudolf Nureyev, it was at the Porte de Clignancourt flea market. We made a game of trying to find haute-couture clothes and he bet that I could not find anything of interest that day, and if I did, he'd make dinner for me that evening. We spent many hours looking at things, him so beautiful with his high boots and cashmere shawl over his shoulder. Dealers ogled what must have been a very strange couple scouring the market that day. Well, naturally, any challenge is fun for me, and of course, he did make the best dinner, as I found some Schiaparelli gloves that day. It would be the last time I would see him with his usual extraordinary energy and strength before he fell ill.

Schiaparelli, as an artist and as a historical subject, was so inspirational to many people. My research into her and her life will be never-ending. It all boils down to love and its symbolism. Her work seemed to have been a constant search for unattainable love. I have the profound conviction that each and every life we lead, and the life I myself have in the here and now, is essential for the wisdom our souls require to advance forward. I have come to understand that life is a balance and that whatever suffering I may have had within my life has been equaled with ebullient joy in experiences related to Schiaparelli. My soul has chosen to undergo this adventure I have lived so far, choices I planned in advance for my return from the plane of non-linear time to this earth at this moment. I learned that there is no such thing as death. I did not learn this only intellectually, but more importantly I learned it truly metaphysically with something that can only be akin to Quantum physics and a very rich and profound paranormal experience. Everything and everyone I have come into contact with has made this journey with Schiaparelli more intense and satisfying. I am not a fashionista, or necessarily interested in fashion the way most people are. My story with Schiap is not about fashion. It's about her and the universe and where my place in it is. Fashion is just the excuse, the alibi that is apparent to those exterior to me and my soul. It's the tip of the iceberg. I am convinced that my soul has been somehow connected to Schiaparelli's for a very long time. She has appeared in my dreams and has been a spiritual guide to me. I am indebted to Schiaparelli and hope I have passed on some of my own lessons and knowledge to whomever I am supposed to guide, both now and later. One thing is very sure, absolute, and that is I have this very strong feeling, I wake with this feeling in the morning and go to sleep with it at night. My work with Schiaparelli is not over but only starting. I know that a new stage of expressing who she was and the work she did and her deeply spiritual side will come and I will now be able to better show the world at large. I even modeled my house to be able to show, document, and share what I have learned and what I have collected in the most advantageous way possible. I know my own work as an artist is more than ever before in a state of, without exaggeration, awe and wonderment. This is due to my soul's enrichment thanks to Schiap. I feel as if the voyage with Elsa Schiaparelli is just beginning despite the extraordinary things I have lived up until now. It's all rather thrilling.

Author Erich Fromm, in his book *The Forgotten Language: An Introduction to the Understanding of Dreams, Fairy Tales, and Myths*, makes a strong statement on symbolism which, to my eyes, relates particularly to the work of Schiaparelli and my predestined adventure with her in this lifetime: "I believe that symbolic language is the one foreign language that each of us must learn. Its understanding brings us in touch with one of the most significant sources of wisdom, that of the myth. Indeed, both dreams and myths are important communications from ourselves to ourselves."[1]

Aside from Schiaparelli's design contributions and her extraordinary life, my respect for her, my reason for collecting her work, and the reason I feel so close to her, can be understood by the few words she chose at beginning of her autobiography. They represent the basis of my gratitude and total immersion into the universe of Elsa Schiaparelli:

Birth is not the beginning
Death is not the end.[2]

The last chapter in her autobiography alludes to her worldliness and the result of a life filled with appreciation for just about everything. I have an enchanting image of the serene Schiaparelli, wedded to her philosophy of life with which I had identified as a very young man all those years ago. I felt the book, and that last chapter in particular, was a long good-bye letter to me. I see her so clearly in my head, blended with the memory of brief encounters as a child in which she radiated her aura so intensely in my direction:

> Schiap is in Hammamet, lying in the twilight of the *moucharabia* . . . a terrace that is neither a room nor a porch, nor yet the open air. It is surrounded by woodwork so fine and with such complicated patterns and transparency that the sun and the wind can come freely through. . . .
>
> And here is Schiap in her small human way absorbing the world while outside a storm lashes the cypresses and the eucalyptuses, and drenches this land of sunshine and dreams.
>
> At her feet lies her white Tibetan dog Gourou Gourou, indifferent and royal. They both listen to a small bird which has taken refuge under the *moucharabia* roof in a moment of panic, singing in English:
>
> "Open the door . . . open the door . . . open the dooorr . . ."[3]

Schiap's book ends there, well . . . almost. I know as a fact that someone finally opened that door and that the small bird flew away free. He was wearing a funny little hat with a gold insect on it.

NOTES

BillyBoy* wishes to thank all writers, journalists, and historians whose research and knowledge have contributed to and supported his own exploration of Schiaparelli's life and work.

I: "OH, IT'S A HAT"

1. A soul contract is an accord made before birth with another soul—human or perhaps an animal—where a promise is made to protect, help, and guide each other in life. It does not matter if both parties are alive at the same time because soul contracts are made in a nonlinear time-space. When the universe sends you a message you cannot ignore it. The universe is very demanding, especially because we ourselves have the *libre-arbitre* to make our various lives on earth exactly what they are. Depending on whom you ask, some feel that every sleeping and waking moment on earth was sketched out by ourselves in our former selves when we were still in that nonlinear place, that limbo prior to our own decision to return to this school we call earth. Though few people believe this, this happens to be the way I see things. I put myself here and I decided to do this long before I was physically born back in 1960. Some people reading these very words will entirely understand what I mean, whereas some will undoubtedly not. I am writing these words for all of you. Those who see things the way I do will "get" my story with Schiap probably a bit more easily, if not much more so. Those who do not may start to see things this way. Regardless of which way you see life in your current incarnation, I think most people will understand my passion because most people in some form or another have a passion of their own.

II: PARIS—LONDON—PARIS

1. *New Woman*, Volume 12, Issues 6–11 (1982), p. 10

17: ELSA'S CHILDHOOD

1. Translated as: To those I love / To those who love me / To those who made me suffer. It is the dedication in her first book of poems.
2. Elsa Schiaparelli, *Shocking Life: The Autobiography of Elsa Schiaparelli* (London: V&A Publishing, 2007), 24.

18: ELSA AS A YOUNG WOMAN

1. Schiaparelli, *Shocking Life*, 27.
2. Ibid., 28.
3. Ibid., 29.
4. Ibid., 29.
5. Ibid.
6. Ibid., 32.
7. The exhibition took place from February 17 to March 15, 1913
8. From an interview in *Constellation* in March 1954.

19: ELSA IN PARIS

1. BillyBoy* in conversation with Bettina Bergery, early 1980s.
2. Boris Kochno, as written in a personal letter to BillyBoy*, late 1970s.
3. BillyBoy* in conversation with Perrine de Wilde (née Poiret), late 1970s.
4. *Harper's Bazaar*, 1934.
5. As explained in a press release from the House of Schiaparelli in 1978, when it was under the artistic direction of Serge Lepage.
6. Janet Flanner, "Comet," *The New Yorker*, June 18, 1932.
7. BillyBoy* in conversation with Aroosiag Azarian (née Mikaëlian) a.k.a. Mike, late 1970s.
8. BillyBoy* in conversation with Aroosiag Azarian (née Mikaëlian) a.k.a. Mike, late 1970s.
9. Dilys Blum, *Shocking! The Art and Fashion of Elsa Schiaparelli* (Philadelphia: Philadelphia Museum of Art, 2003).
10. Janet Flanner, "Comet."
11. As quoted from Gluck in Diana Souhami, *Gluck: Her Biography*, Quercus, 1988.
12. Diana Souhami, *Gluck: Her Biography*, Quercus Pandora, 1988.

20: "SCHIAP" 1929-1933

1. Susan Goldman Rubin, *Hot Pink: The Life and Fashions of Elsa Schiaparelli* (New York: Abrams, 2015).
2. Elsa Schiaparelli *Shocking Life*, Random House, New York, 1954

3. BillyBoy* and Bettina Bergery in conversation, early 1980s.

4. BillyBoy* and Eileen Agar in conversation, mid-1970s.

5. *New York Herald Tribune,* August 7, 1928.

6. Schiaparelli, *Shocking Life,* 48.

7. BillyBoy* and Cecil Beaton in conversation, mid-1970s.

8. BillyBoy* and Bettina Bergery in conversation, early 1980s.

9. BillyBoy* and Bettina Bergery in conversation, according to Bergery, early 1980s.

10. BillyBoy* and Bettina Bergery in conversation, according to Bergery, early 1980s.

11. BillyBoy* and Bettina Bergery in conversation, early 1980s.

12. *Vogue* 1933

13. Ibid.

14. Schiaparelli *Shocking Life,* 49–50.

15. BillyBoy* and Bettina Bergery in conversation, early 1980s.

16. British *Vogue,* September 16, 1931.

17. BillyBoy* and Bettina Bergery in conversation, early 1980s.

18. Schiaparelli, *Shocking Life,* 48.

19. Edna Woolman Chase and Ilka Chase, *Always in Vogue* (New York: Doubleday & Company Inc.,1954).

20. "The Fashion for Scottish Tartan—Schiaparelli" French *Vogue,* July 1933.

21. According to an undated pre-war Schiaparelli press statement.

22. BillyBoy* in conversation with Eliane Bonabel, late 1970s.

21: 1934

1. "Haute Couture," *Time,* August 13, 1934.

2. Schiaparelli press release, 1934.

3. *Women's Wear Daily,* July 31, 1934.

4. Bettina Bergery, conversation with the author, early 1980s.

5. Simone Mirman, conversation with the author, late 1970s.

22: 1935–1940

1. Schiaparelli press release, 1935.

2. Schiaparelli press release, 1931.

3. Schiaparelli, *Shocking Life,* 64.

4. Bettina Bergery, conversation with the author.

5. Schiaparelli, *Shocking Life,* 94–95.

6. Mme Alix Grès, conversation with the author, late 1970s.

7. Ibid.

8. This was not the only time Schiap dressed children; she also designed clothes for her own daughter and her clients' children. After the war, she designed for children on a larger basis.

9. *The Christian Science Monitor,* February 25, 1974.

10. Cecil Beaton, "Fun at the Openings," British *Vogue*, April 1, 1935.

11. Bettina Bergery, conversation with the author, late 1970s.

12. Charles James, conversation with the author, mid-1970s.

13. Bettina Bergery, conversation with the author, late 1970s.

14. Schiaparelli press release, 1936.

15. Bettina Bergery, conversation with the author, late 1970s.

16. Eileen Agar, conversation with the author, late 1988.

17. These "vein" gloves may have been designed by Meret Oppenheim; although a sketch of hers of a similar idea is dated 1942–45, Oppenheim was known to revisit themes from earlier years.

18. "Impossible Interview," *Vogue*, June 15, 1936.

19. This was one of the first times the collaboration between Dalí and Schiap was promoted as such.

20. Schiaparelli press release, 1937.

21. Ibid.

22. Associated Press, October 1937.

23. Leonor Fini, conversation with the author, late 1970s.

24. Yves Saint Laurent, foreword, in Palmer White, *Elsa Schiaparelli: Empress of Paris Fashion* (London: Aurum Press, 1996).

25. Bettina Ballard, *In My Fashion* (New York: Van Rees Press, 1960), 61.

26. Diana Vreeland, *D.V.* (New York: Alfred A. Knopf, 1984), 95.

27. Roger Vivier, conversation with the author, late 1970s.

28. Cecil Beaton, conversation with the author, mid-1970s.

29. Bettina Bergery, conversation with the author, late 1970s.

30. René Gruau, conversation with the author, late 1970s.

31. Claude Arnaud, *Jean Cocteau* (Paris: Gallimard, 2003).

32. Bettina Bergery, conversation with the author, late 1970s.

33. Ibid.

34. *Life*, 1937.

35. *Women's Wear Daily*, December 1937.

36. Bettina Bergery, conversation with the author, late 1970s.

37. Gala Dalí, , conversation with the author, mid-1970s

38. It was available in the hat departments at Jay Thorpe in New York and I. Miller in New York. Some retailers reduced it to an abstract form so as not to be too avant-garde for clients in shops that claimed to have the hat, they adapted it even further to make it more "wearable."

39. *Life*, 1937.

40. Gala Dalí, conversation with the author, mid-1970s.

41. Schiaparelli press release 1937.

42. Ibid.

43. Ibid.

44. Jean Schlumberger, conversation with the author, late 1970s.

45. Schiaparelli press release, 1939. Some of the early ads were drawn by the artist Robert Falcucci as well as Vertès.
46. Also referred as the "Forest" collection for mid-season, shown on April 28 for autumn 1938.
47. "Collection Caviar" was the title of a short-lived feature in *Vogue* during the 1930s that showed a few pieces of the most notable accessories of the year in question.
48. Jean Schlumberger, conversation with the author, mid-1970s
49. Roger Vivier, conversation with the author, late 1970s.
50. "Collection Caviar," *Vogue*, March 15, 1939.
51. *Vogue*, 1938.
52. French *Vogue*, December 1939.
53. Carmel Snow, *Harper's Bazaar*, August 28, 1939.
54. Ibid.
55. Diana Vreeland, conversation with the author, mid-1970s

23: THE WAR YEARS

1. Dante Alighieri, *The Divine Comedy of Dante Alighieri*, trans. John Aitken Carlyle, Thomas Okey, and Philip H. Wicksteed (New York: Random House, 1950).
2. Schiaparelli, *Shocking Life*, TK.
3. The show took place between October 14 and November 7, 1942, at the Coordinating Council of French Relief Societies on Madison Avenue in New York City.
4. Sidney Janis, foreword in Andre Bréton and Marcel Duchamp, *The First Papers of Surrealism* (New York: Coordinating Council of French Relief Societies, 1942), n.p. Catalog of an exhibition held at the Coordinating Council of French Relief Societies, Inc., New York, October 14–November 7, 1942.
5. She would become Comtesse Hayden by marriage to the Russian aristocrat the Comte Hayden.
6. Schiaparelli, *Shocking Life*, 120.
7. Etienne Drian would continue to do the sketches for the house during the war years.
8. Schiaparelli, *Shocking Life*, 120. This story was told and retold by word of mouth in Paris, even into the 1980s. It's become something of an urban legend.
9. Ibid.
10. As seen in year's *L'Officiel de la Couture*—Paris, illustrated by Schompré.
11. Arletty, "Pour ou contre les pantalonées," *L'oeuvre*, February 7, 1942.

24: POST-WAR 1945

1. Schiaparelli, *Shocking Life*, 94.
2. French *Vogue*, Liberation Issue, January 1945.
3. The word *guipure* is used to describe embroidered lace or a robust woven lace that is produced in northern France. The French also call Irish crochet laces *la guipure Irlan-*

daise. The word is derived from the French term *se guiper*, from the fourteenth century, which can be loosely translated to mean "dressed exquisitely in silk."

4. According to M. Cardin, though I believe it was in the summer of 1945, just after his work at Paquin under Castillo and just before his engagement at Dior in 1946. Billy-Boy* in conversation with M. Cardin, mid-1970s.

5. Elsa Schiaparelli, "Smartness Aloft," *Ladies' Home Journal*, March 1930.

6. Schiaparelli, *Shocking Life*, 159.

7. The collection was shown on February 21, 1946.

8. *L'Art de la Mode*, illustrated by Pierre Simon.

9. The collection was shown on April 26, 1946.

10. This bustle style, called *tournures*, evokes the French Republic of 1873.

11. In January of that year, Schiaparelli's perfume company moved to the new perfume laboratory in the French suburbs, Bois-Colombes.

12. One of these dresses was in the wardrobe of Mme. Lesage, Albert Lesage's wife.

13. The collection was shown on February 5, 1947.

14. Ballard, *In My Fashion*, 60.

15. Personal letter from the Duchess of Windsor to Elsa Schiaparelli, circa 1947. Collection BillyBoy*.

16. Shown in *Harper's Bazaar*, August 1948.

17. Notation on undated press photo. Collection BillyBoy*.

18. Ballard, *In My Fashion*, 61–62.

19. Ibid, 62.

20. The collection was shown on November 3, 1947.

21. As seen in the April issue of *Vogue*, 1948.

22. Notation on undated press photo. Collection BillyBoy*.

23. The collection was shown on February 4, 1948.

24. *Harper's Bazaar*, circa 1947 to 1948.

25. Notation on undated press photo. Collection BillyBoy*.

26. Uundated press photo. Collection BillyBoy*.

27. The collection was shown on November 3, 1948.

28. "Schiaparelli robe sans couture," *Paris Match*, no. 34 (November 12, 1949). "Schiaparelli wants to launch this season the dress without seams. It is composed of a bra and band of 4.5 meters of material in black jersey which wraps around the body in an intricate movement. Though the dress doesn't have seams, it has one button. This one buttons plays a key role. If it unhooks the dress falls apart. The seamless dress is not exactly an innovation, this technique has already been employed for beach dresses but nobody had thought until now to use it for formal dresses. Once finished nothing distinguishes the dress without seams from a dress with."

29. Dagmar Freuchen-Gale (née Cohn).

30. The collection was shown in May 1949.

31. Schiaparelli press release.

32. Schiaparelli, press release.

33. Hubert de Givenchy, conversation with the author, late 1970s.

34. Jean-Noël Liaut, *Hubert de Givenchy: Entre Vies et Légendes* (B.Grasset, 2000).

35. Ibid.

36. Hubert de Givenchy, conversation with the author, late 1970s.

37. Susan Train, conversation with the author, mid-1980s.

38. Hubert de Givenchy, conversation with the author, mid-1980s.

39. "Schiaparelli the Shocker," *Newsweek*, September 26, 1949.

25: THE 1950S

1. *Flair*, April 1950.

2. They were in unusual materials such as Everest wool by Bisville, Moscowa by Labbey, silk chiffons by Bianchini-Férier or Bucol velvets.

3. Schiaparelli cosmetics mentioned in *Vogue*, September 15, 1950, 128.

4. This item was given to me by Beatrice Laval, the famous New York art collector.

5. The packaging read, *"a l'intention exclusive des amis du champagne Mumm Reims-France"* ("for the exclusive intention of the friends of Mumm-Reims, France").

6. Press photo of gown given to author by Horst. Collection BillyBoy*. The text to the Horst photo claimed, "Schiaparelli's Chinese lantern pleats in an overskirt turned back on itself to make an apron. Dress, in silk organdy, imported by Bergdorf Goodman. Lipstick, Schiaparelli's 'Paris Pink'."

7. This dress is very much in the taste and style of Serge Matta who worked for Schiap these years.

8. A *cagoule* is a fully encompassing hood usually worn for winter sports. The photo was by Burzin.

9. The collection was shown on April 29, 1952.

10. The text over the photo read, "This suede sweater, encrusted with knit tone on tone, is by Schiaparelli. It symbolizes everything that is sportswear: high collar, fullness, large sleeves, but it is all very practical for life in Paris, to do your errands, to have lunch in a restaurant or to stroll around the Left Bank. These 'sweaters' this winter, will serve a thousand purposes. This is what you'll learn reading our issue where these sweaters are on nearly all the pages."

11. The collection was shown on August 1, 1952.

12. It was founded in 1948 with the goal to create a Musée du Costume Français, which only would actually start taking form in the late 1970s in collaboration with the Louvre.

13. The collection was shown on February 5, 1953.

14. This line was produced by McKay Products Corporation and commercialized by Daniel F. Sheehy and Company in the United States.

15. The collection was shown on April 22, 1953.

16. The collection was shown on July 30, 1953.

17. Artists that Zika Ascher worked with included Jean Cocteau, Jean Hugo, and Christian Bérard but also Henri Matisse, Marie Laurencin, Jean Malclès, Pedro Flores, Nicolas de Staël, Zao Wou Ki, Alexander Calder, Mario Nissim, Ascher award winner

Enrico Baj, Barbara Hepworth, Ivon Hitchens, John Piper, Scottie Wilson, Ben Nicholson, Julian Trevelyan, Felix Topolski, Robert Colquhoun, Graham Sutherland, André Dérain, Antoni Clavé, and Henry Moore, among many others.

18. Valerie D. Mendes, *Fabric, Art, Fashion: Zika and Lida Ascher* (London: Victoria and Albert Museum, 1987).

19. The famous Peynet dolls that were extremely popular throughout the 1960s were made by the French company Technigom.

20. This was designed by Michel de Brunhoff for Schiaparelli.

21. Schiaparelli, *Shocking Life*, 206, 207.

26: 1954–1970

1. Alison Settle, *Clothes Line* (London: Methuen and Company, 1937).

2. In fact, in the year 1953, the manufacturers of her licenses and ready-to-wear would sell over eighteen million items and many others would be signed as of that date.

3. Personal letter from The Honorable Mrs. Reginald "Daisy" Fellowes to Bettina Bergery, undated but circa 1953. Collection BillyBoy*.

4. Robert Riley, *The Fashion Makers* (New York: Crown, Publishers, Inc. 1968)K. It had photos by Walter Vecchio.

5. Private first-draft writings destined for publication in *Vogue* by Bettina Bergery, early 1960s. Collection BillyBoy*.

6. Much like the kind of thing seen on Nova Pilbeam, child movie star who was dressed by Schiaparelli. There is the possibility that it was this line of hats and clothes that were worked on by Maxime de la Falaise.

7. "Skylark Hats," *Vogue*, September 15, 1931, 78.

8. Ballard, *In My Fashion*, 61–62.

9. Some were manufactured by the Glentex company in America, some later made in Japan some of which were hand-painted and marked on the label as such.

10. Andy Warhol, "Sunday, April 27, 1986" in *The Andy Warhol Diaries*.

11. Schiap's legwear names included Apple Flakes, Gold Flakes, Silver Flakes, Crystal Flakes, Grapefruit Flakes, Eggnog Flakes, Cosmetique, Taupe Mode, Mystic, Black Widow, Black Nightingale, Minuet, Witchcraft, Fire and Smoke, Grasshopper, Seashell, Pebble Beach, Coffee Bean, Crushed Mint, Brown Orchid, Sugar and Spice, Ripe Oats, Spun Sugar, Dark Horizon, Dark Legend, Seven Seas, French Navy (that sounds terribly sexy!), Flaming Youth, Beauty Cue, Bouquet (with flower appliqués), Bluebell, Blue Dew, Lady Blue, Blue Smoke, Smoky Pearl, Fleur Rouge, Phoenix, Blush, Rose Wine, Basque Red, Watermelon, Plum Perfect, Colleen Green, Green Goddess, Blue Violet, Forbidden Fruit, Beauty Mist, Blonde Martini, Sparkle, Eternelle, Definitely Neutral (described as "taupe with a rosy nuance"), High Stepping ("a deep toned beige"), Gala Venture ("a subtle golden beige"), Boutique Brown, Nude, Stunning Blend, Banker Gray, Smart Gray, Gray Frost (a wet-look nylon that

glistened on the legs as if one had just stepped out of the ocean!), Florentine Velvet, Sun Worship, Sunny Day, and Sun Tint.

12. I found this quote on a printed pamphlet inside a Schiaparelli stocking case shaped like a satin parasol, from the 1950s.

13. From print advertising soliciting Schiaparelli licensing agreements in trade papers, early 1960s.

14. These were made by N. Wagman and Co., Inc., New York, and sometimes shown with Willi Wear clothes.

15. Schiapettes were small decorated ladies' wallets.

16. Schiaparelli men's ties advertising copy, mid-1960s.

17. Rene Magritte, "Les mots et les images," *La Révolution surréaliste*, 1929.

18. Schiaparelli "Snuff" men's perfume advertising copy, 1950s and 60s.

19. These garments have a big shocking pink and black label, marked *modèle déposé*.

20. Yves Saint Laurent, foreword, in Palmer White, *Elsa Schiaparelli: Empress of Paris Fashion*.

21. Untitled French magazine clipping, translated by the author. Collection BillyBoy*.

22. *New York Times*, September 1971.

23. *Le Journal du Dimanche*, November 1973. Translated by the author. Collection BillyBoy*.

24. Ibid.

25. Marisa Berenson, "Schiap, My Grandmother," Paris *Vogue*, March 1974.

26. Notably an extraordinary show at Musée Jacquemard André featuring the court dresses of Imperial Russia from the Hermitage in Moscow with traditional ones. The show was entirely sponsored by YSL.

27: ARTISTIC COLLABORATIONS

1. The business was located on Hollywood Boulevard and did beading and embroidery work for designers like Galanos, Jean-Louis, Irene, and Adrian. The samples were sometimes sent directly from Paris.

2. Triolet wrote the remarkable novel *Roses à Crédit* (1959)

3. Every bead was accounted for and strategically planned in the design, as with each of her creations.

4. It was model No. 38 in Triolet's sketchbook and was drawn showing eleven "eggs" with a matching belt.

5. Schlumberger was born in 1907 into a traditional French family in Alsace, France, and died August, 29, 1987.

6. Luc Bouchage donated several hundred documents to the museum after painstakingly preserving the drawings, cleaning them, removing old glue and tape, and archiving them with help from Franco Maria Ricci, the luxury book publisher in Paris. Ricci used his famous blue paper to create archival folders and a special label with Jean Schlumberger's name upon them.

7. Illustrated in *Harper's Bazaar*, September 15, 1938.

8. Roland Penrose, *Picasso: His Life and Work* (New York: Harper and Brothers, 1958). This painting, finished in summer 1937, was shown in Les Cahiers d'Art in 1939 to illustrate a poem of Eluard dedicated to his wife, "Je veux qu'elle soit reine" ("I Want Her to Be Queen").

9. One fabric made into a blouse shown in the expo from my collection. Roger Rouffiange did a drawing of one of Schiap's dress ensembles with a huge scarf of one of these prints in 1935, the drawing now in the Musée de la Mode et du Costume—Palais Galliéra, in Paris.

10. The Musée Nationale d'Art Moderne du Centre Georges-Pompidou has one of the double portraits in its collection.

11. The revue was published only for six short years, between 1933 and 1939. It was launched by André Breton, the ringleader in the world of Surrealism, and Albert Skira, the publisher. The third and the fourth issues were published simultaneously on December 12, 1933.

12. From the Winter 1933–34 collection, which was shown in August 1933.

13. The Crazy Coxcomb is now in my collection. The triangular variation of the Madcap eventually became the Crazy Coxcomb hat, evoking exactly that. It was in black crochet and knit wool with a fringed top and the one in my collection was the first one, shown in the Winter 1933–34 collection.

14. Schiaparelli, *Shocking Life*, 91.

15. Jean Ubel was noticed by Schiap around 1927, when he was twenty-seven years old, a painter who had graduated from the École des Beaux-Arts. He also had a degree in chemistry, which he used to great effect in his clever usage of plastics and other synthetics, often incorporating them into Schiaparelli creations.

16. This ensemble was photographed by Hoyningen-Huene on February 1, 1932, on Madame Toulgouat.

17. Photographed by Hoyningen-Huene in the November 1932 issue of *Vogue*.

18. According to the author's diaries.

19. According to the author's diaries.

20. Schiaparelli, *Shocking Life*, 91.

21. François Hugo went on to create his own collections of jewelry as well, becoming one of France's most famous costume jewelry makers. His title is known in the milieu as a *parurier*.

EPILOGUE

1. Erich Fromm, *The Forgotten Language: An Introduction to the Understanding of Dreams, Fairy Tales, and Myths* (New York: Rinehart & Co., 1951), 10.

2. Chuang Tzu (400 B.C.), *The Wisdom of the Chinese: Their Philosophies in Sayings and Proverbs*, Brian Brown, ed. (1920; repr. Kessinger Publishing, 2005), 133.

3. Schiaparelli, *Shocking Life*, 209. Antoine. *Antoine*. New York: Prentice-Hall, 1954.

SELECTED BIBLIOGRAPHY

Antoine. *Antoine*. New York: Prentice-Hall, 1954.

Arletty. *Je suis comme je suis*. Paris: Carrère, 1987.

Baldwin, Neil. *Man Ray: American Artist*. New York: Clarkson Potter, 1988.

Ballard, Bettina. *In My Fashion*. New York: Van Rees Press, 1960.

Balmain, Pierre. *My Years and Seasons*. London: Cassell, 1964.

Batterberry, Michael, and Ariane Batterberry. *Fashion: The Mirror of History*. London: Columbus Books, 1982.

Beaton, Cecil. *The Glass of Fashion*. New York: Doubleday, 1954.

Bettina. *Bettina par Bettina*. Paris: Flammarion, 1964.

BillyBoy*. *Hommage à Elsa Schiaparelli*. Paris: *Ville de Paris*, Musée de la Mode et du Costume, 1984.

BillyBoy*. "Hommage à Schiaparelli". Paris: Femme Nouvelle N°26, June 1986.

Blum, Dilys E. *Shocking! The Art and Fashion of Elsa Schiaparelli*. New Haven: Yale University Press, 2004.

Bonney, Thérèse, and Louise Bonney. *A Shopping Guide to Paris*. New York: Robert M. McBride and Company, 1929.

Botta, Luigi. *Giovanni Virginio Schiaparelli - l'Uomo, Lo Scienziato*. Savigliano, Italy: Associazione Cristoforo Beggiami, 2004.

Brecourt Villars, Claudine. *Les mots d'Arletty*. Paris: Fanval, 1988.

Charles-Roux, Edmonde. *Chanel and Her World*. New York: Vendome, 1981.

Charles-Roux, Edmonde, et al. *Le Théatre de la Mode*. Paris: Du May, 1990.

Daché, Lilly. *Lilly Daché's Glamour Book*. Philadelphia: Lippincott, 1956.

————. *Talking Through My Hats*. New York: Coward-McCann, 1946.

Dalí, Salvador. *Hidden Faces.* London: Nicholson & Watson, 1947.

———. *The Secret Life of Salvador Dalí.* New York: Dial Press, 1944.

Demornex, Jacqueline. *Le siècle en chapeaux : Claude Saint-Cyr, Histoire d'une modiste.* Paris: Du May, 1991.

———. *Vionnet.* Paris: Editions du Regard, 1990.

Deslandres, Yvonne, and Florence Muller. *L'Histoire de la Mode au XX siècle.* Paris: Somogy, 1986.

Deslandres, Yvonne. *Mode des années 40.* Paris: Editions du Regard, 1992.

———. *Poiret.* New York: Rizzoli, 1987.

Dior, Christian. *Christian Dior et moi.* Paris: Bibliothèque Intercontinentale des Nouveautés, 1956.

Ewing, William E. *Hoyningen-Huene, L'Élégance des Années 30.* Paris: Denoël, 1986.

Fairchild, John. *The Fashionable Savages.* New York: Doubleday, 1965.

Farneti Cera, Deanna, ed. *Jewels of Fantasy: Costume Jewelry of the 20th Century.* New York: Abrams, 1991.

Flanner, Janet. *Paris Journal, 1944–1955.* New York: Harvest Books, 1988.

———. *Paris Journal, 1956–1964.* New York: Harvest Books, 1988.

———. *Paris Journal, 1965–1970.* New York: Harvest Books, 1988.

———. *Paris Was Yesterday, 1925–1939.* New York: Viking, 1972.

Frazer, Kennedy. *The Fashionable Mind.* New York: Knopf, 1981.

Garnier, Guillaume. *Paris-Couture-Années-Trente.* Paris: Musée de la Mode et du Costume, 1987.

Giroud, Françoise, and Sacha Van Dorssen. *Christian Dior.* Paris: Editions du Regard, 1987.

Gosselin, Nathalie. *Elsa Triolet – 25ème Festival Culturel Saint-Étienne-du-Rouvray.* France: catalogue published by the City, 1980s.

Hawes, Elisabeth. *Fashion Is Spinach.* New York: Random House, 1938.

Hoffmeyer, Valérie. *Dans la maison du fou d'Elsa.* Switzerland, Fémina Fashion, April 2008.

Join-Diéterle, Catherine, et al. *Givenchy : 40 ans de création.* Paris: Musée de la Mode et du Costume, 1991.

Lalanne, Dorothée. *Shocking ou la légende d'Elsa Schiaparelli.* Paris: Vogue Beauté N°1, 1983.

Längle, Elisabeth. *Pierre Cardin: Fifty Years of Fashion and Design.* London: Thames & Hudson, 2005.

Lawford, Valentine. *Horst: His Work and His World.* New York: Knopf, 1984.

Liaut, Jean-Noël. *Hubert de Givenchy.* Paris: Grasset, 2000.

Martin, Richard. *Fashion and Surrealism.* New York: Rizzoli, 1987.

Mears, Patricia, and G. Bruce Boyer. *Elegance in an Age of Crisis: Fashions of the 1930s.* New Haven: Yale University Press, 2014.

Milbank, Caroline Rennolds. *Couture: The Great Designers.* New York: Stewart, Tabori & Chang, 1985.

Müller, Florence. *Costume Jewelry for Haute Couture.* New York: Vendome, 2006.

Mulvagh, Jane. *"Vogue": History of 20th Century Fashion.* New York/London: Viking, 1988.

Musée de la Mode et du Costume. *Paul Poiret et Nicole Groult, Maîtres de la Mode Art Déco.* Paris: Musée de la Mode et du Costume, 1986.

O'Hara, Georgina. *The Encyclopaedia of Fashion*. London: Thames & Hudson, 1986.

Packer, William. *Fashion Drawing in "Vogue."* London: Thames & Hudson, 1983.

Parkins, Ilya. *Poiret, Dior and Schiaparelli*. Oxford: Berg, 2012.

Penrose, Roland. *Man Ray*. Paris: Chêne, 1975.

Picken, Mary Brooks, and Dora Loues Miller. *Dressmakers of France*. New York: Harper, 1956.

Poiret, Paul. *En habillant l'époque*. Paris: Grasset, 1930.

Rubinstein, Helena. *My Life for Beauty*. New York: Simon & Schuster, 1964.

Saint Laurent, Yves, et al. *Yves Saint Laurent*. New York: The Metropolitan Museum of Art/Clarkson Potter, 1983.

Schiaparelli Berenson, Marisa. *Elsa Schiaparelli's Private Album*. London: Double-Barrelled Books, 2014.

Schiaparelli, Elsa. *Shocking Life*. New York: Dutton, 1954

Séguret, Olivier. *Entrée des fournisseurs*. Paris: Assouline: Maeght, 1991.

Sotheby's. *The Duke & Duchess of Windsor*. New York: Sotheby's, 1997.

Souhami, Diana. *Gluck, 1895—1978: Her Biography*. London: Pandora, 1991.

Triolet, Elsa. *Colliers de Paris*. Berlin: Ebersbach, 1999.

Vaudoyer, Marie. *Le Livre de la Haute Couture*. Neuilly: V & O Editions, 1990.

Vertes, Marcel. *Art and Fashion*. New York/London: The Studio Publications, 1944.

Vieuille, Chantal. *Gala*. Paris: Favre, 1988.

Vivier, Roger, and Cynthia Hampton. *Les souliers de Roger Vivier*. Paris: Musée des Arts de la Mode, 1987.

Vreeland, Diana *Allure*. New York: Doubleday, 1980.

———. *D.V.* New York: Da Capo Press, 1997.

White, Palmer. *Elsa Schiaparelli: Empress of Paris Fashion*. London: Aurum Press, 1986.

———. *Poiret le magnifique*. Paris: Payot, 1986.

Woodman Chase, Edna, and Ilka Chase. *Always in Vogue*. New York: Doubleday, 1954.

GRATEFUL THANKS AND ACKNOWLEDGMENT TO THE FOLLOWING FOR ACCESS TO THEIR ARCHIVES:

Art de la Mode, Paris.

Elle, Paris.

Fémina, Paris.

Flair, New York.

Harper's Bazaar, New York.

Le Jardin des Modes, Paris.

L'Officiel de la Couture et de la Mode, Paris.

Vogue, Paris, London, New York.

Press dossiers, 1927—1979. Maison Schiaparelli, Paris.

Press dossiers and photos, 1927—1979. BillyBoy* personal collection, Delémont, Switzerland.

Personal documents (including letters) of Elsa Schiaparelli. BillyBoy* personal collection, Delémont, Switzerland.

Arletty, (née Léonie Marie Julie Bathiat), Paris.

Ascher, Zika, London.

Balmain, Pierre, Paris.

Bacall, Lauren, Paris, New York.

Beaurepaire, André, Paris.

Bergé, Pierre, Paris.

Bergery, Bettina. Papers. Yale University Beinecke Rare Book and Manuscript Library, New Haven.

Birks, Beverley, New York.

Bonibel, Elaine, Paris.

Burroughs, William S., New York.

Clarke, Henri, Paris.

Chevalier, Jean, Paris.

Comte de Beaumont, Henri, Paris.

Count Taffin de Givenchy, Hubert James Marcel, Paris.

Countess Alain Le Bailly de La *Falaise, Maxime, Paris, New York*

Courrèges, Roger, Paris.

Costume Department of the Victoria and Albert Museum, London.

Costume Institute of the Metropolitan Museum of Art, New York.

Dagmar, Freuchen-Gale, Paris.

Dalí, Salvador and Gala, Paris, New York.

De Boisson, Ghislaine, Paris.

Delair, Suzy, (née Suzanne Delaire), Paris.

Deslandres, Yvonne, Paris.

Dietrich, Marlene, Paris.

di Pietri, Stephen, Paris, New York

Doisneau, Robert, Paris.

Don *Emilio Pucci*, Marchese di Barsento, Florence, Paris, New York.

Eliane, Bonibel, Paris.

Forster Willi, Saint Gallen, Switzerland.

Fini, Leonor, Paris.

Gabor, Jolie, (née Tillman), New York.

Gabor, Zsa Zsa (née Sari Gábor), Los Angeles.

Grant, Cary (né Archibald Alexander Leach), Los Angeles.

Graziani, Bettina, Paris.

Grès (Madame) née (Germaine Émilie Krebs), Paris.

Griffe, Jacques, Paris.

Gruau, René, Paris.

Gysin, Brion, Paris.

Horst, Horst P., New York.

Hughes, Fred, New York.

Hulanicki, Barbara, London.

Jacques Griffe, Paris.

SELECTED BIBLIOGRAPHY

Jakob Schlaepfer, Saint Gallen, Switzerland.

James, Charles, New York.

Kelly, Eugene Curran "Gene", Los Angeles

Klein, William, Paris.

Leary, Timothy, Los Angeles

Maison Ardor, Paris.

Maison Pierre Cardin, Paris.

Maison *Countess Cis* Zoltowska, Los Angeles.

Maison Claude St. Cyr, Paris.

Maison André Courrèges, Paris.

Maison Givenchy, Paris.

Maison Massaro, Paris.

Maison François Lesage, Paris.

Maison Robert Goossens, Paris.

Maison Gripoix, Paris.

Maison Lemarié, Paris.

Maison Roger, Jean-Pierre, Paris

Maison Roger Scemama, Paris.

Maison Roger Vivier, Paris.

Maison Philippe Venet, Paris.

Maison Yves Saint Laurent, Paris.

Mortensen Erik, Paris.

Musée de la Mode, Union Française des Arts du Costume (UFAC), Paris.

Palais Galléria, Musée de la mode, Paris

Per Spook, Paris.

Philadelphia Museum of Art, Philadelphia

Romain de Tirtoff, a.k.a *Erté*, Paris.

Schlumberger, Jean, Paris.

Tabard, Maurice, Paris.

Triolet, Elsa. Archives. Collection Ville de Saint-Etienne-du-Rouvray, Saint-Etienne-du-Rouvray, France.

Van Den Akker, Koos, New York.

Villain-Marais, Jean-Alfred, Paris.

Vivier, Roger, Paris.

Vreeland, Diana. New York.

Warhol, Andy, New York.

FOR FURTHER ARTICLES RELATED TO ELSA SCHIAPARELLI
AND THE AUTHOR:

www.fondationtanagra.com
www.mdvanii.ch

ACKNOWLEDGMENTS

Eternal gratitude to Dee and Benjamin, my adoptive parents, who allowed and encouraged me to be a totally free spirit.

Medal of eternal love for my husband, Lala, for being the enlightened being he is and for the endless help in keeping me safe and happy and working beside me step by step on this book.

Gratitude to my son, Alec Jiri, for his dedication, for being such a dear, and for accepting that he is forever doomed to schlepping crates of Schiaparelli haute couture around for his father.

Heartfelt thanks to my unwavering friend and literary agent Jeffrey Simmons who has been, since I was a teenager, unbelievably supportive—especially for this book, Lord knows.

Sincere thanks to my publisher, Charles Miers, and the editors who worked so hard to help create this book, trimming down a 1,500-page manuscript to a readable form, most notably Giulia Di Filippo. I must say, I have never seen such a perfectionist in making sure this book could be the very best it could be. Thank you.

And most naturally, to Elsa Schiaparelli for having shone her intense spiritual light in my direction those times we met and ever since. What a trip it's been so far!